LYLE PRICE GUIDE
MILITARIA
ARMS &
ARMOUR

While every care has been taken in compiling the information contained in this volume, the publishers cannot accept any liability for loss, financial or otherwise, incurred by reliance placed on the information herein.

The publishers wish to express their sincere thanks to the following for their involvement and assistance in the production of this volume:

Editor	TONY CURTIS
Text By	EELIN McIVOR
Editorial	ANNETTE CURTIS
	DONNA RUTHERFORD
	JACQUELINE LEDDY
Art Production	CATRIONA DAY
	DONNA CRUICKSHANK
	ANGIE DE MARCO
	NICKY FAIRBURN
Graphics	JAMES BROWN
	MALCOLM GLASS
	DOROTHY GLASS

A CIP catalogue record for this book is available from the British Library.

ISBN 86248-148-1

Copyright © Lyle Publications MCMXCIII
Glenmayne, Galashiels, Scotland.

Typeset by Word Power, Berwickshire
Printed and bound in Great Britain by
Butler & Tanner Ltd, Frome and London

LYLE PRICE GUIDE

MILITARIA ARMS & ARMOUR

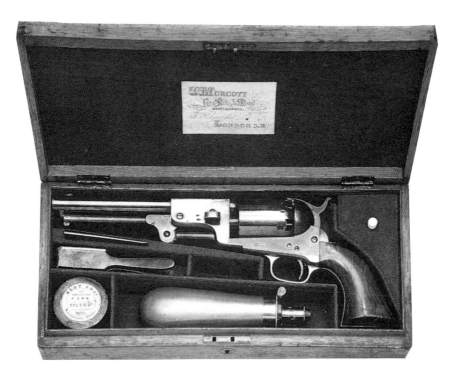

TONY CURTIS

CONTENTS

Acknowledgements

Bearnes, Rainbow, Avenue Road, Torquay TQ2 5TG

Bonhams, Montpelier Street, Knightsbridge, London SW7 1HH

Bonhams Chelsea, 65–69 Lots Road, London SW10 0RN

Bonhams West Country, Dowell Street, Honiton, Devon

Butterfield & Butterfield, 220 San Bruno Avenue, San Francisco CA 94103, USA

Butterfield & Butterfield, 7601 Sunset Boulevard, Los Angeles CA 90046, USA

Christie's Scotland, 164–166 Bath Street Glasgow G2 4TG

Christie's South Kensington Ltd., 85 Old Brompton Road, London SW7 3LD

Christie's, 8 King Street, London SW1Y 6QT

Christie's East, 219 East 67th Street, New York, NY 10021, USA

Christie's, 502 Park Avenue, New York, NY 10022, USA

Christie's, Cornelis Schuytstraat 57, 1071 JG Amsterdam, Netherlands

Christie's SA Roma, 114 Piazza Navona, 00186 Rome, Italy

Christie's Swire, 1202 Alexandra House, 16–20 Chater Road, Hong Kong

Christie's Australia Pty Ltd., 1 Darling Street, South Yarra, Melbourne,
   Victoria 3141, Australia

Du Mouchelles Art Galleries Co., 409 E. Jefferson Avenue, Detroit,
   Michigan 48226, USA

Eldred's, Box 796, E. Dennis, MA 02641, USA

James of Norwich, 33 Timberhill, Norwich NR1 3LA

John Nicholson, 1 Crossways Court, Fernhurst, Haslemere, Surrey GU27 3EP

Phillips Manchester, Trinity House, 114 Northenden Road, Sale,
   Manchester M33 3HD

Phillips Son & Neale SA, 10 rue des Chaudronniers, 1204 Genève, Switzerland

Phillips West Two, 10 Salem Road, London W2 4BL

Phillips, 11 Bayle Parade, Folkestone, Kent CT20 1SQ

Phillips, 49 London Road, Sevenoaks, Kent TN13 1UU

Phillips, 65 George Street, Edinburgh EH2 2JL

Phillips, Blenstock House, 7 Blenheim Street, New Bond Street,
   London W1Y 0AS

Phillips Marylebone, Hayes Place, Lisson Grove, London NW1 6UA

Phillips, New House, 150 Christleton Road, Chester CH3 5TD

Skinner Inc., Bolton Gallery, Route 117, Bolton MA, USA

Henry Spencer, 40 The Square, Retford, Notts. DN22 6DJ

Spink & Son Ltd, 5-7 King St., St James's, London SW1Y 6QS

Wallis & Wallis, West Street Auction Galleries, West Street, Lewes,
   E. Sussex BN7 2NJ

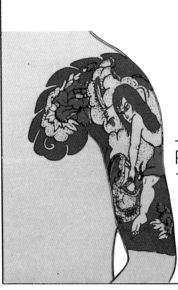

MILITARIA ARMS & ARMOUR

On first consideration Arms & Armour would appear to be one of the most esoteric of collecting fields, appealing to the select cognoscenti. In reality, however, this is far from being the case. Given that Britain was, not so long ago, the policeman of the world, there was hardly a corner of it in which we have not fought. It was, therefore, perfectly natural that, when soldiers and administrators came back from far flung lands, they should bring with them souvenirs of their service, often in the form of the weapons and militaria which had been a daily part of their lives there. All of these items would have their story or memories attached, and from such origins collecting passions can often grow.

The squeamish may shy away from the fact that such items are, first and last, instruments of death, but, partly because of that very fact, they are also the subjects of superb, precise and meticulous craftsmanship, and it is easy to see how these qualities, plus the fact that when handling them one knows one is handling a vivid piece of history, make them so irresistible to so many.

Interest has been heightened too by the fact that, in the last year or so, an arguably unprecedented number of major weapons collections have come under the hammer. Some items have, indeed, had such historical associations as to merit front page headlines in the national press. One such was the Colt revolver with which Bob Ford shot Jesse James in 1882. It was, in fact, James' own gun, which he had laid on a bed in his room while he dusted a picture! Ford, a new member of the James gang, who had done a deal with Governor Crittenden to bring in Jesse alive or dead, seized his chance and the gun and shot Jesse through the forehead as he turned on hearing the gun cock. Ford and his brother were imprisoned but later pardoned. While in prison, Ford gave the gun to Corydon Craig, son of Marshal Craig, who had kept the brothers supplied with sweets, good food etc. during their incarceration. In

JESSE JAMES 1847-1882

The 6 shot .44 Smith & Wesson Number 3 New Model single action revolver with which Bob Ford killed Jesse James, serial no. 3766, 6in. barrel. (Wallis & Wallis) £105,000

1900 Craig sold it to E. Stanley Gary of Baltimore, who had it engraved.

A claim that the piece had been stolen in 1968, while on loan to a Missouri museum, led to a dispute of title which gave the present auction extra spice in that, almost up to the very day of the sale there was doubt as to whether the gun could actually be offered. This was resolved just in time, however, and the Sussex specialist auctioneers, Wallis & Wallis, went on to sell it for £105,000 to an American telephone bidder.

Also trailing with it all the aura and glamour of the Old West was the Winchester owned by Annie Oakley, which was sold by Christie's in London. Oakley, born Phoebe Ann Moses in 1860 in Ohio, came of a poor family and started shooting at an early age for the pot. Her skill led her to compete in local turkey shoots, at one of which she outshot her future husband and manager, the itinerant sharpshooter Frank Butler. She later joined Sells Brothers circus and then Buffalo Bill's Wild West Show, where she was a sensation, even being adopted by Sitting Bull, who called her Little Sure-Shot. With the Show, she toured the UK several times as well as the Continent, where she played a certain role in European history by saving Prince Luitpold of Bavaria from an enraged bronco, and, as some said, missed her chance to avert the First World War by successfully shooting the ash from a cigarette held in the mouth of the future Kaiser Wilhelm II!

It was on one of her visits to Britain that she was befriended by the Clarke family from Shropshire, with whom she stayed on a number of occasions, and she presented the Winchester to Richard Clarke in 1891. It sold for £84,000.

At the same sale a deformed 1890 halfpenny was offered, being one of the coins thrown in the air for Oakley to hit during her act. These were then stamped *Oakley* and handed out to members of the audience. It fetched £1,380.

Though both the above examples sold in Britain, many of the main collections have been offered in the USA, which is perhaps where, in all the world, Arms & Armour are most avidly collected.

And it is, of course, in the United States that both the Winchester and the Colt originated.

Oliver Winchester was born in Boston in 1810. After trying his hand at both carpentry and the building trade he opened a mens' clothing store in Baltimore in 1848, before establishing the nation's first shirt factory in New Haven, CT. The success of this venture gave him the wherewithal to invest, in 1855, in the Volcanic Repeating Arms Co., which had been formed with the purpose of developing and marketing a repeating rifle. When the company failed in 1857, Winchester, with a shrewd eye to the potential of the product, was in a position to buy out the other stockholders, and he became President and Treasurer of the reorganised New Haven Arms Co. One of his inspired decisions was to employ Benjamin Henry, a superb gunsmith, to transform the old, weak Volcanic lever action and ammunition into something much more efficient. Within three years the first Henry rifle was ready for the market, with the new Henry .44 calibre cartridge which propelled a 216 grain bullet at 1,200 ft. per second. This invention, the first practical magazine-fed, breechloading, repeating firearm, was, however, rejected by the US Army, who distrusted its novelty. But in the Civil War, local militias were quick to avail themselves of the new weapon, and the army found itself having to buy 5 million rounds of the new ammunition for the Volunteer regiments! It did eventually purchase 1,200 of the rifles too. In 1866, the first true Winchester, the model 1866 or the New Model Winchester as it was known, appeared.

A rare Winchester .44 WCF Model 1873 lever action repeating smoothbore rifle, the body of the stock inset with steel plaque inscribed Presented by Annie Oakley to W R C Clarke 1891. 20in. barrel.
(Christie's)   £84,000

An engraved Winchester Model 1866 saddle ring carbine with raised carved ivory stock, .44 calibre, 20in. round barrel, profuse Nimschke style scroll engraving on frame, barrel and buttplate.
(Butterfield & Butterfield)   £248,918

Winchester was an astute and far seeing business man and the Winchester Repeating Arms Co., as it was renamed in 1867, owed much of its success to his ability to organise efficient distribution services for his products, his decision to go into the general metallic cased ammunition business, and perhaps most of all to his introduction of the latest techniques to cut manufacturing costs and encourage mass production, reducing the cost of making rifle barrels, for example, from $800 per hundred to just under $80 per hundred. Winchester died in 1880, and his son's brother in law, William Converse succeeded him as President of the company.

The early history of Samuel Colt was just as chequered, though Colt was fascinated by guns themselves from an early age. The story goes that in 1830, while serving as crew on an East Indiaman bound for Calcutta, he spent most of his free time whittling away at a wooden model of a pistol. The model still exists as evidence of this. Home again, Colt continued his experiments while earning his living by, among other things, touring with a medicine show. In 1835, he patented his first revolver, a 6-shot weapon, and in 1836 the Patent Arms Manufacturing Co. of Paterson, NJ, was formed. This did not last long, but Colt Paterson pistols and rifles were bought by the US Army and the Republic of Texas also purchased some pistols for naval use. These were later reissued to Texas Rangers, who used them successfully against the Comanches, and surviving examples are now very valuable.

Portrait of Captain Samuel Hamilton Walker, Capt. of Texas Rangers and later of the US Mounted Rifles, killed in action at Humamantla, Mexico, in 1847.

The Mexican War of 1846–8 saw an upswing in Colt's fortunes, when he became re-established as an arms manufacturer with help from former Texas Ranger and admirer of his pistols, Samuel Walker. At Walker's behest Colt redesigned his revolver and one thousand of the new .44 calibre pistols were purchased by the government. These massive sidearms, known as Colt Walker pistols, are now both rare and valuable.

Rare Colt 1847 Walker Model revolver, 9in. part octagon barrel marked 'Address Sam'l Colt New York City', 44 calibre square back brass trigger and guard, numbered 'D Company No 81'. (Butterfield & Butterfield) £13,750

Their initial success helped Colt to set up a manufactory at his home town of Hartford CT, where it continues today. His pistols were exhibited at the Great Exhibition of 1851, and such was the ensuing demand for them that he set up a further manufactory in London. He made valuable contracts with the British and Russian governments, which led to his products being used both in South Africa and subsequently in the Crimean War. When Colt died in 1862, he was reputedly worth $3 million, his factory had doubled in size, and his guns were achieving, in the course of the American Civil War, a popularity which they were never to lose.

Original Colt Factory Display Board made for Scheyler, Hartley & Graham, Military Goods dealer in New York City, circa 1877.

Not only guns but knives too have achieved a high profile over the last months, with Butterfield & Butterfield in the United States selling Bowie knives from the collections of Herbert Tannenbaum, Robert Berryman and Charles Schreiner. Like the Colt and the Winchester, the Bowie knife embodies all the romance of the Old West. It was devised, however, not by the legendary Jim Bowie, with whom it has come to be associated, but by his brother Rezin, following an incident with a young bull. Bowie's rifle missed fire and when he attempted to plunge his hunting knife into

the bull's head, the force of its attack drove the knife back into his hand which was impaled on a horn. This would not have happened had the knife possessed a guard, so Rezin Bowie had a new one made to his own design by a blacksmith on his plantation, with a straight blade 9$\frac{1}{4}$in. long and 1$\frac{1}{2}$in. wide and with a single edge down the guard. Rezin found the knife more useful for hunting and self-defence than the then common swordstick or Spanish dagger, both of which were eventually superseded by the Bowie knife. He also gave one to his brother James, and it was Col. James Bowie's use of the knife which caused it to catch the public imagination, when he was involved in 1827 in a duel fought on a sandbar in the Mississippi opposite Natchez. The Bowies, with their cousins the Cunys and the Wells, had a long standing feud with some newcomers to Louisiana, a Major Wright and Dr Maddox from Maryland, and Col. Crain and the Blanchards from Virginia. Major Wright had once fired at the unarmed Bowie, and it was this that led Rezin to give James a knife for his protection. In the case of the Sandbar Duel, General Montford Wells and Dr Maddox were the principals. The duel was fought and no one hurt, then Samuel Cuny approached Col. Crain and suggested that 'this is a good time to settle our difficulty'. Crain was standing with a loaded pistol in each hand, and without answering fired one at Cuny and the other at Bowie, who was moving up to act as Cuny's second. Cuny was mortally wounded and there followed a melée in which Crain, Maddox, Blanchard and Wright all attacked Bowie, who saved his life by using his knife when Wright came at him with his swordstick. Wright was killed and Bowie severely wounded, but finally recovered. It is this duel which passed, suitably embellished, into legend, and the Bowie knife became hugely popular as a result. It is interesting to note that Jim Bowie used his knife in a distinctive manner, holding it as one would a sword. Once beyond the opponent's guard, the thrust was deadly. And the veteran knife fighter C. M. Clay of Kentucky wrote this prescription for successful use of the knife ... 'One should drive to the hilt on a line with the navel, a move which produces great shock and almost invariably puts an end to the encounter'.

Limited edition bronze portrait sculpture in high relief of James Bowie, signed Runtsch, copyright 1982, mounted on walnut plaque. (Butterfield & Butterfield)
£311

pioneers, settlers, and the prospectors of California in the succeeding years. The UK also got in on the act, and in the course of the 19th century many thousands were produced in Sheffield for the American market.

When high profile pieces such as the Jesse James gun make the headlines, you can be sure that a good few other similar items will follow them out of the woodwork. Thus, Wallis & Wallis have for sale in autumn 1993 a .22 calibre Winchester which belonged to both Frank James and Cole Younger, another Jesse James revolver, the gun which killed Wild Bill Hickok, Hermann Goering's sporting rifle, and a gun specially made for Adolf Eichmann.

JAMES "WILD BILL" BUTLER HICKOK
1837-1876

In 1832, the brothers visited Philadelphia, where Rezin gave a cutler the model of the Bowie knife. He improved it, reducing the blade to 8in. and making a curve on one side of the point, and then placed it on the market.

James Bowie had meanwhile become a naturalised Texan, and received a charter to set up cotton and woollen mills at Saltillo. In 1831, he married Marie Ursula de Veramendi, the daughter of his patron, but after only three years of marriage she and their two infant sons died of cholera. Thereafter, Bowie entered the service of his adopted state, acting as adjutant to Sam Houston and as a Colonel of the Texas Volunteers. His short but distinguished military career led to his death, Bowie knife in hand, at the Alamo in 1836, where his heroism has been immortalised in film and literature. And at the battle of San Jacinto, where the deaths at the Alamo were bloodily avenged, the independence of Texas was literally won with the Bowie knife, as the Texans, having emptied their pistols and carbines, used the knives as bayonet, sword and dagger combined. It was this versatility which led to the knife's virtual universal use by

One of the most problematic aspects of offering such items for sale is establishing their genuine provenance, surrounded as they often are by myth and legend. The James/Younger Winchester comes with a formal deposition dated Jan 13 1950, and signed by Harry Younger Hall, nephew of Cole Younger, Mrs Robert James, wife of Frank James' son Kearney, and Charles Kemper, a friend of the James-Younger families.

FRANK JAMES 1843–1915

On the other hand, Mr Roy Butler of Wallis & Wallis has also been offered a derringer by an elderly gentleman whose grandfather, as a boy, had run errands for Zorelda James Samuels, Jesse James' mother. She gave the derringer to the boy in thanks for his help, telling him that Jesse had always kept it in the back of his boot, so that he would never be caught without a gun. A charming story, and no doubt quite true, but with absolutely no supporting documentation, making it a nightmare for a reputable auctioneer.

COLE YOUNGER 1844–1916

Wallis & Wallis had, with great regret, to turn it down.

But high profile items apart, one of the most reassuring things about the fields of militaria, arms and armour is their stability. Pieces don't surge in value overnight, according to the whim of the moment, but neither is there any corresponding collapse as they go out of fashion. Instead one sees a general, gentle, ongoing upward trend in just about all the various categories. There is, of course, the odd surprise, as, for example, when Wallis and Wallis offered a rare First pattern Sykes-Fairbairn commando knife. First patterns fetch, on average, £250–350 (2nd and 3rd patterns are much more common and rarely attract more than £100). On this occasion, however, two determined American bidders took it all the way to £850. Inevitably, again, on the heels of this, a further flurry of First patterns emerged, but although the first few went for perhaps slightly more than normal, prices soon settled back down again.

And it would be a stagnant market indeed where, from time to time, there were no upsurges of interest in particular categories. Just at the moment Islamic items are particularly in vogue, perhaps as a result of the increasing wealth of many Middle Eastern collectors. The Japanese, too are showing great interest in repatriating their own arms and armour, an enthusiasm fuelled no doubt by the reverence in which traditional and hereditary items are held in that culture. They had a rare opportunity in June and October 1992 when Christie's in New York offered the massive Walter Compton collection of Japanese swords and sword fittings. A Bitchu chu-Aoe tachi dated 1347, for example, fetched $154,000.

So arms and armour collecting has, in the past year, attracted unprecedented attention from the general press, and while newsworthy items such as the Jesse James gun continue to appear it seems unlikely that such interest will wane. It is, of course, unlikely that this will have any great effect on the mainstream, bread and butter side of the market, but on the premise that there is no such thing as bad publicity, it may well inspire a whole clutch of new collectors into what is already a very rewarding and thriving field.

EELIN McIVOR

BAYONETS

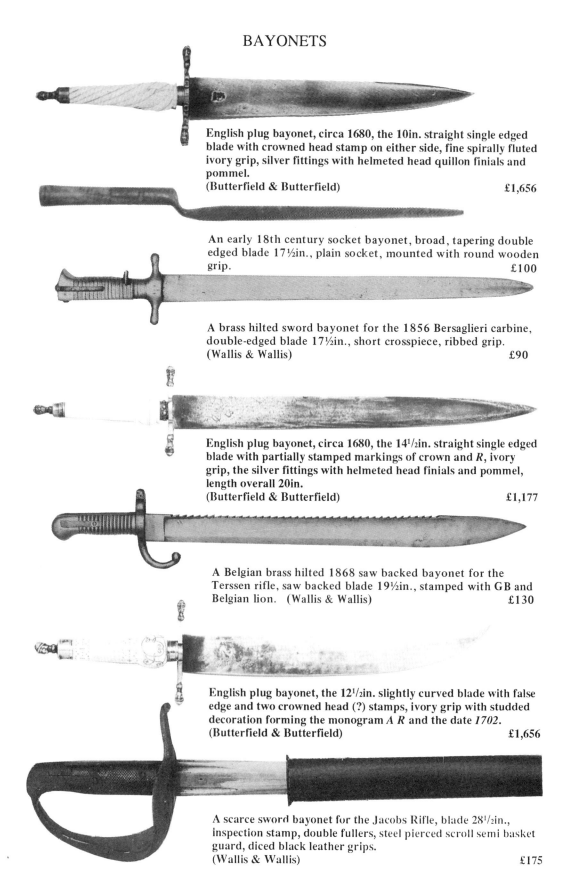

English plug bayonet, circa 1680, the 10in. straight single edged blade with crowned head stamp on either side, fine spirally fluted ivory grip, silver fittings with helmeted head quillon finials and pommel.
(Butterfield & Butterfield)   £1,656

An early 18th century socket bayonet, broad, tapering double edged blade 17½in., plain socket, mounted with round wooden grip.   £100

A brass hilted sword bayonet for the 1856 Bersaglieri carbine, double-edged blade 17½in., short crosspiece, ribbed grip.
(Wallis & Wallis)   £90

English plug bayonet, circa 1680, the 14½in. straight single edged blade with partially stamped markings of crown and *R*, ivory grip, the silver fittings with helmeted head finials and pommel, length overall 20in.
(Butterfield & Butterfield)   £1,177

A Belgian brass hilted 1868 saw backed bayonet for the Terssen rifle, saw backed blade 19½in., stamped with GB and Belgian lion.   (Wallis & Wallis)   £130

English plug bayonet, the 12½in. slightly curved blade with false edge and two crowned head (?) stamps, ivory grip with studded decoration forming the monogram *A R* and the date *1702*.
(Butterfield & Butterfield)   £1,656

A scarce sword bayonet for the Jacobs Rifle, blade 28½in., inspection stamp, double fullers, steel pierced scroll semi basket guard, diced black leather grips.
(Wallis & Wallis)   £175

16

BAYONETS

A Prussian 1871 pattern brass hilted dress sword bayonet, saw-back blade 20in., by W.K.C., German silver crossguard, in its lacquered brass mounted leather scabbard. (Wallis & Wallis)   £85

A Nazi Hitler Youth bayonet, blade 8in., steel mounts, stylised eagle's head pommel, diced black grips, in its black painted metal scabbard. (Wallis & Wallis)   £80

A Nazi Wehrmacht dress bayonet, plated blade 9¾in., by Everitz, plated mounts, stylized eagle's head pommel, real staghorn grips, in its black painted steel scabbard with leather frog. (Wallis & Wallis)   £70

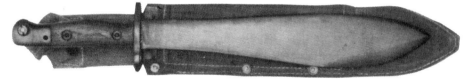

An Australian M.1944 Machete Paratroopers bayonet Bolo blade 11in., steel mounts, wood grip. (Wallis & Wallis)   £75

A Nazi Wehrmacht dress bayonet, plated blade 9½in., by Robert Klaas, etched with "Zur Erinnerung an Meine Dienstzeit". (Wallis & Wallis)   £45

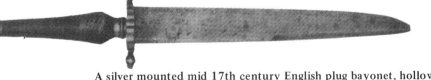

A silver mounted mid 17th century English plug bayonet, hollow ground, blade 9¾in., with false edge. Silver crosspiece and ribbed silver ferule.   £450

A mid 19th century Spanish plug bayonet, single edged straight blade with spear point, blade 8½in., etched at forte 'FBCA Nl. De Toledo Ano De 1843', in its fish skin covered wooden scabbard.   £200

Large Mexican Bowie knife by Aragon, 20th century, 13in. clip point etched blade with Mexican eagle, snake and the motto *No me presto ni me doy solo de mi dueno soy*, brass mounted hilt with antler grip, 18³/₄in. overall.
(Butterfield & Butterfield) £932

Spanish military Bowie-style side knife, Toledo, circa 1870, 11⁷/₁₆in. clip point blade stamped *Artileria Toledo*, ebony grip flanked by an iron crossguard and pommel cap.
(Butterfield & Butterfield) £435

An old Indian Bowie knife, clipped back blade 9in., stamped *Arnachellum Salem*, reversed steel crosspiece, staghorn hilt, in its leather sheath with belt tongue.
(Wallis & Wallis) £260

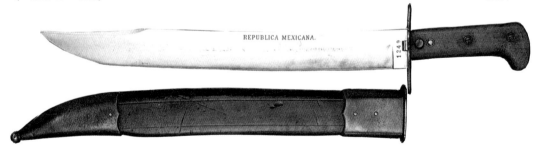

Large Mexican military style Bowie knife, 20th century, 16⁵/₁₆in. blade stamped *Republica Mexicana*, wooden grip with iron crossguard, 21¹/₄in. overall.
(Butterfield & Butterfield) £466

Mexican Bowie knife, 20th century, 10⁹/₁₆in. clip point etched blade with the motto *El Valiente Que Me Ataje Lo Despacho a un Largo Viaje*, brass mounted hilt with eagle head pommel and bone grip, 16⁷/₈in. overall.
(Butterfield & Butterfield)   £497

Bowie knife by Beach, Salisbury, circa 1860, 8⁵/₁₆in. clip point blade etched *For Stags & Buffaloes*, and stamped *Hunters Companion*, German silver mounted hilt stag grip scales, 13¹/₂in. overall.
(Butterfield & Butterfield)   £3,418

Bowie style knife, unmarked, possibly made in India, circa 1880, 8⁷/₈in. clip point blade, iron mounted hilt, guard and stag grip, 13⁵/₁₆in. overall.
(Butterfield & Butterfield)   £466

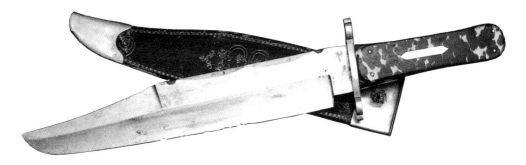

Large Bowie knife, unmarked, possibly American, circa 1840, 11⁵/₁₆in. spear point blade with sharpened false edge, German silver crossguard with tortoise shell hilt inset with escutcheon plate, 16⁹/₁₆in. overall.
(Butterfield & Butterfield)   £4,350

Bowie knife by Wolf & Clark, New York, circa 1840, 12¹/₈in. clip point blade, dark walnut grip scales, German silver hilt, studs, escutcheon plaques and turned quillons, 16³/₁₆in. overall. (Butterfield & Butterfield)   £5,593

Bowie knife by English & Huber, Philadelphia, circa 1835, 9⁹/₁₆in. clip point blade, iron cross guard, German silver mounted hilt with studded ivory grip bearing two escutcheon plates, 14¹/₂in. overall.
(Butterfield & Butterfield)   £2,331

Fighting Bowie knife, unmarked, American, circa 1835, 10in. clip point blade with decorative notch, coin silver mounted grip with silver studs bearing escutcheon plates marked *L. Kimball* and on the reverse *Vicksburg*, 14¹/₁₆in. overall.
(Butterfield & Butterfield)   £24,860

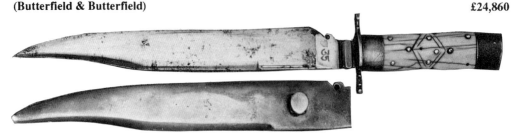

Unmarked Bowie knife, American, circa 1845, 10⁷/₁₆in. clip point blade with sharpened false edge and decorative Spanish notch, silver mounted hilt with ivory grip bearing decorative silver studs, 14³/₈in. overall.
(Butterfield & Butterfield)   £16,780

Rare American patriotic Bowie knife by Chevalier, New York, circa 1860, 8¹³/₁₆in. clip point blade stamped *Chevalier Union Knife*, on obverse *Death to Traitors*, brass mounted hilt with chequered ebony grips, 13³/₁₆in. overall.
(Butterfield & Butterfield)   £3,107

AMERICAN

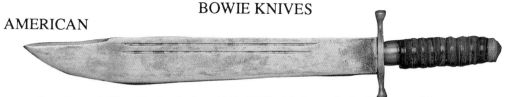

Bowie knife by Collins, Hartford, circa 1880, 13$^{1}/_{4}$in. blade marked with arm and hammer *Legitimus Collins & Co., Hartford*, brass mounted hilt with turned wooden handle, 18$^{1}/_{2}$in. overall. (Butterfield & Butterfield) £373

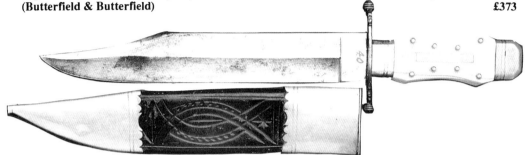

Rare American Bowie knife, Philadelphia, circa 1835, 10$^{7}/_{16}$in. clip point blade marked on ricasso *Sheffield Works 2*, iron crossguard, German silver and ivory hilt set with German silver studs and escutcheon plates, 15$^{1}/_{2}$in. overall. (Butterfield & Butterfield) £9,322

Rare Bowie knife by Schively, Philadelphia, circa 1835, 7$^{1}/_{16}$in. spear point blade, German silver pommel cap and guard, finely chequered horn grip, with old replacement sheath, 12$^{1}/_{4}$in. overall. (Butterfield & Butterfield) £2,952

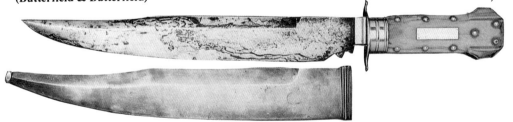

Rare outstanding gold mounted Bowie knife, unmarked, American, circa 1835, 10$^{1}/_{8}$in. clip point blade with decorative Spanish notch, the ivory grip surrounded by gold ricasso, crossguard, bolster, pommel cap, and set with gold studs and escutcheon plates, 14$^{1}/_{2}$in. overall. (Butterfield & Butterfield) £15,537

Rare Bowie knife by Rose, New York, circa 1830, 12$^{7}/_{16}$in. spear point blade marked *Rose New York*, German silver mounted hilt with spiral carved grip, 17$^{7}/_{8}$in. overall. (Butterfield & Butterfield) £2,175

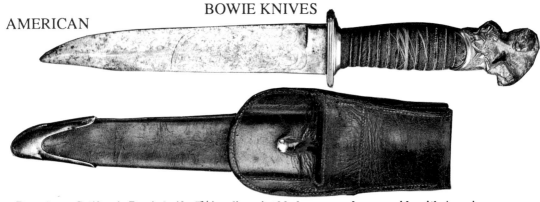

Rare Ames California Bowie knife, 7³/₄in. clip point blade engraved on one side with American eagle and *E Pluribus Unum riband* with a strapwork border and on the reverse with an intertwined riband inscribed *Ames Mfg. Co. Chicopee Mass.*
(Butterfield & Butterfield)   £8,829

Rare Confederate Bowie knife, unmarked, circa 1862, 11⁷/₈in. clip point blade, ground from file stock, brass mounted hilt with wood grip, 17¹/₄in. overall.
(Butterfield & Butterfield)   £2,641

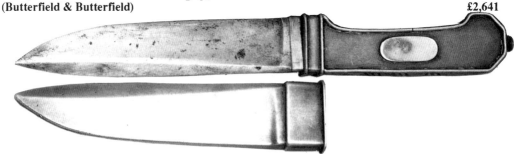

Rare California gold and silver mounted Bowie knife, unmarked, San Francisco, circa 1850, 5³/₄in. semi spear point blade with the ricasso bound in silver, silver hilt trimmed in gold borders and two gold escutcheon plates, 10¹/₂in. overall.
(Butterfield & Butterfield)   £4,972

Rare gold mounted California Bowie knife, unmarked, San Francisco, circa 1855, 6in. spear point blade, German silver mounted hilt inlaid with gold and abalone shell, 10¹/₂in. overall.
(Butterfield & Butterfield)   £10,565

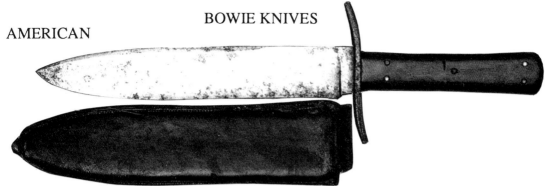

Bowie knife by H. H. Rowell, California, circa 1870, 8in. spear point blade marked *H. H. Rowell* on the ricasso, iron mounted hilt with walnut handle, with original scabbard covered in old leather sheath.
(Butterfield & Butterfield) £1,554

Rare American Bowie knife by Samuel Jackson, Baltimore, circa 1850, $7^{11}/_{16}$in. spear point blade, ivory hilt bound in German silver and set with escutcheon plate, $12^3/_4$in. overall.
(Butterfield & Butterfield) £2,797

Rare silver mounted Bowie knife, American, circa 1835, the $13^5/_8$in. clip point blade with bevelled sharpened false edge and Spanish notch, inscribed near throat *T. Wells* and *Nashville*.
(Butterfield & Butterfield) £33,110

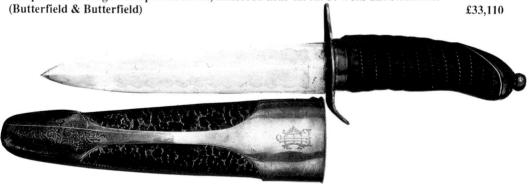

Rare Texas presentation Bowie knife, American, circa 1857, 7in. spear point blade etched in foliate motif, spiral wooden hilt with silver fittings and wire wrap, $12^7/_8$in. overall.
(Butterfield & Butterfield) £4,040

Large Bowie knife, unmarked, American, circa 1840, unusual extra heavy 10in. blade, the top
portion ⁵/₈ths of an inch in width, German silver crossguard, ferrule and grip plaques engraved
with delicate zig-zag borders and primitive floral motifs, hickory grip.
(Butterfield & Butterfield)   £7,358

Rare large American Bowie knife by Alfred Hunter, circa 1840, 12¹/₁₆in. clip point blade stamped
Alfred Hunter on the ricasso, ornate incised carved ivory grip bearing escutcheon plaque engraved
J.L.L.
(Butterfield & Butterfield)   £10,565

Rare historic California Bowie knife by H. McConnell, San Francisco, circa 1852, 6in. spear point
blade marked *H. McConnell San Francisco* (only known specimen), iron mounted hilt with stag
handle, together with a French cavalry sword inscribed *Garde National 1830*, with documenting
letters stating knife and sword were carried by Major General Joshua Pierce Haven into battle
with Indians during the 1850's.
(Butterfield & Butterfield)   £34,182

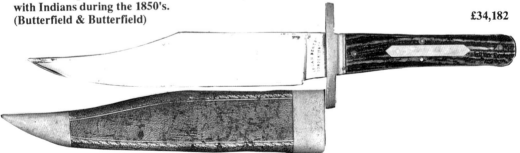

Bowie knife by Corsan, Denton, Burdering & Co., circa 1860, 6¹⁵/₁₆in. clip point blade with etched
panel of spread American eagle and motto *Americans Must and Shall Rule America*, German silver
guard and stag grip scales with escutcheon plaque, 11³/₈in. overall.
(Butterfield & Butterfield)   £2,175

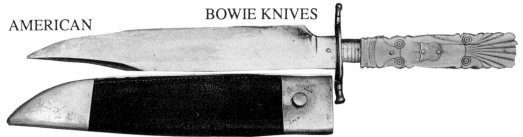

Rare American Bowie knife by Alfred Hunter, circa 1845, 8¹⁵/₁₆in. clip point blade, German silver guard capped by an ornate incised carved ivory grip, bearing an escutcheon plaque, German silver mounted scabbard.
(Butterfield & Butterfield)   £3,418

Historic massive Bowie knife by Graveley & Wreaks, 16in. spear point blade, originally owned by Captain Charles Alexis Berry, sea captain and entrepreneur, born near Mt. Vernon, Virginia in 1810.
(Butterfield & Butterfield)   £18,395

Rare massive frontier Bowie knife, unmarked, American, circa 1830, 12¹/₁₆in. clip point blade, full silver plated, silver plated crossguard and stag grip neatly incised with letter *F* on pommel, 17⁷/₁₆in. overall.
(Butterfield & Butterfield)   £16,159

Rare massive Bowie knife, unmarked, American, circa 1847, 14¹/₄in. clip point blade, the hilt composed of iron crossguard, ferrules, and incised carved ivory grip with silver pommel, inscribed on throat *J. Leach, San Antonio, 1847*, 19³/₄in. overall
(Butterfield & Butterfield)   £18,645

COFFIN HILT

Coffin hilt Bowie knife by W&S Butcher, Sheffield, circa 1855, 9in. sharpened clip point blade marked *Manufactured by W. & S. Butcher, Sheffield*, German silver hilt with rosewood grip scales bearing studs and escutcheon plates on either side, 14½in. overall.
(Butterfield & Butterfield)   £3,418

Coffin hilt Bowie knife, circa 1830, unmarked 10³/₁₆in. spear point blade, coin silver pommel and bolster, walnut grips with silver studs, 14³/₄in. overall.
(Butterfield & Butterfield)   £2,797

Rare coffin hilt Bowie knife by Marks and Rees, Cincinnati, circa 1835, 6½in. clip point blade, rosewood grip scales mounted in German silver and set with escutcheon plate, coin silver overlay on tang, ricasso and brass crossguard, 11½in. overall.
(Butterfield & Butterfield)   £6,836

Rare and important guardless American coffin hilt Bowie knife, unmarked, circa 1830, 13½in. clip point blade, silver mounted hardwood grip with rope edged borders, studs and escutcheon plates on either side, right plate engraved *Bowie No. 1*, 18½in. overall.
(Butterfield & Butterfield)   £19,888

Coffin hilt Bowie knife, unmarked, Sheffield, circa 1835, 9in. spear point blade with sharpened false edge floral etched with the motto *Take Care in Getting Woltish*, 15in. overall.
(Butterfield & Butterfield)   £4,661

Rare coffin hilt Bowie knife marked *Graveley & Weeks*, Sheffield, circa 1835, 8¹/₂in. semi-clip point blade fully etched in florals with the motto *Arkansas Toothpick*, and stamped *Gravely & Weeks, New York*, German silver bound rosewood grip, 14¹/₄in. overall.
(Butterfield & Butterfield)   £22,374

Rare early guardless coffin hilt Bowie knife, American, circa 1830, unmarked 9in. spear point blade, dark walnut scales bearing coin silver studs and escutcheon plates on either side, silver pommel marked with scratched initials *R.P.*, 14in. overall.
(Butterfield & Butterfield)   £9,322

Bowie knife, unmarked, possibly French, circa 1850, 8⁷/₈in. spear point blade etched with blued foliate designs, bone grip bound in German silver, 14in. overall.
(Butterfield & Butterfield)   £1,243

Rare Bowie knife possibly French, circa 1840, 8¹⁵/₁₆in. clip point blade etched *Arkansan Toothpick* and on the back *Manufactured for F.C. Goergen, New Orleans*, German silver mounted hilt with chequered ebonised grip, 13⁵/₈in. overall.
(Butterfield & Butterfield)   £4,350

Bowie knife, unmarked, possibly French, circa 1840, 9¹³/₁₆in. spear point blade profusely etched with hunting scenes against a gold ground, German silver crossguard, pommel cap, and chequered ebony grip.
(Butterfield & Butterfield)   £1,119

Rare half-horse half-alligator hilt Bowie knife by E. Barnes, Sheffield, circa 1840, 11¹/₂in. clip point blade elaborately etched with American eagle clutching riband, inscribed *American Bowie Knife* over the word *Toothpick*, and flanked by patriotic inscriptions, 15⁷/₁₆in. overall. (Butterfield & Butterfield)   £6,836

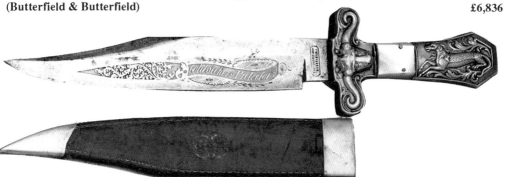

Rare half-horse-half-alligator hilt Bowie knife by Thomas Short, Sheffield, circa 1850, 8¹/₄in. spear point blade with deeply etched motto *Gold Seekers Protector*, German silver hilt with raised buffalo head crossguard and mother-of-pearl grip scales, 13³/₄in. overall. (Butterfield & Butterfield)   £21,131

Rare half-horse/half-alligator hilt Bowie knife by Barnes, Sheffield, circa 1840, 10in. clip point blade, German silver mounted hilt with ivory scales set with an escutcheon plate, 14in. overall. (Butterfield & Butterfield)   £5,593

Rare half-horse-half-alligator hilt Bowie knife by Wragg, Sheffield, circa 1840, 12in. spear point blade, German silver hilt with horn grip scales, 16¹/₂in. overall. (Butterfield & Butterfield)   £3,729

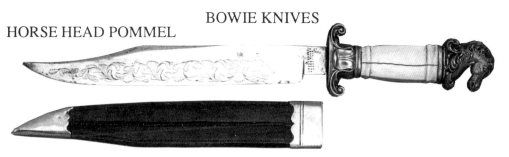

Rare horse head pommel Bowie knife by J. Walters, Sheffield, circa 1850, 11^1/$_2$in. clip point blade, German silver and ivory grip hilt, 17^1/$_8$in. overall.
(Butterfield & Butterfield)   £5,593

Rare horse head pommel Bowie knife by Bunting, Sheffield, circa 1840, 7^3/$_8$in. clip point blade marked *Hawksworth & Mores Celebrated Cast Steel*, German silver mounted hilt with American eagle and shield motifs below horse head, ivory grip scales and coiled snake quillons, 12^{13}/$_{16}$in. overall.
(Butterfield & Butterfield)   £3,729

Rare horse head pommel Bowie knife by Edward Barns, Sheffield, circa 1850, 8^7/$_{16}$in. spear point blade, German silver mounted hilt with rosewood grips, 14^9/$_{16}$in. overall.
(Butterfield & Butterfield)   £4,040

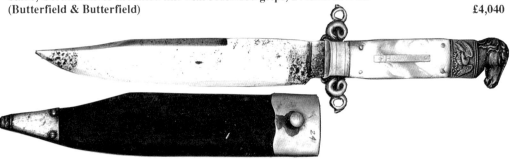

Rare horse head pommel Bowie knife, Sheffield, circa 1840, 8^5/$_{16}$in. clip point blade, German silver hilt featuring coiled snake quillons and American eagle and shield with *E. Pluribus Unum* motto at pommel base, 13^3/$_4$in. overall.
(Butterfield & Butterfield)   £3,729

JOSEPH ROGERS

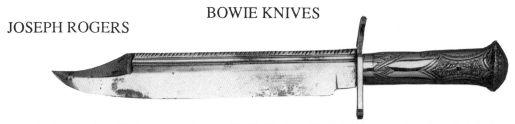

Exhibition Bowie knife by Joseph Rogers, Sheffield, circa 1890, 13³/₈in. serrated clip point blade marked *Joseph Rogers & Sons Cutlers to their Majesties 6 Norfolk St. Sheffield*, profusely decorated cast plated hilt, 19⁷/₈in. overall.
(Butterfield & Butterfield)   **£1,554**

An Edwardian Bowie knife by Joseph Rogers and Sons, clipped back blade 6in., thick white metal crosspiece integral with gripstrap and pommel, two piece rivetted staghorn grips.
(Wallis & Wallis)   £360

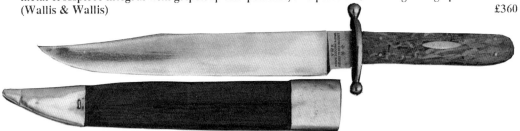

Inscribed English Bowie knife, Sheffield, 9¹/₈in. clip point blade marked *V R/Joseph Rogers & Sons/Cutlers to Her Majesty* at the ricasso, German silver crossguard, staghorn grip scales.
(Butterfield & Butterfield)   **£1,030**

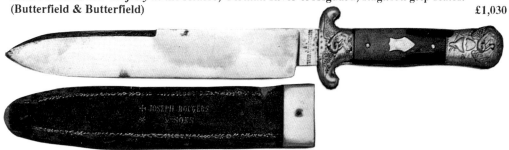

Bowie knife by Joseph Rogers, Sheffield, circa 1860, 8¹/₁₆in. spear point blade marked on ricasso *W. (Crown) R. Joseph Rogers & Sons, Cutlers to her Majesty*, horn grip scales surrounded by German silver crossguard with raised spread eagle and pommel bearing eagle, shield, liberty cap and scales of justice, 12⁷/₈in. overall.
(Butterfield & Butterfield)   **£1,119**

Exhibition Bowie knife by Joseph Rogers, Sheffield, circa 1880, 15⁵/₁₆in. clip point blade, brown composition handle mounted with elaborately engraved Britannia mountings, 21⁵/₁₆in. overall.
(Butterfield & Butterfield)   **£1,709**

JOSEPH ROGERS

Bowie knife by Joseph Rogers, Sheffield, circa 1840, 9³/₁₆in. clip point blade, the ricasso marked, *V (crown) R Joseph Rogers & Sons Cutlers to Her Majesty*, German silver and ivory hilt set with escutcheon plates, 14¹⁵/₁₆in. overall.
(Butterfield & Butterfield)   £2,020

Large Bowie knife by Joseph Rogers, Sheffield, circa 1880, 12in. spear point blade, German silver bound hilt with stag grip scales, with original leather scabbard bearing large German silver mounts.
(Butterfield & Butterfield)   £1,057

Large Bowie knife by Joseph Rogers, Sheffield, circa 1860, 12¹/₄in. clip point blade, stag hilt with German silver serrated guard, 18in. overall.
(Butterfield & Butterfield)   £1,243

Bowie knife by Joseph Rogers, Sheffield, circa 1900, 11⁷/₈in. clip point blade marked on the ricasso *6 (crown) RJ. Rogers & Sons No. 6 Norfolk Street, Sheffield, England*, stag handle with German silver crossguard.
(Butterfield & Butterfield)   £1,398

Bowie knife by J. Rogers, Sheffield, circa 1860, 7⁹/₁₆in. clip point blade, stag handle with German silver crossguard, 12in. overall.
(Butterfield & Butterfield)   £435

BOWIE KNIVES

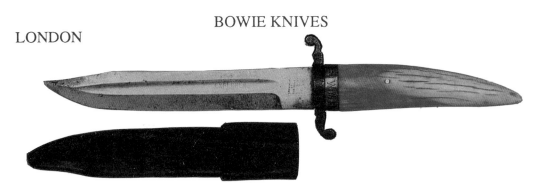

Bowie knife by Cranswick, London, circa 1870, 7³/₄in. clip point blade marked *Explorer* in fuller, iron crossguard and walrus tusk grip with silver band, 13³/₄in. overall.
(Butterfield & Butterfield)   £932

Bowie knife by Holtzapffel, London, circa 1860, 6⁷/₈in. clip point blade marked *Holtzapffel* on the ricasso, iron crossguard and stag grip, 11³/₈in. overall.
(Butterfield & Butterfield)   £233

Bowie knife by W. Thornhill, London, circa 1870, 9¹/₄in. spear point blade marked *W. Thornhill London*, brass crossguard with stag handle and German silver pommel cap, 14⁵/₁₆in. overall.
(Butterfield & Butterfield)   £808

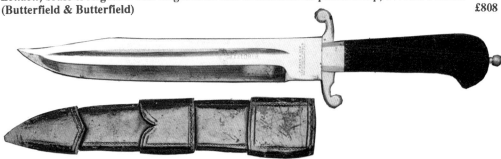

Bowie knife by J. Drew, London, circa 1890, 10in. clip point blade marked on fuller *Explorer*, chequered ebony grip and German silver crossguard, 16in. overall.
(Butterfield & Butterfield)   £746

Large Bowie knife by Booth, Sheffield, circa 1850, 10³/₄in. spear point blade bearing engraved and etched panels on left side with deep serrations on the obverse and reverse, with horn and mother-of-pearl scales and two piece silver plated crossguard, 16⁷/₈in. overall.
(Butterfield & Butterfield)   £3,729

Bowie knife by T. Ellin, Sheffield, circa 1845, 8¹³/₁₆in. clip point blade etched *Prarie Knife*, German silver and ivory hilt set with German silver bands, 13⁵/₈in. overall.
(Butterfield & Butterfield)   £2,952

Bowie knife by Fisher, Sheffield, circa 1860, 10¹/₂in. spear point blade marked *George Fisher, Sheffield*, the ricasso stamped *S.D.*, stag handle with German silver crossguard, 15¹/₄in. overall.
(Butterfield & Butterfield)   £621

English style Bowie knife, unmarked, circa 1880, 11¹/₂in. spear point blade, coin silver mounted hilt with celluloid grip, 17¹/₈in. overall.
(Butterfield & Butterfield)   £218

Bowie knife by C. Congreve, Sheffield, circa 1835, 9¹¹/₁₆in. clip point blade with Spanish notch marked *CELEBRATED AMERICAN BOWIE KNIFE*, German silver and ivory hilt, 14¹/₄in. overall.
(Butterfield & Butterfield)   £9,944

Large Bowie knife by Greaves, Sheffield, circa 1840, 11⁵/₈in. double edged spear point blade, German silver mounted hilt with ivory grip scales bearing escutcheon plates on either side, 16¹/₂in. overall.
(Butterfield & Butterfield)   £4,661

SHEFFIELD

Bowie knife by Thompson, Sheffield, circa 1850, 12^1/$_{16}$in. blade, German silver crossguard with chequered ebony handle, 17^5/$_{16}$in. overall.
(Butterfield & Butterfield)   £404

Bowie knife by Lingard, Sheffield, circa 1850, 8^7/$_8$in. clip point blade etched with 8 florals, eagle carrying bag of gold in beak and clutching riband displaying *Draw me not in haste*, 14^1/$_8$in. overall.
(Butterfield & Butterfield)   £311

Bowie knife by Samuel Robinson, Sheffield, circa 1840, 11^1/$_{16}$in. clip point blade stamped with scenes of early trains and hounds chasing deer, ornate copper plated base metal handle and crossguard, 17^3/$_8$in. overall.
(Butterfield & Butterfield)   £808

Bowie knife by Tillotson, Sheffield, circa 1850, 9^7/$_8$in. clip point blade etched *Hunters Companion*, German silver mounted hilt, oval crossguard and horn grip scales, 17^1/$_2$in. overall.
(Butterfield & Butterfield)   £1,398

Rare alligator hilt Bowie knife by Woodhead and Hartley, Sheffield, circa 1845, 7^3/$_{16}$in. clip point blade etched and stamped *American Hunting Knife*, German silver and ivory hilt set with German silver medallion plaque, 12^1/$_4$in. overall.
(Butterfield & Butterfield)   £2,486

Bowie knife by Wragg, Sheffield, circa 1845, 7^5/$_8$in. clip point blade marked *Alabama Hunting Knife, For Use, Surpass All Try Me*, with figures of hound, buffalo, sphinx, soldier and centaur, ornate cutlery hilt.
(Butterfield & Butterfield)   £528

Bowie knife by James Westa, Sheffield, circa 1850, 7^{1}/$_{16}$in. spear point blade, German silver bound hilt with mother-of-pearl grip scales, 11^{7}/$_{16}$in. overall.
(Butterfield & Butterfield)   £994

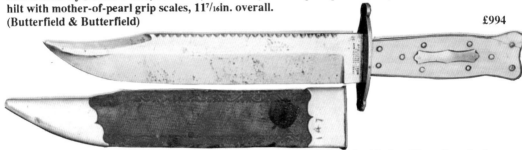

Rare Bowie knife by James Rogers, Sheffield, circa 1845, 9in. clip point blade with scalloped edge marked *ARKANSAS TOOTHPICK*, German silver and ivory hilt with escutcheon plates on either side, 14in. overall.
(Butterfield & Butterfield)   £4,350

Bowie knife by James Rogers, Sheffield, circa 1850, 9in. spear point blade, German silver and wood hilt with escutcheon plaques marked *R.B.P.* and *Pollard* on the reverse, 14^{1}/$_{4}$in. overall.
(Butterfield & Butterfield)   £1,709

Bowie knife by Tillotson, Sheffield, circa 1850, 10in. clip point blade elaborately etched with foliate scrolls, *E Pluribus Unum* motto, stars, spread American eagle, cannon and draped flags, length overall 15^{1}/$_{2}$in.
(Butterfield & Butterfield)   £1,839

Bowie knife by Wilson Hawkworth, Sheffield, circa 1850, 8^{3}/$_{16}$in. clip point blade with etched panel of British Royal seal surrounded by floral designs, German silver cutlery handle with original German silver mounted scabbard, 13^{1}/$_{16}$in. overall.
(Butterfield & Butterfield)   £497

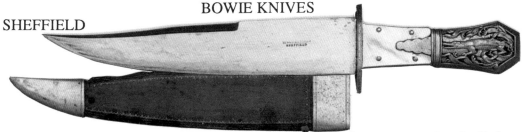

Rare alligator hilt Bowie knife by Butcher, Sheffield, circa 1840, 8⁵/₈in. sharpened clip point blade, German silver and mother-of-pearl hilt, 13³/₁₆in. overall. (Butterfield & Butterfield)

£6,215

Bowie knife by E. Barnes, Sheffield, circa 1860, 6¹/₈in. clip point blade, floral etched and marked *Independence*, ornate German silver hilt with horn grip, scales inlaid with mother-of-pearl, 10¹/₈in. overall. (Butterfield & Butterfield)

£559

Bowie knife by Westa, Sheffield, circa 1845, 8in. spear point blade etched *To Our Brave Volunteers*, German silver mounted hilt with Mexican eagle and snake motifs and stag grip scales, 14³/₈in. overall. (Butterfield & Butterfield)

£5,283

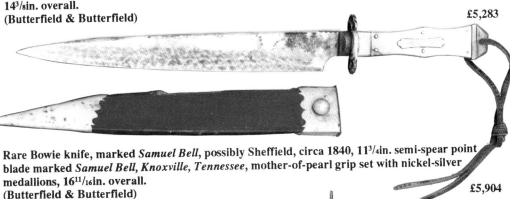

Rare Bowie knife, marked *Samuel Bell*, possibly Sheffield, circa 1840, 11³/₄in. semi-spear point blade marked *Samuel Bell, Knoxville, Tennessee*, mother-of-pearl grip set with nickel-silver medallions, 16¹¹/₁₆in. overall. (Butterfield & Butterfield)

£5,904

Bowie knife by Rogers, Sheffield, circa 1850, 8¹¹/₁₆in. clip point blade, the ricasso stamped *James Rodgers Royal Cutlery, Sheffield*, ornate German silver cutlery hilt, 15¹/₄in. overall. (Butterfield & Butterfield)

£435

Rare large half-horse-half alligator hilt Bowie knife, unmarked, Sheffield, circa 1850, 14¹/₂in. spear point blade stamped *Cast Steel Bowie* with large *H. California Knife* etched on blade, stag grip mounted in German silver, 19¹/₄in. overall.
(Butterfield & Butterfield)   £2,641

Rare half-horse-half-alligator hilt Bowie knife by Woodhead & Hartley, Sheffield, circa 1845, 9³/₁₆in. clip point blade bearing patriotic and foliate etching, German silver hilt with ivory scales set with an escutcheon plaque, 13¹/₂in. overall.
(Butterfield & Butterfield)   £4,972

Rare horse head pommel Bowie knife by James Rogers, Sheffield, circa 1850, 9in. spear point blade marked *Cast Steel Bowie Knife* and *James Rogers Royal Cutlery Sheffield*, German silver hilt with stag grip, 15¹/₁₆in. overall.
(Butterfield & Butterfield)   £2,797

Large half-horse-half-alligator hilt Bowie knife, unmarked, Sheffield, circa 1840, 12⁷/₁₆in. clip point blade, German silver hilt with ivory grip scales and escutcheon plate, 17¹/₈in. overall.
(Butterfield & Butterfield)   £2,797

A late Victorian Bowie knife, clipped back blade 7in. stamped *Ibbotson Brothers & Co Limited Sheffield*, with globe, pressed horn hilt inlaid with mother-of-pearl diamonds.
(Wallis & Wallis)   £150

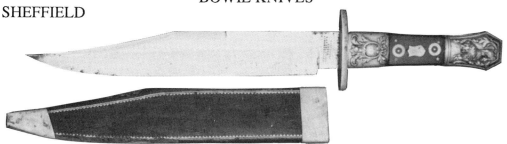

Lion pommel Bowie knife by William Jackson, Sheffield, circa 1845, 8^{15}/$_{16}$in. clip point blade etched with scrolls and the intertwined legend *A SURE DEFENCE*, German silver hilt with rosewood scales set with mother-of-pearl and silver medallion plaque, 14in. overall.
(Butterfield & Butterfield)   £3,107

Bowie knife by Butcher, Sheffield, circa 1850, 9^{1}/$_{8}$in. clip point blade, German silver cutlery handle and guard, with original scabbard, 14^{5}/$_{8}$in. overall.
(Butterfield & Butterfield)   £1,181

Bowie knife by Butcher, Sheffield, circa 1835, 8^{3}/$_{4}$in. clip point blade with Spanish notch, German silver mounted rosewood hilt, complete with original period composition scabbard, 13^{3}/$_{4}$in. overall.
(Butterfield & Butterfield)   £2,486

Rare lion head pommel Bowie knife by J. Nicholson, Sheffield, 10^{3}/$_{8}$in. clip point blade, German silver mounted with pearl grips, with original scabbard embossed *CALIFORNIA GOLD FINDER*, 14^{1}/$_{2}$in. overall.
(Butterfield & Butterfield)   £2,797

Bowie knife, unmarked, Sheffield, circa 1840, 9¼in. clip point blade with coin silver overlay on ricasso, ivory grip flanked by German silver guard, bolster and pommel of shell motif, 13⅞in. overall.
(Butterfield & Butterfield)   £6,215

Bowie knife by Butcher, Sheffield, circa 1835, 8½in. clip point blade with Spanish notch, German silver and rosewood hilt bearing escutcheon plates on either side, 13⅛in. overall.
(Butterfield & Butterfield)
                                                                                                            £5,593

Bowie knife by Tillotson, Sheffield, circa 1850, 10¹/₁₆in. blade profusely etched with foliate scrolls, American eagle, stars, cannon and *Gold Hunters' Knife, E. Pluribus Unum, Palo Alto*, German silver S guard, reclining llon pommel and mother-of-pearl scales bearing an escutcheon plate, 14⅜in. overall.
(Butterfield & Butterfield)   £10,565

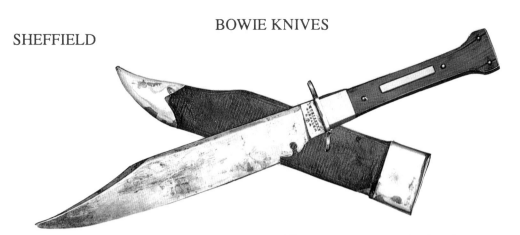

Rare Bowie knife by Butcher, Sheffield, circa 1835, 8⁹/₁₆in. clip point blade with Spanish notch,
German silver bound hilt with rosewood grip, 13¹/₂in. overall.
(Butterfield & Butterfield)   £4,040

Bowie knife by Woodhead, Sheffield, circa 1850, 9in. clip point blade elaborately etched with
panel scenes of the Golden Gate, spread American eagle and running buffalo, marked
*Manufactured by G. Woodhead, California at The Diggings, the United States the Land of the Free
and the Home of the Brave protected by her noble and brave Volunteers* and *Celebrated American
Bowie knife,* 14¹/₂in. overall.
(Butterfield & Butterfield)   £9,322

Bowie knife by Enoch Drabble, Sheffield, circa 1840, 8¹/₂in. clip point blade, elaborately etched
with floral scrolls and the legends *My Country,* the reverse *My Steel its Protection,* ivory hilt with
German silver mounts and escutcheon plate, 12¹/₂in. overall.
(Butterfield & Butterfield)   £4,972

Bowie knife by E. Barnes, Sheffield, circa 1860, 7^{1}/$_{16}$in. spear point blade marked *The Real U.S. Knife, Hunters Companion*, stag hilt, 13^{7}/$_{16}$in. overall.
(Butterfield & Butterfield)   £280

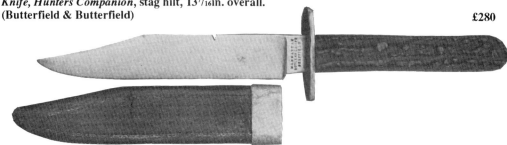

English Bowie knife by Manhattan Cutlery Company, Sheffield, 5^{3}/$_{4}$in. clip point blade, German silver quillons, staghorn grip scales.
(Butterfield & Butterfield)   £110

Bowie knife by Tillotson, Sheffield, circa 1850, 10in. clip point blade etched with bold ornate scrolls and legend *Hunters' Companion*, 14^{1}/$_{2}$in. overall.
(Butterfield & Butterfield)   £3,729

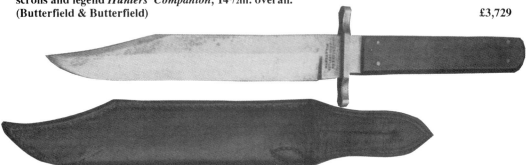

English Bowie knife by Manhattan Cutlery Company, Sheffield, the 7in. clip point blade marked *Manhattan/Cutlery Comp/Sheffield* on the ricasso, horn grip scales.
(Butterfield & Butterfield)   £405

Engllsh Bowie knife by Manhattan Cutlery Company, Sheffield, 5^{1}/$_{2}$in. clip point blade, German silver quillons, staghorn grip scales with rectangular silver inset.
(Butterfield & Butterfield)   £92

Sheffield Bowie knife by Edward Barnes, having an 8³/₄in. clipped point blade etched on the left side with American eagle over riband with maker's name and motto *American Bowie Knife*, length overall 13³/₄in.
(Butterfield & Butterfield)   £1,656

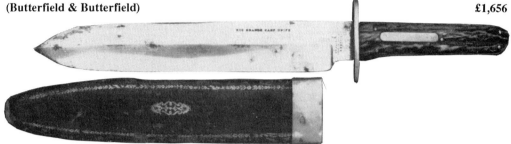

Bowie knife by William Jackson, Sheffield, circa 1860, 10¹/₁₆in. blade marked *Rio Grand Camp Knife*, the ricasso stamped *Wm. Jackson Sheaf Island Works Sheffield*, German silver mounted stag hilt, 15in. overall.
(Butterfield & Butterfield)   £1,398

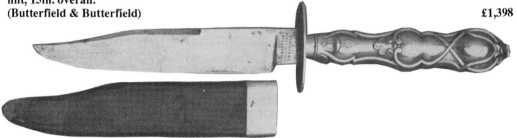

English Bowie knife by Manhattan Cutlery Company, Sheffield, 6¹/₄in. clip point blade etched with florals and the motto *Americans Ask For Nothing But What Is Right/And will Submit To Nothing Wrong* and *OK*.
(Butterfield & Butterfield)   £313

Bowie knife by William Jackson, Sheffield, circa 1860, 7¹/₁₆in. spear point blade marked *Rio Grande Camp Knife*, German silver crossguard and stag handle, 11¹/₈in. overall.
(Butterfield & Butterfield)   £994

Bowie knife by Edward Barnes, Sheffield, circa 1860, 7⁷/₁₆in. spear point blade, stag handle with German silver guard and pommel cap, 12¹/₈in. overall.
(Butterfield & Butterfield)   £264

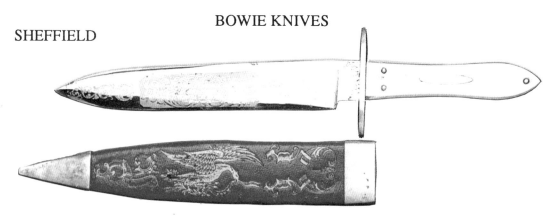

Bowie knife by G. Nixon, Sheffield, circa 1860, 6^{13}/$_{16}$in. spear point blade etched with foliate designs and decorative panel bearing the motto *The Land of the Free and Home of the Brave*, ivory hilt with German silver guard, 10^{7}/$_{8}$in. overall.
(Butterfield & Butterfield)   £2,641

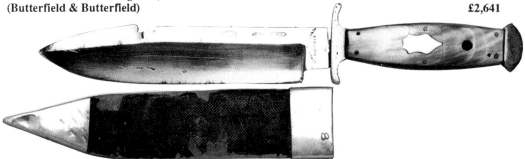

Bowie knife by Corsan Denton & Co., Sheffield, circa 1850, 8in. notched spear point blade marked *Warranted* and *Of The Best Quality*, brass bound hilt with horn grip scales, 13^{3}/$_{16}$in. overall.
(Butterfield & Butterfield)   £684

Rare Bowie knife by Broomhead and Thomas, Sheffield, circa 1835, 10^{11}/$_{16}$in. clip point blade with Spanish notch, the ricasso marked *Broomhead and Thomas Celebrated American Hunting Knife*, 16in. overall.
(Butterfield & Butterfield)   £8,701

Bowie knife by Horrabins, Sheffield, circa 1847, 8in. blade stamped *Rough and Ready, Old Zack, Buena Vista* and depicting mounted hunter with dogs chasing buffalo, 12^{7}/$_{16}$in. overall.
(Butterfield & Butterfield)   £9,322

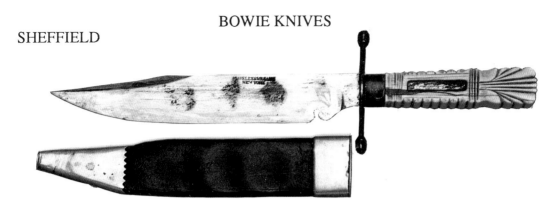

Rare Bowie knife marked *Gravely & Wreaks, Sheffield*, circa 1840, 8^{1}/$_{4}$in. etched clip point blade with Spanish notch, iron crossguard and incised carved ivory handle set with escutcheon plate, 12^{7}/$_{8}$in. overall.
(Butterfield & Butterfield)   £2,020

Bowie knife by Manson, Sheffield, circa 1865, 7^{3}/$_{16}$in. spear point blade, floral etched with the legend *A Sure Defense*, German silver cutlery handle, 12^{1}/$_{4}$in. overall.
(Butterfield & Butterfield)   £528

Rare massive Bowie knife by Broomhead & Thomas, Sheffield, circa 1835, 10^{11}/$_{16}$in. clip point blade with Spanish notch, marked on ricasso *Broomhead & Thomas, Celebrated American Hunting Knife*, the ornate German silver and mother-of-pearl hilt fitted with crowned pommel, 15^{3}/$_{4}$in. overall.
(Butterfield & Butterfield)   £26,103

Bowie knife by Webster, Sheffield, circa 1850, 10^{3}/$_{16}$in. spear point blade elaborately etched on left side with floral scrolls, the motto *I Am For Use, Try Me* and panel scenes of a steam locomotive and sailing ship with the word *Dispatch* overhead, 15^{3}/$_{4}$in. overall.
(Butterfield & Butterfield)   £3,729

Large Bowie knife, unmarked, possibly Sheffield, circa 1860, 12⁷/₁₆in. spear point blade stamped with winged horse on ricasso, German silver crossguard and stag grip, with original leather scabbard bearing German and coin silver mounts, 17³/₂₁in. overall.
(Butterfield & Butterfield)   £870

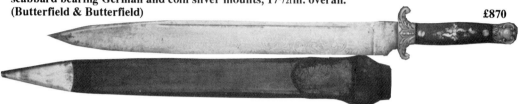

Large Bowie knife, unmarked, probably Sheffield, circa 1860, 16¹/₂in. spear point blade fully etched in ornate foliate motif, horn grip inlaid with floral mother-of-pearl designs on one side, 22¹/₂in. overall.
(Butterfield & Butterfield)   £1,554

Bowie knife by J. Lingard, Sheffield, circa 1860, 7¹³/₁₆in. clip point blade marked on ricasso *John Lingards Celebrated Bowie Knife, Peacroft, Sheffield*, ornate German silver hilt with American eagle and shield in a central panel flanked by mother-of-pearl scales, 12⁹/₁₆in. overall.
(Butterfield & Butterfield)   £1,398

Large Bowie knife by Bunting, Sheffield, circa 1850, 13³/₁₆in. clip point blade marked *R. Bunting & Sons, Cutlers to their Majesties*, German silver hilt with ivory grip scales bearing an escutcheon plaque, 18¹/₈in. overall.
(Butterfield & Butterfield)   £3,729

Bowie knife by William Jackson, Sheffield, circa 1850, 10¹/₈in. spear point blade marked *Rio Grande Camp Knife*, the ricasso stamped *William Jackson, Sheaf Island Works, Sheffield*, stag hilt with German silver guard and escutcheon plate, 15in. overall.
(Butterfield & Butterfield)   £932

Massive Bowie knife by Wragg, Sheffield, circa 1840, 16^1/$_8$in. clip point blade marked *Cast Steel Bowie Knife, Samuel C. Wragg, No. 25 Funice Hill, Sheffield,* German silver hilt with bone grip scales bearing escutcheon plates on either side, 21^5/$_8$in. overall.
(Butterfield & Butterfield)   £3,107

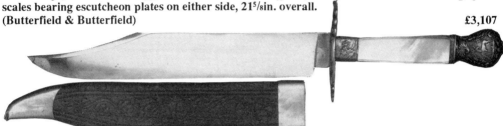

Large Bowie knife, unmarked, Sheffield, 11^1/$_2$in. clip point blade, mother-of-pearl grip with ornate German silver mounts, pommel bears floral and stag motifs, 18^3/$_8$in. overall.
(Butterfield & Butterfield)   £2,952

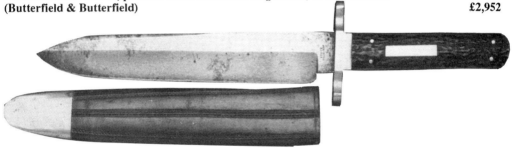

Bowie knife by Stacy, Sheffield, circa 1860, 7^{15}/$_{16}$in. semi-spear point blade, German silver crossguard and stag grip set with an escutcheon plate, 12^1/$_2$in. overall.
(Butterfield & Butterfield)   £590

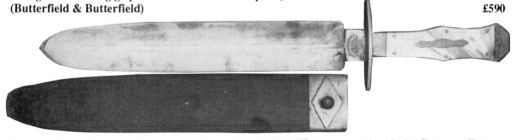

Bowie knife by Unwin & Rogers, Sheffield, circa 1845, 11^1/$_8$in. spear point blade, German silver hilt with mother-of-pearl scales bearing an escutcheon plate, 16^1/$_8$in. overall.
(Butterfield & Butterfield)   £2,175

Bowie knife by Haywood, Sheffield, circa 1850, 8^7/$_8$in. clip point blade marked on ricasso *Joseph Haywood & Company Makers, Sheffield,* teapot stamped on obverse, German silver and chequered horn hilt, 14^3/$_{16}$in. overall.
(Butterfield & Butterfield)   £1,709

Large Bowie knife by George Wostenholm, Sheffield, circa 1850, 11½in. clip point blade, marked *Wostenholm & Sons, Washington Works, IXL* and *The Real IXL Knife, Hunters Companion*, chequered horn grip, 17in. overall.
(Butterfield & Butterfield)   £1,181

Small Bowie knife by G. Wostenholm, Sheffield, circa 1850, 5⁷/₁₆in. spear point blade marked *G. Wostenholm & Sons, Washington Works, Sheffield* and *The real IXL Knife, the Hunters Companion*, ornate German silver mounts with mother-of-pearl grip scales, 9½in. overall.
(Butterfield & Butterfield)   £1,057

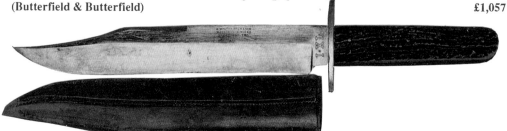

Bowie knife by Wostenholm, Sheffield, circa 1900, 9⁷/₈in. clip point blade marked *G. Wostenholm & Son, Washington Works, Sheffield, England*, German silver crossguard with stag handle, 15in. overall.
(Butterfield & Butterfield)   £746

Bowie knife by Wostenholm, Sheffield, circa 1860, 10³/₁₆in. clip point blade marked *G. Wostenholm & Son, Washington Works, Sheffield*, spread eagle and *The Real IXL Knife, The Hunters' Companion*, German silver and stag hilt set with escutcheon plate, 15½in. overall.
(Butterfield & Butterfield)   £1,864

IXL Bowie knife by Wostenholm, Sheffield, circa 1840, 8¹⁵/₁₆in. clip point blade with sharpened false edge, German silver mounted hilt with ivory grip scales bearing escutcheon plates on either side, 13½in. overall.
(Butterfield & Butterfield)   £3,418

WOSTENHOLM

Bowie knife by Wostenholm, Sheffield, circa 1850, $9^7/_8$in. clip point blade marked *G. Wostenholm & Son Washington Works, IXL The Real IXL Knife and the Hunters Companion*, the ricasso stamped with General Taylor on horseback, 15in. overall.
(Butterfield & Butterfield)   £2,641

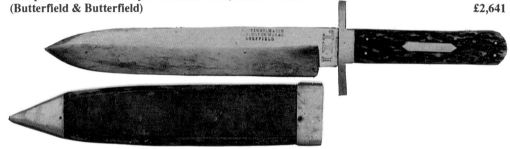

Bowie knife by Wostenholm, Sheffield, circa 1860, $8^7/_{16}$in. spear point blade, German silver crossguard with stag handle set with escutcheon plate, $13^3/_4$in. overall.
(Butterfield & Butterfield)   £1,181

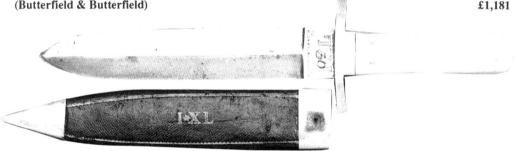

Bowie knife by Wostenholm, Sheffield, circa 1850, $6^{15}/_{16}$in. spear point blade, German silver guard and mother-of-pearl grip scales, $11^1/_8$in. overall.
(Butterfield & Butterfield)   £1,057

Bowie knife by Wostenholm, Sheffield, circa 1850, $11^9/_{16}$in. clip point blade marked *G. Wostenholm & Son Washington Works. IXL The Real IXL Knife, The Hunters' Companion, None are genuine, but those marked IXL and etched G. Wostenholm and Son celebrated California Knife*, 17in. overall.
(Butterfield & Butterfield)   £9,322

Large I.X.L. Bowie knife by Wostenholm, Sheffield, circa 1850, $12^5/_{16}$in. clip point blade, stag hilt with German silver crossguard, $17^1/_2$in. overall.
(Butterfield & Butterfield)   £1,398

BOWIE KNIVES

Rare outstanding exhibition Bowie knife by George Wostenholm, Sheffield, circa 1870, 13^1/$_2$in. clip point blade elaborately etched with panel scenes of Mt. Vernon flanked by standing Indians, mother-of-pearl grip marked *Avoir Patrie* under a raised carved profile of George Washington, 21^1/$_2$in. overall.
(Butterfield & Butterfield)   £74,580

Small Bowie knife by Wostenholm, the 5^1/$_4$in. double edged spear point blade marked *I-X-L/ George/Wostenholm/Celebrated/Cutlery*, hilt with ivory scales and German silver quillons and pommel.
(Butterfield & Butterfield)   £294

Rare ornate Bowie knife by Wostenholm, Sheffield, circa 1850, 10^1/$_4$in. clip point blade, coin silver mounted hilt with full fluted ivory grips and elaborately engraved quillons in the form of dolphins, 15^3/$_4$in. overall.
(Butterfield & Butterfield)   £9,944

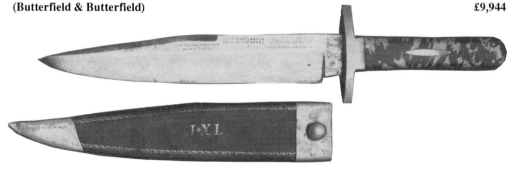

English IXL Bowie knife, 8in. clip point blade marked *None Are Genuine But Those/Marked IXL, G. Wostenholm & Son/Washington Works, The Real IXL Knife, The Hunters Companion*, and *IXL*, grip with tortoise shell with German silver escutcheon.
(Butterfield & Butterfield)   £809

A good early 19th century Persian dagger, 12³/₄in., finely watered single edged blade 6³/₄in., with chiselled ribs along back edge, floral and foliate engraved silver bolster, one piece walrus ivory hilt.
(Wallis & Wallis)   £625

An unusual 19th century Ottoman enamelled Qama, 22¹/₂in., broad double-edged fullered blade 13³/₄in., thickly silver damascened at forte with foliage, copper hilt and sheath.
(Wallis & Wallis)   £280

Silver mounted dagger, probably late 18th/early 19th century, the 7in. sharply tapered blade with false edge and serrated back, the tapered silver hilt with plain fluted channels alternating with repoussé floral panels.
(Butterfield & Butterfield)   £405

A 19th century Tibetan silver mount dagger, pattern welded straight single edged blade 11¹/₄in., fluted sharkskin covered grip, pommel pierced with foliage and set with 2 turquoise.
(Wallis & Wallis)   £170

An Indian dagger with watered slightly curved double-edged blade cut with lines forming ridges along its entire lengths on both sides, mutton-fat jade hilt with fish-tail pommel and swelling grip, 19th century, 16¹/₂in. long.
(Christie's)   £3,850

An unusual Bosnian dagger with bird shaped hilt, 12³/₄in., bi-fullered single edged blade 7in. with bird shaped brass forte, one piece horn hilt carved in the form of a bird, with inlaid ivory eyes.
(Wallis & Wallis)   £90

A rare dagger of a member of the French Mameluk Guard, imitating a jambiya, the slender curved double-edged blade of hollow triangular section, etched *Coulaux Frères* on one face and *Mfture de Klingenthal* on the other, 1801–4, 21in.
(Christie's)   £2,090

DAGGERS

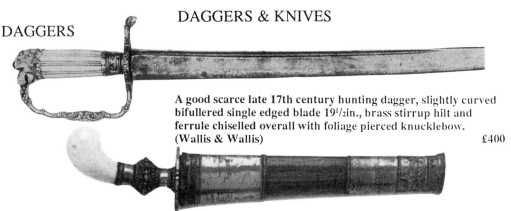

A good scarce late 17th century hunting dagger, slightly curved bifullered single edged blade 19¹/₂in., brass stirrup hilt and ferrule chiselled overall with foliage pierced knucklebow.
(Wallis & Wallis)   £400

Southeast Asian dagger, having a 9in. undulating blade, the low grade silver hilt with ivory pistol grip, with silver mounted wood scabbard, length overall 13in.
(Butterfield & Butterfield)   £147

An Indian dagger with watered slight curved double-edged blade reinforced towards the point, rock-crystal hilt decorated with shaped gold panels set with green foiled cabochon gems, probably 17th century, 12in. long.
(Christie's)   £968

A large 19th century Indian silver mounted dagger, 17¹/₄in. broad straight single edged blade 9¹/₂in., nicely engraved with scrolling palmettes, in its green velvet covered sheath with silver mounts.
(Wallis & Wallis)   £330

A good 19th century Indo Persian scissors dagger, 10¹/₂in., fluted steel blades gold damascened with foliage, scroll pierced brass handles with traces of gilding.
(Wallis & Wallis)   £150

A scarce 19th century Burmese dagger, straight single edged blade 9¹/₄in., brass crosspiece with nicely chiselled and chased lion's head finials, two piece chequered ivory grips.
(Wallis & Wallis)   £110

BADE BADE

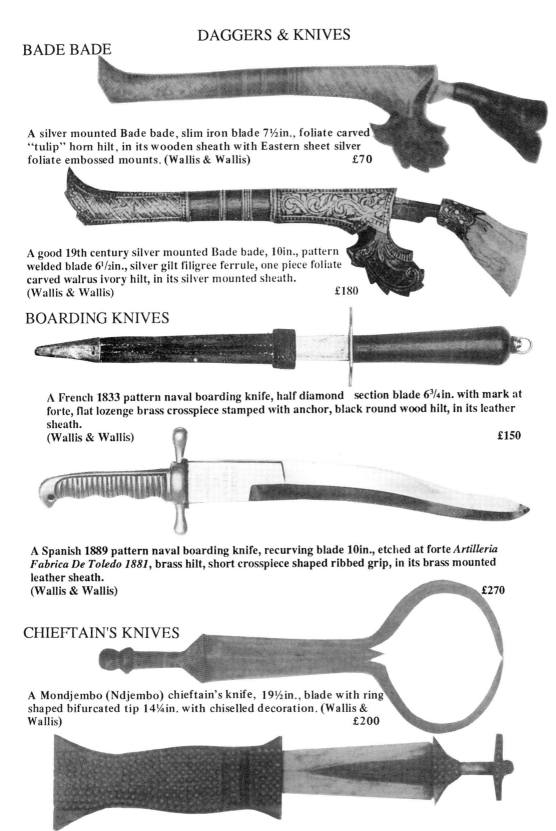

A silver mounted Bade bade, slim iron blade 7½in., foliate carved "tulip" horn hilt, in its wooden sheath with Eastern sheet silver foliate embossed mounts. (Wallis & Wallis)   £70

A good 19th century silver mounted Bade bade, 10in., pattern welded blade 6½in., silver gilt filigree ferrule, one piece foliate carved walrus ivory hilt, in its silver mounted sheath. (Wallis & Wallis)   £180

BOARDING KNIVES

A French 1833 pattern naval boarding knife, half diamond section blade 6¾in. with mark at forte, flat lozenge brass crosspiece stamped with anchor, black round wood hilt, in its leather sheath.
(Wallis & Wallis)   £150

A Spanish 1889 pattern naval boarding knife, recurving blade 10in., etched at forte *Artilleria Fabrica De Toledo 1881*, brass hilt, short crosspiece shaped ribbed grip, in its brass mounted leather sheath.
(Wallis & Wallis)   £270

CHIEFTAIN'S KNIVES

A Mondjembo (Ndjembo) chieftain's knife, 19½in., blade with ring shaped bifurcated tip 14¼in. with chiselled decoration. (Wallis & Wallis)   £200

A Chief's knife, Empute, of the Nkundo-Ekonda tribe of the Central Basin of Zaire, broad blade 12¾ x 3¼in. at widest. (Wallis & Wallis)   £140

An 18th century Indian dagger kard, thick heavy single edged watered steel blade 12in., steel ferrules and gripstrap with brass pommel band, two piece thick ivory grips of good colour. (Wallis & Wallis)   £290

A well made Indo Persian dagger kard, circa 1800, watered steel blade 8in., floral and foliate gold damascened bolsters and gripstrap. (Wallis & Wallis)   £115

An unusual late 18th century Ottoman Turkish dagger kard, $15^{1}/_{2}$in., slightly T section blade $8^{1}/_{2}$in. of sham damascus watered pattern, foliate chiselled brass ferrule, one piece walrus ivory hilt.
(Wallis & Wallis)   £340

A 19th century Caucasian dagger kard, watered steel single edged blade 7in., tapered cylindrical watered steel hilt.
(Wallis & Wallis)   £160

An 18th century Persian dagger kard, very finely watered polished single edged hollow ground blade $8^{3}/_{4}$in., of Kirk Nardaban pattern, steel gripstrap and bolsters, two-piece polished ivory grips. (Wallis & Wallis)   £110

Indo-Persian dagger, kard, having a $9^{1}/_{2}$in. watered single edged blade decorated at the hilt with gold koftgari inlay, the steel hilt entirely inlaid with gold koftgari florals, length overall $13^{3}/_{4}$in. (Butterfield & Butterfield)   £478

DAGGER PESH KABZ

A good Indian gold damascened dagger pesh kabz circa 1800, 13$^{1}/_{2}$in., finely watered recurved single edged blade 8$^{3}/_{4}$in. of dark tight whorled pattern, large steel hilt thickly gold damascened with flowers and foliage in panels and borders, faceted button to pommel.
(Wallis & Wallis) £220

A good 18th century Persian dagger pesh kabz, 14in. long, recurved T section blade 9$^{1}/_{2}$in., finely watered with raised central rib and edges, applied with shaped device on each side.
(Wallis & Wallis) £400

A fine quality 18th century Indo-Persian dagger pesh kabz, 13$^{3}/_{4}$in., recurved blade 9in. of hollow ground T section, finely watered dark kirk nardaban pattern, fluted back edge, thickened armour piercing top.
(Wallis & Wallis) £575

A gold damascened Indo Persian dagger pesh kabz circa 1800, 15$^{1}/_{2}$in., 'T' section blade 11in. with swollen point, damscened with foliate and floral designs at forte.
(Wallis & Wallis) £190

An attractive Indo Persian copper gilt mounted dagger pesh kabz, circa 1800, 18in., re-curved 'T' section blade 9$^{3}/_{4}$in. with thickened armour piercing tip. (Wallis & Wallis) £180

Large Indo-Persian dagger, pesh-kabz, the 13in. blade inscribed on right side *Henry Waghorn 1880*, the massive hilt with marine ivory plaquettes, length overall 17$^{1}/_{4}$in.
(Butterfield & Butterfield) £203

DIRK KNIVES

Dirk knife by Butcher, Sheffield, circa 1860, 6¹/₈in. double edged spear point blade with finely etched panel eagle over the motto *U.S. Land of the Free and Home of the Brave*, 10¹/₂in. overall. (Butterfield & Butterfield)

£1,554

English dirk knife by Manhattan Cutlery Company, Sheffield, 3³/₄in. spear point blade, German silver quillons, bone grip scales with two circular horn insets. (Butterfield & Butterfield)

£74

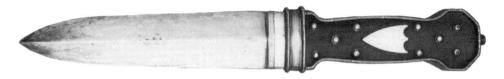

Rare California gold and silver mounted dirk knife, unmarked, San Francisco, circa 1850, 6¹/₄in. double edged blade, the horn hilt bound in silver and set with gold medallion plaques, the horn central portion set with gold name plaque, 11¹/₂in. overall. (Butterfield & Butterfield)

£10,565

Dirk knife by Wilson Swift, Sheffield, circa 1860, 8¹⁵/₁₆in. double edged spear point blade with floral etched panel surrounding the legend *America the Land of the Free and the Home of the Brave*, the hilt with German silver crossguard and horn grip scales set with round mother-of-pearl inlays, 14¹/₄in. overall. (Butterfield & Butterfield)

£1,398

English dirk knife, 6³/₄in. spear point blade etched *Watt/Sheffield*, steel crossguard, one piece ivory grip with German silver ferrule and pommel plate. (Butterfield & Butterfield)

£1,030

English dirk knife by Manhattan Cutlery Company, Sheffield, 6in. single edge spear point blade, German silver quillons, length overall 10in. (Butterfield & Butterfield)

£276

DIRK KNIVES

Dirk knife by Hill & Son, London, circa 1860, 7¹/₂in. double edged spear point blade etched *Death to Traitors*, iron crossguard and chequered ebony grip, 12¹/₂in. overall.
(Butterfield & Butterfield)   £2,641

English dirk knife by Manhattan Cutlery Company, Sheffield, 7in. spear point blade, German silver quillons, staghorn grip scales with German silver escutcheon.
(Butterfield & Butterfield)   £184

Dirk knife by M. Price, San Francisco, circa 1860, 5¹/₄in. spear point blade, iron mounted hilt with walrus ivory handle.
(Butterfield & Butterfield)   £1,864

Dirk knife, unmarked, Sheffield, circa 1860, 6⁹/₁₆in. double edged spear point blade, etched *Never Draw Me Without Reason Nor Sheath Me Without Honor*, ivory grip, crossguard bears the legend *Liberty and Union*, 11in. overall.
(Butterfield & Butterfield)   £497

English dirk knife, 6³/₄in. spear point blade marked *J. Lockley/V R/Warranted* on the ricasso, German silver grip with horn inlaid bone scales and cutlery style mounts featuring Mexican eagle and snake on pommel.
(Butterfield & Butterfield)   £957

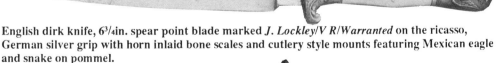

English dirk knife by Manhattan Cutlery Company, Sheffield, 4³/₄in. spear point blade, German silver quillons, bone grip scales.
(Butterfield & Butterfield)   £59

DIRKS

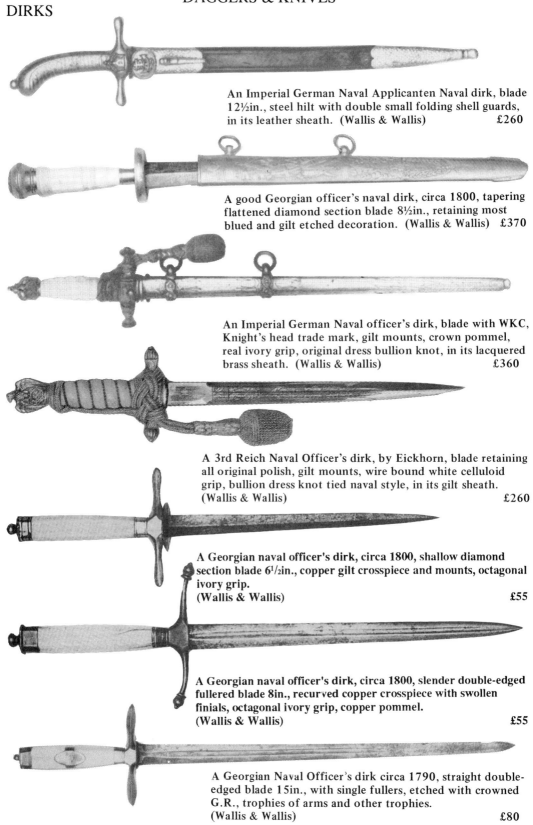

An Imperial German Naval Applicanten Naval dirk, blade 12½in., steel hilt with double small folding shell guards, in its leather sheath. (Wallis & Wallis) £260

A good Georgian officer's naval dirk, circa 1800, tapering flattened diamond section blade 8½in., retaining most blued and gilt etched decoration. (Wallis & Wallis) £370

An Imperial German Naval officer's dirk, blade with WKC, Knight's head trade mark, gilt mounts, crown pommel, real ivory grip, original dress bullion knot, in its lacquered brass sheath. (Wallis & Wallis) £360

A 3rd Reich Naval Officer's dirk, by Eickhorn, blade retaining all original polish, gilt mounts, wire bound white celluloid grip, bullion dress knot tied naval style, in its gilt sheath. (Wallis & Wallis) £260

A Georgian naval officer's dirk, circa 1800, shallow diamond section blade 6¹/₂in., copper gilt crosspiece and mounts, octagonal ivory grip. (Wallis & Wallis) £55

A Georgian naval officer's dirk, circa 1800, slender double-edged fullered blade 8in., recurved copper crosspiece with swollen finials, octagonal ivory grip, copper pommel. (Wallis & Wallis) £55

A Georgian Naval Officer's dirk circa 1790, straight double-edged blade 15in., with single fullers, etched with crowned G.R., trophies of arms and other trophies. (Wallis & Wallis) £80

DIRKS

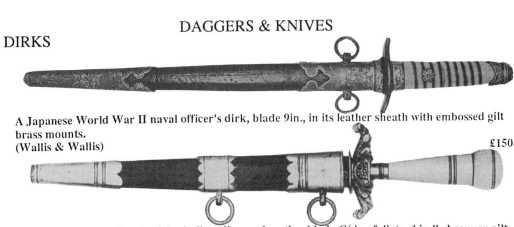

A Japanese World War II naval officer's dirk, blade 9in., in its leather sheath with embossed gilt brass mounts.
(Wallis & Wallis)   £150

A Georgian naval officer's dirk, shallow diamond section blade 6¼in., foliate chiselled copper gilt crosspiece and ferrule, turned ivory grip and swollen pommel with good patina.
(Wallis & Wallis)   £210

A Georgian officer's dirk, circa 1800, straight double-edged fullered blade 16in., copper gilt mounts, recurved crosspiece, reeded ivory grip, in its leather sheath.
(Wallis & Wallis)   £75

Small silver mounted dirk, having an unmarked 5⅜in. leaf shaped blade, the silver hilt of oval section with plain pommel and quillons with acorn finials.
(Butterfield & Butterfield)   £313

A scarce American silver hilted midshipman's dirk, circa 1820, shallow diamond section blade 5½in., pressed silver hilt with helmet pommel and scaled grips.
(Wallis & Wallis)   £175

Rare and historic presentation Confederate naval dirk, unmarked, Continental, circa 1860, 7⅛in. spear point blade etched *Presented to John T. Wood* and on the reverse *From His Shipmates Aboard C.S.S. Virginia, March 9, 1862*, 13¼in. overall.
(Butterfield & Butterfield)   £23,617

A Victorian dirk, shallow diamond section blade 5¼in., stamped crowned *VR* above *Paget* London, copper gilt hilt in the form of entwined sea monster with quillons and pommel en-suite.
(Wallis & Wallis)   £115

FIGHTING KNIVES

A World War I/II Dutch commando knife, blade 8in., retaining some blued finish, oval steel crosspiece, shaped ribbed wood hilt, in its leather sheath.
(Wallis & Wallis)   £85

A French World War I trench knife, spear point blade 6¼in., stamped at forte *41 Gonon*, steel crosspiece, wooden hilt, in its steel sheath with belt loop.
(Wallis & Wallis)   £70

A scarce 1st pattern field service fighting knife, blade 6in. engraved *F.A.A.* with square shank etched *Wilkinson Sword* and *The FS Fighting Knife* plated reversed crosspiece, diced plated hilt.
(Wallis & Wallis)   £190

A good World War I French fighting trench knife, blade 8in. struck with mark of an archer, steel crosspiece, rivetted wooden grips, in its steel sheath.
(Wallis & Wallis)   £45

A US M1917 knuckleduster trench knife, triangular blade 8½in., traces of blued finish, steel knuckleduster knucklebar, shaped wood grip.
(Wallis & Wallis)   £60

A 1st Pattern Field Service fighting knife, tapering double-edged square shank flattened diamond section blade 6½in. by Wilkinson Sword, chequered plated hilt.
(Wallis & Wallis)   £210

FIGHTING KNIVES

A Nazi fighting knife, spear blade 6½in., Nazi control stamp at forte, steel narrow crosspiece, wood grips, in its black painted metal sheath.
(Wallis & Wallis)   £80

A World War II Dutch commando knife, blued blade 8in., steel crosspiece, ribbed wooden grip with swollen pommel, in its leather sheath with copper riveted frog.
(Wallis & Wallis)   £150

A 2nd Pattern FS fighting knife, blade 6½in. etched with label 'Wilkinson Sword, etc', and within scrolls 'Hand Forged by Tom Beasley, the Famous Sword Smith'. (Wallis & Wallis)
£120

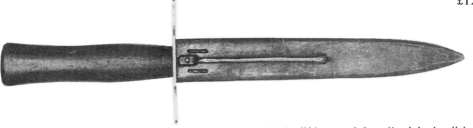

A French World War I fighting knife, spear shaped blade 6½in., retaining all original polish, stamped *41. Gonon*, flat steel crosspiece, rounded wooden hilt.
(Wallis & Wallis)   £70

A U.S. World War I Mark I brass hilt fighting knife, blade 7in., hilt marked *US 1918 L.F. & C* **1918 and pricker engraved with initials, in its metal sheath** stamped at throat.
(Wallis & Wallis)   £130

A scarce Belgian World War I combat knife, tapered blade 8in., stamped *(Sand)erson Brothers Newbould* with faint *Sheffield*, oval steel guard, wooden grip, steel sheath with pierced steel belt loop.
(Wallis & Wallis)   £100

FOLDING KNIVES

English folding knife/circa 1860, 4½in. blade marked *Of the Best Quality* with faint Sheffield maker's mark, mother-of-pearl inlaid horn plaquettes, German silver cutlery style pommel. (Butterfield & Butterfield)   £203

A late Victorian folding Bowie type knife, blade 4in., embossed mounts incorporating classical masks amid foliage and scrolls, flat horn sideplates, copper suspension ring. (Wallis & Wallis)   £145

An unusual late 19th century Indian hunting knife with assorted implements built into the 'penknife' style hilt, clipped back blade 8½in., gold damascened with two tigers and an antelope. (Wallis & Wallis)   £340

European folding knife, 19th century, 4in. blade etched with florals and birds, wood grips inlaid with ivory floral and scroll designs, German silver mounts. (Butterfield & Butterfield)   £258

A late 19th century Indian combination Bowie knife, clipped back blade 8½in., damascened with 2 tigers and antelope, with stipple engraved foliage on reverse. (Wallis & Wallis)   £300

English folding knife, circa 1860, 4¼in. blade marked *US* and *Edward Barnes & Sons*, horn plaquettes with German silver inlay, German silver cutlery style pommel. (Butterfield & Butterfield)   £331

HUNTING KNIVES

Bowie or hunting knife by John Coe, Sheffield, circa 1860, $15^{13}/_{16}$in. clip point blade, German silver hilt with ivory and horn grip scales, $21^{1}/_{2}$in. overall.
(Butterfield & Butterfield)   £2,175

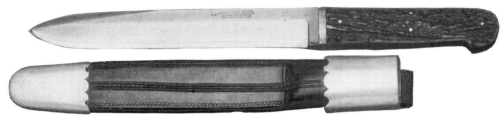

Bowie or hunting knife by Joseph Rogers, Sheffield, circa 1890, $10^{3}/_{4}$in. spear point blade, stag horn grip and nickel silver mounted leather sheath, $14^{1}/_{2}$in. overall.
(Butterfield & Butterfield)   £1,181

Elaborate French hunting knife, circa 1850, $11^{5}/_{8}$in. spear point blade, profusely floral etched on ricasso and towards tip, marked *L. Chobert-Arquer à Paris*, the stag handle flanked by an iron guard and pommel cap, $17^{1}/_{4}$in. overall.
(Butterfield & Butterfield)   £4,040

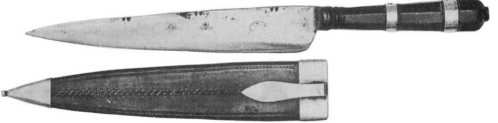

A Victorian hunting knife, broad tapered single edged polished blade $8^{1}/_{2}$in., moulded horn octagonal grip with silver bands in the form of buckled straps, in its leather sheath.
(Wallis & Wallis)   £160

An Imperial Russian hunting dagger from the Zlatoust Arsenal, double-edged blade $6^{3}/_{4}$in. etched with rabbits, flowers, foliage and *Zlatoust* in Cyrillic within fuller.
(Wallis & Wallis)   £220

JAMBIYA

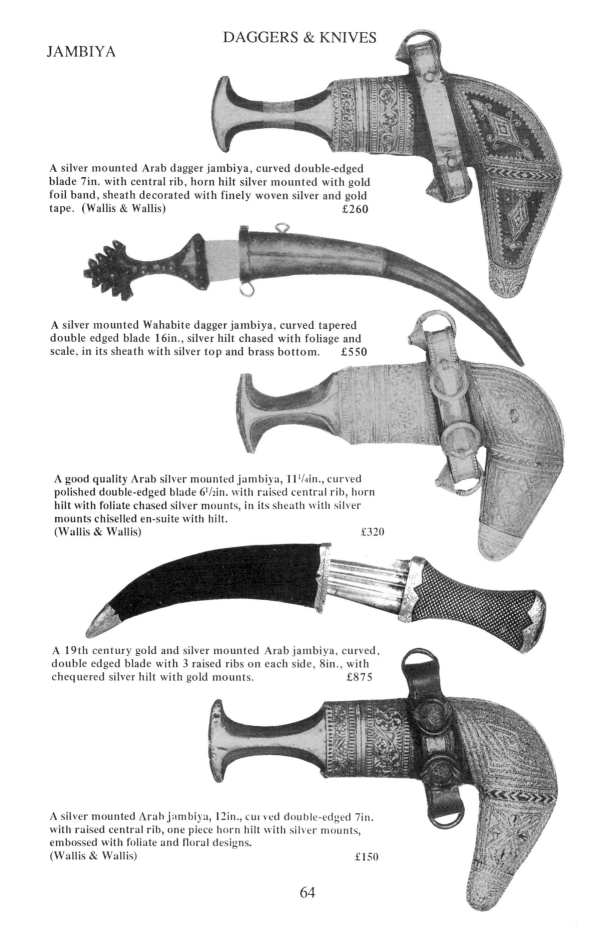

A silver mounted Arab dagger jambiya, curved double-edged blade 7in. with central rib, horn hilt silver mounted with gold foil band, sheath decorated with finely woven silver and gold tape. (Wallis & Wallis) £260

A silver mounted Wahabite dagger jambiya, curved tapered double edged blade 16in., silver hilt chased with foliage and scale, in its sheath with silver top and brass bottom. £550

A good quality Arab silver mounted jambiya, 11$\frac{1}{4}$in., curved polished double-edged blade 6$\frac{1}{2}$in. with raised central rib, horn hilt with foliate chased silver mounts, in its sheath with silver mounts chiselled en-suite with hilt. (Wallis & Wallis) £320

A 19th century gold and silver mounted Arab jambiya, curved, double edged blade with 3 raised ribs on each side, 8in., with chequered silver hilt with gold mounts. £875

A silver mounted Arab jambiya, 12in., curved double-edged 7in. with raised central rib, one piece horn hilt with silver mounts, embossed with foliate and floral designs. (Wallis & Wallis) £150

JAPANESE DAGGERS

Japanese bone mounted dagger, having a 9in. slightly curved blade, the hilt and scabbard relief carved with scenes of personages bearing scrolls.
(Butterfield & Butterfield)   £203

A fine quality Japanese dagger tanto, blade 28.7cm., signed *Mito Yokoyama Suke Mitsu*, dated Meiji 2nd year (= 1869 A.D.), unokubizukuri, gunome hamon, bold nie, itame hada.
(Wallis & Wallis)   £2,250

Japanese ivory mounted dagger, having a 7½in. slightly curved blade, the ivory hilt and scabbard finely carved with a palace scene of the Seven Lucky Gods sporting with children.
(Butterfield & Butterfield)   £809

A Shinshinto Edo suishinshi kozuka blade, Edo period (circa 1850), signed *Taikei Naotane Kore-o Saku*, small rounded point with long kaeri, regular shape tang with sloping file marks and signature on outside of blade, in silk brocade storage bag, 9.3cm. long.
(Christie's)   £1,637

Japanese bone mounted dagger, having a 7in. curved blade, the bone hilt and scabbard carved in low relief with warriors and brocade motifs.
(Butterfield & Butterfield)   £129

A silver mounted Japanese dagger, aikuchi, blade 25.3cm., mumei, hira zukuri, tight itame hada, hiro-suguha hamon, with Higo binding and black lacquered sheath.   £1,000

KATAR

A fine late 18th century Indian katar, 14$^{1}/_{2}$in., thick burnished blade 7$^{1}/_{2}$in. with deeply chiselled fullers, swollen tip, steel hilt entirely covered with gold damascene including 3 grip bars. (Wallis & Wallis) £300

A heavy 18th century chiselled steel katar, 14$^{1}/_{4}$in., deeply chiselled blade 7$^{1}/_{2}$in. with swollen armour piercing tip, engraved central rib, steel hilt with twin grip bars. (Wallis & Wallis) £140

A 17th century Southern Indian katar, double edged fullered blade 14$^{1}/_{2}$in. with chiselled forte and swollen tip, steel hilt with sail shaped guard chiselled with flowers and foliage. £430

An 18th century katar, 18in., blade 9$^{1}/_{2}$in., swollen tip, hilt covered with sheet silver, foliate engraved, in its black leather sheath. (Wallis & Wallis) £120

A fine 18th century Indian silver inlaid katar, 18in., double-edged blade 11$^{1}/_{2}$in., double fullered with raised central rib and thickened armour piercing tip, steel hilt thickly inlaid overall with engraved silver decoration. (Wallis & Wallis) £400

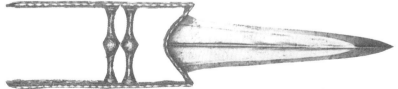

A good 17th century Indian Moghul inlaid thrusting dagger katar, 14$^{3}/_{4}$in., double edged blade 8$^{1}/_{2}$in., with swollen tip and raised ribs, steel hilt with swollen grip bars and flared wings, inlaid overall with copper gilt flowers and foliage chiselled in relief. (Wallis & Wallis) £200

KHANJAR

Indo-Persian dagger, khanjar, the 9in. curved blade with slightly thickened tip, median ridge and chiselled with lappets in low relief at the hilt, the hilt of pale green jade carved with leaves and blossoms in low relief.
(Butterfield & Butterfield) **£809**

A khanjar, 22cm. watered blade, milky white jade hilt with a floral pattern in gold, cabochon rubies and diamonds, contained in its cloth covered scabbard. **£2,000**

A khanjar, 23.5cm. watered blade with twin fullers and reinforced point chiselled at the forte, the jade hilt lightly carved with leaves and decorated with native cut diamonds and cabochon rubies set in gold. **(Phillips)** **£460**

An Indian khanjar, recurved double edged polished blade with raised rib 12in., steel ferrule of shaped form with stylised twin scroll guard, pale green jade hilt, in its leather covered sheath. **£300**

An Indian khanjar with finely watered recurved double-edged blade with three gold-damascened lines over nearly its entire length on both sides, the forte chiselled in low relief on each side with arabesques and flowering foliage, 18th/19th century, 15³/₄in. long.
(Christie's) **£4,950**

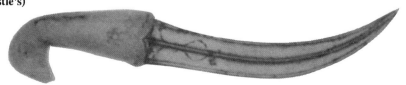

An Indian 19th century Moghul jade hilted dagger khanjar, curved watered blade 8½in.
(Wallis & Wallis) **£700**

KINDJAL

Caucasian dagger, Kindjal, the 14in. blade with offset fullers, the silver hilt and scabbard decorated on the front with silver filigree overlay and niello panels and inset with ivory panels decorated with incised gilt florals.
(Butterfield & Butterfield)   £736

Caucasian dagger, Kindjal, the 13in. blade with offset fullers and maker's mark *Osman* in Cyrillic, the silver hilt and scabbard with niello decorated repoussé floral designs alternating with beaded panels.
(Butterfield & Butterfield)   £441

Caucasian dagger, Kindjal, the 13½in. blade with needle point and triple floral etched fullers, the fine Russian hallmarked silver hilt and scabbard with chiselled floral panels framed by niello and beaded borders.
(Butterfield & Butterfield)   £1,251

Caucasian dagger, Kindjal, the 10in. blade with small double fullers etched with wavy lines, ivory hilt with simple brass studs, black leather covered scabbard with niello silver mounts.
(Butterfield & Butterfield)   £405

Fine Caucasian kindjal, the broad 16in. blade blued overall except for the offset fullers and a narrow strip beside each, marine ivory hilt with niello silver mounts signed and dated *1209* (1794).
(Butterfield & Butterfield)   £2,023

Indo-Persian dagger, of kindjal form, the watered 12¼in. straight double edged blade with raised median ridge terminating in a simple lappet at the hilt, one piece marine ivory grip.
(Butterfield & Butterfield)   £441

KNIFE PISTOLS

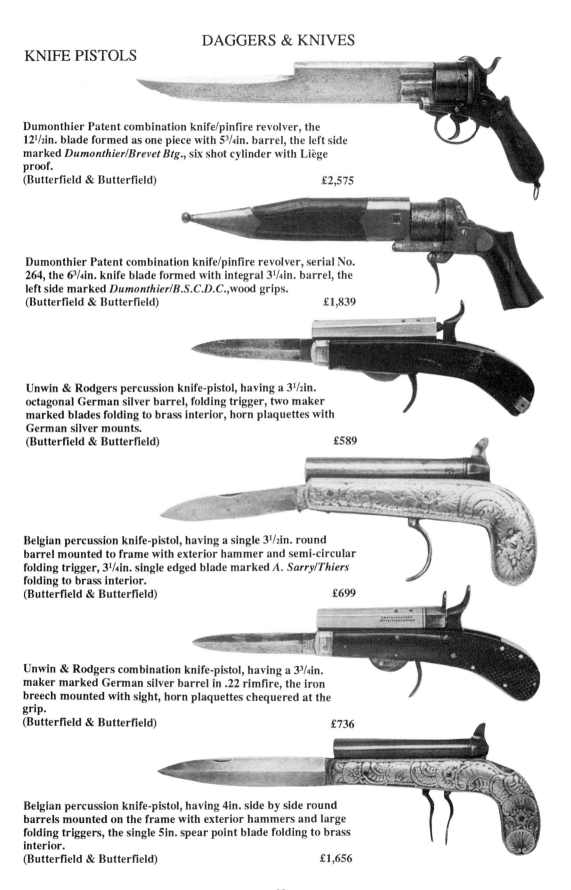

Dumonthier Patent combination knife/pinfire revolver, the 12$^{1}/_{2}$in. blade formed as one piece with 5$^{3}/_{4}$in. barrel, the left side marked *Dumonthier/Brevet Btg.*, six shot cylinder with Liège proof.
(Butterfield & Butterfield)   £2,575

Dumonthier Patent combination knife/pinfire revolver, serial No. 264, the 6$^{3}/_{4}$in. knife blade formed with integral 3$^{1}/_{4}$in. barrel, the left side marked *Dumonthier/B.S.C.D.C.*,wood grips.
(Butterfield & Butterfield)   £1,839

Unwin & Rodgers percussion knife-pistol, having a 3$^{1}/_{2}$in. octagonal German silver barrel, folding trigger, two maker marked blades folding to brass interior, horn plaquettes with German silver mounts.
(Butterfield & Butterfield)   £589

Belgian percussion knife-pistol, having a single 3$^{1}/_{2}$in. round barrel mounted to frame with exterior hammer and semi-circular folding trigger, 3$^{1}/_{4}$in. single edged blade marked *A. Sarry/Thiers* folding to brass interior.
(Butterfield & Butterfield)   £699

Unwin & Rodgers combination knife-pistol, having a 3$^{3}/_{4}$in. maker marked German silver barrel in .22 rimfire, the iron breech mounted with sight, horn plaquettes chequered at the grip.
(Butterfield & Butterfield)   £736

Belgian percussion knife-pistol, having 4in. side by side round barrels mounted on the frame with exterior hammers and large folding triggers, the single 5in. spear point blade folding to brass interior.
(Butterfield & Butterfield)   £1,656

French percussion combination knife/pistol, the 8½in. straight
double edged blade marked *Dumonthier/Brevet Btg*, and flanked
by 3½in. round barrels, fluted silver grip, complete with silver
tipped brown leather scabbard.
(Butterfield & Butterfield)   £2,207

Scottish percussion combination knife/pistol, the 12¼in. straight
single edged blade with two fullers and serrated back edge, the
German silver hilt fitting with integral 3in. octagonal barrel.
(Butterfield & Butterfield)   £1,177

A French Dumonthier patent combined hunting dagger and
double-barrelled percussion pistol with signed fullered double-
edged blade, and original leather-covered scabbard with white-
metal mounts, circa 1850, 16½in. (Christie's)   £1,150

Interesting English knife-form percussion pistol, having a
diminutive combination barrel/folding trigger and hammer with
ivory knife grip carved with a lion-form pommel.
(Butterfield & Butterfield)   £2,391

French percussion combination knife/pistol, of Dumonthier type
but unmarked, the 14½in. straight double edged blade etched
with floral meander, birds and a dragon on a gilt ground, finely
chequered ebony grips. (Butterfield & Butterfield)   £2,756

European flintlock combination knife/pistol, probably English,
late 18th century, the 12in. leaf shaped blade with 5in. ricasso
fitted on the right side with a 4½in. brass three stage cannon
barrel with oval bore. (Butterfield & Butterfield)   £1,104

KNIVES

A rare German Hauswehr with heavy single-edged blade curving up to meet the decoratively notched point, struck at the base on one face with two orb and cross marks, iron handle conforming to the shape of the tang and comprising deep rectangular ferrule, early 16th century, 16½in. long.
(Christie's)   £1,540

An Ngombe tribal war knife Welo from Ubangi Province of Zaire, circa 1900, pierced swollen blade 19½in. with geometric tooled ribs and 2 copper inlays, brass and copper wound wooden hilt with leather covered pommel.
(Wallis & Wallis)   £35

A South American silver mounted Gaucho knife, spear point blade 8½in., scallop top edge, etched with mounted huntsmen chasing stag, birds in foliage, South American embossed silver hilt decorated with bull's heads, patterns, Gorgon's head, and engraved with small armorial crest.
(Wallis & Wallis)   £35

An early 19th century Afghan khyber knife, "T" section blade 27in. with narrow fullers, faceted steel ferrules with gold damascened flowers and foliage, gripstrap gold damascened with Persian inscriptions, large 2-piece ivory grips.
(Wallis & Wallis)   £90

Rare elaborate California dress knife by M. Price, San Francisco, circa 1860, 7in. spear point blade, the ivory hilt ensconced in intricately etched coin silver, the ivory surface fitted with ten gold studs, 12in. overall.
(Butterfield & Butterfield)   £29,832

An Ottoman sheath-knife with slightly curved single-edged blade inlaid with silver stars, with reinforced back-edged point and narrow fuller along the back on each face, and beaked handle with rounded wooden grip-scales, first half of the 17th century, 11¾in.
(Christie's)   £3,300

A good early 19th century Afghan khyber knife, 'T' section blade 26$\frac{1}{4}$in. deeply chiselled with scrolling foliage, and bands of foliate and geometric ornament for full length. (Wallis & Wallis)
£125

An Italian Fascist Colonial police knife, double edged broad leaf-shaped blade 7$\frac{1}{2}$in., oval steel crosspiece, shaped black horn grips inset with oval brass cartouche.
£175

A good Spanish Ripol type knife, 17$\frac{1}{2}$in., broad tapered single edged blade 11$\frac{1}{2}$in. chiselled brass sheath and hilt mounts. (Wallis & Wallis)
£80

A late 19th century S. American bush knife, massive Bowie shaped blade 12$\frac{1}{4}$in., stamped no. 910-G, nickel hilt with eagle's head pommel and scale grip, in its tooled leather sheath. (Wallis & Wallis)
£165

An Indian knife pichingatti, blade of ram dao form 7in., silver hilt with gold crescent pommel mount and ornamental rivet heads, silver inlaid tang sides, in its silver mounted sheath with length of silver chain. (Wallis & Wallis)
£165

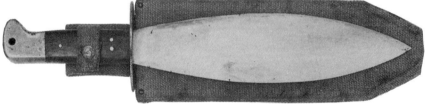

A World War II 'Smatchet', leaf blade 10in., oval metal guard, squared brass pommel with WD arrow and 5, wood grips, in its canvas sheath. (Wallis & Wallis)
£220

A heavy diver's knife, broad straight single edged blade 6$\frac{1}{4}$in., one piece brass hilt stamped *Heinke & Co London*, pierced for lanyard, in its heavy brass sheath cast *Heink London*, sprung to retain knife. (Wallis & Wallis)
£120

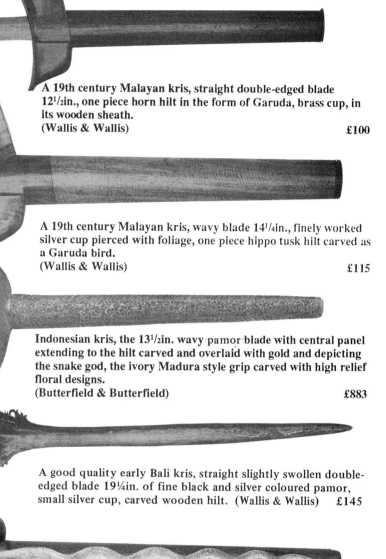

A 19th century Malayan kris, straight double-edged blade 12½in., one piece horn hilt in the form of Garuda, brass cup, in its wooden sheath.
(Wallis & Wallis)   £100

A 19th century Malayan kris, wavy blade 14¼in., finely worked silver cup pierced with foliage, one piece hippo tusk hilt carved as a Garuda bird.
(Wallis & Wallis)   £115

Indonesian kris, the 13½in. wavy pamor blade with central panel extending to the hilt carved and overlaid with gold and depicting the snake god, the ivory Madura style grip carved with high relief floral designs.
(Butterfield & Butterfield)   £883

A good quality early Bali kris, straight slightly swollen double-edged blade 19¼in. of fine black and silver coloured pamor, small silver cup, carved wooden hilt. (Wallis & Wallis)   £145

A 19th century Sumatran kris, wavy pamor blade 15in., one piece hippo tusk ivory hilt carved as stylised Garuda bird with deeply incised scroll work, in its wooden sheath with nicely grained top.
(Wallis & Wallis)   £140

A silver mounted Sumbawa executioner's kris, straight blade 15¾in., wooden Garuda hilt, silver cup, in its wooden sheath with foliate engraved silver mounts.
(Wallis & Wallis)   £100

KUKRI

A good quality 19th century Nepalese silver mounted kukri, 20¼in., blade 13¼in., geometric chiselled back edge, one piece ivory hilt with foliate carved bands, good patina.
(Wallis & Wallis)   £425

A Gurkha kukri belonging to Major Rambahadur Limbu VC, M.V.O., who won his Victoria Cross as Lance Corporal in Indonesia with the 10th Princess Mary's Own Gurkha Rifles during their 1963–66 posting.
(Wallis & Wallis)   £270

A good quality silver mounted Nepalese kukri, blade 13½in., chiselled with foliage, horn hilt with grotesque animal head pommel, in its blue velvet sheath.
(Wallis & Wallis)   £190

A silver mounted Nepalese kukri, blade 11½in., brass mounted bone hilt, in its leather sheath with silver mounts.   £200

An attractive gold mounted kukri, blade 13in. horn hilt with gold ferrule, in its black leather sheath with pierced gold mounts. (Wallis & Wallis)   £360

74

LEFT HAND DAGGERS

A rare Saxon left-hand dagger, the stout leaf-shaped blade of flattened hexagonal section changing to flattened diamond section at the point, with central fuller on each face and fluted ricasso, the hilt of blackened iron, circa 1570, 16¼in. (Christie's S. Ken) £12,100

A left-hand dagger with sharply tapering blade of flattened diamond section with oblong ricasso recessed on each face, faceted globular pommel, and wire-bound wooden grip, early 17th century, 15¾in. (Christie's) £805

A Spanish left-hand dagger with tapering single-edged blade double-edged towards the point, the back of the forte cusped and notched, the broad ricasso decorated en suite, pierced for sword breaking, late 17th century, 22½in. (Christie's) £920

A fine left-hand dagger with tapering blade of flattened hollow diamond section with rectangular ricasso, iron hilt comprising straight quillons widening slightly towards the rounded tips, late 16th century, 17¾in. (Christie's S. Ken) £8,800

A fine Saxon left-hand dagger with broad tapering blade of flattened diamond section with narrow central fuller on each side of the forte, the iron hilt with strongly-arched flat quillons with spatulate 'fish-tail' ends with central flutes, circa 1610, 20½in. (Christie's) £6,600

DAGGERS & KNIVES

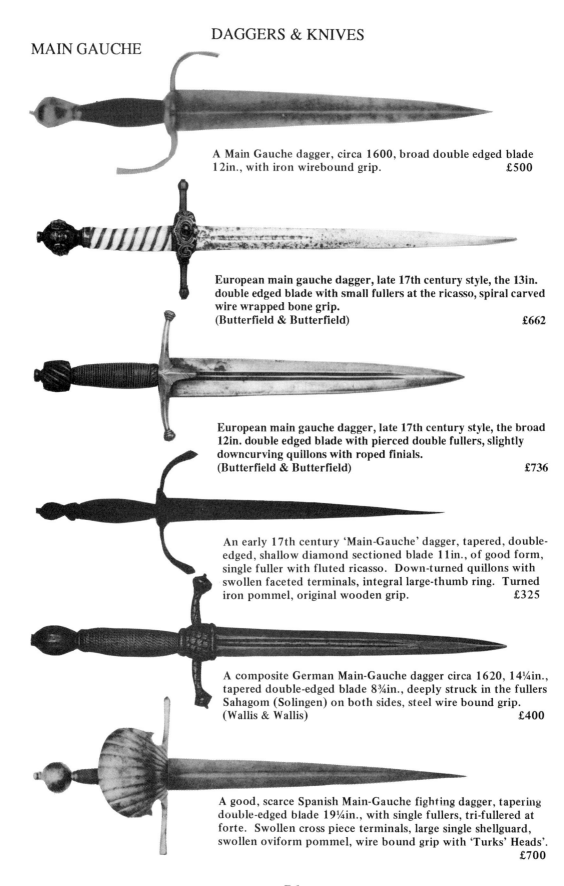

A Main Gauche dagger, circa 1600, broad double edged blade 12in., with iron wirebound grip. £500

European main gauche dagger, late 17th century style, the 13in. double edged blade with small fullers at the ricasso, spiral carved wire wrapped bone grip.
(Butterfield & Butterfield) £662

European main gauche dagger, late 17th century style, the broad 12in. double edged blade with pierced double fullers, slightly downcurving quillons with roped finials.
(Butterfield & Butterfield) £736

An early 17th century 'Main-Gauche' dagger, tapered, double-edged, shallow diamond sectioned blade 11in., of good form, single fuller with fluted ricasso. Down-turned quillons with swollen faceted terminals, integral large-thumb ring. Turned iron pommel, original wooden grip. £325

A composite German Main-Gauche dagger circa 1620, 14¼in., tapered double-edged blade 8¾in., deeply struck in the fullers Sahagom (Solingen) on both sides, steel wire bound grip.
(Wallis & Wallis) £400

A good, scarce Spanish Main-Gauche fighting dagger, tapering double-edged blade 19¼in., with single fullers, tri-fullered at forte. Swollen cross piece terminals, large single shellguard, swollen oviform pommel, wire bound grip with 'Turks' Heads'. £700

NAZI DAGGERS

A Nazi **Water Customs officer's dagger** by Horster, white metal mounts, silver wire bound navy blue leather covered grip, in its navy blue leather covered metal sheath.
(Wallis & Wallis) £330

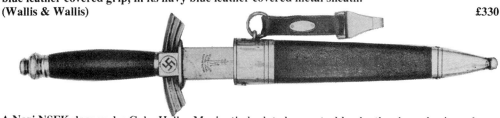

A Nazi **NSFK dagger**, by Gebr Heller Marienthal, plated mounts, blue leather bound grip and sheath covering, in its metal sheath with plated mounts.
(Wallis & Wallis) £390

A Nazi M 1933 **SS dagger**, by Boker, blade retaining some original polish, German silver mounts in its German silver mounted sheath.
(Wallis & Wallis) £410

A good **Nazi 2nd Pattern Luftwaffe officers dagger**, by E Pack & Sohne Siegfried Waffen, grey metal mounts, silver wire bound white grip, in its grey metal sheath with scarce original cardboard makers label attached of "Packis Blanke Waffen".
(Wallis & Wallis) £200

A Nazi **model 1936 S.S. officer's dagger**, by Boker, German silver mounts, in its metal sheath with plated mounts and hanging chains and belt clip. (Wallis & Wallis) £750

A Nazi **1933 SS dagger**, blade etched with maker's mark of *Boker, Solingen*, in its black sheath with plated mounts.
(Wallis & Wallis) £525

NAZI DAGGERS

A Nazi Army officer's dagger, by Eickhorn, blade retains most original polish, plated hilt, orange grip, in its plated sheath with original hanging straps. (Wallis & Wallis)   £130

A scarce Nazi NPEA student's dagger, by Karl Burgsmuller, plain hilt with plated mounts, in its bright steel sheath, with K98 type leather frog.
(Wallis & Wallis)   £750

A Nazi Luftwaffe officer's 2nd Pattern dagger, by Eickhorn, grey metal mounts, silver wire bound yellow grip, in its grey metal sheath with original bullion dress knot and hanging straps.
(Wallis & Wallis)   £170

A rare Nazi Diplomat's dagger by Eickhorn, blade retaining some original polish, plated mounts.
(Wallis & Wallis)   £1,250

A Nazi S.S. officer's 1936 model dagger, by Bertram Reinh., with German silver mounts, in its metal sheath with plated mounts and hanging chains with belt clip.   £750

A Nazi SA dagger, by Gustav Wirth, plated mounts, in its metal sheath with plated mounts, and retaining original spring catch.
(Wallis & Wallis)   £140

NAZI DIRKS

A Nazi Naval officer's dirk, by Eickhorn, plain double fullered blade, gilt mounts, white grip, in its gilt sheath with bullion dress knot. (Wallis & Wallis)   £150

A Nazi naval officer's dirk, by Clemen & Jung, blade retaining much original polish, etched with entwined dolphins, fouled anchor and foliage, wire bound white celluloid grip. (Wallis & Wallis)   **£220**

A Nazi Naval officer's dirk, by W.K.C., blade retaining virtually all original polish, wire bound white celluloid grip, in its gilt brass sheath. (Wallis & Wallis)   £145

A good Nazi naval officer's dirk, by Horster, blade retaining all original polish, etched with fouled anchor, entwined dolphins and foliage. (Wallis & Wallis)   **£180**

A Nazi Naval officer's dirk, plain blade by Eickhorn, gilt mounts, wire bound white celluloid grip, in its gilt sheath with original bullion dress knot. (Wallis & Wallis)   £115

A Nazi naval officer's dirk, by Eickhorn, blade etched with fouled anchor, entwined dolphins, and foliage, brass mounts, brass wire bound white celluloid grip, in its brass sheath. (Wallis & Wallis)   **£115**

PIA KAETTA

A large 18th century Ceylonese dagger pia kaetta, 13½in., broad straight single edged blade 8½in., silver damascened foliage at forte, brass fullers, brass mount chiselled with foliage and flowers.
(Wallis & Wallis) £220

A Sinhalese dagger, pia kaetta, blade 5½in., overlaid at forte with silver scrolls, foliate scrolled brass mount, foliate carved horn grips, with similarly decorated pommel cap and mounts, in its wooden sheath with Eastern silver sheet mount. £100

A large 17th century Sinhalese knife pia kaetta, blade 8½in., with some foliate engraved inlaid brass decoration, brass root with foliate carved ivory grips of fine ancient colour with some white metal overlay. £100

Exceptional Sinhalese pia-kaetta, the heavy blade with silver inlay at upper edge and silver overlay decorated with scrolling vines in relief, the brass ricasso cap cast with scrollwork and inlaid with silver.
(Butterfield & Butterfield) £883

A Sinhalese dagger, pia kaetta, iron blade 7in., partly sheathed in brass, bone carved hilt with brass scroll decorated base, silver sheet embossed pommel cap. £200

A good quality 18th century Ceylonese dagger pia kaetta, 11¾in., blade 8in., fullers and back edge inlaid with foliate engraved sheet silver, two piece horn grips finely scroll carved.
(Wallis & Wallis) £80

PUSH DAGGERS

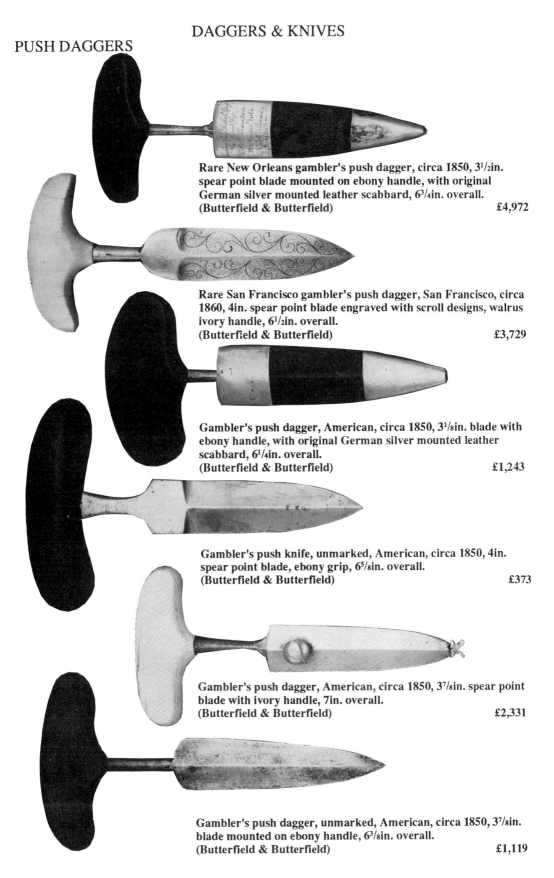

Rare New Orleans gambler's push dagger, circa 1850, $3^{1}/_{2}$in.
spear point blade mounted on ebony handle, with original
German silver mounted leather scabbard, $6^{3}/_{4}$in. overall.
(Butterfield & Butterfield)   £4,972

Rare San Francisco gambler's push dagger, San Francisco, circa
1860, 4in. spear point blade engraved with scroll designs, walrus
ivory handle, $6^{1}/_{2}$in. overall.
(Butterfield & Butterfield)   £3,729

Gambler's push dagger, American, circa 1850, $3^{1}/_{8}$in. blade with
ebony handle, with original German silver mounted leather
scabbard, $6^{1}/_{4}$in. overall.
(Butterfield & Butterfield)   £1,243

Gambler's push knife, unmarked, American, circa 1850, 4in.
spear point blade, ebony grip, $6^{5}/_{8}$in. overall.
(Butterfield & Butterfield)   £373

Gambler's push dagger, American, circa 1850, $3^{7}/_{8}$in. spear point
blade with ivory handle, 7in. overall.
(Butterfield & Butterfield)   £2,331

Gambler's push dagger, unmarked, American, circa 1850, $3^{7}/_{8}$in.
blade mounted on ebony handle, $6^{3}/_{8}$in. overall.
(Butterfield & Butterfield)   £1,119

Cased Highland regimental dirk, the 10³/₄in. blade marked *Sanderson & Co./Edinburgh* and etched on one side *The Queen's Own Cameron Highlanders* with battle honours and sphinx badge, the obverse with crowned *VR*, highland motifs and the regimental number *79* within laurels. (Butterfield & Butterfield) £957

An officer's dirk of the 93rd Sutherland Highlanders with 10¹/₄in. notched back fullered blade, cairngorm pommel and white metal mounted black leather covered scabbard. (Christie's) £770

A Victorian Scottish dirk set, plain blade 11¹/₂in. with single fuller, part carved wooden hilt with thistle decoration, GS mirror pommel and base mount with beaded decoration, in its patent leather covered wooden sheath. (Wallis & Wallis) £150

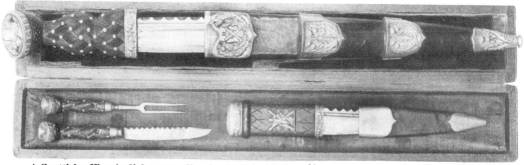

A Scottish officer's dirk set, scallop back plain blade 10¹/₂in. by Hamilton Crighton & Co Edinburgh, retaining much original polish, copper gilt mounted hilt, corded wood hilt mounted with gilt studs, thistle decoration to base mount, contained in a leather covered purple velvet lined fitted case. (Wallis & Wallis) £870

A silver mounted Scottish dress dirk with signed partly hollow ground single edged blade, stamped *McLeod,* circa 1830, and a silver mounted sgian dubh, with fullered single edged blade, early 19th century, 17in. and 8½in. (Christie's S. Ken) £660

A good Victorian Scottish officer's dirk set of the Seaforth Highlanders, scallop back blade 10in., with broad and narrow fullers, retaining all original polish, etched with crown, *V.R.* Thistles, foliage, crown, *"L"*, Elephant "Assaye" and *"Cuidich'n Righ"*. (Wallis & Wallis) £1,100

SCOTTISH DIRKS

Silver mounted Highland dirk, the straight 11in. blade unmarked, the carved wood hilt of typical form, the hallmarked silver mounts on hilt and scabbard engraved with Celtic strapwork.
(Butterfield & Butterfield)   £699

Cased Highland dirk set, the 10¹/₂in. blade with etched panel at grip with thistle motif and monogram *T.H.C.*, hilt carved with brass tacked strapwork, gilt brass mounts cast with thistle motifs, the scabbard throat with St. Andrew.
(Butterfield & Butterfield)   £1,251

A good Victorian silver mounted officer's Scottish dirk, spear point blade 12in., single back fuller, finely corded wood hilt; with plain silver mounts, in its blind tooled leather sheath with silver mounts.
(Wallis & Wallis)   £650

A good quality Victorian Scottish dirk of The 78th (Ross-shire Buffs) Regt., straight single edged bifullered blade 12in. etched with crowned 'VR' cypher, '78 Highland' beneath elephant. (Wallis & Wallis)   £950

A good silver mounted officer's dress dirk of the Argyle and Sutherland Highlanders, 31cm. blade with faceted back edge by Brook & Son, George St., Edinburgh etched with scrolls and regimental badges, hallmarked Edinburgh 1883.
(Phillips)   £1,500

A Scottish Highland dirk with straight fullered single edged blade (some pitting) back edged towards the point, brass mounted root wood handle carved with interlace, early 18th century, 15½in. (Christie's S. Ken)   £880

STILETTOS

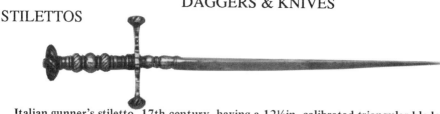

Italian gunner's stiletto, 17th century, having a 12½in. calibrated triangular blade with turned ricasso and fluted quillons, the steel hilt with fluted pommel of flattened ovoid section. (Butterfield & Butterfield) £441

An Italian late 17th century gunner's stiletto, triangular section blade 11¼in. engraved with Cattaneo's scale from 1 to 120. (Wallis & Wallis) £300

An all steel dagger stiletto, circa 1700, hollow ground triangular section blade 8¼in., nicely baluster turned steel crosspiece and grip. (Wallis & Wallis) £160

TROUSSE

An unusual 19th century Turkish H.M. silver mounted trousse, 15½in., the three knives with curved fullered single edged blades 6¼in. to 4½in., hilts made from jade. (Wallis & Wallis) £360

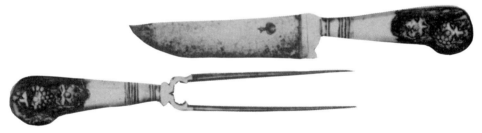

A good late 17th century German (Augsburg) knife and fork trousse, knife blade 4in., struck with cutler's mark of a fir cone within an orb, both mounted on stepped German silver hilt with integral grip straps, natural stag horn grips with rivet heads in the form of fir cones. £300

A Continental eating trousse circa 1800, comprising knife, two pronged fork and sharpening steel, knife blade 5¼in. stamped with maker's mark of splayed footed cross. (Wallis & Wallis) £210

Japanese bone mounted sword, having a 25in. slightly curved blade, the bone hilt and scabbard with low relief carving of Japanese personages, length overall 35in.
(Butterfield & Butterfield)   £239

Japanese helmetbreaker, Hachiwara, 11in. blade inscribed on both sides, scabbard and hilt with brown and red lacquer finish, length overall 18in.
(Butterfield & Butterfield)   £331

A Bizen Osafune ken, Nambokucho period, dated *Meitoku 5* (1394), signed *Bishu Osafune (no) ju Morimitsu*, length (nagasa): 7 sun, 6 bu (23.2cm.); carving (horimono): goma-bashi and bonji on both sides.
(Christie's)   £10,912

A large ho-o-no-dachi, the blade honzukuri and torii-zori, ihorimune and nagagissaki, with dragon and tama horimono on omote and rendai and bonji on ura, with itame hada and gonome-midare hamon (point chipped), ubu nakago, unsigned, probably 18th century, 28in.
(Christie's)   £3,450

Japanese short sword, with signed 19½in. slightly curved blade having double fullers at the back edge, the brass bound bronze tsuba chiselled with a dragon among rolling waves, length overall 24in.
(Butterfield & Butterfield)   £441

An unusual efu-no-dachi with kabuto-gane shaped as a baku head, the blade honzukuri and shallow torii-zori, ihorimune and chugissaki with itame hada, ko-midare hamon, midare komi boshi, and suriage nakago with five mekugi-ana, a kirikomi on the mune just below the yokote, unsigned, probably 17th century, 27½in.
(Christie's)   £2,760

A Mino Seki katana, Muromachi period (circa 1500), signed (*Orikaeshi-mei*) *Izumi (no) Kami Kanesada*, with longitudinal ridge line (shinogi-zukuri), tri-bevelled back (mitsu-mune) and medium point (chu-kissaki); length (nagasa): 1 shaku, 4 sun, 4 bu (52.8cm.).
(Christie's)
£1,909

An Osaka Tamba katana, Edo period (circa 1660), signed *Yamato (no) Kami Yoshimichi*, attributed to Yoshimichi II, with longitudinal ridge line (shinogi-zukuri), shallow peaked back (iori-mune) and medium point (chu-kissaki); length (nagasa): 2 shaku, 3 sun, 7 bu (72.1cm.).
(Christie's)
£10,230

A Kaga katana, Muromachi period (early 16th century), inscribed *Kiyomitsu*, with longitudinal ridge line (shinogi-zukuri), shallow peaked back (iori-mune) and medium point (chu-kissaki); length 73.9cm.
(Christie's)
£1,525

A Mino Seki katana, Muromachi period (circa 1530), signed *Kanenaga*, with longitudinal ridge line (shinogi-zukuri), shallow peaked back (iori-mune) and medium point (chu-kissaki); length 60.7cm.
(Christie's)
£1,178

A Kaga Fujishima katana, Edo period (circa 1640), signed with three kin-zogan cutting attestations and kin-zogan-mei, *Kanemaki Saku*, with longitudinal ridge line (shinogi-zukuri), and medium point (chu-kissaki); length (nagasa): 2 shaku, 3 sun (69.9cm.); curvature (sori): koshi-zori of 1.3cm.; increase in width of blade (fumbari): 0.9cm..
(Christie's)
£8,184

A Yamato katana, Edo period (circa 1675), signed *Fujiwara Kaneshige*, with longitudinal ridge line (shinogi-zukuri), shallow peaked back (iori-mune) and medium point (chu-kissaki); length (nagasa): 2 shaku, 3 sun, 4 bu (71.1cm.).
(Christie's)
£2,728

KATANA

A Showa Gunto Totomi katana, Showa era (circa 1940), signed *Toto (No) Ju Minamoto Yoshiharu*, with longitudinal ridge line (shinogi-zukuri), shallow peaked back (iori-mune) and medium point (chu-kissaki); length 66.3cm.
(Christie's)   £554

A katana, dated *1939*, signed *Oite Toyama Mitsuru o Tsukamoto Ikkanshi Okimasa Saku*, with longitudinal ridge line (shinogi-zukuri), shallow peaked back (iori-mune) and medium point (chu-kissaki); length (nagasa): 2 shaku, 2 sun, 2 bu (67.3cm.).
(Christie's)   £3,751

A Shinshinto Inaba Jukaku katana, Edo period (circa 1820), signed *Toshizane*, with longitudinal ridge line (shinogi-zukuri), shallow peaked back (iori-mune) and medium point (chu-kissaki); length (nagasa): 2 shaku, 1 sun, 9.5 bu (66.7cm.).
(Christie's)   £1,909

An Osaka Ikkanshi katana, Edo period, dated *Empo 5* (1677), signed *Settsu (no) Kami Minamoto Tadayuki*, of flat, wedge section (hira-zukuri), shallow peaked back (iori-mune) and medium point (chu-kissaki); length (nagasa): 2 shaku, 2 sun, 9 bu (69.4cm.).
(Christie's)   £4,774

An Osaka Inoue katana, Edo period (circa 1680), signed *Kitamado Harukuni Tsukuru* (Harukuni I), with longitudinal ridge line (shinogi-zukuri), shallow peaked back (iori-mune) and medium point (chu-kissaki); length (nagasa): 2 shaku, 3 sun, 3 bu (70.6cm.) increase in width of blade (fumbari): 1.1cm.
(Christie's)   £5,115

An Echizen Seki katana, Edo period (circa 1660), signed *Yamato Daijo Fujiwara Masanori*, attributed to Masanori II, with longitudinal ridge line (shinogi-zukuri), shallow peaked back (iori-mune) and medium point (chu-kissaki); length (nagasa): 2 shaku, 4 sun, 5 bu (74.3cm.).
(Christie's)   £4,433

KATANA

A katana, the blade honzokuri and torii-zori, ihorimune and chugissaki with ko-itame hada and suguba midare hamon of ko-nie omaru boshi and ubu nakago, signed *Hisakatsu*, circa 1400, 25¹/₂in.
(Christie's)   £2,990

A katana blade, honzukuri and torii-zori, ihorimune and chugissaki with itame-mokume hada, pointed gonome hamon, omaru boshi and suriage nakago with kinzogan mei Kanetomo, 14th century, 27¹/₄in.
(Christie's)   £4,370

A later Soshu katana, Muromachi period (circa 1550), with longitudinal ridge line (shinogi-zukuri), shallow peaked back (iori-mune) and medium point (chu-kissaki); length 74.8cm.
(Christie's)   £6,237

A koto katana, probably Nambokucho period (14th century), attributed to the Yamashiro Nobukuni school, with longitudinal ridge line (shinogi-zukuri), shallow peaked back (iori-mune) and medium point (chu-kissaki); length (nagasa): 2 shaku, 1 sun, 5 bu (65.3cm.).
(Christie's)   £8,184

A Chikuzen Samonji katana, Nambokucho period (circa 1345), attributed to Sa Hiroyuki, with longitudinal ridge line (shinogi-zukuri), shallow peaked back (iori-mune) and large point (o-kissaki); length 70.3cm.
(Christie's)   £6,930

A later Soshu katana, Muromachi period, dated *Tenmon 13* (1544), signed *Hiroie*, with longitudinal ridge line (shinogi-zukuri), shallow peaked back (iori-mune) and boar's neck point (ikubi-kissaki); length (nagasa): 2 shaku, 4 sun, 5 bu (74.3cm.).
(Christie's)   £10,230

A fine katana, the blade honzukuri and shallow torii-zori, ihorimune and chugissaki with itame-masame hada, with many chikei, gonome-midare hamon of nioi, sunagashi, and inazuma, komaru boshi, so no kurikara horimono on omote, and Marishi-ten inscription on ura, uba nakago with two mekugi-ana, unsigned, 19th century, 26¹/₄in.
(Christie's)   £4,370

KATANA

An Echizen Seki katana, Edo period (circa 1625), signed *Echizen [No] Ju/Harima Daijo Fujiwara Shige* [Taka], with longitudinal ridge line (shinogi-zukuri), shallow peaked back (iori-mune) and medium point (chu-kissaki); length 68.7cm.
(Christie's)   £4,158

A Mino Seki chiisa-katana, Muromachi period (second half 16th century), signed *Kanemoto*, with longitudinal ridge line (shinogi-zukuri), shallow peaked back (iori-mune) and medium point (chu-kissaki); length 53.6cm.
(Christie's)   £1,525

A Mino Seki katana, Muromachi period (circa 1395), signed *Noshu Kaneaki*, with longitudinal ridge line (shinogi-zukuri), shallow peaked back (iori-mune) and medium point (chu-kissaki); length 80.3cm.
(Christie's)   £7,623

An Osaka Kunisuke katana, Edo period (circa 1670), attributed to Naka Kawachi Kunisuke (Kunisuke II), with longitudinal ridge line (shinogi-zukuri), shallow peaked back (iori-mune) and medium point (chu-kissaki); length (nagasa): 2 shaku, 5 sun, 0.5 bu (76cm.); curvature (sori): torii-zori of 1.7cm.
(Christie's)   £34,100

A Bizen Osafune katana, Muromachi period (circa 1550), signed *Bizen [No] Kuni [No] Ju Osafune Kiyomitsu Saku*, with longitudinal ridge line (shinogi-zukuri), shallow peaked back (iori-mune) and medium point (chu-kissaki); length 69.9cm.
(Christie's)   £17,325

A Shinshinto Edo Suishinshi katana, Edo period, dated *Bunsei 11* (1828), signed *Dewa (no) Kami Shonau (no) ju Ikeda Kazuhide Nyudo Ryuken*, with longitudinal ridge line (shinogi-zukuri), shallow peaked back (iori-mune) and medium point (chu-kissaki); length (nagasa): 2 shaku, 2 sun, 4 bu (68cm.).
(Christie's)   £4,433

A fine katana, the blade honzukuri and shallow torii-zori, ihorimune and chugissaki with itame-masame hada, sudare-midare hamon with profuse nie, komaru boshi and ubu nakago with one mekugi-ana, unsigned, possibly by Tamba no Kami Yoshimichi, 17th century, 24^{1}/$_{2}$in.
(Christie's)   £4,830

KATANA

An Echizen Shimosaka katana, Edo period (circa 1660), signed *(Aoi-mon) Yasutsugu (ni) Oite Echizen Kore(o) Saku* (Shirozaemon Yasutsugu III), with longitudinal ridge line (shinogi-zukuri), shallow peaked back (iori-mune) and medium point (chu-kissaki); length (nagasa): 2 shaku, 3 sun, 4 bu (70.9cm.).
(Christie's)   £6,479

A katana, the blade honzukuri with full length wide grooves on omote and ura, shallow torii-zori, ihorimune and chugissaki, the hada obscured by shallow rubbing with wide suguba hamon of konie, komaru boshi and ubu nakago, signed *Echizen ju Harima Dai jo Fujiwara Shigetaka*, circa 1661, 28in.
(Christie's)   £3,450

A later Soshu katana, Edo period, dated *Kanei 8* (1631), signed *Hoki (no) Kuni Kurayoshi (no) ju Sai No-o Shichirosaemon (no) jo Morihiro Saku*, with longitudinal ridge line (shinogi-zukuri), shallow peaked back (iori-mune) and medium point (chu-kissaki); length (nagasa): 2 shaku, 4 sun, 5 bu (74.6cm.).
(Christie's)   £10,912

A Chikuzen katana, probably Nambokucho period (circa 1350), signed *Moritaka*, with longitudinal ridge line (shinogi-zukuri), and small point (ko-kissaki); length 72.4cm.
(Christie's)   £970

A Kii Ishido katana, Edo period (circa 1660), signed *Kii (no) Kuni Yasutsuna*, with longitudinal ridge line (shinogi-zukuri), shallow peaked back (iori-mune) and medium point (chu-kissaki); length (nagasa): 2 shaku, 1 sun, 8 bu (66.2cm.).
(Christie's)   £1,909

A fine katana, the blade honzukuri and torii-zori, ihorimune and chugissaki, with mokume hada and gonome-midare hamon of konie, komaru boshi and machi-okiri nakago with kirijiri, signed *Kazusa Suke Fujiwara Kaneshige*, mid-17th century, 27³/₄in.
(Christie's)   £4,830

TACHI

A Bizen Osafune tachi, dated *1960*, signed *Bizen (no) Kuni Osafune (no) ju Fujiwara Toshimitsu* [b. 1898] *Tsukuru*, with longitudinal ridge line (shinogi-zukuri), shallow peaked back (iori-mune) and medium point (chu-kissaki); length (nagasa): 2 shaku, 3 sun, 8.5 bu (72.6cm.).
(Christie's) £4,092

A Bizen tachi, Kamakura period (probably mid-13th century), signed *Yoshifusa*, with longitudinal ridge line (shinogi-zukuri), shallow peaked back (iori-mune) and small point (ko-kissaki); length (nagasa): 2 shaku, 4 sun, 1 bu (73.2cm).
(Christie's) £1,317

A Ko-Bizen tachi, Heian period (circa 1000), signed *Bizen (No) Kuni Tomonari Saku*, with longitudinal ridge line (shinogi-zukuri), shallow peaked back (iori-mune) and medium point (chu-kissaki); length (nagasa): 2 shaku, 3 sun, 6.5 bu (71.9cm.).
(Christie's) £20,460

A Chikuzen Kongo Byoe tachi, mid-Nambokucho period (circa 1350–1370), attributed to Reizen Sadamori, with longitudinal ridge line (shinogi-zukuri), shallow peaked back (iori-mune) and medium point (chu-kissaki); length (nagasa): 2 shaku, 2 sun, 5.5 bu (68.1cm.).
(Christie's) £25,916

A Bitchu Chu-aoe tachi, Nambokucho period, dated Jowa 3 (1347), signed *Bitchu (No) Kuni (No) ju Tsugunao saku*, with longitudinal ridge line (shinogi-zukuri), rounded back (maru-mune), and short, medium point (chu-kissaki); length (nagasa): 2 shaku, 9 sun, 6 bu (89.8cm.).
(Christie's) £95,480

A Bizen Osafune tachi, Nambokucho period (circa 1350), signed *Nagamitsu*, attributed to Nagamitsu III, with longitudinal ridge line (shinogi-zukuri), shallow peaked back (iori-mune) and small point (ko-kissaki); length (nagasa): 2 shaku, 1 sun, 6 bu (65.5cm.).
(Christie's) £7,502

TACHI

A Hizen Tadayoshi tachi, Edo period (circa 1750), signed *Hizen (no) Kuni Tadahiro* (Tadahiro V), with longitudinal ridge line (shinogi-zukuri), shallow peaked back (iori-mune) and medium point (chu-kissaki); length (nagasa): 2 shaku, 3 sun, 3 bu (70.7cm.).
(Christie's) £10,230

A Bizen Osafune tachi, Nambokucho period (circa 1360), signed *Bishu Osafune* [Kanemitsu], attributed to Masamitsu and dated *Enbun* [?], with longitudinal ridge line (shinogi-zukuri), shallow peaked back (iori-mune) and small boar's neck point (ikubi-kissaki); length (nagasa): 2 shaku, 2 sun, 1 bu (67cm.).
(Christie's) £23,870

A tachi, the blade honzukuri and torii-zori, mitsumune and chugissaki with ken and futasuji-bi on omote, and rendai, bonji and futasuji-bi on ura, with itame hada becoming slightly tsukare, suguba hamon and komaru boshi, ubu nakago, signed *Soshu ju Hiromasa*, circa 1500, 29³/₄in.
(Christie's) £3,680

A fine itomaki-no-tachi, the blade honzukuri and torii-zori, ihorimune and chugissaki with full length wide grooves on each side, ko-itame hada, mimigata-midare hamon with many ko-nie, komaru boshi and suriage nakago, signed *Chikugo Kurume ju Fujiwara Takekuni* and dated *Teikyo ninen* (1685) ni-gatsu no hi, and a tameshigiri inscription *jidoko*, 25³/₄in.
(Christie's) £9,775

A tachi, the blade honzukuri and torii-zori, ihorimune and chugissaki, with dragon, plum and bonji horimono, itame hada and midare hamon, suriage nakago with four mekugi-ana, inscribed *Nagamitsu*, probably 16th century with later horimono, 26¹/₄in.
(Christie's) £1,265

A massive exhibition tachi, the hilt and saya of ivory sections elaborately carved with scenes of agricultural and peasant life, the large ivory tsuba carved with dragons, unsigned, late 19th century, 50¹/₂in. long.
(Christie's) £1,955

TACHI

A tachi with unsigned 19th century Bizen blade, 70.7cm. long, with shari-nashiji scabbard with aoimon and umemon, with silvered metal mounts and gilt crane menuki.   £4,000

A late Japanese sword tachi, blade 66.4cm., inscribed Tadamitsu, muji hada, chu suguha hamon, brass aoi tsuba, tsuka, dragon menuki, nashiji lacquered saya.   £1,750

An itomaki-no-tachi, the blade honzukuri and torii-zori, ihorimune and chugissaki with mokume hada, nokogiri midare hamon, komaru boshi and suriage nakago with two mekugi-ana, signed *Bizen Kuni ju Nobufusa*, 16th century, 26½in.
(Christie's)   £2,990

A late Japanese ito maki-no-tachi, blade 68.7cm., mumei, itame hada, gunome hamon, tape bound tsuka, black lacquered saya.   £800

An attractively mounted Japanese sword tachi, blade 51.3cm., signed *Tajima Nokami Kanemitsu*, copper gilt mounts engraved with imperial chrysanthemum mons and tendrils overall, same tsuka with gilt rice barrels.
(Wallis & Wallis)   £1,550

An Ito Maki tachi, 72.4cm. blade with three mekugi-ana, midare hamon, fully bound tsuka with shakudo fuchi and kabuto gane decorated with gilt flowers.   £2,200

TANTO

A Shinshinto Edo Yamaura yoroi-doshi tanto after a 14th century example, Edo period, dated *Ansei 5* (1858), signed *Minamoto Masao*, of thick, flat, wedge section (hira-zukuri) with shallow peaked back (iori-mune); length (nagasa): 9 sun (27.4cm.); curvature (sori): none (muzori). (Christie's)   £6,820

An Osaka Gassan school tanto, dated *1960*, signed *Gokamei Motte Yotetsu Ryusen Sadatsugu Kore(o) Saku/Kotaishi Denka Goseikon Kinon*, of flat, wedge section (hira-zukuri) with tri-bevelled back (mitsu-mune) and uchizori; length (nagasa): 7 sun, 5 bu (22.9cm.). (Christie's)   £4,092

A Showa tanto after Rai Kunitoshi, dated *1966*, signed *Utsushi Rai Kunitoshi Miyairi Shohei* (b. 1913), with longitudinal ridge line (shinogi-zukuri) with tri-bevelled back (mitsu-mune); length (nagasa): 8 sun, 8 bu (26.7cm.); curvature (sori): uchizori of 0.2cm. (Christie's)   £5,115

A Bizen Osafune tanto after Bizen Kagemitsu, dated *1967*, signed *Bizen (no) Kuni Osafune (no) ju Toshimitsu* (b. 1898), of flat, wedge section (hira-zukuri) with shallow peaked back (iori-mune); length (nagasa): 8 sun, 6 bu (26cm.). (Christie's)   £4,092

A Bizen Osafune tanto, Muromachi period, dated *Bunan 6* (1449), signed *Bishu Osafune Sukemitsu*, of flat, wedge section (hira-zukuri) with shallow peaked back (iori-mune); length (nagasa): 9 sun, 4 bu (28.4cm.); curvature (sori): almost none (muzori); carving (horimono): inside (ura): a single bonji; outside (omote): Fudo Myo-o descending on a dragon. (Christie's)   £6,138

A tanto, dated *1980*, signed *Yoshindo* (b. 1942), of flat, wedge section (hira-zukuri), shallow peaked back (iori-mune); length (nagasa): 8 sun, 5 bu (25.6cm.); curvature (sori): uchizori of 0.1cm. (Christie's)   £3,751

An Echizen Shimosaka Utsushi Sadamune tanto, Edo period (circa 1605), signed *Oite Bushu Echizen Yasutsugu* (Yasutsugu I), of flat, wedge section (hira-zukuri) with tri-bevelled back (mitsu-mune); length (nagasa): 1 shaku, 2 bu (30.8cm.); curvature (sori): almost none.
(Christie's)   £7,502

A Yamashiro Nobukuni tanto, Muromachi period (circa 1400), signed Genzaemon (No) jo Nobukuni, of flat, wedge section (hira-zukuri); length (nagasa): 1 shaku, 1 bu (30.5cm.); curvature (sori): none (mu-zori) with slight uchizori; carving (horimono): bo-hi ni tsure-hi on both sides.
(Christie's)   £16,368

An Etchu Uda Utsushi tanto, Muromachi period (circa 1430), signed *Uda Kunishige*, of flat, wedge section (hira-zukuri), with shallow peaked back (iori-mune) and slight uchizori; length (nagasa): 7 sun, 1 bu (21.4cm.).
(Christie's)   £4,774

A Kyo Korikawa tanto, Edo period (circa 1620), signed *Dewa Daijo Fujiwara Kunimichi* (attributed to Kunimichi I), of flat, wedge section (hira-zukuri) with tri-bevelled back (mitsu-mune); length (nagasa): 9 sun, 6 bu (29.3cm.); curvature (sori): unsigned (muzori).
(Christie's)   £15,004

A Bizen Osafune tanto, Nambokucho period (circa 1380), signed *Bizen (no) Kuni Osafune* (attributed to Yoshimitsu), of flat, wedge section (hira-zukuri) with tri-bevelled back (mitsu-mune); length (nagasa): 8 sun, 8 bu (26.8cm.); carving (horimono): inside (ura): bonji; outside (omote): kurikara above bonji.
(Christie's)   £2,046

A Yamashiro Rai tanto, Kamakura period (circa 1320), signed *Rai Kunitoshi*, of flat, wedge section (hira-zukuri), tri-bevelled back (mitsu-mune) and small point (ko-kissaki); length 23cm.
(Christie's)   £5,544

TANTO

A Mino Shizu tanto,Nambokucho/Yoshino period (mid-14th century), signed *Kanetsugu*, of flat, wedge section (hira-zukuri) with tri-bevelled back (mitsu-mune) and a drop in the back towards the tip (uchizori); length (nagasa): 6 sun, 9 bu (20.8cm.).
(Christie's)   £3,751

A Mino Seki tanto, Muromachi period (circa 1500), signed *Kanetomo*, of flat, wedge section (hira-zukuri) with shallow peaked back; length 22.6cm.
(Christie's)   £3,465

A Yamashiro Horikawa tanto after Myoju, Edo period, bearing a date of *Kan-ei 3* (1626), inscribed *Yamashiro (no) Kuni Nishijin (no) ju Umetada Myoju Hori Dosaku*, inside (ura): kiriha-zukuri and with extraordinarily wide shinogi; outside (omote): of flat, wedge section (hira-zukuri); tri-bevelled back (mitsu-mune); length (nagasa): 9 sun, 2 bu (27.8cm.).
(Christie's)   £3,069

A Mino Seki tanto, Momoyama period (circa 1600), signed *Hida (no) Kami Fujiwara Ujifusa*, of curved, wedge section (ohira-zukuri) with tri-bevelled back (mitsu-mune); length (nagasa): 1 shaku, 1 sun, 3 bu (34.3cm.).
(Christie's)   £8,866

An Echizen Shimosaka tanto, Edo period (circa 1615), with red lacquer attestation by Sato Kanzan to Yasutsugu I, of flat, wedge section (hira-zukuri), with tri-bevelled back (mitsu-mune); length (nagasa): 1 shaku (30.3cm.); carving (horimono): inside (ura): unusual configuration of naginata-hi ni tsure-hi; outside (omote): kurikara.
(Christie's)   £4,092

A Bizen Osafune tanto, Momoyama period, dated *Tensho 2* (1574), signed *Bishu Osafune Sukesada*; silver mounts by Funada Ikkin, of flat, wedge section (hira-zukuri) with shallow peaked back (iori-mune); length (nagasa): 7 sun, 7 bu (23.4cm.); curvature (sori): strong dropped back (uchizori).
(Christie's)   £3,751

TANTO

A Kyo Horikawa Kunihiro tanto, Edo period (circa 1624), signed *Awa (no) Kami Fujiwara Ariyoshi*, of flat, wedge section (hira-zukuri) with tri-bevelled back (mitsu-mune); length (nagasa): 9 sun, 6.5 bu (29.3cm.).
(Christie's)   £11,594

A Mino Seki tanto in Muramasa style, Muromachi period (circa 1560), signed *Kanefusa*, flat (hira-zukuri) with shallow peaked back (iori-mune); length 30.7cm.
(Christie's)   £2,079

A Shimosaka or Horikawa tanto, Edo period (mid-17th century), inside (ura): of flat, wedge section (hira-zukuri) with tri-bevelled back (mitsu-mune); outside (omote): Shobu-zukuri; length (nagasa): 9 sun, 4 bu (28.5cm.).
(Christie's)   £21,824

A Shinshinto Osaka Gassan tanto, Edo period, dated *Keio 4* (1868), signed *Naniwa Gassan Minamoto Sadakazu Tsukuru*, with a narrowed back in the upper half and with the ridge line continuing directly to the point (shobu-zukuri), with shallow peaked back (iori-mune) and rather thick, approaching the proportions of a yoroi-doshi and with the point dropping 0.1cm.; length (nagasa): 8 sun, 1 bu (24.6cm.).
(Christie's)   £3,751

A Koto tanto, possibly Yamato or Mikawa, probably Nambukucho/early Muromachi period (circa 1400), signed *Sadayoshi*, of flat, wedge section (hira-zukuri) with shallow peaked back (iori-mune); length 27.8cm.
(Christie's)   £1,663

A Bizen Osafune tanto, Kamakura period, dated *Showa 2* (1313), signed *Bishu Osafune Kagemitsu*, kanmuriotoshi-zukuri (the shinogi decreases in thickness in the upper half and the shinogi extends to meet the point), with shallow peaked back (iori-mune); length (nagasa): 8 sun, 3 bu (25.4cm).
(Christie's)   £10,395

WAKIZASHI

A Bizen Yoshii wakizashi, Muromachi period, dated *Oei 12* (1405), signed *Yoshinori* (Yoshinori II), with longitudinal ridge line (shinogi-zukuri), shallow peaked back (iori-mune) and medium point (chu-kissaki); length (nagasa): 1 shaku, 6 sun, 2 bu (49.1cm.).
(Christie's)   £5,456

A Wakasa Fuyuhiro ko-wakizashi, Edo period (circa 1610), signed *Fuyuhiro Saku*, of flat, wedge section (hira-zukuri) with shallow peaked back (iori-mune); length (nagasa): 1 shaku, 2 sun (36.5cm.); curvature (sori): almost none.
(Christie's)   £2,182

A Mino Seki ko-wakizashi, Muromachi period (circa 1450), signed *Kanemoto*, attributed to Kanemoto I, of flat, wedge section (hira-zukuri) with tri-bevelled back (mitsu-mune); length (nagasa): 1 shaku, 2 sun, 8 bu (38.7cm.).
(Christie's)   £3,751

A Soshu ko-wakizashi, Muromachi period (circa 1525), signed *Soshu (no) ju Tsunahiro*, of flat, wedge section (hira-zukuri), with tri-bevelled back (mitsu-mune); length (nagasa): 1 shaku, 4 sun, 4 bu (43.7cm.); curvature (sori): shallow, 0.7cm.
(Christie's)   £3,956

An Osaka Ikkanshi wakizashi, early Edo period (circa 1680), signed *Awataguchi Omi (no) Kami Tadatsuna*, attributed to Tadatsuna II, with longitudinal ridge line (shinogi-zukuri), shallow peaked back (iori-mune) and medium point (chu-kissaki); length (nagasa): 1 shaku, 7 sun, 2 bu (52.1cm.).
(Christie's)   £4,774

A Bizen Osafune ko-wakizashi, Muromachi period, bearing a date of *Eikyo 2* (1430), inscribed *Bishu Osafune Yasumitsu*, of flat, wedge section (hira-zukuri) with shallow peaked back (iori-mune); length (nagasa): 1 shaku, 1 sun, 1 bu (33.5cm.); carving (horimono): maru-dome katana ni tsure hi on both sides (traces of the secondary hi visible).
(Christie's)   £1,773

WAKIZASHI

A later Soshu wakizashi, Muromachi period (circa 1470), signed *Soshu [No] Ju Hirotsugu Saku*, attributed to Hirotsugu I, with longitudinal ridge line (shinogi-zukuri), shallow peaked back (iori-mune) and medium point (chu-kissaki); length 55.3cm.
(Christie's)   £4,504

A Hizen Tadayoshi wakizashi, Edo period (circa 1665–70), signed *Omi Daijo Fujiwara Tadahiro* (Tadahiro II), with longitudinal ridge line (shinogi-zukuri), shallow peaked back (iori-mune) and medium point (chu-kissaki); length (nagasa): 1 shaku, 8 sun, 6 bu (56.5cm.).
(Christie's)   £5,115

A Hizen Tadayoshi wakizashi, Edo period (circa 1675), signed *Omi Daijo Fujiwara Tadahiro*, with longitudinal ridge line (shinogi-zukuri), shallow peaked back (iori-mune) and medium point (chu-kissaki); length (nagasa): 1 shaku, 8 sun, 1.5 bu (55cm.).
(Christie's)   £4,092

A Bizen Osafune wakizashi, Muromachi period, dated *Bunmei 9* (1477), signed *Bishu Osafune ?*, with longitudinal ridge line (shinogi-zukuri), shallow peaked back (iori-mune) and medium point (chu-kissaki); length 53.3cm.
(Christie's)   £1,663

A Hizen Tadayoshi wakizashi, Edo period (circa 1625), signed *Hizen (no) Kuni (no) ju Tosa (no) Kami Fujiwara Tadayoshi* (Tadayoshi II), with longitudinal ridge line (shinogi-zukuri), shallow peaked back (iori-mune) and long medium point (chu-kissaki); length (nagasa): 1 shaku, 3 sun, 3 bu (40.5cm.).
(Christie's)   £4,433

An Echizen Takai wakizashi, Edo period (circa 1675), signed *(Kiku-mon) Echizen (no) Kami Minamoto Nobuyoshi*, with longitudinal ridge line (shinogi-zukuri), shallow peaked back (iori-mune) and medium point (chu-kissaki); length (nagasa): 1 shaku, 4 sun, 8 bu (45.1cm.); curvature (sori): koshi-zori of 0.7cm.
(Christie's)   £2,387

WAKIZASHI

An Osaka Ikkanshi style wakizashi, Edo period, dated *Genroku 5* (1692), inscribed *Awataguchi Ikkanshi Tadatsuna,* with longitudinal ridge line (shinogi-zukuri), shallow peaked back (iori-mune) and large point (o-kissaki); length (nagasa): 1 shaku, 2 sun, 8 bu (38.7cm.); curvature (sori): torii-zori of 1cm.
(Christie's) £5,797

An Osaka Gassan school ko-wakizashi after Yasutsugu, dated *1968,* signed *Yasutsugu (no) Hoto(o) Utsushi Tatematsuru/Ryuoji Sadatsugu, kao/(Aoi-mon) Hono Bishu Atsuta Daimyojin,* of flat, wedge section (hira-zukuri) with tri-bevelled back (mitsu-mune); length (nagasa): 1 shaku, 1 sun, 8 bu (35.8cm.).
(Christie's) £17,732

A Shinshinto Kii wakizashi, Edo period (circa 1805), signed *Kishu To Yoshikawa Minamoto Toshiyuki,* with longitudinal ridge line (shinogi-zukuri), shallow peaked back (iori-mune) and medium point (chu-kissaki); length (nagasa): 1 shaku, 6 sun, 3 bu (49.6cm.).
(Christie's) £4,092

A Shinshinto Edo Suishinshi ko-wakizashi, Edo period, dated *Tempo 8* (1837), signed *Fujiwara Masatsugu* with kao, with longitudinal ridge line (shinogi-zukuri), shallow peaked back (iori-mune) and large point (o-kissaki); length (nagasa): 1 shaku, 5 sun, 4 bu (46.7cm.); curvature (sori): torii-zori of 1.2cm.
(Christie's) £6,138

An Echizen Seki wakizashi, Edo period (circa 1600–15), signed *Oite Namban Tetsu Esshu Sukemune,* with longitudinal ridge line (shinogi-zukuri), shallow peaked back (iori-mune) and medium point (chu-kissaki); length (nagasa): 1 shaku, 8 sun, 3 bu (55.6cm.); curvature (sori): torii-zori of 1.3cm.
(Christie's) £5,456

An Osaka Inoue wakizashi, Edo period, dated *Kanbun 6* (1666), signed *Inoue Izumi (no) Kami Kunisada* (Inoue Shinkai), with longitudinal ridge line (shinogi-zukuri), shallow peaked back (iori-mune) and medium point (chu-kissaki); length (nagasa): 1 shaku, 5 sun, 3 bu (46.4cm.); curvature (sori): koshi-zori of 0.9cm.
(Christie's) £25,916

WAKIZASHI

A later Satsuma Masafusa wakizashi, Edo period (circa 1715), signed *(Aoimon) Mondo (no) Sho Masakiyo* (attributed to Masakiyo I), with longitudinal ridge line (shinogi-zukuri), and large point (o-gissaki); length (nagasa): 1 shaku, 2 sun, 9 bu (39.3cm.).
(Christie's) £2,728

A Hizen Tadayoshi wakizashi, Momoyama period (circa 1600), signed *Hi Tadayoshi* (Tadayoshi I), outside (omote): hira-zukuri; inside (ura): shobu-zukuri; tri-bevelled back (mitsu-mune); length (nagasa): 1 shaku, 2 sun, 9 bu (39.2cm.); curvature (sori): rather strong (0.6cm.).
(Christie's) £15,004

An Echizen ko-wakizashi, Edo period (first half 17th century), attributed to Shigetaka, of deep, flat, wedge section (ohira-zukuri) with tri-bevelled back (mitsu-mune); length (nagasa): 1 shaku, 3 sun, 5 bu (41cm.).
(Christie's) £8,184

An o-wakizashi, the blade honzukuri and torii-zori, ihorimune and chugissaki, with mokume hada with wild midare hamon, with tobiyaki, hakkakeru boshi, ubu nakago with one mekugi-ana, inscribed *Hizen Kuni ju Tadayoshi* (possibly made at Kuwana in Ise Province), early 17th century, 20³/₄in.
(Christie's) £2,875

Cloisonné mounted Japanese wakazashi, having a 15in. slightly curved blade having a single fuller at back edge extending from hilt to 3in. from tip, the grip of cloisonné decorated with dragons and peonies on a beige ground.
(Butterfield & Butterfield) £2,391

A Bizen wakizashi in full Mino style mounts, the blade, Muromachi period (circa 1500), with longitudinal ridge line (shinogi-zukuri), shallow peaked back (iori-mune) and medium point (chu-kissaki); length 45.6cm.
(Christie's) £2,911

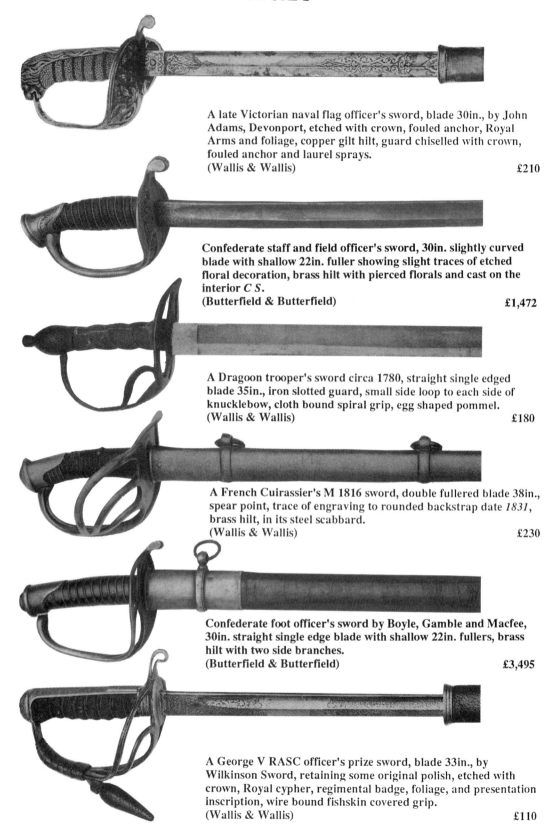

A late Victorian naval flag officer's sword, blade 30in., by John Adams, Devonport, etched with crown, fouled anchor, Royal Arms and foliage, copper gilt hilt, guard chiselled with crown, fouled anchor and laurel sprays.
(Wallis & Wallis) £210

Confederate staff and field officer's sword, 30in. slightly curved blade with shallow 22in. fuller showing slight traces of etched floral decoration, brass hilt with pierced florals and cast on the interior *C S*.
(Butterfield & Butterfield) £1,472

A Dragoon trooper's sword circa 1780, straight single edged blade 35in., iron slotted guard, small side loop to each side of knucklebow, cloth bound spiral grip, egg shaped pommel.
(Wallis & Wallis) £180

A French Cuirassier's M 1816 sword, double fullered blade 38in., spear point, trace of engraving to rounded backstrap date *1831*, brass hilt, in its steel scabbard.
(Wallis & Wallis) £230

Confederate foot officer's sword by Boyle, Gamble and Macfee, 30in. straight single edge blade with shallow 22in. fullers, brass hilt with two side branches.
(Butterfield & Butterfield) £3,495

A George V RASC officer's prize sword, blade 33in., by Wilkinson Sword, retaining some original polish, etched with crown, Royal cypher, regimental badge, foliage, and presentation inscription, wire bound fishskin covered grip.
(Wallis & Wallis) £110

SWORDS

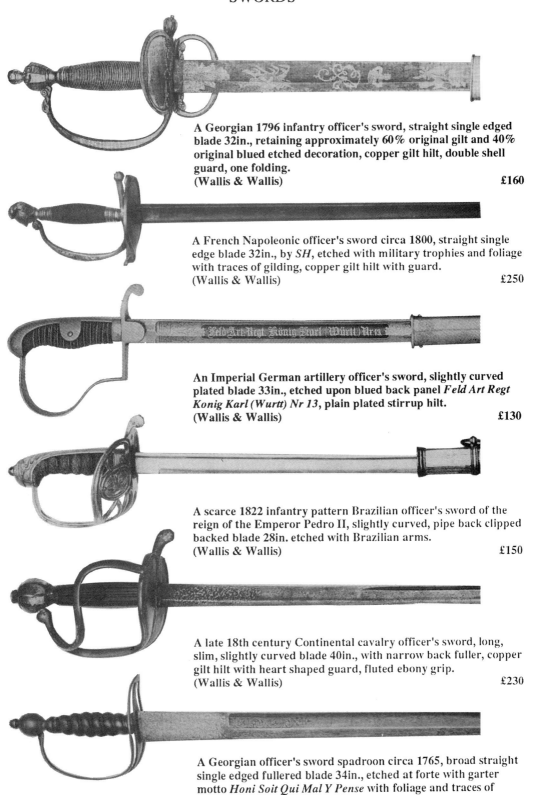

A Georgian 1796 infantry officer's sword, straight single edged blade 32in., retaining approximately 60% original gilt and 40% original blued etched decoration, copper gilt hilt, double shell guard, one folding.
(Wallis & Wallis) £160

A French Napoleonic officer's sword circa 1800, straight single edge blade 32in., by *SH*, etched with military trophies and foliage with traces of gilding, copper gilt hilt with guard.
(Wallis & Wallis) £250

An Imperial German artillery officer's sword, slightly curved plated blade 33in., etched upon blued back panel *Feld Art Regt Konig Karl (Wurtt) Nr 13*, plain plated stirrup hilt.
(Wallis & Wallis) £130

A scarce 1822 infantry pattern Brazilian officer's sword of the reign of the Emperor Pedro II, slightly curved, pipe back clipped backed blade 28in. etched with Brazilian arms.
(Wallis & Wallis) £150

A late 18th century Continental cavalry officer's sword, long, slim, slightly curved blade 40in., with narrow back fuller, copper gilt hilt with heart shaped guard, fluted ebony grip.
(Wallis & Wallis) £230

A Georgian officer's sword spadroon circa 1765, broad straight single edged fullered blade 34in., etched at forte with garter motto *Honi Soit Qui Mal Y Pense* with foliage and traces of gilding.
(Wallis & Wallis) £170

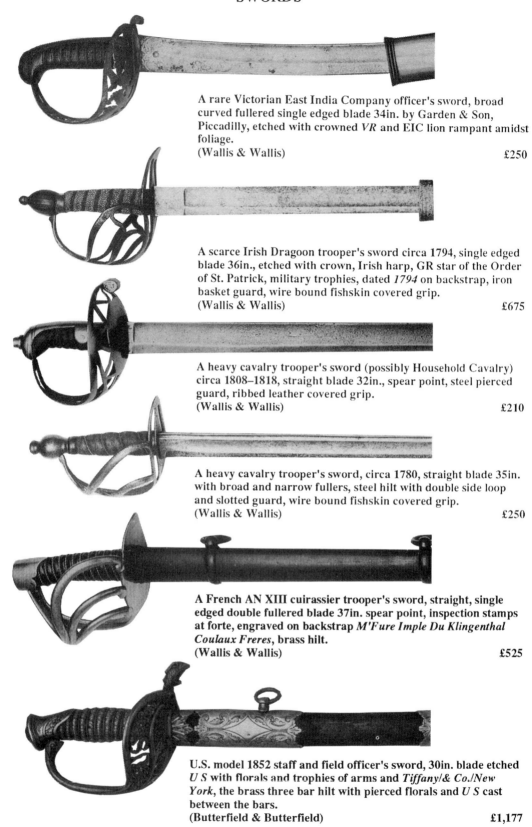

A rare Victorian East India Company officer's sword, broad curved fullered single edged blade 34in. by Garden & Son, Piccadilly, etched with crowned *VR* and EIC lion rampant amidst foliage.
(Wallis & Wallis)   £250

A scarce Irish Dragoon trooper's sword circa 1794, single edged blade 36in., etched with crown, Irish harp, GR star of the Order of St. Patrick, military trophies, dated *1794* on backstrap, iron basket guard, wire bound fishskin covered grip.
(Wallis & Wallis)   £675

A heavy cavalry trooper's sword (possibly Household Cavalry) circa 1808–1818, straight blade 32in., spear point, steel pierced guard, ribbed leather covered grip.
(Wallis & Wallis)   £210

A heavy cavalry trooper's sword, circa 1780, straight blade 35in. with broad and narrow fullers, steel hilt with double side loop and slotted guard, wire bound fishskin covered grip.
(Wallis & Wallis)   £250

A French AN XIII cuirassier trooper's sword, straight, single edged double fullered blade 37in. spear point, inspection stamps at forte, engraved on backstrap *M'Fure Imple Du Klingenthal Coulaux Freres*, brass hilt.
(Wallis & Wallis)   £525

U.S. model 1852 staff and field officer's sword, 30in. blade etched *U S* with florals and trophies of arms and *Tiffany/& Co./New York*, the brass three bar hilt with pierced florals and *U S* cast between the bars.
(Butterfield & Butterfield)   £1,177

SWORDS

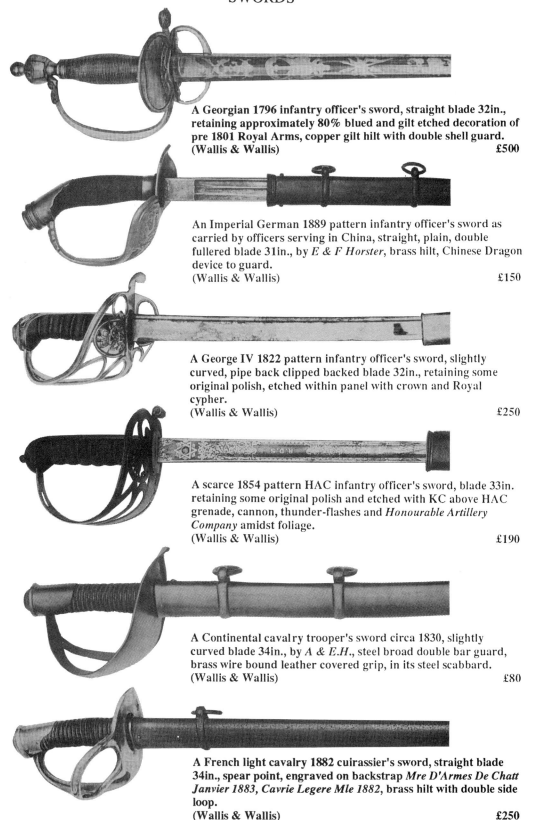

A Georgian 1796 infantry officer's sword, straight blade 32in., retaining approximately 80% blued and gilt etched decoration of pre 1801 Royal Arms, copper gilt hilt with double shell guard.
(Wallis & Wallis)   £500

An Imperial German 1889 pattern infantry officer's sword as carried by officers serving in China, straight, plain, double fullered blade 31in., by *E & F Horster*, brass hilt, Chinese Dragon device to guard.
(Wallis & Wallis)   £150

A George IV 1822 pattern infantry officer's sword, slightly curved, pipe back clipped backed blade 32in., retaining some original polish, etched within panel with crown and Royal cypher.
(Wallis & Wallis)   £250

A scarce 1854 pattern HAC infantry officer's sword, blade 33in. retaining some original polish and etched with KC above HAC grenade, cannon, thunder-flashes and *Honourable Artillery Company* amidst foliage.
(Wallis & Wallis)   £190

A Continental cavalry trooper's sword circa 1830, slightly curved blade 34in., by *A & E.H.*, steel broad double bar guard, brass wire bound leather covered grip, in its steel scabbard.
(Wallis & Wallis)   £80

A French light cavalry 1882 cuirassier's sword, straight blade 34in., spear point, engraved on backstrap *Mre D'Armes De Chatt Janvier 1883, Cavrie Legere Mle 1882*, brass hilt with double side loop.
(Wallis & Wallis)   £250

A good English Civil War period Mortuary backsword, straight single edge bi-fullered blade 33¼in., struck in the fullers *xx Hermen xx Keisser xx*, four times, with crowned maker's stamp at forte.
(Wallis & Wallis)   £875

A good Cromwellian basket hilted backsword, straight single edged blade 35½in., with narrow fullers, deeply struck with running wolf, from a group of identical swords preserved at Nostel Priory, Wakefield, Yorkshire
(Wallis & Wallis)   £825

A good early 17th century English basket hilted backsword, straight single edged blade 33in. of unusual section, flat one side with chamfered edge, twin short narrow fullers stamped *Andrea Ferara* with orb and various maker's stamps.
(Wallis & Wallis)   £700

A composite English basket-hilted cavalry backsword with fullered single-edged blade double-edged towards the point, guard of flattened hemispherical shape formed of a rectangular trellis of slender bars of circular section, circa 1740, 31¾in. blade.
(Christie's)   £805

An English backsword with single-edged blade back-edged towards the point, the back bordered by a single groove on each face stamped respectively *Spes Mea* and *Est Deo*, wire-bound shagreen-covered wooden grip, circa 1640–50, 35in. blade.
(Christie's)   £1,380

A Cromwellian cavalry officer's backsword, straight tullered blade 33in. stamped in the fullers "Andria Ferara", fluted guard with thumbscroll. (Wallis & Wallis)   £600

BROADSWORDS

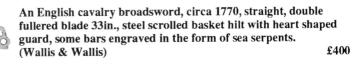

An English cavalry broadsword, circa 1770, straight, double
fullered blade 33in., steel scrolled basket hilt with heart shaped
guard, some bars engraved in the form of sea serpents.
(Wallis & Wallis)   £400

A good quality early 19th century copy of a late medieval
broadsword, broad tapered shallow diamond section blade 34in.,
down turned quillons with pierced swollen finials.
(Wallis & Wallis)   £150

A George V 1865 Scottish officer's military broadsword, double-
edged blade 31$\frac{1}{2}$in. by Wm. Anderson & Sons, Edinburgh and
Glasgow, etched with crown, Royal cypher, thistles, foliage and
A.A. Pitcairn The Black Watch within panel.
(Wallis & Wallis)   £500

A good Scottish basket hilted broadsword, circa 1760, double
edged blade 29$\frac{3}{4}$in., deeply struck 6 times with the maker's
mark of crowned pincers with initials "W.W.", copper wire
bound sharkskin covered grip with brass ferrules.
(Wallis & Wallis)   £600

A Scottish basket-hilted broadsword with broad double-edged
blade of flattened oval section struck with a leaf-shaped mark on
one face, iron guard of characteristic form made of fluted flat
bars, early 18th century, 37in. blade.
(Christie's)   £1,725

A good Elizabeth II 1865 pattern Scottish officer's Military
broadsword, blade 32in., by Wilkinson Sword, etched with
thistles, plated basket hilt with red cloth fronted white leather
liner.
(Wallis & Wallis)   £550

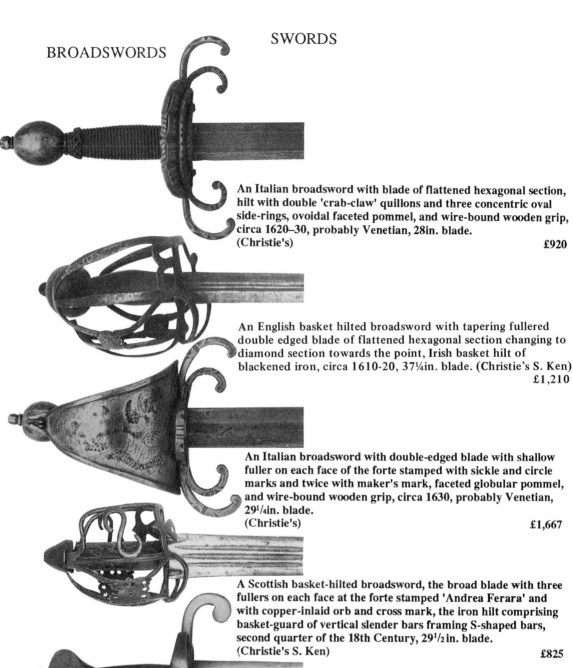

An Italian broadsword with blade of flattened hexagonal section, hilt with double 'crab-claw' quillons and three concentric oval side-rings, ovoidal faceted pommel, and wire-bound wooden grip, circa 1620–30, probably Venetian, 28in. blade.
(Christie's)   £920

An English basket hilted broadsword with tapering fullered double edged blade of flattened hexagonal section changing to diamond section towards the point, Irish basket hilt of blackened iron, circa 1610-20, 37¼in. blade. (Christie's S. Ken)
£1,210

An Italian broadsword with double-edged blade with shallow fuller on each face of the forte stamped with sickle and circle marks and twice with maker's mark, faceted globular pommel, and wire-bound wooden grip, circa 1630, probably Venetian, 29¼in. blade.
(Christie's)   £1,667

A Scottish basket-hilted broadsword, the broad blade with three fullers on each face at the forte stamped 'Andrea Ferara' and with copper-inlaid orb and cross mark, the iron hilt comprising basket-guard of vertical slender bars framing S-shaped bars, second quarter of the 18th Century, 29½in. blade.
(Christie's S. Ken)   £825

A good Scandinavian broadsword circa 1620 with Sinclair hilt, straight tapered double edged blade 32¼in., struck with maker's mark of a splayed foot cross.
(Wallis & Wallis)   £650

A George V Scottish infantry officer's cruciform hilted broadsword, blade 32¼in. etched with crowned GVR cypher and Royal Arms amidst foliage, plated crosspiece and pommel.
(Wallis & Wallis)   £130

CHINESE SWORDS

Chinese sword, the 17³/₄in. straight double edged blade of diamond section, spirally carved wood grip, the brass hilt and scabbard mounts with relief decoration of dragons, dragon heads and dragon head meander.
(Butterfield & Butterfield)   £203

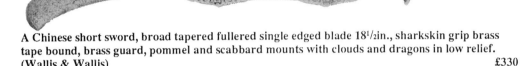

A Chinese short sword, broad tapered fullered single edged blade 18¹/₂in., sharkskin grip brass tape bound, brass guard, pommel and scabbard mounts with clouds and dragons in low relief.
(Wallis & Wallis)   £330

A Chinese double sword, double edged blades 17½in., brass crosspiece, pommel and mounts, decorated with traditional patterns, fluted wood grips, in its wooden scabbard with brass chapes similarly decorated.   £200

An unusual Chinese sword, diamond section blade 22in., inlaid with brass dragons and symbols on one side with two shallow fullers to the other, cast white metal crossguard, engraved white metal mounted tape bound hilt, the triangular pommel similarly decorated, in its fish-skin covered white metal mounted scabbard, top and bottom mounts engraved with dragons and mythical scenes, the central suspension loop mounted with a lizard.   £250

A good Chinese sword, curved blade 27in., with scrolled gilt sprays at forte, elaborately pierced oval gilt metal guard with designs of dragons within foliage, squared pommel and mounts similarly decorated, blue cord bound grip and blue tassel, in its vellum covered scabbard.   £400

Chinese sword, the 18¹/₂in. straight double edged blade of diamond section, spirally fluted wood grip, the brass quillons with dragon's head in relief, the lobed pommel with dragon head meander.
(Butterfield & Butterfield)   £276

COURT SWORDS

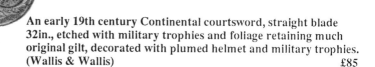

An early 19th century Continental courtsword, straight blade 32in., etched with military trophies and foliage retaining much original gilt, decorated with plumed helmet and military trophies. (Wallis & Wallis) £85

A mid 19th century Danish courtsword, straight slim blade 27½in., shell guard chiselled with arms of Denmark. (Wallis & Wallis) £70

An Imperial Russian courtsword, straight double-edged slim blade 26in. of flattened diamond section, hilt with traces of gilding, shell guard with Imperial eagle, twist grip. (Wallis & Wallis) £110

An Imperial Prussian courtsword (Degen), slim blade 29½in., retaining all original polish, by WKC, gilt hilt with double shell guard, foliate chiselled urn pommel, wire bound grip, in its leather scabbard with gilt mounts. (Wallis & Wallis) £45

A Spanish silver gilt hilted court sword with narrow single edged hollow ground blade double edged towards the point, silver marks and Barcelona assay mark, early 19th century, 32in. blade. (Christie's S. Ken) £440

A cut steel hilted court sword, plain, triangular, tapering blade 30½in., polished steel hilt, with shellguard, knucklebow and urn shaped pommel decorated with cut steel faceted studs, in its patent leather scabbard. £175

CUTLASS

A French 1833 pattern naval boarding cutlass, slightly curved blade 26½in. engraved on backstrap "Manufre Rle De Chatellerault 1839". (Wallis & Wallis) £65

A late 19th century cutlass, slightly curved blade 31in., by "Robt. Mole & Sons, Birmingham", inspection stamps at forte. (Wallis & Wallis) £50

An interesting Georgian experimental naval boarding cutlass circa 1820, broad straight single edged 28½in. with crowned *GR* 3 inspector's stamp and government disposal marks, boat shaped steel guard stamped *BO* with broad arrow, pierced twice with diamond shaped brass label. (Wallis & Wallis) £310

A Georgian 'Figure of eight' naval cutlass, single edged blade 28½in., stamped *Gill* on backstrap, traces of crown, *GR*, ribbed grip and iron guard painted black. (Wallis & Wallis) £125

A good Georgian "Double disc pommel" naval boarding cutlass, broad straight blade 28¾in. deeply stamped with crowned "GR", government inspector's mark and rack No 21. (Wallis & Wallis) £350

An American revolutionary war period cutlass, slightly curved blade 26in., narrow back fuller, iron hilt with disc guard, narrow single knucklebow. (Wallis & Wallis) £290

SWORDS

A Burmese silver mounted shortsword dha, blade 10in., octagonal ivory hilt with silver ferrule, covered sheath en-suite. £150

A silver mounted Burmese sword dha, blade 19¼in., sheet and hilt silver mounted, chased with foliage. £250

A good quality 19th century Burmese silver mounted sword dha, curved swollen fullered single edged blade 24¾in. thickly silver damascened with many groups of figures including swordsmith, amidst foliage with profuse inscriptions.
(Wallis & Wallis) £320

A good quality 19th century silver mounted Burmese sword dha, curved single edged fullered blade 20½in., silver damascened on both sides and back edge with flowering foliage.
(Wallis & Wallis) £300

Burmese dha, the slightly curved 20in. blade with multiple fullers and punched designs, the silver covered hilt with banded designs, rattan-wrapped grip and large fluted pommel.
(Butterfield & Butterfield) £221

A 19th century silver mounted Burmese sword dha, 17½in. overall, single edged blade 10¼in., octagonal silver ferrule and ivory hilt, in its copper sheath with extensive silver and filigree bands.
(Wallis & Wallis) £240

112

DRESS SWORDS

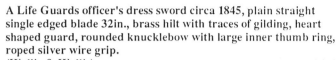

A Life Guards officer's dress sword circa 1845, plain straight single edged blade 32in., brass hilt with traces of gilding, heart shaped guard, rounded knucklebow with large inner thumb ring, roped silver wire grip.
(Wallis & Wallis) £625

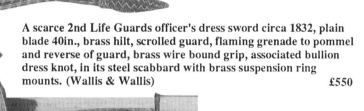

A scarce 2nd Life Guards officer's dress sword circa 1832, plain blade 40in., brass hilt, scrolled guard, flaming grenade to pommel and reverse of guard, brass wire bound grip, associated bullion dress knot, in its steel scabbard with brass suspension ring mounts. (Wallis & Wallis) £550

A US Army officer's dress sword, circa 1900, blade 29in. by Ridabock New York, retaining some original polish, etched with US eagle, military trophies and foliage, brass hilt with traces of gilding.
(Wallis & Wallis) £115

A rare Household Cavalry officer's 1814 pattern dress sword, straight, double fullered blade 34in., half basket copper gilt hilt, with crowned lion upon crown badge, circular pommel.
(Wallis & Wallis) £1,600

An EIIR RAF officer's dress sword, blade 32in., by Wilkinson Sword, retaining much original polish, etched with Royal Arms, blank scrolls and laurel sprays, gilt hilt, with royal cypher, eagle's head pommel, original bullion dress knot, gilt wire bound white fishskin covered grip.
(Wallis & Wallis) £220

A 1796 heavy cavalry officer's dress sword, straight tapering double-edged blade 32in. signed in the short fullers *J.J. Runkel Solingen*, copper gilt hilt, boat shaped guard, ovoid pommel, silver wire bound grip.
(Wallis & Wallis) £130

EASTERN SWORDS

A 19th century Nepalese sacrificial sword Ram Dao, 32in., broad curved tapered heavy single edged blade 23in. chiselled with the seeing eyes, trisula, flower head and geometric devices. (Wallis & Wallis) £75

A 19th century Afghan sword Pulouar, curved fullered single edged blade 31in., steel hilt of traditional form, downturned quillons with stylised animal head finials. (Wallis & Wallis) £30

A Singhalese gold and silver mounted kastana with short slightly curved single edged blade struck with a mark on one side at the forte, the hilt comprising knuckle guard and downturned quillons each terminating in a dragon's head, 23¾in. (Christie's S. Ken) £1,210

A very unusual 19th century Borneo Dyak sword Parang Ilang, swollen single edged blade 24½in., engraved brass ferrule, bone hilt carved with foliage. (Wallis & Wallis) £300

A scarce early 19th century Dyak Parang Latok, heavy swollen single edged fullered blade 20in. emanating from fluted brass inlaid forte, silver covered grip, foliate carved horn hilt. (Wallis & Wallis) £85

A good 17th century Tanjore sword firangi, straight single edged bi-fullered blade 38in., hilt finely chiselled and pierced overall with palmettes, foliage, beaded bands, twin stylised tiger's heads at forte. (Wallis & Wallis) £320

EASTERN SWORDS

An early 18th century Indian gauntlet sword Pata, straight double-edged blade 30in. with raised central rib, scroll chiselled langet, multibar basket hilt with guard of keel section terminating in grotesque head finial.
(Wallis & Wallis)   £180

A good early 19th century Indian hunting sword Shamshire Shikargar, broad blade 29½in. with thickened tip, deeply chiselled in low relief on both sides with an assortment of animals fighting.
(Wallis & Wallis)   £360

A good Dyak headhunter's sword Mandau, swollen hollow ground single edged blade 17¾in., bone hilt finely carved with jaws, teeth and scrolls and set with dyed coloured goat's hair.
(Wallis & Wallis)   £85

An early Indian gauntlet hilted shortsword pata, 31in. overall, double edged blade 26in. with raised rib, pierced reinforcing langets, engraved sail shaped guard with nicely chiselled grotesque animal's head finial.
(Wallis & Wallis)   £160

A North Indian shortsword of Khyber knife type, single edged wootz blade 20in. struck with Hindi mark, two piece ivory grips of good colour, in its wooden scabbard.
(Wallis & Wallis)   £180

A good 19th century silver mounted Moro sword barong, swollen single edged heavy blade 19in., hilt of nicely shaped form of iridescent grained wood, large silver ferrule.
(Wallis & Wallis)   £100

EXECUTIONER'S SWORDS

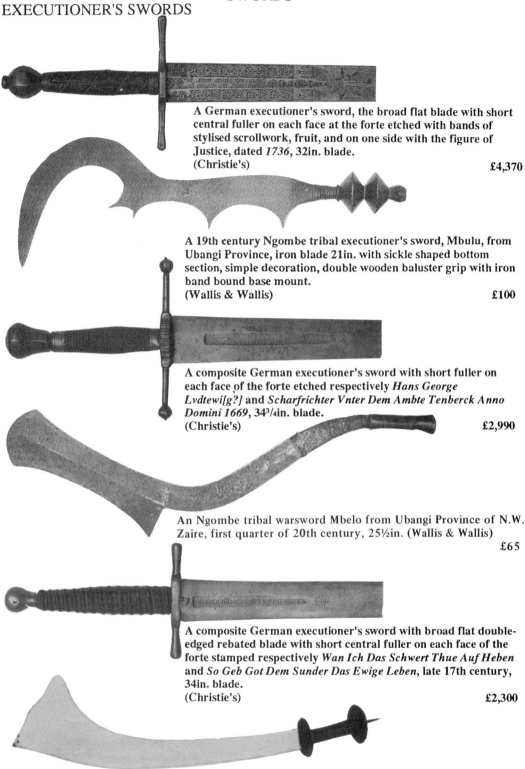

A German executioner's sword, the broad flat blade with short central fuller on each face at the forte etched with bands of stylised scrollwork, fruit, and on one side with the figure of Justice, dated *1736*, 32in. blade.
(Christie's)   £4,370

A 19th century Ngombe tribal executioner's sword, Mbulu, from Ubangi Province, iron blade 21in. with sickle shaped bottom section, simple decoration, double wooden baluster grip with iron band bound base mount.
(Wallis & Wallis)   £100

A composite German executioner's sword with short fuller on each face of the forte etched respectively *Hans George Lvdtewi[g?]* and *Scharfrichter Vnter Dem Ambte Tenberck Anno Domini 1669*, 34³/₄in. blade.
(Christie's)   £2,990

An Ngombe tribal warsword Mbelo from Ubangi Province of N.W. Zaire, first quarter of 20th century, 25½in. (Wallis & Wallis)
                                                                 £65

A composite German executioner's sword with broad flat double-edged rebated blade with short central fuller on each face of the forte stamped respectively *Wan Ich Das Schwert Thue Auf Heben* and *So Geb Got Dem Sunder Das Ewige Leben*, late 17th century, 34in. blade.
(Christie's)   £2,300

A Nepalese executioner's heavy kora, plain, curved blade 23in., inlaid at top with brass geometric design, plain steel hilt, in its leather covered wooden scabbard.   £150

HANGERS

A Georgian silver hilted hanger of the type favoured by naval officers circa 1775, slightly curved bi-fullered single edged blade 24½in. etched with foliate decoration, one piece spiral carved horn grip.
(Wallis & Wallis)   £470

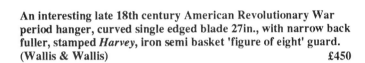

An interesting late 18th century American Revolutionary War period hanger, curved single edged blade 27in., with narrow back fuller, stamped *Harvey*, iron semi basket 'figure of eight' guard.
(Wallis & Wallis)   £450

An unusual military style presentation hanger, probably Post Office, curved fullered single edged blade 21¾in., brass stirrup hilt, sharkskin grip, brass pommel.
(Wallis & Wallis)   £105

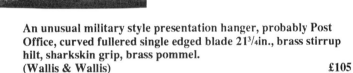

A brass hilted militia hanger circa 1750, slightly curved blade 24in., narrow back fuller, trace of running fox mark.
(Wallis & Wallis)   £130

An English hanger, the curved single edge blade with two broad fullers on each face, in original leather covered wooden scabbard (slightly damaged) with gilt iron locket and chape chased with rococo strapwork and trophies, circa 1750, 21in. blade. (Christie's S. Ken)   £715

A rare English hanger circa 1635, probably made in the sword factory at Hounslow, broad slightly curved blade 24in., with false edge at tip, fullers stamped "Gloreia Sole Deo" with orbs.
Vallis & Wallis)   £900

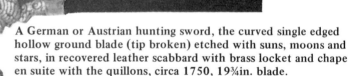

A late 18th century Continental hunting sword, curved fullered single edged blade 28½in. etched with trophies of arms and foliage, downturned brass crosspiece with stylised eagle head finials.
(Wallis & Wallis)   £145

A German hunting sword, with tapering single-edged blade back-edged towards the point and with narrow central fuller on each face, etched and gilt with running foliage below a band of bolder foliage bordering the back, early 19th century, probably French, the blade German, early 18th century, 23½in. blade.
(Christie's)   £605

A German or Austrian hunting sword, the curved single edged hollow ground blade (tip broken) etched with suns, moons and stars, in recovered leather scabbard with brass locket and chape en suite with the quillons, circa 1750, 19¾in. blade.
(Christie's S. Ken)   £462

A good George II period hallmarked silver hilted English hunting sword (1741), curved blade 22in., narrow back fullers signed *Ferara*, finely chiselled silver hilt with shell guard with mask bordered by scallops.
(Wallis & Wallis)   £650

A German hunting sword with curved single-edged blade back-edged at the point and etched at the forte with rococo scrollwork, scenes of the chase, trophies of arms and buildings, all with traces of gilding, brass hilt comprising downturned shell, mid-18th century, 21½in. blade.
(Christie's)   £550

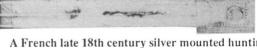

A French late 18th century silver mounted hunting sword, straight, double fullered, double-edged tapering blade 20in., crosspiece chiselled in the form of hounds' heads.
(Wallis & Wallis)   £700

MAMELUKE

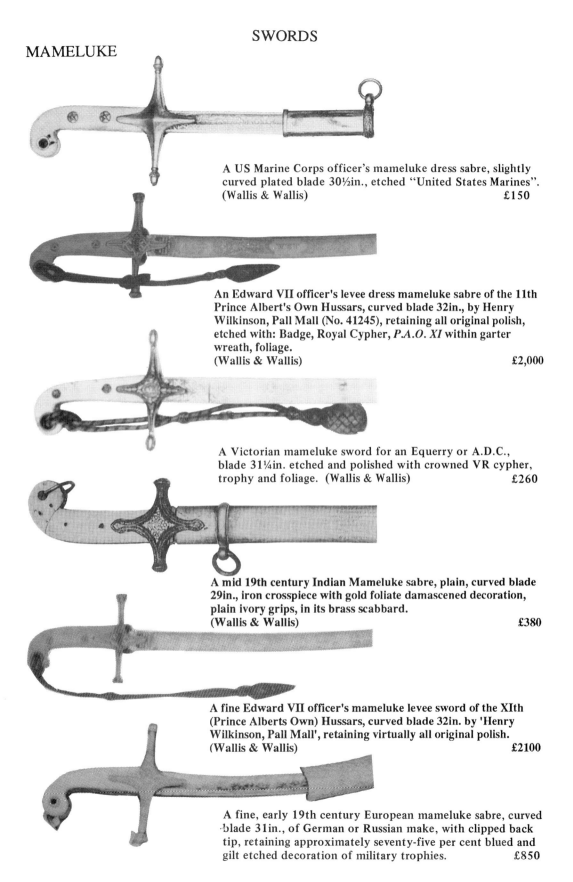

A US Marine Corps officer's mameluke dress sabre, slightly curved plated blade 30½in., etched "United States Marines".
(Wallis & Wallis)   £150

An Edward VII officer's levee dress mameluke sabre of the 11th Prince Albert's Own Hussars, curved blade 32in., by Henry Wilkinson, Pall Mall (No. 41245), retaining all original polish, etched with: Badge, Royal Cypher, *P.A.O. XI* within garter wreath, foliage.
(Wallis & Wallis)   £2,000

A Victorian mameluke sword for an Equerry or A.D.C., blade 31¼in. etched and polished with crowned VR cypher, trophy and foliage. (Wallis & Wallis)   £260

A mid 19th century Indian Mameluke sabre, plain, curved blade 29in., iron crosspiece with gold foliate damascened decoration, plain ivory grips, in its brass scabbard.
(Wallis & Wallis)   £380

A fine Edward VII officer's mameluke levee sword of the XIth (Prince Alberts Own) Hussars, curved blade 32in. by 'Henry Wilkinson, Pall Mall', retaining virtually all original polish.
(Wallis & Wallis)   £2100

A fine, early 19th century European mameluke sabre, curved blade 31in., of German or Russian make, with clipped back tip, retaining approximately seventy-five per cent blued and gilt etched decoration of military trophies.   £850

MEDIEVAL SWORDS

A fine Italian medieval sword with flat tapering double-edged blade of flattened hexagonal section with a wide shallow central fuller on each face of the forte inlaid in copper with a triangle surmounted by a cross, and inscribed on one face in Nashki script, early 14th century, 33³/₄in. blade.
(Christie's)   £30,800

A medieval cruciform sword, in excavated condition, the flat straight tapering double-edged blade with shallow central fuller on each face of the forte, straight trumpet-shaped quillons of polygonal section, first half of the 14th century, 38in. blade.   £2,750

A medieval cruciform sword, in excavated condition, the broad flat slightly tapering straight blade with wide central fuller on each face, one inlaid with an inscription in Roman and Lombardic characters and a cross, 12th/13th century, 34³/₄in. blade.
(Christie's)   £12,100

A rare 13th century medieval sword, double edged blade 32½in., with traces of central fuller, straight iron crossguard of square form, 'Brazil nut' pommel, in excavated condition (blade tip missing).   £1,000

A fine Italian knightly sword with broad sharply tapering double edged blade of flattened hexagonal section changing to flattened diamond section towards the point, circa **1400**, 32in. blade. (Christie's S. Ken)   £11,000

NAZI SWORDS

A Nazi Naval Officer's sword, curved plated blade 31in., by
W.K.C., gilt hilt with large and small folding shell guards,
gilt wire bound white celluloid grip, lion head pommel inset
with red and green glass eyes, in its leather scabbard.
(Wallis & Wallis)   £625

A Nazi Luftwaffe officer's sword, blade 18½in., by Eickhorn,
with chiselled lions head pommel inset with red glass eyes.
                                                          £150

A Nazi cavalry officer's sword, curved plated blade by WKC, gilt
hilt with stirrup knucklebow, chiselled lion's head pommel inset
with red glass eyes.
(Wallis & Wallis)   £170

A Nazi artillery officer's Sabel, curved plated blade 37in.,
by Eickhorn, plated plain hilt with stirrup guard, wire bound,
black grip, in its black painted steel scabbard. (Wallis & Wallis)
                                                          £230

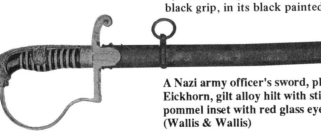

A Nazi army officer's sword, plated curved blade 30in. by
Eickhorn, gilt alloy hilt with stirrup knucklebow, lion's head
pommel inset with red glass eyes, Nazi eagle to langet.
(Wallis & Wallis)   £150

A Nazi army officer's sword, slightly curved plated blade 31in. by
Eickhorn, brass hilt, lion's head pommel with red glass eyes,
stirrup knucklebow decorated with oak leaves.
(Wallis & Wallis)   £90

PRESENTATION SWORDS

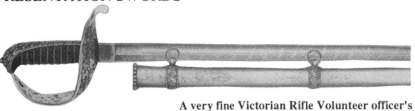

A very fine Victorian Rifle Volunteer officer's silver mounted presentation sword, blade 32in., by Pillin, finely etched for entire length with regiment *38th Middlesex (The Artists) Rifle Voltrs*. (Wallis & Wallis)   £1,600

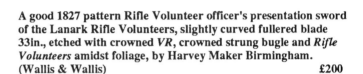

A good 1827 pattern Rifle Volunteer officer's presentation sword of the Lanark Rifle Volunteers, slightly curved fullered blade 33in., etched with crowned *VR*, crowned strung bugle and *Rifle Volunteers* amidst foliage, by Harvey Maker Birmingham. (Wallis & Wallis)   £200

A good Victorian 1821 pattern Light Cavalry officer's presentation sword, blade 35in., etched for most of length with blued and gilt etched decoration. (Wallis & Wallis)
                                      £380

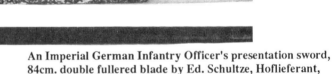

An Imperial German Infantry Officer's presentation sword, 84cm. double fullered blade by Ed. Schultze, Hoflieferant, Potsdam, etched and gilt for half its length with scrolls and inscription.
(Phillips)   £1,900

A good, Victorian 1822 pattern Artillery Volunteer Officer's presentation sword, slightly curved blade 34½in., by "Hobson, Windmill St.", etched with crown "V.R.", officer's crest and initials, and presentation inscription within scrolls. Plated guard and mounts, wire bound fishskin covered grip, in its plated metal scabbard.   £200

A very fine Victorian rifle volunteer officer's silver mounted presentation sword, blade 32in., by Pillin, finely etched for entire length, with regiment '38th Middlesex (The Artists) Rifle Voltrs'.
                                      £700

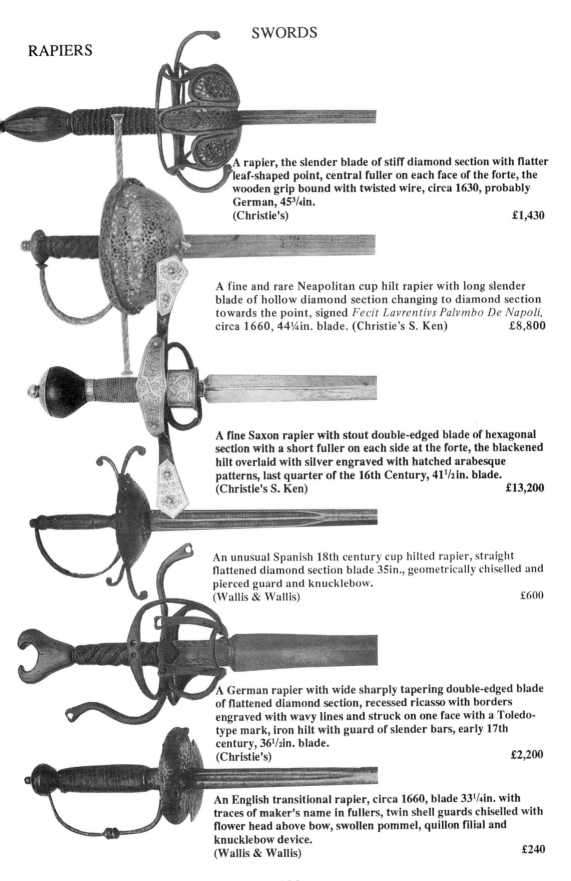

A rapier, the slender blade of stiff diamond section with flatter leaf-shaped point, central fuller on each face of the forte, the wooden grip bound with twisted wire, circa 1630, probably German, 45³/₄in.
(Christie's)   £1,430

A fine and rare Neapolitan cup hilt rapier with long slender blade of hollow diamond section changing to diamond section towards the point, signed *Fecit Lavrentivs Palvmbo De Napoli*, circa 1660, 44¼in. blade. (Christie's S. Ken)   £8,800

A fine Saxon rapier with stout double-edged blade of hexagonal section with a short fuller on each side at the forte, the blackened hilt overlaid with silver engraved with hatched arabesque patterns, last quarter of the 16th Century, 41¹/₂in. blade.
(Christie's S. Ken)   £13,200

An unusual Spanish 18th century cup hilted rapier, straight flattened diamond section blade 35in., geometrically chiselled and pierced guard and knucklebow.
(Wallis & Wallis)   £600

A German rapier with wide sharply tapering double-edged blade of flattened diamond section, recessed ricasso with borders engraved with wavy lines and struck on one face with a Toledo-type mark, iron hilt with guard of slender bars, early 17th century, 36¹/₂in. blade.
(Christie's)   £2,200

An English transitional rapier, circa 1660, blade 33¹/₄in. with traces of maker's name in fullers, twin shell guards chiselled with flower head above bow, swollen pommel, quillon filial and knucklebow device.
(Wallis & Wallis)   £240

RIDING SWORDS

A Swedish riding sword with tapering double-edged blade incised with a central wavy line on each face at the forte, iron hilt decorated on the outside with punched flowers and foliage, heart-shaped pommel, and wire-bound wooden grip, circa 1640–50, 35¼in. blade.
(Christie's) £1,437

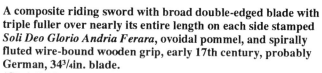

A composite riding sword with broad double-edged blade with triple fuller over nearly its entire length on each side stamped *Soli Deo Glorio Andria Ferara*, ovoidal pommel, and spirally fluted wire-bound wooden grip, early 17th century, probably German, 34¾in. blade.
(Christie's) £1,725

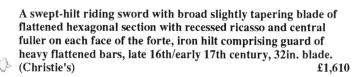

A swept-hilt riding sword with broad slightly tapering blade of flattened hexagonal section with recessed ricasso and central fuller on each face of the forte, iron hilt comprising guard of heavy flattened bars, late 16th/early 17th century, 32in. blade.
(Christie's) £1,610

A riding sword with broad straight two-edged fullered blade with long oblong ricasso, the hilt of polished iron with guard comprising vertically recurved flat quillons, the front one forming a knuckle-guard, spirally-ribbed wooden grip bound with brass wire, early 17th Century, probably German, 39½in. blade.
(Christie's S. Ken) £1,540

An unusual riding sword with associated broad double-edged blade of flattened hexagonal section with wide fuller on each side at the forte, the forte etched with suns, stars and the letters *IF*, steel hilt comprising slender moulded knuckle-guard, circa 1640, probably German, 31in. blade.
(Christie's) £1,150

SABRES

A Georgian 1796 Light Cavalry officer's sabre, curved blade 32½in. etched with 1801-16 Royal Arms, mounted cavalry trooper, crown, "GR", military trophies, pineapple and urn. (Wallis & Wallis)   £135

A Georgian Grenadier Company officer's sabre, circa 1795, curved blade 33½in., etched with crown, "GR", military trophies.   (Wallis & Wallis)   £80

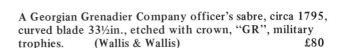

A rare 1788 Light Cavalry trooper's sabre, curved blade 35in. engraved on backledge *R. Sohlingen*, etched with: mounted trooper, *17th Light Dragoons*, Military trophies, plain steel hilt with single knucklebow and lozenge langets. (Wallis & Wallis)   £625

A very rare Swiss sabre (Schweizersäbel) with long single-edged slightly curved blade double-edged towards the point, and with broad shallow fuller bordering the back on each face, the guard of blackened iron, a saltire-shaped guard of slender round bars, circa 1600, 38¼in. (Christie's S. Ken)   £27,500

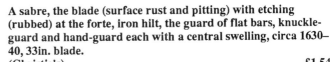

A sabre, the blade (surface rust and pitting) with etching (rubbed) at the forte, iron hilt, the guard of flat bars, knuckle-guard and hand-guard each with a central swelling, circa 1630–40, 33in. blade. (Christie's)   £1,540

Presentation model 1860 cavalry officer's sabre, 34in. curved blade with 24in. fullers etched with florals, military trophies and with *U.S.* on left side, gilt bronze three bar hilt cast with scrolling florals.
(Butterfield & Butterfield)   £1,656

A French M 1822 light cavalry trooper's sabre, curved blade 36in., engraved on backstrap *Mre D'Armes de Chatt Obre 1878 Cavrie Lre Mle 1822*, triple bar brass hilt, wire bound leather covered grip, in its steel scabbard.
(Wallis & Wallis)   £150

A rare Polish sabre with curved single-edged blade with yelman and two wide fullers on each face, the forte etched on each face with a horseman in mid-17th century costume, an arm holding flowers issuing from a cloud, and Latin inscriptions, mid-17th century, 33in. blade.
(Christie's)   £2,420

A scarce Georgian 1803 pattern officer's sabre of the Royal Scots, curved blade 31in., etched with crown above order of the Thistle badge above *The Royal* within scroll with traces of gilt decoration, copper wire bound white fishskin grip.
(Wallis & Wallis)   £320

A rare sabre (karabella) with slightly curved single-edged blade double-edged towards the point, short ricasso and, on each face, double fullers struck four times with a 'castle' mark and letters, the cross-guard and scabbard mounts Turkish, second half of the 16th century, the remainder late 17th century, 30$^1/_2$in. blade.
(Christie's)   £6,050

An Imperial Russian 1826 pattern cavalry trooper's sabre, curved blade 33in., Russian inscription to backstrap and date *1832*, brass hilt, ribbed leather grip set with single brass lozenge, in its steel scabbard.
(Wallis & Wallis)   £290

SCHIAVONA

A Venetian schiavona with double-edged blade stamped within the fullers at the forte *Johannes* and *Zuchini*, guard involving three flat diagonal bars, 17th/18th century, 33in. blade. (Christie's) £977

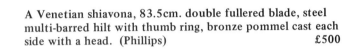

A Venetian shiavona, 83.5cm. double fullered blade, steel multi-barred hilt with thumb ring, bronze pommel cast each side with a head. (Phillips) £500

A 17th century Venetian sword schiavona, double edged, tapering blade 33in., struck at ricasso with crowned mark and engraved with zig-zag pattern at forte. Good looped and rayed iron basket guard with thumb ring and curved back quillon, wire bound leather covered grip, eared pommel. £400

A late 17th century Venetian sword schiavona, plain double edged blade 34in., iron basket guard with thumb ring, ribbed leather covered grip, cast brass eared pommel. £1,250

A good Venetian sword schiavona, circa 1580, straight, single edged, fullered blade 40in., with contemporary repair. Multi-bar swept hilt, wrought from one piece, incorporating large thumb ring, integral square sectioned quillon with swollen finial. Brass pommel of eared form, wire bound grip with brass ferrules. £700

A 17th century schiavona, single edged multi-fullered straight blade 36in., with clip back point with traces of Andria Ferrara in fullers, basket guard of good form with thumb ring, struck with two armourers' marks possibly the lion of St. Marks. £500

127

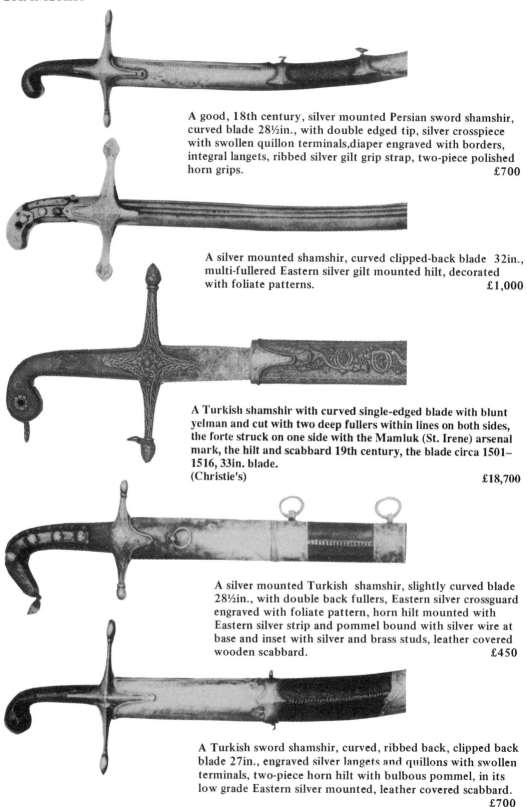

A good, 18th century, silver mounted Persian sword shamshir, curved blade 28½in., with double edged tip, silver crosspiece with swollen quillon terminals,diaper engraved with borders, integral langets, ribbed silver gilt grip strap, two-piece polished horn grips. £700

A silver mounted shamshir, curved clipped-back blade 32in., multi-fullered Eastern silver gilt mounted hilt, decorated with foliate patterns. £1,000

A Turkish shamshir with curved single-edged blade with blunt yelman and cut with two deep fullers within lines on both sides, the forte struck on one side with the Mamluk (St. Irene) arsenal mark, the hilt and scabbard 19th century, the blade circa 1501–1516, 33in. blade.
(Christie's) £18,700

A silver mounted Turkish shamshir, slightly curved blade 28½in., with double back fullers, Eastern silver crossguard engraved with foliate pattern, horn hilt mounted with Eastern silver strip and pommel bound with silver wire at base and inset with silver and brass studs, leather covered wooden scabbard. £450

A Turkish sword shamshir, curved, ribbed back, clipped back blade 27in., engraved silver langets and quillons with swollen terminals, two-piece horn hilt with bulbous pommel, in its low grade Eastern silver mounted, leather covered scabbard. £700

SHASQUA

A scarce, Soviet World War II period military shasqua, curved blade 31½in., dated "1940" at forte, with other Russian stamps, brass mounted spiral wood grip, the 'beaked' pommel with Soviet emblem, "C.C.C.P.".   £200

Silver mounted Russian sabre, shasqua, the 29in. curved blade with median ridge, three narrow fullers at the back edge and slight hatchet tip, the hilt of gold washed niello silver.
(Butterfield & Butterfield)   £625

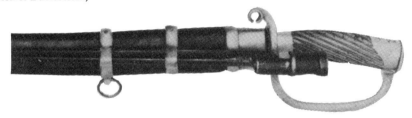

A model 1881 Imperial Russian Dragoon shasqua, slightly curved fullered blade 34in., dated at forte 1895, together with sundry military and arsenal stamps. Regulation brass stirrup hilt, spiral carved wooden grip. In its brass mounted leather covered scabbard with Moisin Nagant bayonet attached to fittings.   £300

Silver mounted Russian shasqua, the 31¹/₂in. slightly curved, watered blade with gold inlaid Turkish maker's mark and narrow fuller at back edge, the hilt of chiselled and repoussé niello silver.
(Butterfield & Butterfield)   £1,324

A fine niello and silver mounted Caucasian shasqua, curved, clipped back blade 33in., multi-fullered and deeply struck with a mark of star form with letters inside on both sides, the eared hilt covered with Eastern nielloed silver decorated with foliate patterns and with struck Caucasian hallmark in its leather covered wooden scabbard.   £700

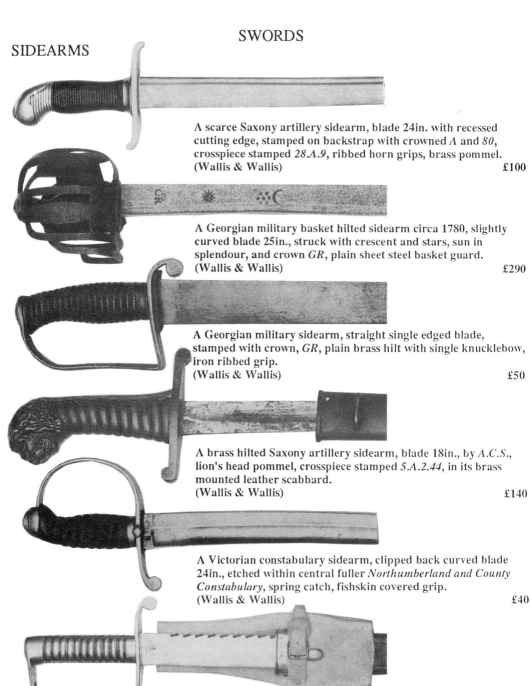

A scarce Saxony artillery sidearm, blade 24in. with recessed cutting edge, stamped on backstrap with crowned *A* and *80*, crosspiece stamped *28.A.9*, ribbed horn grips, brass pommel. (Wallis & Wallis) £100

A Georgian military basket hilted sidearm circa 1780, slightly curved blade 25in., struck with crescent and stars, sun in splendour, and crown *GR*, plain sheet steel basket guard. (Wallis & Wallis) £290

A Georgian military sidearm, straight single edged blade, stamped with crown, *GR*, plain brass hilt with single knucklebow, iron ribbed grip. (Wallis & Wallis) £50

A brass hilted Saxony artillery sidearm, blade 18in., by *A.C.S.*, lion's head pommel, crosspiece stamped *5.A.2.44*, in its brass mounted leather scabbard. (Wallis & Wallis) £140

A Victorian constabulary sidearm, clipped back curved blade 24in., etched within central fuller *Northumberland and County Constabulary*, spring catch, fishskin covered grip. (Wallis & Wallis) £40

A brass hilted 1856 pioneer sidearm, saw backed blade 22in. ribbed hilt, stamped above quillon *9.96 V.24 Mx 9* in its brass mounted leather scabbard with buff leather frog. (Wallis & Wallis) £120

An 1871 pattern brass hilted Prussian dress sidearm, slightly curved blade, lined grip, in its brass mounted leather scabbard. £115

SMALL SWORDS

A good Irish hallmarked silver hilted smallsword c. 1770, colichemarde shaped hollow ground blade 32½in., etched with military trophies and figure of agriculture seated upon crossed bow and quiver.
(Wallis & Wallis)   £2,000

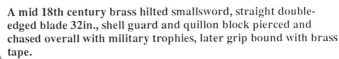

A mid 18th century brass hilted smallsword, straight double-edged blade 32in., shell guard and quillon block pierced and chased overall with military trophies, later grip bound with brass tape.
(Wallis & Wallis)   £74

A French chiselled and pierced steel hilted smallsword, circa 1750, hollow ground blade 31¼in. etched and gilt with heart displayed above *Vigelandum* on both sides with putti, birds, trophies, strapwork and foliage.
(Wallis & Wallis)   £380

A cut steel hilted smallsword, slim tapering triangular blade 31in., foliate etched, shell guard, urn pommel and hilt with some stud decoration, in its patent leather scabbard.
(Wallis & Wallis)   £110

A steel hilted smallsword circa 1770, colichemarde triangular tapering blade 31in., finely chiselled and pierced double shell guard in foliate patterns, knucklebow and ovoid pommel similarly pierced and decorated.
(Wallis & Wallis)   £330

A 19th century Continental white metal hilted smallsword, straight single edged fullered blade 32¼in., twin shellguard with raised hobnail decoration, dragon's head finial to knucklebow, foliate quillons, one piece grip.
(Wallis & Wallis)   £220

A French silver hilted smallsword (hallmarked *Paris 1798*), hollow ground triangular tapering blade 31in. etched with military trophies and foliage, with some gilding remaining.
(Wallis & Wallis)   £525

SPADROONS

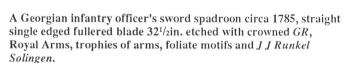

A Georgian infantry officer's sword spadroon circa 1785, straight single edged fullered blade 32½in. etched with crowned *GR*, Royal Arms, trophies of arms, foliate motifs and *J J Runkel Solingen*.
(Wallis & Wallis)   £120

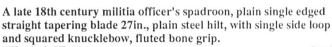

A late 18th century militia officer's spadroon, plain single edged straight tapering blade 27in., plain steel hilt, with single side loop and squared knucklebow, fluted bone grip.
(Wallis & Wallis)   £170

A Georgian officer's spadroon circa 1770, straight plain blade 31in., steel slotted hilt, gadrooned ovoid pommel, silver wire and band bound grip.
(Wallis & Wallis)   £200

A Naval officer's spadroon, 85cm. blade engraved and gilt with foliage, Royal arms and cypher, figure of Britannia and signed Osborn's Warranted. (Phillips)   £650

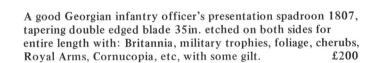

A good Georgian infantry officer's presentation spadroon 1807, tapering double edged blade 35in. etched on both sides for entire length with: Britannia, military trophies, foliage, cherubs, Royal Arms, Cornucopia, etc, with some gilt.   £200

A Napoleonic era Bavarian infantry officer's five ball hilt spadroon, straight slim blade 33in., etched with crown 'M.K.', floral sprays, steel knucklebow and side loop incorporating gilt lion holding Bavarian arms.   £175

SWORD PISTOLS

A scarce combination pinfire revolver and hunting sword, 51.5cm. double fullered blade, the six-shot revolver with 10cm. barrel mounted on the right side, the top strap signed H. G. & F. Brevets.
(Phillips) £1,350

A 55 bore flintlock hunting sword pistol circa 1760, 28in. overall, tapered and swamped turn off barrel 2¹/₄in., with London and maker's proofs at breech, triple fullered blade 23in., the action enclosed by tapered fluted horn grip, foliate chiselled steel pommel and knucklebow.
(Wallis & Wallis) £610

A rare Italian flintlock combined hunting sword and D.B. flintlock pistol with straight tapering single-edged blade back-edged at the point and retaining some etched decoration at the forte, the right side with the etched inscription *Ne me tirez pas sans raison*, signed *Giuseppe Averani Roma*, circa 1770, 17³/₄in. blade.
(Christie's) £1,980

A fine German combined hunting sword and flintlock pistol with straight tapering blade of flattened diamond section, flat disc guard of copper with engraved borders on the inner side, two-stage barrel chiselled on top of the breech with symmetrical scrollwork, by Picart a Freudenthal, early 18th century, 23³/₄in. blade.
(Christie's) £6,600

A German combined hunting sword and flintlock pistol with straight single-edged blade with two narrow fullers, the pistol with two-stage gilt-brass barrel decorated with punched scrolls on the breech, retaining much original gilding throughout, circa 1720–30, 14in. blade.
(Christie's) £1,650

A rare German combined hunting sword and flintlock pistol reconverted from flintlock, with curved single-edged blade double-edged at the point and with one broad and one narrow fuller, the locket housing an iron ramrod, mid-18th century, 21³/₄in. blade.
(Christie's) £1,760

An early 19th century swordstick, 36¼in., broad flattened diamond section blade 29½in., one piece rhino horn hilt with silver escutcheon.
(Wallis & Wallis)   £220

A good Georgian blued and gilt swordstick, blade 29½in. etched with military trophies and foliate ornaments, blued and gilt for first 11in.
(Wallis & Wallis)   £330

A late Georgian ivory mounted sword cane, 36in., straight fullered single edged blade 25in., etched with foliage, trophy of arms and laurel wreath, ivory handle with chequered grip.
(Wallis & Wallis)   £240

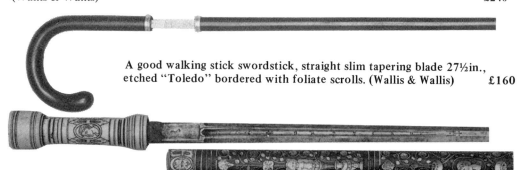

A good walking stick swordstick, straight slim tapering blade 27½in., etched "Toledo" bordered with foliate scrolls. (Wallis & Wallis)   £160

A rare swordstick with long rapier blade of flattened hexagonal section with narrow central fuller on each face of the forte stamped respectively *Sebastian* and *Hernandez*, the ricasso struck on each face with the Toledo mark, early 17th century, 47in.
(Christie's)   £7,475

A Victorian sword cane, 36¾in., square section polished blade 28½in. with narrow fuller, horn handle of 'putter' form, floral embossed copper gilt ferrule, cane handle.
(Wallis & Wallis)   £125

A Victorian sword cane, shallow diamond sectioned blade 27in., blued and gilt with scrolls for half its length. Foliate embossed silver top (not hallmarked) and ferrule engraved 'A.B.', white metal mounted steel tip.   £200

YATAGHAN

A fine silver mounted yataghan, curved blade 24in., struck with armourer's mark, the hilt covered in Eastern sheet silver embossed in foliate patterns, in its sheath entirely covered with Eastern silver embossed in foliate and geometric patterns.   £400

A late 18th century Algerian sword yataghan, swollen 'T' section blade 23in. struck with maker's mark, two piece ivory grips of good colour, nielloed silver gripstrap with gilt vignettes. (Wallis & Wallis)   £300

A Turkish yataghan, the blade damascened in gold with the maker's name *Hajj Muhammed Husam* and owner's name *Osman Agha*, the forte encased in silver-gilt chased with foliage, the hilt entirely covered with silver, dated *1832 AD*, 20³/₄in. (Christie's)   £1,840

A late 18th century Turkish gold damascened sword yataghan, recurved single edged blade 23½in., nicely ribbed back edge, sides gold damascened with foliate cartouches. (Wallis & Wallis)   £260

A large ornate yataghan, blade 23in., large marine ivory eared grips, gilt blade forte mounts, hilt mounts with some coral stone decoration, in its leather covered sheath, two large German silver mounts.   £300

A good Turkish sword yataghan, recurved, single edged blade 22in., inlaid with extensive silver script within scrolls and dog tooth borders. Two-piece eared walrus ivory grips, grip strap and blade mountings of ornamental silver. Silver scabbard with gilt top pierced and worked in relieved bands, integral stylised dragon chape.   £1,500

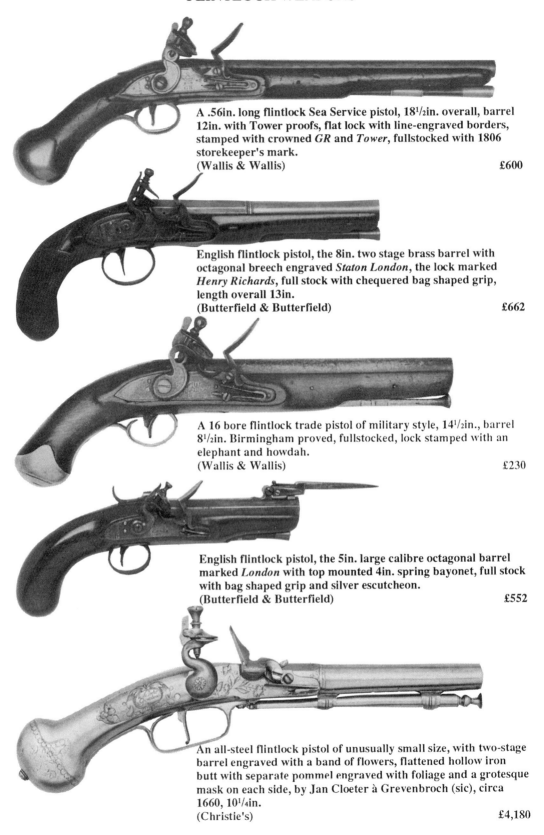

A .56in. long flintlock Sea Service pistol, 18¹/₂in. overall, barrel 12in. with Tower proofs, flat lock with line-engraved borders, stamped with crowned *GR* and *Tower*, fullstocked with 1806 storekeeper's mark.
(Wallis & Wallis)   £600

English flintlock pistol, the 8in. two stage brass barrel with octagonal breech engraved *Staton London*, the lock marked *Henry Richards*, full stock with chequered bag shaped grip, length overall 13in.
(Butterfield & Butterfield)   £662

A 16 bore flintlock trade pistol of military style, 14¹/₂in., barrel 8¹/₂in. Birmingham proved, fullstocked, lock stamped with an elephant and howdah.
(Wallis & Wallis)   £230

English flintlock pistol, the 5in. large calibre octagonal barrel marked *London* with top mounted 4in. spring bayonet, full stock with bag shaped grip and silver escutcheon.
(Butterfield & Butterfield)   £552

An all-steel flintlock pistol of unusually small size, with two-stage barrel engraved with a band of flowers, flattened hollow iron butt with separate pommel engraved with foliage and a grotesque mask on each side, by Jan Cloeter à Grevenbroch (sic), circa 1660, 10¹/₄in.
(Christie's)   £4,180

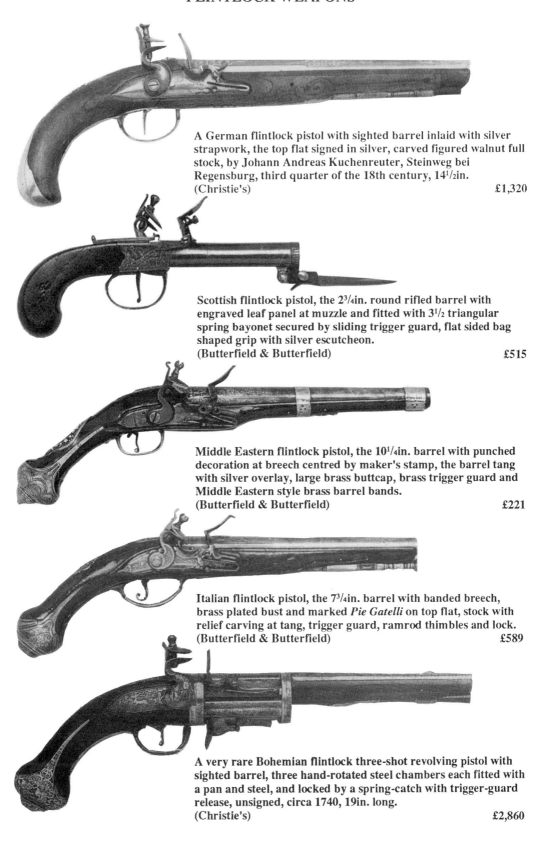

A German flintlock pistol with sighted barrel inlaid with silver strapwork, the top flat signed in silver, carved figured walnut full stock, by Johann Andreas Kuchenreuter, Steinweg bei Regensburg, third quarter of the 18th century, 14$^{1}/_{2}$in. (Christie's) £1,320

Scottish flintlock pistol, the 2$^{3}/_{4}$in. round rifled barrel with engraved leaf panel at muzzle and fitted with 3$^{1}/_{2}$ triangular spring bayonet secured by sliding trigger guard, flat sided bag shaped grip with silver escutcheon. (Butterfield & Butterfield) £515

Middle Eastern flintlock pistol, the 10$^{1}/_{4}$in. barrel with punched decoration at breech centred by maker's stamp, the barrel tang with silver overlay, large brass buttcap, brass trigger guard and Middle Eastern style brass barrel bands. (Butterfield & Butterfield) £221

Italian flintlock pistol, the 7$^{3}/_{4}$in. barrel with banded breech, brass plated bust and marked *Pie Gatelli* on top flat, stock with relief carving at tang, trigger guard, ramrod thimbles and lock. (Butterfield & Butterfield) £589

A very rare Bohemian flintlock three-shot revolving pistol with sighted barrel, three hand-rotated steel chambers each fitted with a pan and steel, and locked by a spring-catch with trigger-guard release, unsigned, circa 1740, 19in. long. (Christie's) £2,860

BELT PISTOLS

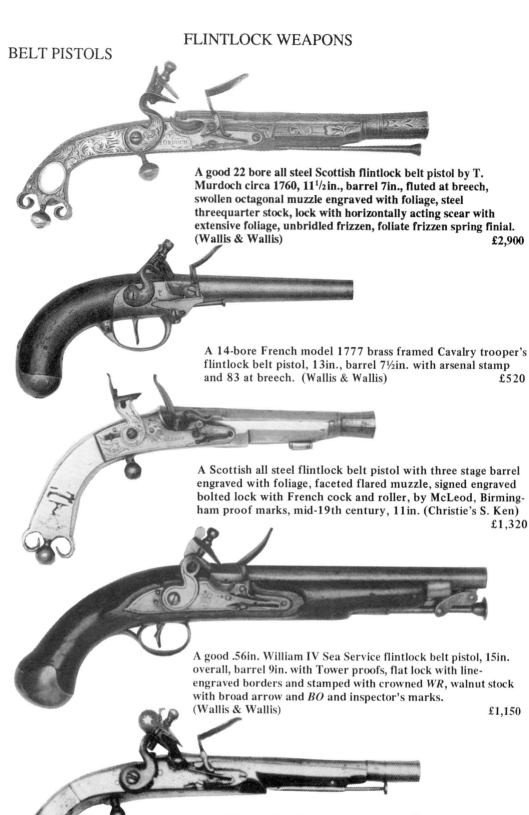

A good 22 bore all steel Scottish flintlock belt pistol by T. Murdoch circa 1760, $11\frac{1}{2}$in., barrel 7in., fluted at breech, swollen octagonal muzzle engraved with foliage, steel threequarter stock, lock with horizontally acting scear with extensive foliage, unbridled frizzen, foliate frizzen spring finial. (Wallis & Wallis) **£2,900**

A 14-bore French model 1777 brass framed Cavalry trooper's flintlock belt pistol, 13in., barrel $7\frac{1}{2}$in. with arsenal stamp and 83 at breech. (Wallis & Wallis) **£520**

A Scottish all steel flintlock belt pistol with three stage barrel engraved with foliage, faceted flared muzzle, signed engraved bolted lock with French cock and roller, by McLeod, Birmingham proof marks, mid-19th century, 11in. (Christie's S. Ken) **£1,320**

A good .56in. William IV Sea Service flintlock belt pistol, 15in. overall, barrel 9in. with Tower proofs, flat lock with line-engraved borders and stamped with crowned *WR*, walnut stock with broad arrow and *BO* and inspector's marks. (Wallis & Wallis) **£1,150**

An 18-bore all steel Scottish flintlock belt pistol, circa 1780, $12\frac{1}{2}$in., barrel 8in., three-quarter stocked, horizontally acting scear, 'ram's horn' butt, elaborately pierced and engraved belt hook. (Wallis & Wallis) **£350**

BELT PISTOLS

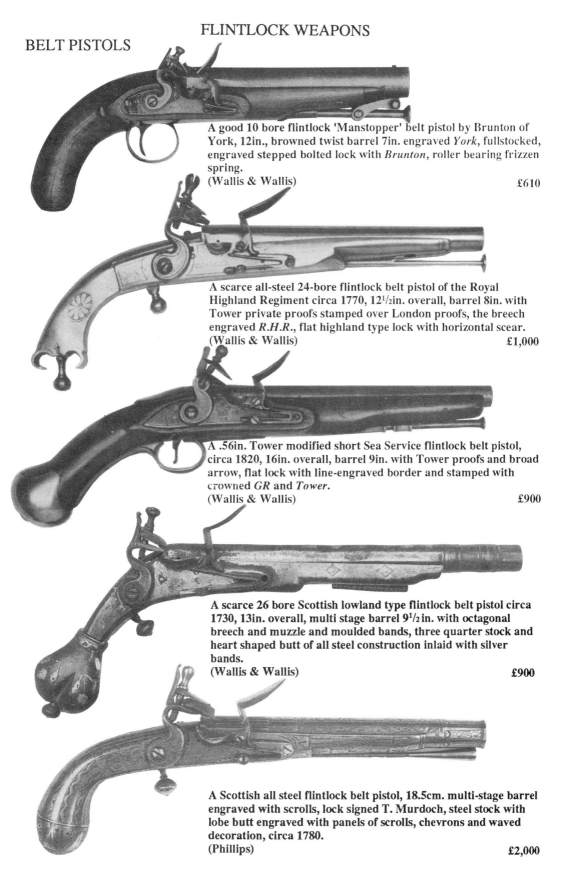

A good 10 bore flintlock 'Manstopper' belt pistol by Brunton of York, 12in., browned twist barrel 7in. engraved *York*, fullstocked, engraved stepped bolted lock with *Brunton*, roller bearing frizzen spring.
(Wallis & Wallis)   £610

A scarce all-steel 24-bore flintlock belt pistol of the Royal Highland Regiment circa 1770, 12½in. overall, barrel 8in. with Tower private proofs stamped over London proofs, the breech engraved *R.H.R.*, flat highland type lock with horizontal scear.
(Wallis & Wallis)   £1,000

A .56in. Tower modified short Sea Service flintlock belt pistol, circa 1820, 16in. overall, barrel 9in. with Tower proofs and broad arrow, flat lock with line-engraved border and stamped with crowned *GR* and *Tower*.
(Wallis & Wallis)   £900

A scarce 26 bore Scottish lowland type flintlock belt pistol circa 1730, 13in. overall, multi stage barrel 9½in. with octagonal breech and muzzle and moulded bands, three quarter stock and heart shaped butt of all steel construction inlaid with silver bands.
(Wallis & Wallis)   £900

A Scottish all steel flintlock belt pistol, 18.5cm. multi-stage barrel engraved with scrolls, lock signed T. Murdoch, steel stock with lobe butt engraved with panels of scrolls, chevrons and waved decoration, circa 1780.
(Phillips)   £2,000

BLUNDERBUSS PISTOLS

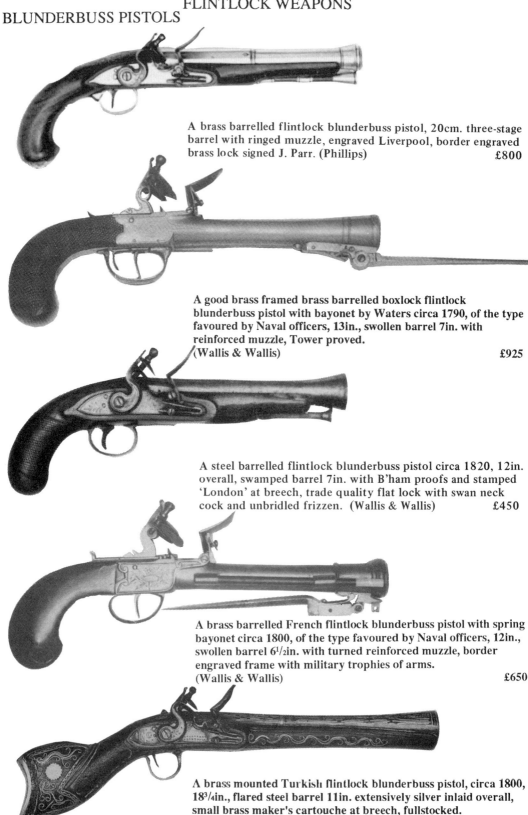

A brass barrelled flintlock blunderbuss pistol, 20cm. three-stage barrel with ringed muzzle, engraved Liverpool, border engraved brass lock signed J. Parr. (Phillips) **£800**

A good brass framed brass barrelled boxlock flintlock blunderbuss pistol with bayonet by Waters circa 1790, of the type favoured by Naval officers, 13in., swollen barrel 7in. with reinforced muzzle, Tower proved. (Wallis & Wallis) **£925**

A steel barrelled flintlock blunderbuss pistol circa 1820, 12in. overall, swamped barrel 7in. with B'ham proofs and stamped 'London' at breech, trade quality flat lock with swan neck cock and unbridled frizzen. (Wallis & Wallis) **£450**

A brass barrelled French flintlock blunderbuss pistol with spring bayonet circa 1800, of the type favoured by Naval officers, 12in., swollen barrel 6$\frac{1}{2}$in. with turned reinforced muzzle, border engraved frame with military trophies of arms. (Wallis & Wallis) **£650**

A brass mounted Turkish flintlock blunderbuss pistol, circa 1800, 18$\frac{3}{4}$in., flared steel barrel 11in. extensively silver inlaid overall, small brass maker's cartouche at breech, fullstocked. (Wallis & Wallis) **£425**

CASED SETS

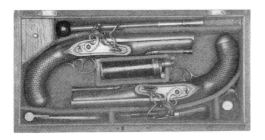

An unusual pair of 16 bore flintlock belt pistols by Tatham and Egg, circa 1810, 11½in., rebrowned barrels 6¼in. engraved on their top flats. £1,900

Cased pair of English flintlock pocket pistols, the frames engraved with trophies of arms and inscribed *W Jones* on one side and *London* on the obverse, flat sided bag shaped grips. (Butterfield & Butterfield) £625

A pair of Royal over-and-under flintlock carriage pistols with rebrowned twist octagonal barrels signed in gold on the top flats and with gold lines at the breeches, gold fore-sights, platinum vents, engraved case-hardened tangs, signed engraved case-hardened locks with blued steel-springs and top jaws, by Durs Egg, No. 132 Strand, London, No, 700, circa 1815, 8¾in. long. £8,800

A fine pair of D.B. flintlock pistols with heavy browned twist barrels signed in full on the rib, silver fore-sights, scroll engraved case-hardened breeches and breech tangs, the former with gold vents and the latter also engraved 1 and 2, by John Dickson & Son, 63 Princes Street, Edinburgh, London proof marks, nos. 4590/1 for 1893, 14¾in. long. £5,500

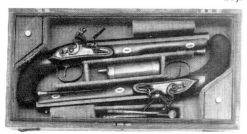

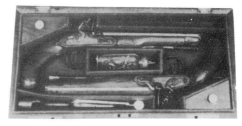

A pair of flintlock holster or duelling pistols, 25cm. sighted octagonal barrels signed H. Nock, London, stepped signed and bolted locks, set triggers, full stocked, the chequered butts with oval silver escutcheons, contained in a baize lined oak case. £1,500

A good pair of 16-bore flintlock duelling pistols by Parsons of Salisbury, circa 1800, 14¾in., octagonal sighted barrels 9in., engraved on the top flat 'Salisbury' with silver foresights, full-stocked in finely figured walnut, linear engraved stepped lockplates. £2,500

A good pair of 48 bore Dutch flintlock duelling pistols refurbished by Tatham & Egg, formerly owned by Sir W. H. Clinton, 15¼ inches browned twist barrels 10 inches with silver inlaid breech lines. £3,000

An unusual pair of Flemish flintlock box-lock pistols with brass cannon barrels and actions of one piece, the latter engraved with a floral and musical trophy on each side, thumbpiece safety-catches also locking the steels, early 19th century, 10in. long. £2,200

An exceptional garniture of flintlock pistols, comprising: a pair of saw-handled duelling pistols with rebrowned octagonal barrels, each with patent breech signed in gold, a single-trigger over-and-under officer's pistol with rebrowned octagonal barrels, and an associated single-trigger over-and-under pocket pistol with blued octagonal barrels, by Joseph Egg, London, circa 1815, 15½in., 13¼in. and 6in. £18,700

Cased pair of English flintlock officer's pistols, each with 6in. large calibre octagon barrel inlaid in gold with two lines at the breech and on top flat *J Egg London.*
(Butterfield & Butterfield) £3,678

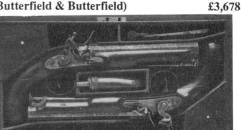

Cased pair of English flintlock officer's pistols, the 8in. large calibre octagon barrels engraved *Westley Richards* and fitted with swivel ramrods, platinum vents, engraved maker marked locks with frizzen spring rollers and push on safeties.
(Butterfield & Butterfield) £3,127

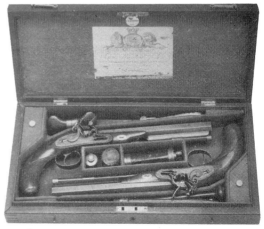

A fine pair of flintlock duelling pistols with heavy rebrowned octagonal polygroove rifled barrels signed in full on the top flats, in original lined and fitted mahogany case, with trade label and accessories including red leather covered flask, by John Manton & Son, 15in. £9,350

DOUBLE BARRELLED

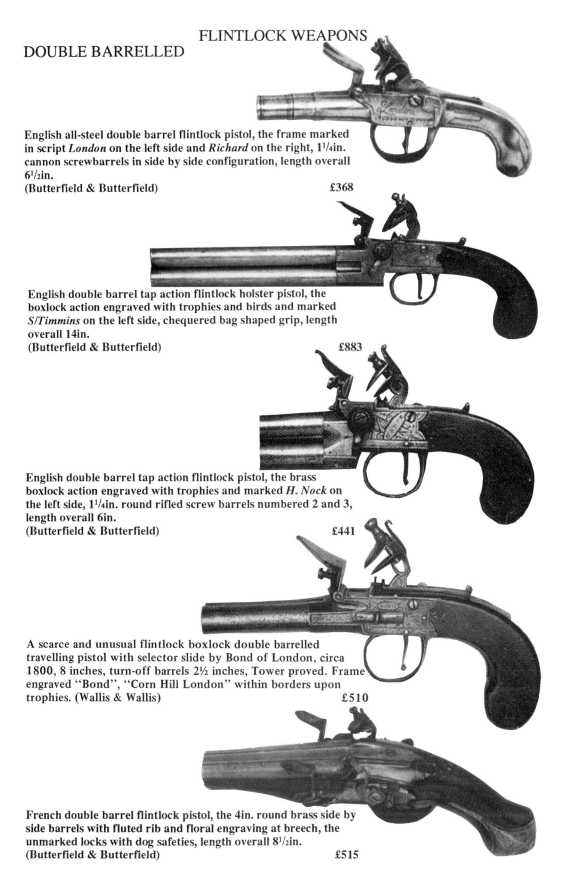

English all-steel double barrel flintlock pistol, the frame marked in script *London* on the left side and *Richard* on the right, 1¼in. cannon screwbarrels in side by side configuration, length overall 6½in.
(Butterfield & Butterfield) £368

English double barrel tap action flintlock holster pistol, the boxlock action engraved with trophies and birds and marked *S/Timmins* on the left side, chequered bag shaped grip, length overall 14in.
(Butterfield & Butterfield) £883

English double barrel tap action flintlock pistol, the brass boxlock action engraved with trophies and marked *H. Nock* on the left side, 1¼in. round rifled screw barrels numbered 2 and 3, length overall 6in.
(Butterfield & Butterfield) £441

A scarce and unusual flintlock boxlock double barrelled travelling pistol with selector slide by Bond of London, circa 1800, 8 inches, turn-off barrels 2½ inches, Tower proved. Frame engraved "Bond", "Corn Hill London" within borders upon trophies. (Wallis & Wallis) £510

French double barrel flintlock pistol, the 4in. round brass side by side barrels with fluted rib and floral engraving at breech, the unmarked locks with dog safeties, length overall 8½in.
(Butterfield & Butterfield) £515

DOUBLE BARRELLED

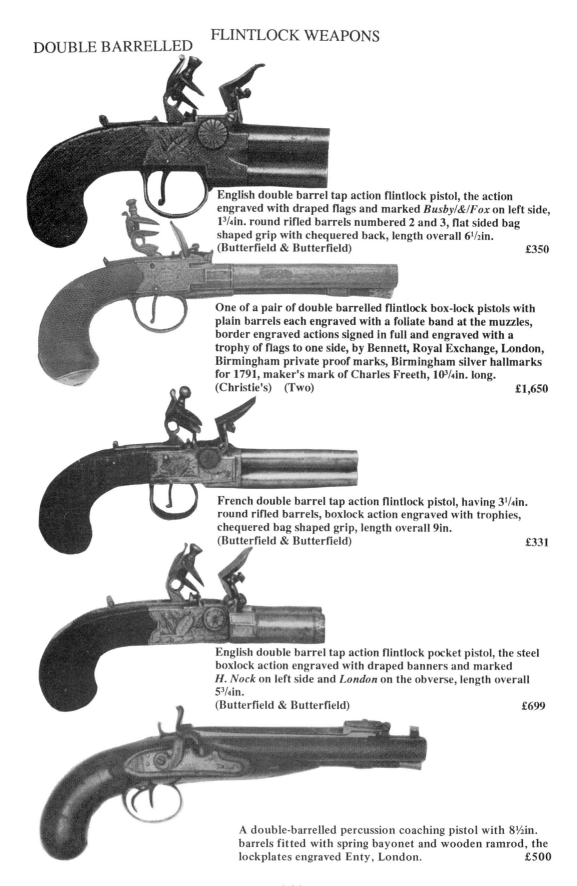

English double barrel tap action flintlock pistol, the action engraved with draped flags and marked *Busby/&/Fox* on left side, 1³/₄in. round rifled barrels numbered 2 and 3, flat sided bag shaped grip with chequered back, length overall 6¹/₂in.
(Butterfield & Butterfield) £350

One of a pair of double barrelled flintlock box-lock pistols with plain barrels each engraved with a foliate band at the muzzles, border engraved actions signed in full and engraved with a trophy of flags to one side, by Bennett, Royal Exchange, London, Birmingham private proof marks, Birmingham silver hallmarks for 1791, maker's mark of Charles Freeth, 10³/₄in. long.
(Christie's)   (Two) £1,650

French double barrel tap action flintlock pistol, having 3¹/₄in. round rifled barrels, boxlock action engraved with trophies, chequered bag shaped grip, length overall 9in.
(Butterfield & Butterfield) £331

English double barrel tap action flintlock pocket pistol, the steel boxlock action engraved with draped banners and marked *H. Nock* on left side and *London* on the obverse, length overall 5³/₄in.
(Butterfield & Butterfield) £699

A double-barrelled percussion coaching pistol with 8½in. barrels fitted with spring bayonet and wooden ramrod, the lockplates engraved Enty, London. £500

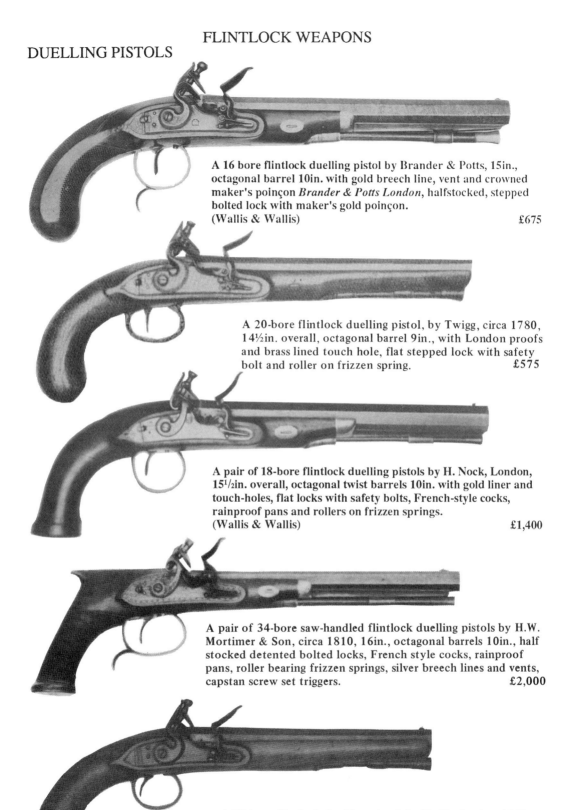

A 16 bore flintlock duelling pistol by Brander & Potts, 15in., octagonal barrel 10in. with gold breech line, vent and crowned maker's poinçon *Brander & Potts London*, halfstocked, stepped bolted lock with maker's gold poinçon.
(Wallis & Wallis) £675

A 20-bore flintlock duelling pistol, by Twigg, circa 1780, 14½in. overall, octagonal barrel 9in., with London proofs and brass lined touch hole, flat stepped lock with safety bolt and roller on frizzen spring. £575

A pair of 18-bore flintlock duelling pistols by H. Nock, London, 15¹/₂in. overall, octagonal twist barrels 10in. with gold liner and touch-holes, flat locks with safety bolts, French-style cocks, rainproof pans and rollers on frizzen springs.
(Wallis & Wallis) £1,400

A pair of 34-bore saw-handled flintlock duelling pistols by H.W. Mortimer & Son, circa 1810, 16in., octagonal barrels 10in., half stocked detented bolted locks, French style cocks, rainproof pans, roller bearing frizzen springs, silver breech lines and vents, capstan screw set triggers. £2,000

A 22-bore flintlock duelling pistol, by H. Nock, circa 1800, 14½in., overall, octagonal barrel 9in., plain flat stepped lock with swan-neck cock and roller on frizzen spring, plain walnut fullstock and rounded butt. £550

HOLSTER PISTOLS

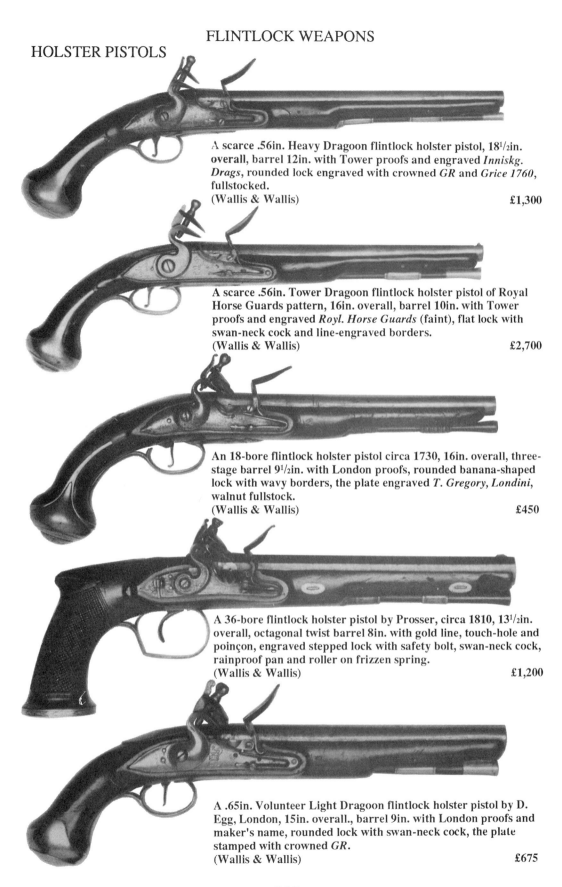

A scarce .56in. Heavy Dragoon flintlock holster pistol, 18½in. overall, barrel 12in. with Tower proofs and engraved *Inniskg. Drags*, rounded lock engraved with crowned *GR* and *Grice 1760*, fullstocked.
(Wallis & Wallis)   £1,300

A scarce .56in. Tower Dragoon flintlock holster pistol of Royal Horse Guards pattern, 16in. overall, barrel 10in. with Tower proofs and engraved *Royl. Horse Guards* (faint), flat lock with swan-neck cock and line-engraved borders.
(Wallis & Wallis)   £2,700

An 18-bore flintlock holster pistol circa 1730, 16in. overall, three-stage barrel 9½in. with London proofs, rounded banana-shaped lock with wavy borders, the plate engraved *T. Gregory, Londini*, walnut fullstock.
(Wallis & Wallis)   £450

A 36-bore flintlock holster pistol by Prosser, circa 1810, 13½in. overall, octagonal twist barrel 8in. with gold line, touch-hole and poinçon, engraved stepped lock with safety bolt, swan-neck cock, rainproof pan and roller on frizzen spring.
(Wallis & Wallis)   £1,200

A .65in. Volunteer Light Dragoon flintlock holster pistol by D. Egg, London, 15in. overall., barrel 9in. with London proofs and maker's name, rounded lock with swan-neck cock, the plate stamped with crowned *GR*.
(Wallis & Wallis)   £675

HOLSTER PISTOLS

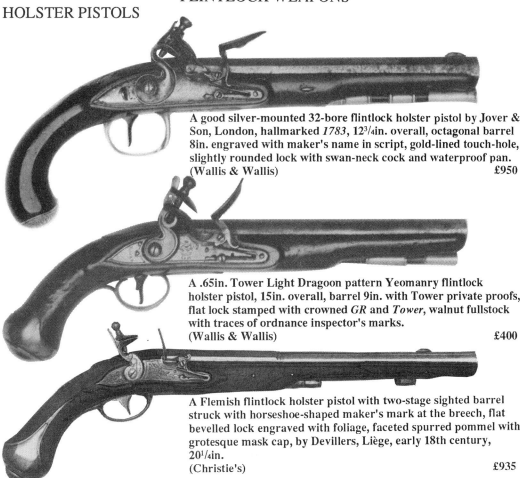

A good silver-mounted 32-bore flintlock holster pistol by Jover & Son, London, hallmarked *1783*, 12¾in. overall, octagonal barrel 8in. engraved with maker's name in script, gold-lined touch-hole, slightly rounded lock with swan-neck cock and waterproof pan.
(Wallis & Wallis)   £950

A .65in. Tower Light Dragoon pattern Yeomanry flintlock holster pistol, 15in. overall, barrel 9in. with Tower private proofs, flat lock stamped with crowned *GR* and *Tower*, walnut fullstock with traces of ordnance inspector's marks.
(Wallis & Wallis)   £400

A Flemish flintlock holster pistol with two-stage sighted barrel struck with horseshoe-shaped maker's mark at the breech, flat bevelled lock engraved with foliage, faceted spurred pommel with grotesque mask cap, by Devillers, Liège, early 18th century, 20¼in.
(Christie's)   £935

FLINTLOCK WEAPONS

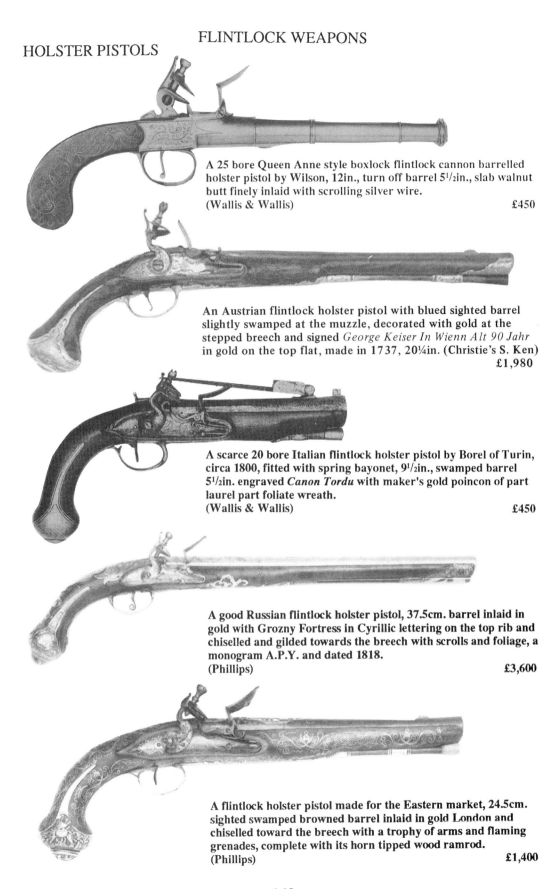

A 25 bore Queen Anne style boxlock flintlock cannon barrelled holster pistol by Wilson, 12in., turn off barrel 5¹/₂in., slab walnut butt finely inlaid with scrolling silver wire.
(Wallis & Wallis) £450

An Austrian flintlock holster pistol with blued sighted barrel slightly swamped at the muzzle, decorated with gold at the stepped breech and signed *George Keiser In Wienn Alt 90 Jahr* in gold on the top flat, made in 1737, 20¹/₄in. (Christie's S. Ken) £1,980

A scarce 20 bore Italian flintlock holster pistol by Borel of Turin, circa 1800, fitted with spring bayonet, 9¹/₂in., swamped barrel 5¹/₂in. engraved *Canon Tordu* with maker's gold poincon of part laurel part foliate wreath.
(Wallis & Wallis) £450

A good Russian flintlock holster pistol, 37.5cm. barrel inlaid in gold with Grozny Fortress in Cyrillic lettering on the top rib and chiselled and gilded towards the breech with scrolls and foliage, a monogram A.P.Y. and dated 1818.
(Phillips) £3,600

A flintlock holster pistol made for the Eastern market, 24.5cm. sighted swamped browned barrel inlaid in gold London and chiselled toward the breech with a trophy of arms and flaming grenades, complete with its horn tipped wood ramrod.
(Phillips) £1,400

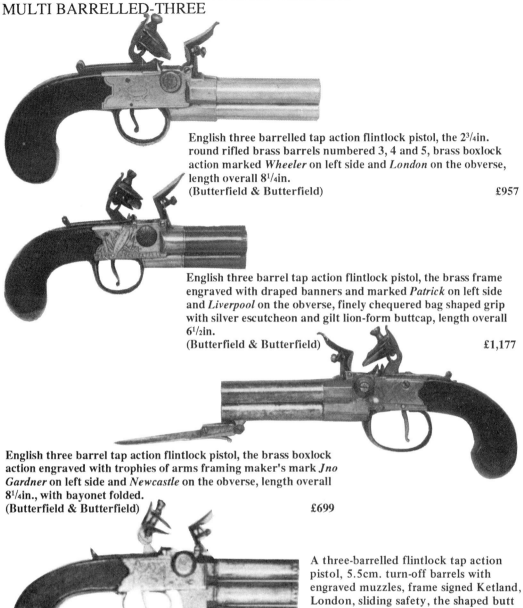

English three barrelled tap action flintlock pistol, the 2³/₄in. round rifled brass barrels numbered 3, 4 and 5, brass boxlock action marked *Wheeler* on left side and *London* on the obverse, length overall 8¹/₄in.
(Butterfield & Butterfield)   £957

English three barrel tap action flintlock pistol, the brass frame engraved with draped banners and marked *Patrick* on left side and *Liverpool* on the obverse, finely chequered bag shaped grip with silver escutcheon and gilt lion-form buttcap, length overall 6¹/₂in.
(Butterfield & Butterfield)   £1,177

English three barrel tap action flintlock pistol, the brass boxlock action engraved with trophies of arms framing maker's mark *Jno Gardner* on left side and *Newcastle* on the obverse, length overall 8¹/₄in., with bayonet folded.
(Butterfield & Butterfield)   £699

A three-barrelled flintlock tap action pistol, 5.5cm. turn-off barrels with engraved muzzles, frame signed Ketland, London, sliding safety, the shaped butt with white metal lion's mask butt cap.
                                                                £400

A flintlock boxlock three-barrelled pistol, 7.5cm. turn-off barrels, frame engraved with trophies of arms and signed Twigg, London, pan selector on left, sliding safety, slab sided wood butt.
                                                                £500

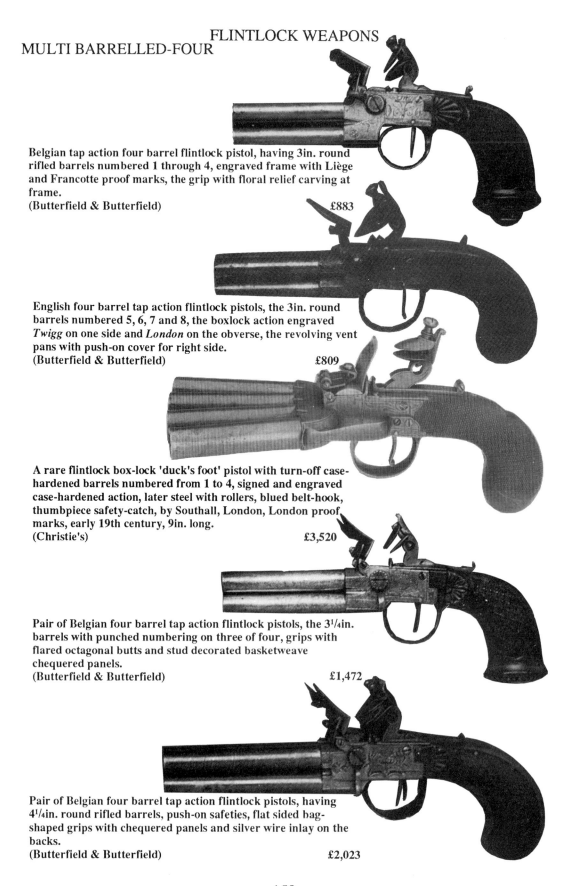

Belgian tap action four barrel flintlock pistol, having 3in. round rifled barrels numbered 1 through 4, engraved frame with Liège and Francotte proof marks, the grip with floral relief carving at frame.
(Butterfield & Butterfield) £883

English four barrel tap action flintlock pistols, the 3in. round barrels numbered 5, 6, 7 and 8, the boxlock action engraved *Twigg* on one side and *London* on the obverse, the revolving vent pans with push-on cover for right side.
(Butterfield & Butterfield) £809

A rare flintlock box-lock 'duck's foot' pistol with turn-off case-hardened barrels numbered from 1 to 4, signed and engraved case-hardened action, later steel with rollers, blued belt-hook, thumbpiece safety-catch, by Southall, London, London proof marks, early 19th century, 9in. long.
(Christie's) £3,520

Pair of Belgian four barrel tap action flintlock pistols, the 3¼in. barrels with punched numbering on three of four, grips with flared octagonal butts and stud decorated basketweave chequered panels.
(Butterfield & Butterfield) £1,472

Pair of Belgian four barrel tap action flintlock pistols, having 4¼in. round rifled barrels, push-on safeties, flat sided bag-shaped grips with chequered panels and silver wire inlay on the backs.
(Butterfield & Butterfield) £2,023

OVER AND UNDER

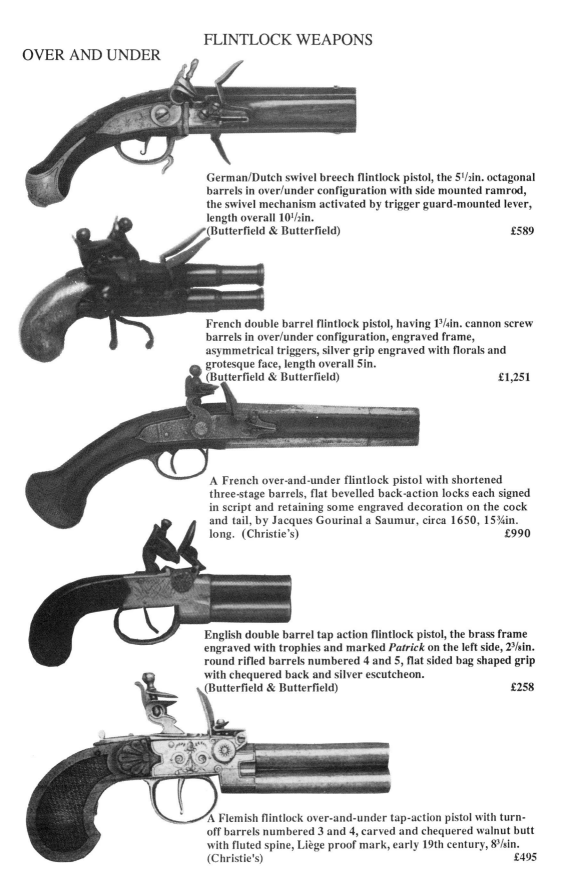

German/Dutch swivel breech flintlock pistol, the 5$^{1}/_{2}$in. octagonal barrels in over/under configuration with side mounted ramrod, the swivel mechanism activated by trigger guard-mounted lever, length overall 10$^{1}/_{2}$in.
(Butterfield & Butterfield)   £589

French double barrel flintlock pistol, having 1$^{3}/_{4}$in. cannon screw barrels in over/under configuration, engraved frame, asymmetrical triggers, silver grip engraved with florals and grotesque face, length overall 5in.
(Butterfield & Butterfield)   £1,251

A French over-and-under flintlock pistol with shortened three-stage barrels, flat bevelled back-action locks each signed in script and retaining some engraved decoration on the cock and tail, by Jacques Gourinal a Saumur, circa 1650, 15$^{3}/_{4}$in. long. (Christie's)   £990

English double barrel tap action flintlock pistol, the brass frame engraved with trophies and marked *Patrick* on the left side, 2$^{3}/_{8}$in. round rifled barrels numbered 4 and 5, flat sided bag shaped grip with chequered back and silver escutcheon.
(Butterfield & Butterfield)   £258

A Flemish flintlock over-and-under tap-action pistol with turn-off barrels numbered 3 and 4, carved and chequered walnut butt with fluted spine, Liège proof mark, early 19th century, 8$^{3}/_{8}$in.
(Christie's)   £495

OVERCOAT PISTOLS

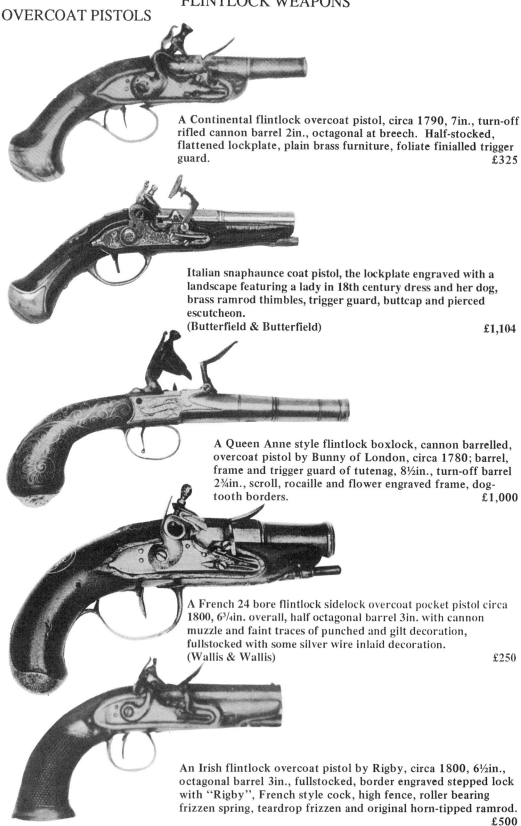

A Continental flintlock overcoat pistol, circa 1790, 7in., turn-off rifled cannon barrel 2in., octagonal at breech. Half-stocked, flattened lockplate, plain brass furniture, foliate finialled trigger guard. £325

Italian snaphaunce coat pistol, the lockplate engraved with a landscape featuring a lady in 18th century dress and her dog, brass ramrod thimbles, trigger guard, buttcap and pierced escutcheon.
(Butterfield & Butterfield) £1,104

A Queen Anne style flintlock boxlock, cannon barrelled, overcoat pistol by Bunny of London, circa 1780; barrel, frame and trigger guard of tutenag, 8½in., turn-off barrel 2¾in., scroll, rocaille and flower engraved frame, dog-tooth borders. £1,000

A French 24 bore flintlock sidelock overcoat pocket pistol circa 1800, 6¾in. overall, half octagonal barrel 3in. with cannon muzzle and faint traces of punched and gilt decoration, fullstocked with some silver wire inlaid decoration.
(Wallis & Wallis) £250

An Irish flintlock overcoat pistol by Rigby, circa 1800, 6½in., octagonal barrel 3in., fullstocked, border engraved stepped lock with "Rigby", French style cock, high fence, roller bearing frizzen spring, teardrop frizzen and original horn-tipped ramrod. £500

POCKET PISTOLS

English flintlock screwbarrel pocket pistol, the brass boxlock with rounded frame marked *H Nock* on left side and *London* on the obverse, chequered bag shaped grip, length overall 6¹/₂in. (Butterfield & Butterfield) £166

An unusual Continental .36 inch rifled cannon barrelled flintlock pocket pistol, circa 1750, 5½ inches, half octagonal strongly reinforced barrel 2½ inches with 12 groove rifling. (Wallis & Wallis) £400

A flintlock cannon barrelled pocket pistol by T. Lane, 7¹/₄in., turn off barrel 2¹/₂in., London proved, halfstocked, lockplate engraved *T. Lane*, brass furniture with simple engraved decoration. (Wallis & Wallis) £330

A flintlock boxlock pocket pistol, by W. Bond, circa 1820, 5¼in. overall, turn-off barrel 1½in. with fern-tip engraved muzzle, Birmingham proved. (Wallis & Wallis) £220

A 55 bore cannon barrelled flintlock boxlock pocket pistol by W. Aston, Manchester, circa 1780, 8in. overall, turn off barrel 2¹/₂in. with London proofs, the frame engraved with stand of flags and maker's name in ovals. (Wallis & Wallis) £320

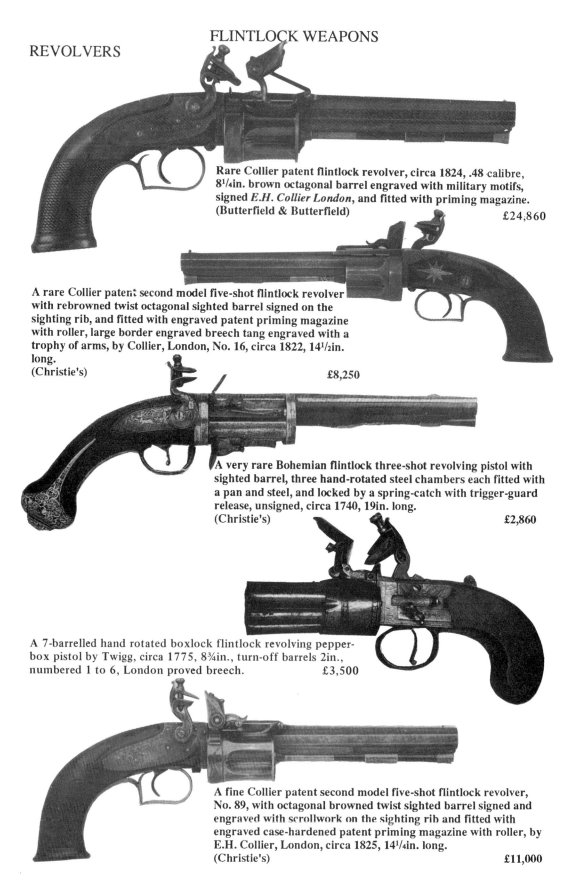

Rare Collier patent flintlock revolver, circa 1824, .48 calibre, 8¼in. brown octagonal barrel engraved with military motifs, signed *E.H. Collier London*, and fitted with priming magazine.
(Butterfield & Butterfield)   £24,860

A rare Collier patent second model five-shot flintlock revolver with rebrowned twist octagonal sighted barrel signed on the sighting rib, and fitted with engraved patent priming magazine with roller, large border engraved breech tang engraved with a trophy of arms, by Collier, London, No. 16, circa 1822, 14½in. long.
(Christie's)   £8,250

A very rare Bohemian flintlock three-shot revolving pistol with sighted barrel, three hand-rotated steel chambers each fitted with a pan and steel, and locked by a spring-catch with trigger-guard release, unsigned, circa 1740, 19in. long.
(Christie's)   £2,860

A 7-barrelled hand rotated boxlock flintlock revolving pepperbox pistol by Twigg, circa 1775, 8¾in., turn-off barrels 2in., numbered 1 to 6, London proved breech.   £3,500

A fine Collier patent second model five-shot flintlock revolver, No. 89, with octagonal browned twist sighted barrel signed and engraved with scrollwork on the sighting rib and fitted with engraved case-hardened patent priming magazine with roller, by E.H. Collier, London, circa 1825, 14¼in. long.
(Christie's)   £11,000

TRAVELLING PISTOLS

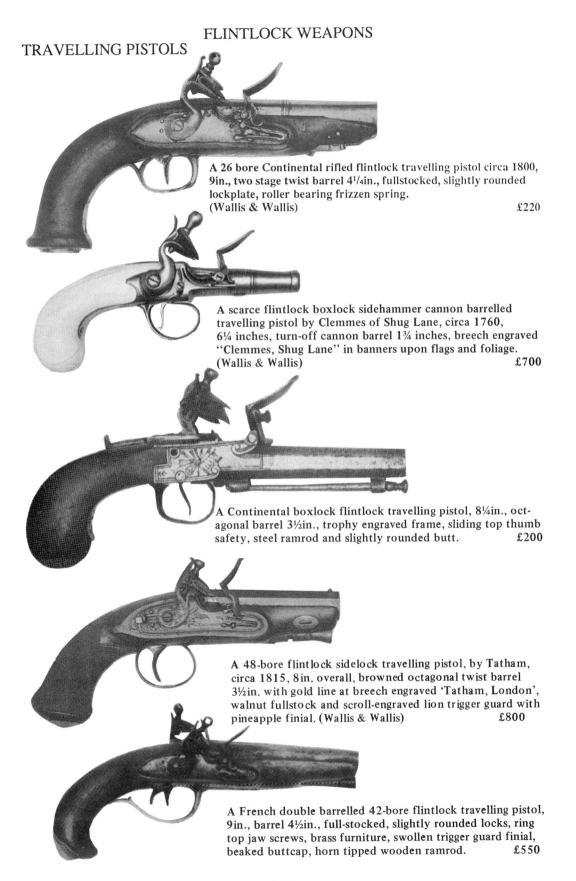

A 26 bore Continental rifled flintlock travelling pistol circa 1800, 9in., two stage twist barrel 4¼in., fullstocked, slightly rounded lockplate, roller bearing frizzen spring.
(Wallis & Wallis)   £220

A scarce flintlock boxlock sidehammer cannon barrelled travelling pistol by Clemmes of Shug Lane, circa 1760, 6¼ inches, turn-off cannon barrel 1¾ inches, breech engraved "Clemmes, Shug Lane" in banners upon flags and foliage.
(Wallis & Wallis)   £700

A Continental boxlock flintlock travelling pistol, 8¼in., octagonal barrel 3½in., trophy engraved frame, sliding top thumb safety, steel ramrod and slightly rounded butt.   £200

A 48-bore flintlock sidelock travelling pistol, by Tatham, circa 1815, 8in. overall, browned octagonal twist barrel 3½in. with gold line at breech engraved 'Tatham, London', walnut fullstock and scroll-engraved lion trigger guard with pineapple finial. (Wallis & Wallis)   £800

A French double barrelled 42-bore flintlock travelling pistol, 9in., barrel 4½in., full-stocked, slightly rounded locks, ring top jaw screws, brass furniture, swollen trigger guard finial, beaked buttcap, horn tipped wooden ramrod.   £550

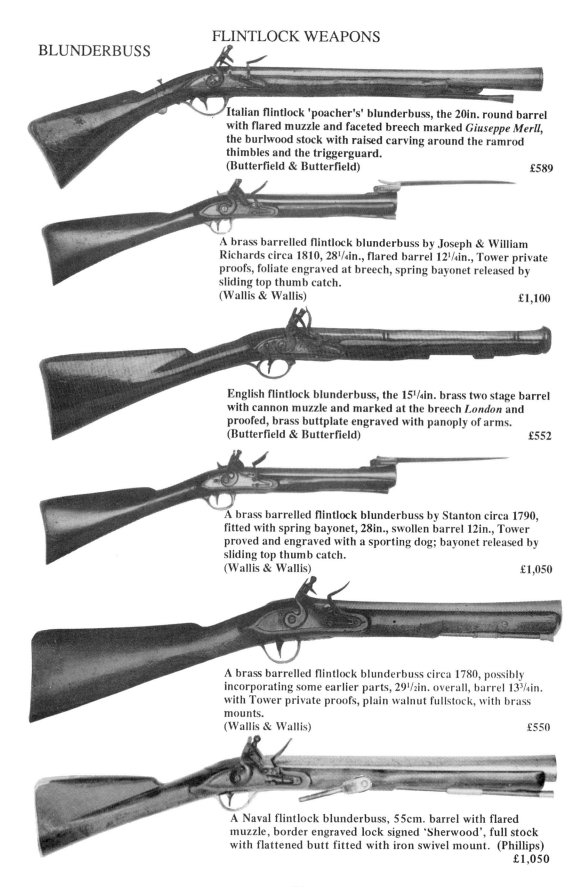

Italian flintlock 'poacher's' blunderbuss, the 20in. round barrel with flared muzzle and faceted breech marked *Giuseppe Merll*, the burlwood stock with raised carving around the ramrod thimbles and the triggerguard.
(Butterfield & Butterfield)   £589

A brass barrelled flintlock blunderbuss by Joseph & William Richards circa 1810, 28$\frac{1}{4}$in., flared barrel 12$\frac{1}{4}$in., Tower private proofs, foliate engraved at breech, spring bayonet released by sliding top thumb catch.
(Wallis & Wallis)   £1,100

English flintlock blunderbuss, the 15$\frac{1}{4}$in. brass two stage barrel with cannon muzzle and marked at the breech *London* and proofed, brass buttplate engraved with panoply of arms.
(Butterfield & Butterfield)   £552

A brass barrelled flintlock blunderbuss by Stanton circa 1790, fitted with spring bayonet, 28in., swollen barrel 12in., Tower proved and engraved with a sporting dog; bayonet released by sliding top thumb catch.
(Wallis & Wallis)   £1,050

A brass barrelled flintlock blunderbuss circa 1780, possibly incorporating some earlier parts, 29$\frac{1}{2}$in. overall, barrel 13$\frac{3}{4}$in. with Tower private proofs, plain walnut fullstock, with brass mounts.
(Wallis & Wallis)   £550

A Naval flintlock blunderbuss, 55cm. barrel with flared muzzle, border engraved lock signed 'Sherwood', full stock with flattened butt fitted with iron swivel mount. (Phillips)
                                                                      £1,050

BLUNDERBUSS

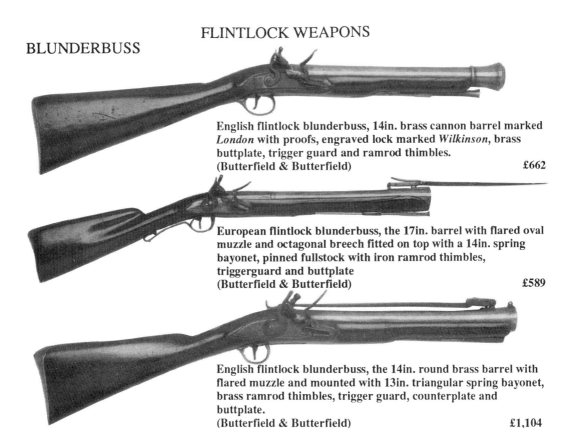

English flintlock blunderbuss, 14in. brass cannon barrel marked *London* with proofs, engraved lock marked *Wilkinson*, brass buttplate, trigger guard and ramrod thimbles.
(Butterfield & Butterfield)   £662

European flintlock blunderbuss, the 17in. barrel with flared oval muzzle and octagonal breech fitted on top with a 14in. spring bayonet, pinned fullstock with iron ramrod thimbles, triggerguard and buttplate
(Butterfield & Butterfield)   £589

English flintlock blunderbuss, the 14in. round brass barrel with flared muzzle and mounted with 13in. triangular spring bayonet, brass ramrod thimbles, trigger guard, counterplate and buttplate.
(Butterfield & Butterfield)   £1,104

A fine and rare Baker's 13 bore 1822 pattern flintlock carbine, 37in., barrel 21in., Birmingham proved with Ezekiel Baker's private proofs, and engraved *Ezekiel Baker & Son Gunmakers to His Majesty London*.
(Wallis & Wallis)   £1,450

A .65in. India pattern Sergeant's flintlock carbine of 1807, 52in., barrel 37in., military proofs, fullstocked, lock engraved *Tower* with crowned *GR* and inspector's stamp, regulation brass mounts, buttcap spur engraved *5*.
(Wallis & Wallis)   £750

A rare 22 bore turnover 'Wender' flintlock carbine by Harman Barne circa 1660, 31in., part octagonal barrels 15³/₄in., screw on pan and frizzen units both engraved *H. Barne*.
(Wallis & Wallis)   £1,55(

A rare .65in. Elliotts patent flintlock carbine, 43¹/₂in., barrel 28in., Tower military proofs, fullstocked, regulation lock with crowned *GR* and *Tower*, regulation brass mounts, steel saddle bar and lanyard ring.
(Wallis & Wallis)   £900

A scarce 10 bore Nock's patent enclosed lock flintlock carbine, 41in., barrel 26in., Tcwer military proved, fullstocked, regulation lock engraved *H. Nock* with inspector's stamp, raised pan shield engraved crowned *GR* cypher.
(Wallis & Wallis)   £2,100

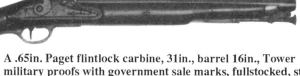

A .65in. Paget flintlock carbine, 31in., barrel 16in., Tower military proofs with government sale marks, fullstocked, stepped bolted lock engraved crowned *GR* with Tower and inspector's stamp.
(Wallis & Wallis)   £800

Rare breechloading German flintlock carbine, first half 18th century, 18³/₄in. rifled octagonal barrel marked *Wilhelm Neupauer* with maker's stamp, the barrel pivoting down at the breech, with removable chamber of one piece with the priming pan and cover.
(Butterfield & Butterfield) £2,023

German flintlock Jaeger carbine, the 26in. octagon barrel with brass front sight, full stock with fluting and incised lines at forestock, chequered wrist with fitting for peep sight.
(Butterfield & Butterfield) £1,030

German flintlock 'poacher's' carbine, 21in. barrel with oval flared muzzle and breech with maker's stamp circled by fleur de lys stamps, the lock marked *Ant Bauman/in Munich*, the stock, jointed at the wrist with relief carving framing the fittings.
(Butterfield & Butterfield) £957

A .65in. Dublin Castle Light Dragoon flintlock carbine, 48¹/₂in., barrel 33in., military proofmarks, fullstocked, flat lock engraved with crowned *GR* and *Dublin Castle*, struck with inspector's mark.
(Wallis & Wallis) £700

A .65in. Paget type flintlock carbine from Dublin Castle, 32in., barrel 16in., Tower proved with Irish Census number *CW-863*, fullstocked, lock with ordnance inspector's stamp, engraved crowned *GR*, with Dublin Castle on tail.
(Wallis & Wallis) £850

A German flintlock sporting carbine with three-stage sighted barrel of small bore turned at the muzzle and rifled with eight grooves, moulded walnut full stock, iron mounts including thin butt-plate with long tang, staghorn patch-box cover engraved with a standing halberdier, late 17th century, 15⁷/₈in. barrel.
(Christie's) £605

FLINTLOCK WEAPONS

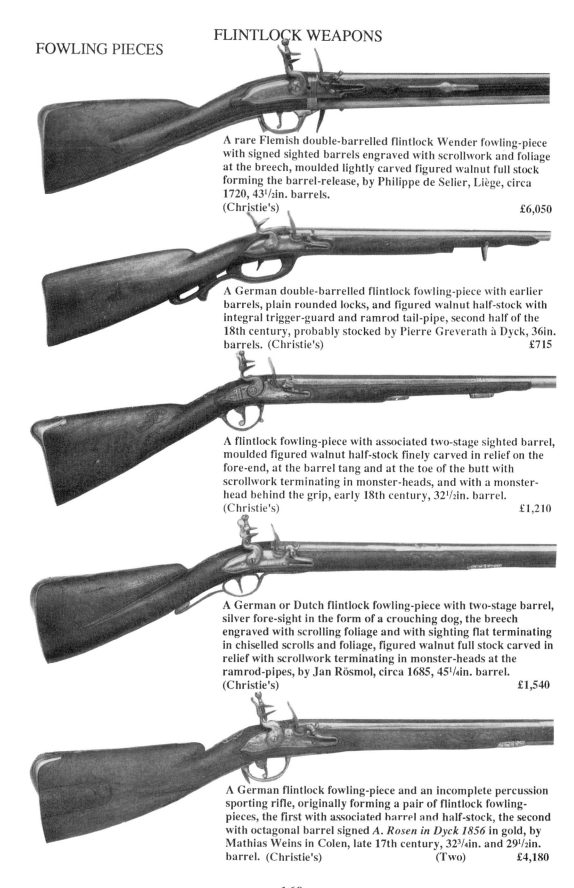

A rare Flemish double-barrelled flintlock Wender fowling-piece with signed sighted barrels engraved with scrollwork and foliage at the breech, moulded lightly carved figured walnut full stock forming the barrel-release, by Philippe de Selier, Liège, circa 1720, 43½in. barrels.
(Christie's)   £6,050

A German double-barrelled flintlock fowling-piece with earlier barrels, plain rounded locks, and figured walnut half-stock with integral trigger-guard and ramrod tail-pipe, second half of the 18th century, probably stocked by Pierre Greverath à Dyck, 36in. barrels. (Christie's)   £715

A flintlock fowling-piece with associated two-stage sighted barrel, moulded figured walnut half-stock finely carved in relief on the fore-end, at the barrel tang and at the toe of the butt with scrollwork terminating in monster-heads, and with a monster-head behind the grip, early 18th century, 32½in. barrel.
(Christie's)   £1,210

A German or Dutch flintlock fowling-piece with two-stage barrel, silver fore-sight in the form of a crouching dog, the breech engraved with scrolling foliage and with sighting flat terminating in chiselled scrolls and foliage, figured walnut full stock carved in relief with scrollwork terminating in monster-heads at the ramrod-pipes, by Jan Rösmol, circa 1685, 45¼in. barrel.
(Christie's)   £1,540

A German flintlock fowling-piece and an incomplete percussion sporting rifle, originally forming a pair of flintlock fowling-pieces, the first with associated barrel and half-stock, the second with octagonal barrel signed A. *Rosen in Dyck 1856* in gold, by Mathias Weins in Colen, late 17th century, 32¾in. and 29½in. barrel. (Christie's)   (Two)   £4,180

FOWLING PIECES

A fine and rare German four-barrel flintlock fowling-piece with blued barrels, the upper pair signed and dated in gold on the rib and with silver fore-sight within a gilt sunburst, figured birchwood full stock inlaid with silver wire lines enclosing engraved silver rosettes on the fore-stock, by Pierre Greverath à Dyck, dated *1797*, 33½in. barrels.
(Christie's) £22,000

A 14 bore flintlock fowling piece by Ketland & Co. built for a youth circa 1770, 46in., barrel 29½in., London proved, maker *TK*, engraved with teardrop, fullstocked, foliate engraved lock, brass furniture, acorn finialled trigger guard.
(Wallis & Wallis) £425

A rare French or Dutch double-barrelled Wender fowling-piece with three-stage sighted barrels, signed flat bevelled back-action lock engraved with flowers and scrolls and with rounded cock with flush-fitting retaining bolt engraved with a flowerhead, by Barroy, circa 1660, 46in. barrels.
(Christie's) £2,860

A German flintlock fowling-piece with two-stage barrel, the fore-sight in the form of a lizard, the breech with sighting flat interrupted by the standing figure of Fame chiselled in relief, and terminating in chiselled foliage and scrolls with monster-heads, moulded figured walnut full stock finely carved in low relief with scrollwork and monster-heads, by Michael Bus, Essen, circa 1700, 45½in. barrel.
(Christie's) £7,700

An English flintlock fowling-piece with signed three-stage sighted barrel engraved with a symmetrical pattern of strawberry foliage at the breech, engraved tang, moulded rootwood full stock, brass mounts including engraved butt-plate with long waved tang in the form of a serpent, by Isaac Bleiberg, London, London proof marks, circa 1700, 43½in. barrel.
(Christie's) £8,800

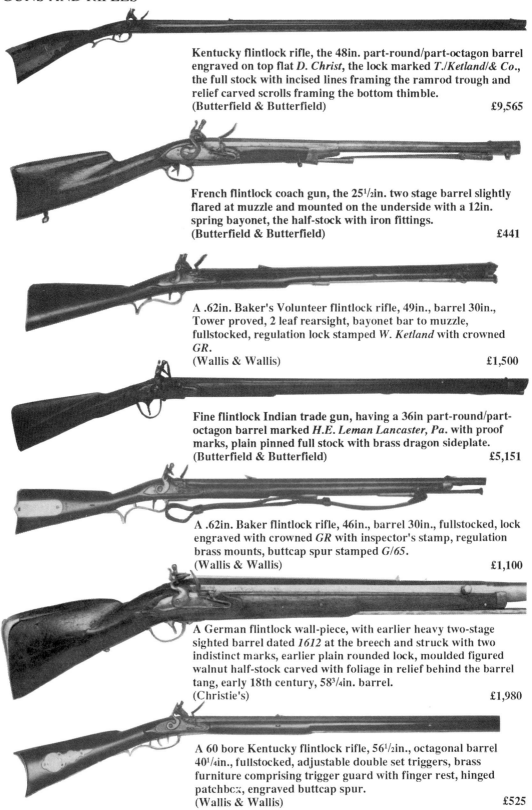

Kentucky flintlock rifle, the 48in. part-round/part-octagon barrel engraved on top flat *D. Christ*, the lock marked *T./Ketland/& Co.*, the full stock with incised lines framing the ramrod trough and relief carved scrolls framing the bottom thimble.
(Butterfield & Butterfield)   £9,565

French flintlock coach gun, the 25$\frac{1}{2}$in. two stage barrel slightly flared at muzzle and mounted on the underside with a 12in. spring bayonet, the half-stock with iron fittings.
(Butterfield & Butterfield)   £441

A .62in. Baker's Volunteer flintlock rifle, 49in., barrel 30in., Tower proved, 2 leaf rearsight, bayonet bar to muzzle, fullstocked, regulation lock stamped *W. Ketland* with crowned *GR*.
(Wallis & Wallis)   £1,500

Fine flintlock Indian trade gun, having a 36in part-round/part-octagon barrel marked *H.E. Leman Lancaster, Pa.* with proof marks, plain pinned full stock with brass dragon sideplate.
(Butterfield & Butterfield)   £5,151

A .62in. Baker flintlock rifle, 46in., barrel 30in., fullstocked, lock engraved with crowned *GR* with inspector's stamp, regulation brass mounts, buttcap spur stamped *G/65*.
(Wallis & Wallis)   £1,100

A German flintlock wall-piece, with earlier heavy two-stage sighted barrel dated *1612* at the breech and struck with two indistinct marks, earlier plain rounded lock, moulded figured walnut half-stock carved with foliage in relief behind the barrel tang, early 18th century, 58$\frac{3}{4}$in. barrel.
(Christie's)   £1,980

A 60 bore Kentucky flintlock rifle, 56$\frac{1}{2}$in., octagonal barrel 40$\frac{1}{4}$in., fullstocked, adjustable double set triggers, brass furniture comprising trigger guard with finger rest, hinged patchbox, engraved buttcap spur.
(Wallis & Wallis)   £525

GUNS AND RIFLES

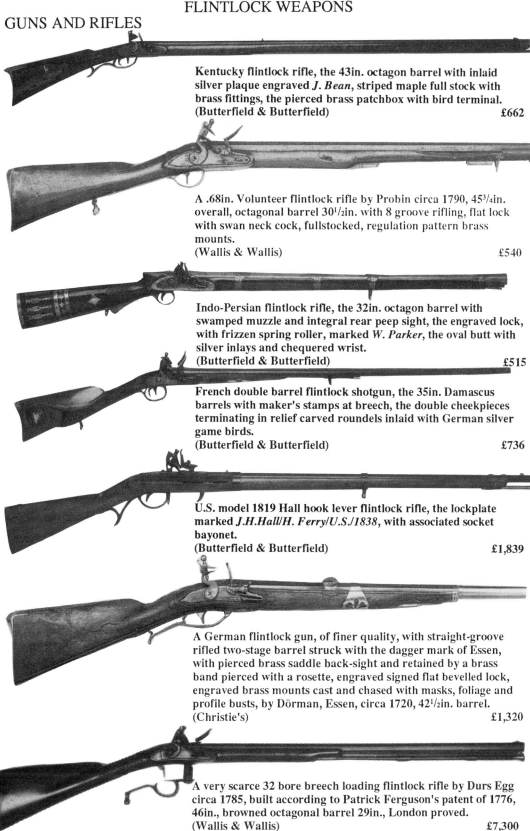

Kentucky flintlock rifle, the 43in. octagon barrel with inlaid silver plaque engraved *J. Bean*, striped maple full stock with brass fittings, the pierced brass patchbox with bird terminal.
(Butterfield & Butterfield) £662

A .68in. Volunteer flintlock rifle by Probin circa 1790, 45³/₄in. overall, octagonal barrel 30¹/₂in. with 8 groove rifling, flat lock with swan neck cock, fullstocked, regulation pattern brass mounts.
(Wallis & Wallis) £540

Indo-Persian flintlock rifle, the 32in. octagon barrel with swamped muzzle and integral rear peep sight, the engraved lock, with frizzen spring roller, marked *W. Parker*, the oval butt with silver inlays and chequered wrist.
(Butterfield & Butterfield) £515

French double barrel flintlock shotgun, the 35in. Damascus barrels with maker's stamps at breech, the double cheekpieces terminating in relief carved roundels inlaid with German silver game birds.
(Butterfield & Butterfield) £736

U.S. model 1819 Hall hook lever flintlock rifle, the lockplate marked *J.H.Hall/H. Ferry/U.S./1838*, with associated socket bayonet.
(Butterfield & Butterfield) £1,839

A German flintlock gun, of finer quality, with straight-groove rifled two-stage barrel struck with the dagger mark of Essen, with pierced brass saddle back-sight and retained by a brass band pierced with a rosette, engraved signed flat bevelled lock, engraved brass mounts cast and chased with masks, foliage and profile busts, by Dörman, Essen, circa 1720, 42¹/₂in. barrel.
(Christie's) £1,320

A very scarce 32 bore breech loading flintlock rifle by Durs Egg circa 1785, built according to Patrick Ferguson's patent of 1776, 46in., browned octagonal barrel 29in., London proved.
(Wallis & Wallis) £7,300

163

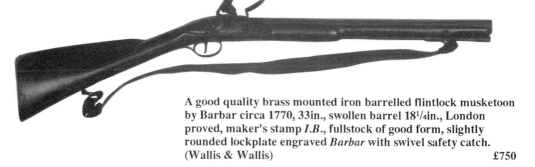

A good quality brass mounted iron barrelled flintlock musketoon by Barbar circa 1770, 33in., swollen barrel 18¼in., London proved, maker's stamp *I.B.*, fullstock of good form, slightly rounded lockplate engraved *Barbar* with swivel safety catch.
(Wallis & Wallis) £750

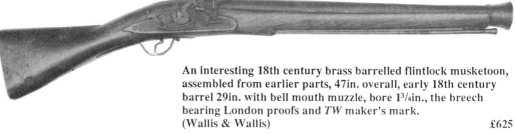

An interesting 18th century brass barrelled flintlock musketoon, assembled from earlier parts, 47in. overall, early 18th century barrel 29in. with bell mouth muzzle, bore 1¾in., the breech bearing London proofs and *TW* maker's mark.
(Wallis & Wallis) £625

French flintlock musketoon, the 31in. barrel with inspector's marks and dated *1831*, the lockplate marked *Mre Rle de St. Etienne*, with socket bayonet.
(Butterfield & Butterfield) £2,207

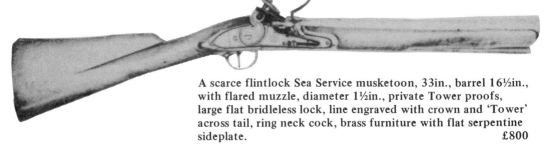

A scarce flintlock Sea Service musketoon, 33in., barrel 16½in., with flared muzzle, diameter 1½in., private Tower proofs, large flat bridleless lock, line engraved with crown and 'Tower' across tail, ring neck cock, brass furniture with flat serpentine sideplate. £800

A scarce and interesting Spanish miquelet flintlock musketoon, circa 1750, 31in., half-octagonal flared barrel 17½in., gold inlaid: "Soy Ed Dn Tadeo Segura", brass maker's poincon crowned "Domingo", fullstocked, scroll engraved cock and frizzen bridles. £2,500

A rare French flintlock musket with swamped octagonal sighted barrel struck at the breech with a crowned *L*, and the maker's name *Journel*, rounded lock, moulded walnut full stock, full iron mounts including rounded scroll side-plate, circa 1700, 46³/₄in. barrel.
(Christie's) £715

A French infantry 1777 model flintlock musket, with dated barrel, the lock inscribed *Manufre Imple de Charleville*, the dated butt with recessed cheek-piece, dated *1809* and *1810*, with an iron socket bayonet, 44³/₄in. barrel.
(Christie's) £660

A French infantry flintlock musket, the lock engraved *M.re imple de Tulle*, walnut full stock and brass and iron mounts, the butt with recessed cheek-piece and stamped with various marks, early 19th century, with an iron socket bayonet, 44⁵/₈in. barrel.
(Christie's) £660

A 10 bore Volunteer Brown Bess flintlock musket by D. Egg, 55in. overall, barrel 39in. with Tower private proofs, rounded lock with swan neck cock, the plate with line engraved border, walnut fullstock with regulation brass mounts.
(Wallis & Wallis) £550

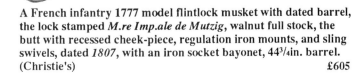

A French infantry 1777 model flintlock musket with dated barrel, the lock stamped *M.re Imp.ale de Mutzig*, walnut full stock, the butt with recessed cheek-piece, regulation iron mounts, and sling swivels, dated *1807*, with an iron socket bayonet, 44³/₄in. barrel.
(Christie's) £605

MUSKETS

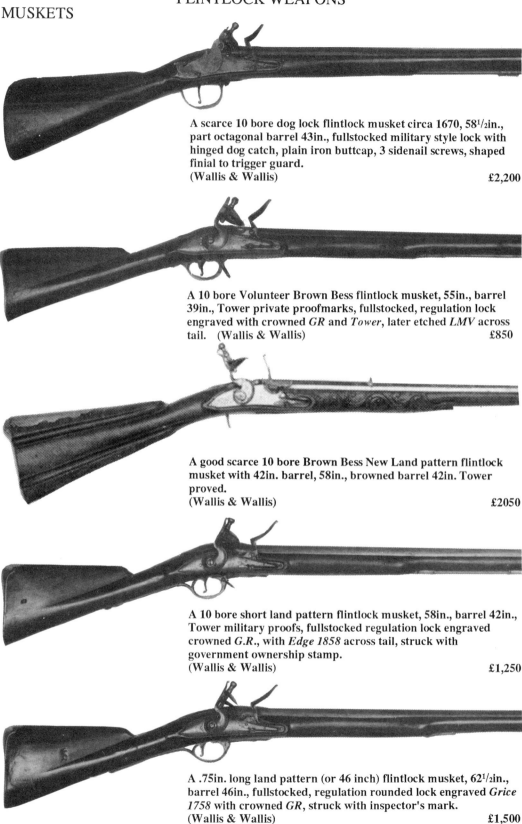

A scarce 10 bore dog lock flintlock musket circa 1670, 58½in., part octagonal barrel 43in., fullstocked military style lock with hinged dog catch, plain iron buttcap, 3 sidenail screws, shaped finial to trigger guard.
(Wallis & Wallis) £2,200

A 10 bore Volunteer Brown Bess flintlock musket, 55in., barrel 39in., Tower private proofmarks, fullstocked, regulation lock engraved with crowned *GR* and *Tower*, later etched *LMV* across tail. (Wallis & Wallis) £850

A good scarce 10 bore Brown Bess New Land pattern flintlock musket with 42in. barrel, 58in., browned barrel 42in. Tower proved.
(Wallis & Wallis) £2050

A 10 bore short land pattern flintlock musket, 58in., barrel 42in., Tower military proofs, fullstocked regulation lock engraved crowned *G.R.*, with *Edge 1858* across tail, struck with government ownership stamp.
(Wallis & Wallis) £1,250

A .75in. long land pattern (or 46 inch) flintlock musket, 62½in., barrel 46in., fullstocked, regulation rounded lock engraved *Grice 1758* with crowned *GR*, struck with inspector's mark.
(Wallis & Wallis) £1,500

FLINTLOCK WEAPONS

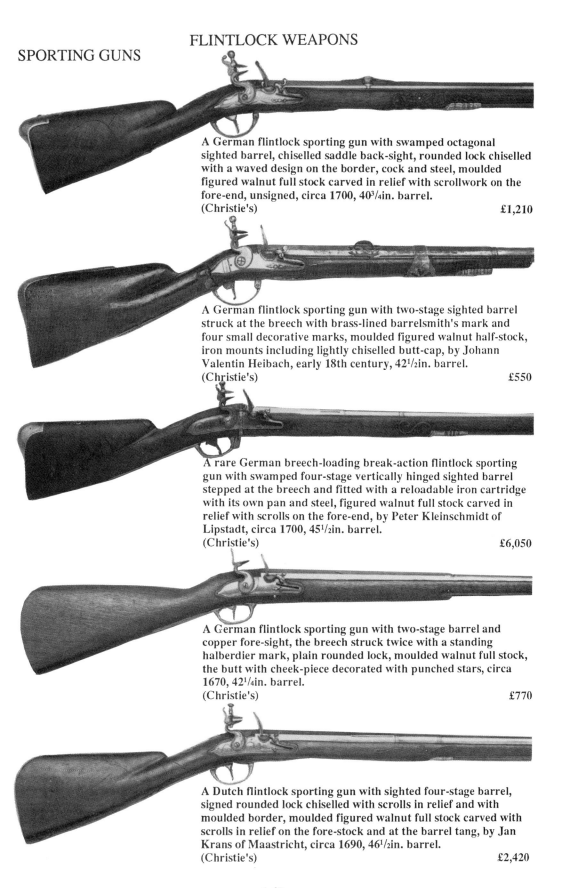

A German flintlock sporting gun with swamped octagonal
sighted barrel, chiselled saddle back-sight, rounded lock chiselled
with a waved design on the border, cock and steel, moulded
figured walnut full stock carved in relief with scrollwork on the
fore-end, unsigned, circa 1700, 40³/₄in. barrel.
(Christie's)   £1,210

A German flintlock sporting gun with two-stage sighted barrel
struck at the breech with brass-lined barrelsmith's mark and
four small decorative marks, moulded figured walnut half-stock,
iron mounts including lightly chiselled butt-cap, by Johann
Valentin Heibach, early 18th century, 42¹/₂in. barrel.
(Christie's)   £550

A rare German breech-loading break-action flintlock sporting
gun with swamped four-stage vertically hinged sighted barrel
stepped at the breech and fitted with a reloadable iron cartridge
with its own pan and steel, figured walnut full stock carved in
relief with scrolls on the fore-end, by Peter Kleinschmidt of
Lipstadt, circa 1700, 45¹/₂in. barrel.
(Christie's)   £6,050

A German flintlock sporting gun with two-stage barrel and
copper fore-sight, the breech struck twice with a standing
halberdier mark, plain rounded lock, moulded walnut full stock,
the butt with cheek-piece decorated with punched stars, circa
1670, 42¹/₄in. barrel.
(Christie's)   £770

A Dutch flintlock sporting gun with sighted four-stage barrel,
signed rounded lock chiselled with scrolls in relief and with
moulded border, moulded figured walnut full stock carved with
scrolls in relief on the fore-stock and at the barrel tang, by Jan
Krans of Maastricht, circa 1690, 46¹/₂in. barrel.
(Christie's)   £2,420

SPORTING GUNS

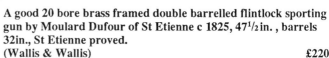

A good 20 bore brass framed double barrelled flintlock sporting gun by Moulard Dufour of St Etienne c 1825, 47$^{1}/_{2}$in. , barrels 32in., St Etienne proved.
(Wallis & Wallis)   £2200

A Flemish flintlock sporting gun, with etched twist octagonal three-stage barrel in the Turkish manner, inlaid with silver at the muzzle and breech, pierced brass saddle back-sight, moulded lightly carved figured full stock, carved patch-box cover, engraved brass mounts including pierced side-plate involving two marine monsters, unsigned, circa 1720, 38$^{1}/_{2}$in. barrel.
(Christie's)   £1,100

An Italian flintlock sporting gun with long two stage sighted barrel, octagonal breech with gold filled maker's stamp and signed *Benedetto Picinardo,* the lock signed *Francesco Donati,* circa 1730-40, 46in. barrel. (Christie's S. Ken)   £550

A Continental double barrelled flintlock sporting gun, 95cm. sighted damascus barrels decorated in gold against a blued ground at the breech and muzzle with scrolls and mythical creatures, the locks with coppered finish, the underside of the butt carved with a classical head with inlaid eyes.
(Phillips)   £3,000

A German flintlock sporting gun with swamped octagonal sighted barrel, iron saddle back-sight with chiselled foliate finials, signed rounded lock with moulded border, moulded figured walnut full stock carved in relief with scrolls inhabited by scenes of the chase on the fore-end and cheek-piece, by Michael Meckelen of Cologne, circa 1690, 40$^{1}/_{4}$in. barrel.
(Christie's)   £3,520

SPORTING RIFLES

A German flintlock sporting rifle with smooth-bored swamped octagonal sighted barrel, plain flat bevelled lock with stepped tail, moulded figured walnut full stock, the butt with cheek-piece and plain patch-box cover, early 18th century, 29³/₄in. barrel.
(Christie's)   £1,320

A German flintlock sporting rifle with swamped octagonal sighted barrel rifled with seven grooves, inlaid with silver around the fore-sight and with silver interlaced designs at the breech enclosing a dog in silver and a squirrel in brass, moulded lightly carved figured walnut full stock, second quarter of the 18th century, 27¹/₄in. barrel.
(Christie's)   £1,100

An Alsatian flintlock sporting rifle with swamped octagonal sighted smoothbore barrel struck twice at the breech with barrelsmith's mark *PS*, figured walnut full stock carved in relief behind the barrel tang and on the cheek-piece with scrollwork, berries and foliage on a punched ground, by Thomas Bader à Strasbourg, late 17th century, 28¹/₄in. barrel.
(Christie's)   £2,860

A German flintlock sporting rifle, the barrel rifled with six grooves, plain rounded lock, moulded lightly carved figured walnut full stock, the butt with carved cheek-piece, the patch-box containing a worm and a powder-measure and with wooden cover carved with scrolls, late 17th century, 29¹/₂in. barrel.
(Christie's)   £1,210

A German flintlock sporting rifle, the barrel with sliding fore-sight and signed *Leonhard Wenger 1629*, rounded lock engraved with foliage, figured walnut full stock inlaid with staghorn plaques variously engraved with marine monsters and flower-heads, late 17th century, 28¹/₈in. barrel.
(Christie's)   £880

A 26-bore Japanese matchlock gun, 51½in., octagonal barrel 39½in., signed Banshu Noju Igawa Terunaga Koresaku, block rearsight, raised ribs to barrel flats, swollen muzzle. £1,100

Interesting Southeast Asian combination matchlock/knife, having a 10½in. European pistol barrel with an 18in. single edge blade extending from the tang.
(Butterfield & Butterfield) £515

A matchlock gun with oak butt and stock, brass match-holder, spring, lock-plate trigger and guard, the octagonal iron barrel signed Goshu Hino Yoshihisa saku, barrel length 77.8cm. (Christie's) £495

An Indian matchlock gun from Scinde, 67in., damascus barrel 51½in., chiselled with scrolls and zoomorphic muzzle upon relief chiselled chevron base, fullstocked, massive Scinde fish tail butt with two foliate punched silver gilt mounts. £500

A superbly decorated matchlock gun, the russet iron octagonal barrel fitted with a set sight on the peep line and a bar sight on the flared muzzle which also bears five gilt applied Tokugawa aoimon, signed *Kunitomo Heiji Shigetoshi, working in Omi*, and dated *March 1820*, 19th century.
(Christie's) £38,500

A 32-bore Japanese matchlock gun, 47in., heavy octagonal barrel 33½in., fullstocked brass lock struck with single character, and wooden ramrod. (Wallis & Wallis)
£475

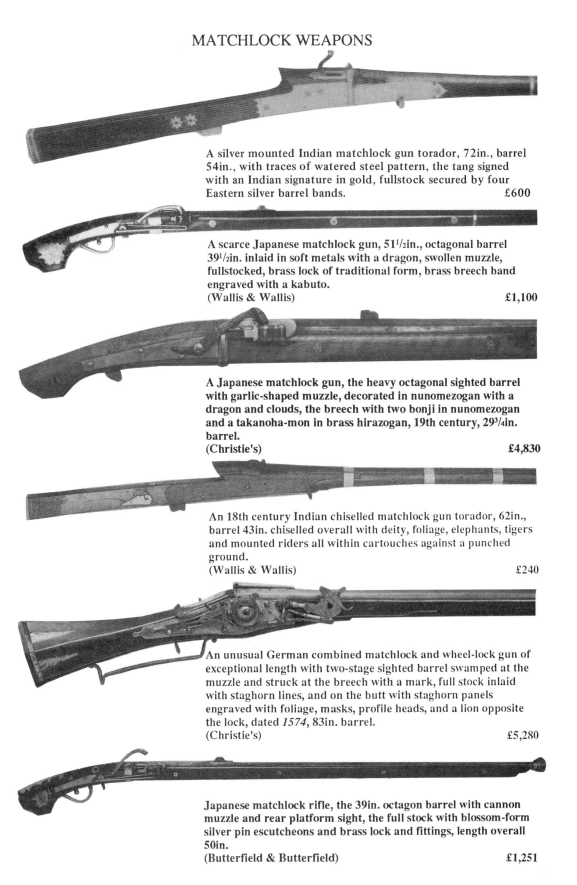

A silver mounted Indian matchlock gun torador, 72in., barrel 54in., with traces of watered steel pattern, the tang signed with an Indian signature in gold, fullstock secured by four Eastern silver barrel bands. **£600**

A scarce Japanese matchlock gun, 51½in., octagonal barrel 39½in. inlaid in soft metals with a dragon, swollen muzzle, fullstocked, brass lock of traditional form, brass breech band engraved with a kabuto.
(Wallis & Wallis) **£1,100**

A Japanese matchlock gun, the heavy octagonal sighted barrel with garlic-shaped muzzle, decorated in nunomezogan with a dragon and clouds, the breech with two bonji in nunomezogan and a takanoha-mon in brass hirazogan, 19th century, 29¾in. barrel.
(Christie's) **£4,830**

An 18th century Indian chiselled matchlock gun torador, 62in., barrel 43in. chiselled overall with deity, foliage, elephants, tigers and mounted riders all within cartouches against a punched ground.
(Wallis & Wallis) **£240**

An unusual German combined matchlock and wheel-lock gun of exceptional length with two-stage sighted barrel swamped at the muzzle and struck at the breech with a mark, full stock inlaid with staghorn lines, and on the butt with staghorn panels engraved with foliage, masks, profile heads, and a lion opposite the lock, dated *1574*, 83in. barrel.
(Christie's) **£5,280**

Japanese matchlock rifle, the 39in. octagon barrel with cannon muzzle and rear platform sight, the full stock with blossom-form silver pin escutcheons and brass lock and fittings, length overall 50in.
(Butterfield & Butterfield) **£1,251**

PISTOLS

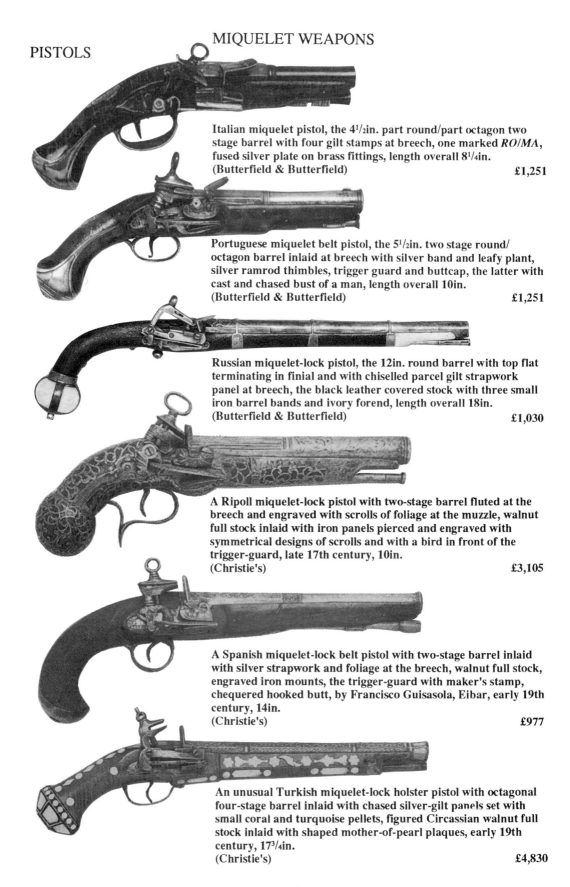

Italian miquelet pistol, the 4½in. part round/part octagon two stage barrel with four gilt stamps at breech, one marked *RO/MA*, fused silver plate on brass fittings, length overall 8¼in. (Butterfield & Butterfield) **£1,251**

Portuguese miquelet belt pistol, the 5½in. two stage round/octagon barrel inlaid at breech with silver band and leafy plant, silver ramrod thimbles, trigger guard and buttcap, the latter with cast and chased bust of a man, length overall 10in. (Butterfield & Butterfield) **£1,251**

Russian miquelet-lock pistol, the 12in. round barrel with top flat terminating in finial and with chiselled parcel gilt strapwork panel at breech, the black leather covered stock with three small iron barrel bands and ivory forend, length overall 18in. (Butterfield & Butterfield) **£1,030**

A Ripoll miquelet-lock pistol with two-stage barrel fluted at the breech and engraved with scrolls of foliage at the muzzle, walnut full stock inlaid with iron panels pierced and engraved with symmetrical designs of scrolls and with a bird in front of the trigger-guard, late 17th century, 10in. (Christie's) **£3,105**

A Spanish miquelet-lock belt pistol with two-stage barrel inlaid with silver strapwork and foliage at the breech, walnut full stock, engraved iron mounts, the trigger-guard with maker's stamp, chequered hooked butt, by Francisco Guisasola, Eibar, early 19th century, 14in. (Christie's) **£977**

An unusual Turkish miquelet-lock holster pistol with octagonal four-stage barrel inlaid with chased silver-gilt panels set with small coral and turquoise pellets, figured Circassian walnut full stock inlaid with shaped mother-of-pearl plaques, early 19th century, 17¾in. (Christie's) **£4,830**

PISTOLS

Late 18th century 64-bore Italian miquelet flintlock holster pistol, 17½in., stepped barrel 12in., fullstocked, stepped Roman style lock, brass furniture, longspur buttcap engraved with trophies and brass tipped wooden ramrod. (Wallis & Wallis) £550

A Spanish miquelet-lock belt pistol the two-stage barrel with turned girdle and moulded muzzle, the forward stage with raised rib and engraved with flower-heads and foliage, plain patilla lock, wooden full stock entirely covered with brass embossed and chased with scrolling foliage of Moorish design, circa 1700, almost certainly Ripoll, 12½in. long. (Christie's) £3,080

A Balkan miquelet lock pistol with plain iron barrel, plain lock, wooden full stock with slightly curved butt and bulbous pommel, 19th century, 20½in. (Christie's S. Ken) £385

A 14-bore miquelet flintlock Spanish belt pistol, by Torento, circa 1800, 10in., half octagonal barrel 5½in., fullstocked, brass furniture with applied silver foil bosses to buttcap, trigger guard bow and escutcheon. (Wallis & Wallis) £440

A 20-bore Cossack nielloed silver mounted miquelet flintlock holster pistol, 17¼in., barrel 11½in., with traces of a little foliate chiselling, fullstocked, lock with maker's stamp to bridle, ribbed frizzen face. (Wallis & Wallis) £575

A Caucasian miquelet-lock pistol, the barrel damascened with silver panels containing gold-damascened arabesques and retained by three white-metal bands engraved with foliage, the full stock covered in black leather and with foliate engraved shaped white-metal mounts, 19th century, 16in. long. (Christie's) £715

Turkish miquelet rifle, the 32in. octagon barrel with swamped muzzle and gold koftgari inlay at muzzle and breech, the stock elaborately inlaid with bone, horn, coloured wood and brass roundels and studs.
(Butterfield & Butterfield) £1,104

A rare Flemish miquelet-lock sporting rifle with swamped three-stage sighted barrel in the Turkish manner rifled with sixteen grooves and inlaid with silver at the muzzle and breech, moulded lightly carved figured walnut half-stock, brass mounts cast and chased with stags, masks and foliage in relief, early 18th century, 41½in. barrel.
(Christie's) £935

An early 18th century Spanish miquelet flintlock musketoon, 41in. overall, half octagonal swamped twist barrel 26in., with brass poincon and keyhole patterns at breech. £1,250

A Sardinian miquelet-lock fowling-piece with octagonal barrel, characteristic lock with traces of incised decoration, and full stock almost encased in steel panels, late 18th century, 45in. barrel.
(Christie's) £805

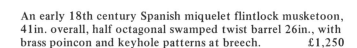

A very fine Italian miquelet-lock sporting gun with swamped octagonal sighted barrel stamped *Lazarino Cominazzo* at the breech, the back-sight with chiselled foliate finial, engraved tang, flat lock chiselled in high relief with a lion at the rear and with a monster at the front, later moulded figured walnut full stock carved in relief with a scroll on the fore-end, circa 1660–80, probably Neapolitan, 31½in. barrel.
(Christie's) £11,000

RIFLES

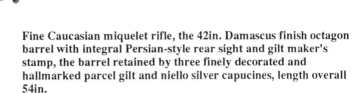

Fine Caucasian miquelet rifle, the 42in. Damascus finish octagon barrel with integral Persian-style rear sight and gilt maker's stamp, the barrel retained by three finely decorated and hallmarked parcel gilt and niello silver capucines, length overall 54in.
(Butterfield & Butterfield)   £3,127

Caucasian miquelet rifle, the 31in. round rifled barrel gold inlaid at the muzzle with diagonal beaded lines and on the tang with maker's signature, niello silver counterplate, trigger plate, ball trigger, wedge escutcheons and butt fitting.
(Butterfield & Butterfield)   £1,656

A Turkish miquelet-lock gun with twist octagonal sighted barrel inlaid with a silver band on the muzzle, breech, and standing back-sight, and retained by four engraved white-metal bands, original iron ramrod, dated *1813*, 35³/₄in. barrel.
(Christie's)   £2,530

Turkish miquelet carbine, the 27in. octagon barrel with swamped muzzle and integral rear peep sight, the muzzle, breech, sight, tang and lock gold inlaid with dense floral designs, the butt and adjoining 4in. inlaid with bone and wood designs.
(Butterfield & Butterfield)   £662

A 26 bore Kurdish miquelet flintlock rifle, 19th century, 38in., swamped octagonal barrel 36in., fullstocked, lock with some engraved silver inlay silver faced and engraved bridle, button trigger.
(Wallis & Wallis)   £810

ROMAN LOCK GUNS

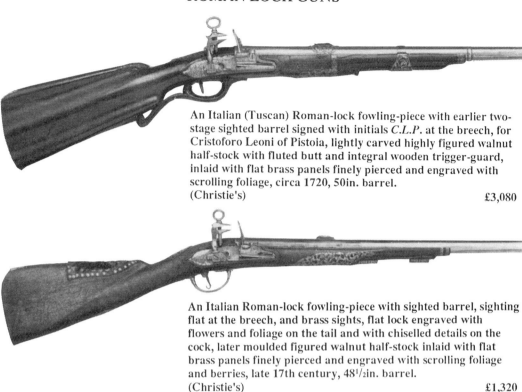

An Italian (Tuscan) Roman-lock fowling-piece with earlier two-stage sighted barrel signed with initials *C.L.P.* at the breech, for Cristoforo Leoni of Pistoia, lightly carved highly figured walnut half-stock with fluted butt and integral wooden trigger-guard, inlaid with flat brass panels finely pierced and engraved with scrolling foliage, circa 1720, 50in. barrel.
(Christie's) £3,080

An Italian Roman-lock fowling-piece with sighted barrel, sighting flat at the breech, and brass sights, flat lock engraved with flowers and foliage on the tail and with chiselled details on the cock, later moulded figured walnut half-stock inlaid with flat brass panels finely pierced and engraved with scrolling foliage and berries, late 17th century, 48½in. barrel.
(Christie's) £1,320

SCHUETZEN RIFLES

Fine German Schuetzen rifle, the 29in. barrel fluted from front sight to forend, the muzzle inlaid with gold and silver lines, the breech with top flat inlaid with gold highlighted silver scrollwork framing the inlaid silver figure of a medieval huntsman below the gilt signature *Theodor Brauer*.
(Butterfield & Butterfield) £8,785

Austrian Schuetzen rifle, the 29¾in. heavy octagon barrel with matte top flat marked *Joh Postler In Wien*, the Martini action etched and engraved with scrolling florals overall, the chequered forestock with relief carved grape leaves at the tip.
(Butterfield & Butterfield) £1,251

Fine German Schuetzen rifle, the 28in. fluted barrel engraved at the muzzle and fitted with two integral ramrod thimbles, the rearmost with sling swivel, the octagonal breech inlaid with gold and silver florals and inlaid in silver *F. Schilling Coburg* on top flat.
(Butterfield & Butterfield) £2,207

SNAPHAUNCE WEAPONS

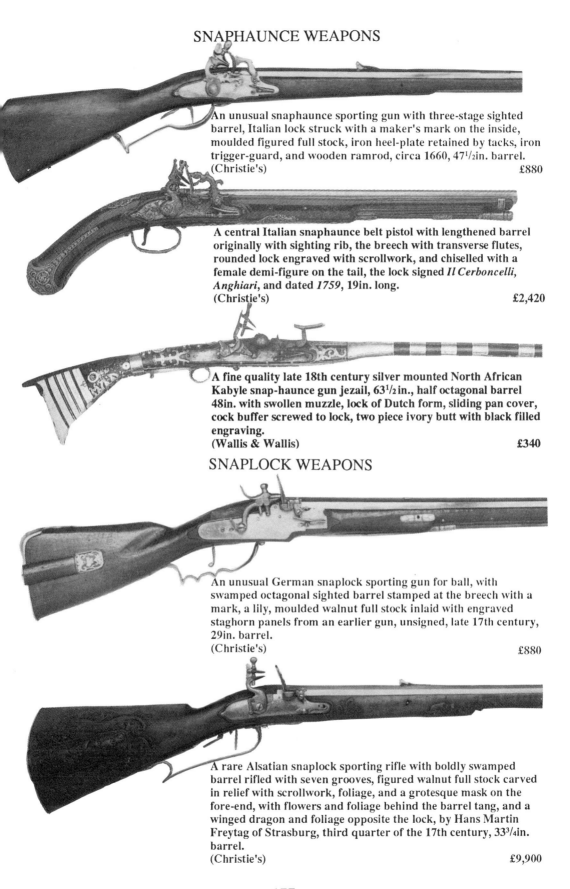

An unusual snaphaunce sporting gun with three-stage sighted barrel, Italian lock struck with a maker's mark on the inside, moulded figured full stock, iron heel-plate retained by tacks, iron trigger-guard, and wooden ramrod, circa 1660, 47½in. barrel. (Christie's) £880

A central Italian snaphaunce belt pistol with lengthened barrel originally with sighting rib, the breech with transverse flutes, rounded lock engraved with scrollwork, and chiselled with a female demi-figure on the tail, the lock signed *Il Cerboncelli, Anghiari,* and dated *1759,* 19in. long. (Christie's) £2,420

A fine quality late 18th century silver mounted North African Kabyle snap-haunce gun jezail, 63½in., half octagonal barrel 48in. with swollen muzzle, lock of Dutch form, sliding pan cover, cock buffer screwed to lock, two piece ivory butt with black filled engraving. (Wallis & Wallis) £340

SNAPLOCK WEAPONS

An unusual German snaplock sporting gun for ball, with swamped octagonal sighted barrel stamped at the breech with a mark, a lily, moulded walnut full stock inlaid with engraved staghorn panels from an earlier gun, unsigned, late 17th century, 29in. barrel. (Christie's) £880

A rare Alsatian snaplock sporting rifle with boldly swamped barrel rifled with seven grooves, figured walnut full stock carved in relief with scrollwork, foliage, and a grotesque mask on the fore-end, with flowers and foliage behind the barrel tang, and a winged dragon and foliage opposite the lock, by Hans Martin Freytag of Strasburg, third quarter of the 17th century, 33¾in. barrel. (Christie's) £9,900

PISTOLS

A fine Nuremberg wheel-lock carbine with swamped sighted three-stage barrel octagonal at the muzzle and breech and spirally fluted between, plain lock with domed wheel-cover, pivoting safety-catch, the plate struck with Nuremberg mark and maker's mark *GS*, third quarter of the 16th century, 19³/₄in. barrel.
(Christie's)   £33,350

A German wheel-lock belt pistol, the barrel struck at the breech with the Nuremberg mark and maker's mark *LH*, a falchion between, late 16th century, 21¹/₄in.
(Christie's)   £8,050

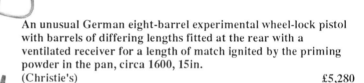

An unusual German eight-barrel experimental wheel-lock pistol with barrels of differing lengths fitted at the rear with a ventilated receiver for a length of match ignited by the priming powder in the pan, circa 1600, 15in.
(Christie's)   £5,280

A Brescian wheel-lock holster pistol with two-stage barrel, flat lock with small wheel-retaining bracket, full stock inlaid with small pierced iron panels, pierced iron fore-end cap, baluster trigger, and original iron-tipped ramrod, circa 1620–30, 25³/₈in. barrel.
(Christie's)   £4,370

A German wheel-lock holster pistol with associated swamped two-stage barrel, plain lock with flat wheel-cover, full stock inlaid with staghorn between staghorn lines, late 16th century, 20³/₄in.
(Christie's)   £4,370

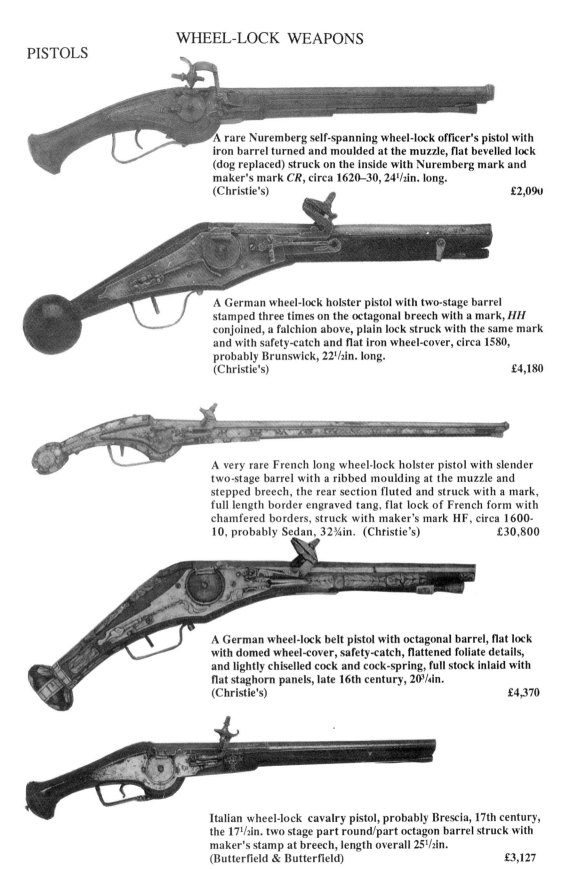

A rare Nuremberg self-spanning wheel-lock officer's pistol with iron barrel turned and moulded at the muzzle, flat bevelled lock (dog replaced) struck on the inside with Nuremberg mark and maker's mark *CR*, circa 1620–30, 24¹/₂in. long. (Christie's) £2,090

A German wheel-lock holster pistol with two-stage barrel stamped three times on the octagonal breech with a mark, *HH* conjoined, a falchion above, plain lock struck with the same mark and with safety-catch and flat iron wheel-cover, circa 1580, probably Brunswick, 22¹/₂in. long. (Christie's) £4,180

A very rare French long wheel-lock holster pistol with slender two-stage barrel with a ribbed moulding at the muzzle and stepped breech, the rear section fluted and struck with a mark, full length border engraved tang, flat lock of French form with chamfered borders, struck with maker's mark HF, circa 1600-10, probably Sedan, 32¾in. (Christie's) £30,800

A German wheel-lock belt pistol with octagonal barrel, flat lock with domed wheel-cover, safety-catch, flattened foliate details, and lightly chiselled cock and cock-spring, full stock inlaid with flat staghorn panels, late 16th century, 20³/₄in. (Christie's) £4,370

Italian wheel-lock cavalry pistol, probably Brescia, 17th century, the 17¹/₂in. two stage part round/part octagon barrel struck with maker's stamp at breech, length overall 25¹/₂in. (Butterfield & Butterfield) £3,127

179

RIFLES

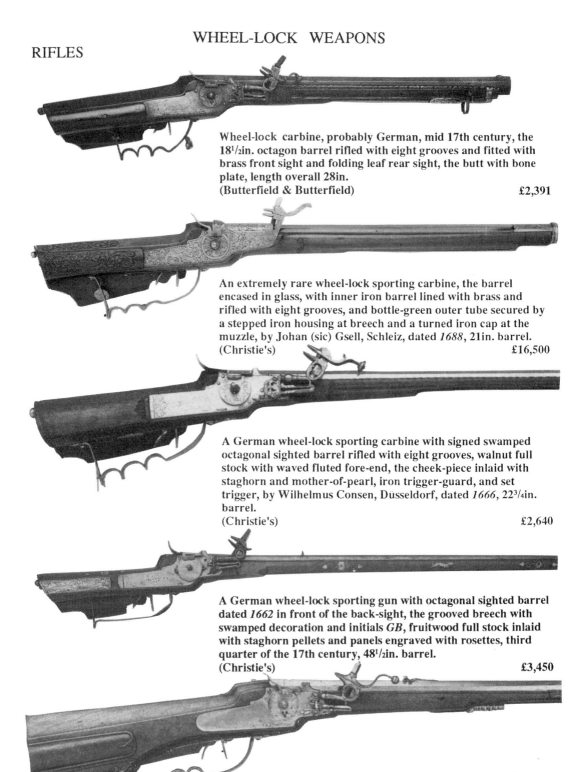

Wheel-lock carbine, probably German, mid 17th century, the 18½in. octagon barrel rifled with eight grooves and fitted with brass front sight and folding leaf rear sight, the butt with bone plate, length overall 28in.
(Butterfield & Butterfield)   £2,391

An extremely rare wheel-lock sporting carbine, the barrel encased in glass, with inner iron barrel lined with brass and rifled with eight grooves, and bottle-green outer tube secured by a stepped iron housing at breech and a turned iron cap at the muzzle, by Johan (sic) Gsell, Schleiz, dated *1688*, 21in. barrel.
(Christie's)   £16,500

A German wheel-lock sporting carbine with signed swamped octagonal sighted barrel rifled with eight grooves, walnut full stock with waved fluted fore-end, the cheek-piece inlaid with staghorn and mother-of-pearl, iron trigger-guard, and set trigger, by Wilhelmus Consen, Dusseldorf, dated *1666*, 22¾in. barrel.
(Christie's)   £2,640

A German wheel-lock sporting gun with octagonal sighted barrel dated *1662* in front of the back-sight, the grooved breech with swamped decoration and initials *GB*, fruitwood full stock inlaid with staghorn pellets and panels engraved with rosettes, third quarter of the 17th century, 48½in. barrel.
(Christie's)   £3,450

A German wheel-lock sporting rifle with signed and dated swamped octagonal sighted barrel rifled with seven grooves, plain lock struck with a mark, a crowned fish on a shield, lightly carved moulded figured walnut full stock, and banded iron fore-end cap, Michael Grienwalt of Munich, dated *1661*, 32½in. barrel.
(Christie's)   £3,520

RIFLES

A Saxon wheel-lock sporting rifle with dated swamped octagonal sighted barrel rifled with eight shallow grooves, plain flat lock with domed brass cover etched with foliated scrollwork and retaining some gilding, full stock profusely inlaid with staghorn plaques, dated *1605*, 35¼in. barrel.
(Christie's)   £6,785

German wheel-lock rifle, Silesia, first half 17th century, the 30in. octagon barrel, with flared muzzle, decorated with punched floral panels alternating with birds and leaves on a lightly crosshatched ground.
(Butterfield & Butterfield)   £6,254

A German wheel-lock sporting rifle with swamped octagonal sighted barrel rifled with eight grooves and struck at the breech with a similar mark, plain lock with crescentic wheel-retaining bracket and lightly engraved cock, full stock with fluted fore-end, third quarter of the 17th century, 28¾in. barrel.
(Christie's)   £1,980

German wheel-lock rifle, the 33½in. octagon barrel with triangular bore, the top flat with sighting channel from breech to rear sight dovetail, the stock inlaid with bone borders and numerous bone plaques carved with geometric forms and depicting sea monsters, shells and faces.
(Butterfield & Butterfield)   £3,679

A fine German wheel-lock gun with octagonal sighted barrel of exceptional length, full stock profusely inlaid throughout its length with staghorn scrolls, pellets, leaves and ball-flowers inhabited by monsters, birds, putti, an owl and a snail, dated *1579*, 51in. barrel.
(Christie's)   £16,500

SPORTING RIFLES

A Saxon wheel-lock sporting rifle with signed and dated
octagonal sighted barrel rifled with six grooves and with grooved
breech, stained walnut full stock with fluted fore-end, the butt
and patch-box cover carved in relief with animals and tendrils in
the manner of the so-called 'Meister der Tierkopfranke', by
Bastian From, Heiligenstadt, dated *1665*, 28in. barrel.
(Christie's)   £3,520

A German wheel-lock sporting rifle with swamped octagonal
sighted barrel rifled with six grooves and struck with indistinct
maker's mark at the breech, fruitwood full stock profusely inlaid
with staghorn lines, scrolls and pellets enclosing plaques
engraved with masks, strapwork, profile heads and scenes of the
chase, second quarter of the 17th century, 25in. barrel.
(Christie's)   £5,500

A German wheel-lock sporting rifle with swamped octagonal
sighted barrel rifled with seven grooves, stained walnut full stock
with fluted fore-end, the butt carved in relief with foliage, a stag,
a hind, a dog, and a rabbit, dated *1682*, perhaps Schwäbish-
Gmünd, 34¼in. barrel.
(Christie's)   £4,950

A wheel-lock sporting rifle with signed and dated swamped
octagonal sighted barrel rifled with seven grooves, figured walnut
full stock and patch-box cover carved in relief with scenes of the
chase within landscapes enriched by flat panels inlaid with
staghorn plaques, the barrel by Hans Stifter of Prague and dated
1660, 33½in. barrel.
(Christie's)   £7,150

A German wheel-lock sporting rifle with swamped octagonal
sighted barrel rifled with eight grooves, figured full stock with
waved fluted fore-end inlaid with staghorn pellets, the butt
carved with a stag-hunt in relief opposite the lock and inlaid with
large staghorn panels engraved with scenes of the chase, dated
1676, 27¾in. barrel.
(Christie's)   £7,150

TSCHINKE

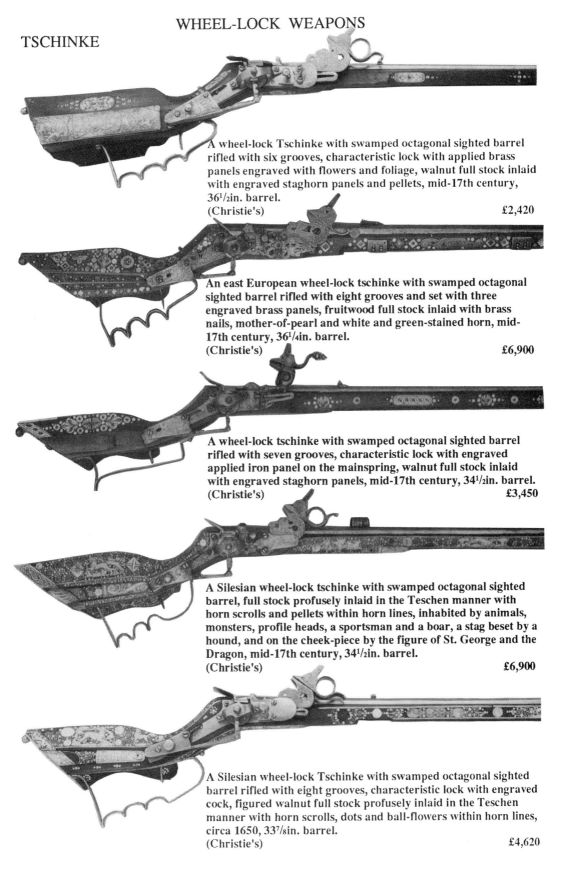

A wheel-lock Tschinke with swamped octagonal sighted barrel rifled with six grooves, characteristic lock with applied brass panels engraved with flowers and foliage, walnut full stock inlaid with engraved staghorn panels and pellets, mid-17th century, 36½in. barrel.
(Christie's) £2,420

An east European wheel-lock tschinke with swamped octagonal sighted barrel rifled with eight grooves and set with three engraved brass panels, fruitwood full stock inlaid with brass nails, mother-of-pearl and white and green-stained horn, mid-17th century, 36¼in. barrel.
(Christie's) £6,900

A wheel-lock tschinke with swamped octagonal sighted barrel rifled with seven grooves, characteristic lock with engraved applied iron panel on the mainspring, walnut full stock inlaid with engraved staghorn panels, mid-17th century, 34½in. barrel.
(Christie's) £3,450

A Silesian wheel-lock tschinke with swamped octagonal sighted barrel, full stock profusely inlaid in the Teschen manner with horn scrolls and pellets within horn lines, inhabited by animals, monsters, profile heads, a sportsman and a boar, a stag beset by a hound, and on the cheek-piece by the figure of St. George and the Dragon, mid-17th century, 34½in. barrel.
(Christie's) £6,900

A Silesian wheel-lock Tschinke with swamped octagonal sighted barrel rifled with eight grooves, characteristic lock with engraved cock, figured walnut full stock profusely inlaid in the Teschen manner with horn scrolls, dots and ball-flowers within horn lines, circa 1650, 33⅞in. barrel.
(Christie's) £4,620

A composite cuirassier armour of bright steel, studded with rivets and with turned edges, early 17th century, probably German.
(Christie's) £6,820

An unusual moyegi-ito-odoshi tosei-gusoku with a fine associated kabuto comprising a sixty-two-plate russet-iron sujibachi, unsigned, probably 18th century.
(Christie's) £6,600

A German fluted 'Maximilian' full armour in early 16th century style, of bright steel, on wooden figure mounted on an octagonal wooden base.
(Christie's) £13,225

A moyegi-ito-odoshi gold lacquered domaru, comprising a fine russet-iron sixty-two-plate koboshi bachi, the interior gilt, signed *Myochin Shigenobu*, second half 16th century.
(Christie's) £10,120

A composite Continental armour mainly in early 17th century style, mounted on a fabric-covered wooden dummy, with realistically-carved, painted and bearded head set with glass eyes.
(Christie's) £3,800

A kon-ito-odoshi mogami haramaki, the kabuto comprising a fine sixty-two plate russet-iron sujibachi with gilt and silvered five-stage yukimochi.
(Christie's) £9,350

A fine kon-ito-shira odoshi domar, comprising a kabuto with a sixty-two plate russet-iron sujibachi with iron mabizashi.
(Christie's)   £8,800

A decorative Italian armour, comprising close helmet, gorget of four plates, breast plate, backplate, front to skirt with tassels of three plates, late 16th century.
(John Nicholson)   £4,500

An important suit of early 17th century Japanese black lacquered metal armour, circa 1620. (Prudential)
£6,100

A decorative composite armour mainly in 16th century style, on a wooden display-stand with square base. (Christie's)
£900

Fine lacquered suit of armour, sixty-two plate kabuto with five-lame shikoro, crescent maedate and gold lacquer kuwagata.
(Skinner Inc.)   £10,086

A Victorian full armour and halberd, 19th century.
£2,750

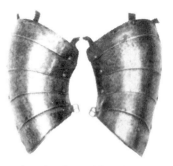

An English Civil War period steel hat liner 'secret' of simple skull cap form. (Wallis & Wallis) £300

A good composite late 16th century Almain collar, hinged gorget with key-hole fastening stud, medial ridge to front plate. (Wallis & Wallis) £825

A pair of spaulders from a late 16th century German Infantry Armour. (Wallis & Wallis) £160

A German gorget, of exceptionally large size, comprising front and back-plates of bright steel pivoted together, bluntly pointed and struck with Nuremberg mark, early 17th century, 6½in. high. (Christie's) £1,045

Early 17th century pikeman's breastplate together with associated simulated five lame tassets. £900

An iron mempo, Edo period, 17th century, the plain iron mask set with two 'S' cheek flanges and with a separate nosepiece. (Christie's) £1,091

An etched Italian gothic pauldron for the right shoulder, of bright steel, covering the outside and back, the top-plate pierced with point holes, circa 1510. (Christie's) £1,430

A European mail shirt entirely of riveted steel rings, with elbow-length sleeves, probably 15th century, 34in. long. (Christie's) £2,070

A rare German 'Maximilian' chanfron, in two halves riveted together horizontally, shaped to the front of the horse's head and decorated with radiating flutes, circa 1520, 24in. long. (Christie's) £11,000

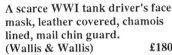

A scarce WWI tank driver's face mask, leather covered, chamois lined, mail chin guard.
(Wallis & Wallis) £180

A German codpiece probably from a black and white armour, of bright steel, traces of tinning inside, mid 16th century, 6in. high. (Christie's) £1,210

An iron skull cap or secrete composed of numerous flattened bars riveted together complete with its original leather liner, 17th century.
(Phillips) £680

A good heavy early 19th century Moro cuirass, composed of shaped brass plates linked together by thick brass mail.
(Wallis & Wallis) £450

A rare pair of Italian vambraces, each comprising a tubular upper-cannon made in two parts linked by a recessed turning joint, early 16th century, 18¼in. long.
(Christie's S. Ken.) £6,050

A boldly modelled russet-iron mempo with one-piece nose and fangs (onimen), with a four-lame yodorekake covered in black leather, the facepiece early 16th century, the mounting 17th century.
(Christie's) £2,200

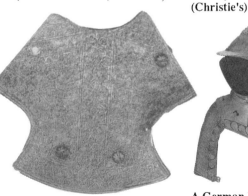

A rare Gothic falling bevor composed of three plates with medial ridge, the top plate with angular outward turn and released by a spring catch, late 15th century, 13½in. high.
(Christie's) £1,100

An etched and gilt pommel plate from a saddle, the upper edges bordered by narrow flanges, probably French, circa 1570, 8in. high.
(Christie's S. Ken.) £440

A German burgonet and almain collar from a black and white armour, the former with one-piece four-sided skull drawn up to a point with an acorn finial, circa 1560.
(Christie's) £2,640

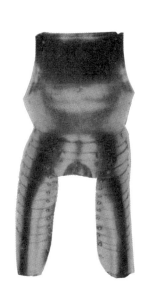

A Cromwellian pikeman's armour, comprising: pot with two-piece skull of crude construction with turned rim, breastplate of peascod form with medial ridge. (Phillips) £520

A breastplate with raised central ridge, gussets with turned edges, fauld of three lames and long attached tassets of ten lames, late 16th century.
(Phillips) £1,700

A Victorian suit of armour in the style of the 16th century, 67in. high. £6,000

A 19th century sugake-laced okegawa-do, unsigned, lacking armour-box. (Christie's) £3,080

A composite armour comprising: lacquered iron four-plate momonari kabuto with four lame shikiro and modern kuwagata, all contained in a wood box, some restoration. (Phillips) £1,400

A 16th century composite Maximilian armour. £25,000

A complete Maximilian suit of fluted armour, circa 1520-30. £17,500

A rare Italian breast-plate, of slightly flattened form with low medial ridge, bold angular turn at the neck, early 16th century, 30¹/₂ in. high.
(Christie's S. Ken.) £5,060

A shira-ito-ni-odoshi kebiki laced tosei-gusoku, the hotoke-do covered with shohei-gawa (stencilled buckskin).
(Christie's) £10,450

Mid 16th century Nuremberg Foot soldier's armour with burgonet helmet. £5,000

A well made Edwardian part suit of armour in the Milanese style comprising high peaked morion, breastplate, deep gorget, and articulated gauntlets. (Wallis & Wallis) £400

A cuirassier's three-quarter armour, circa 1640, the whole mounted on plastic dummy and wooden base. £7,000

A curassier's armour,
comprising close helmet, gorget,
breast plate and backplate,
tassets to the knee and full arms
with gauntlets, 17th century.
(John Nicholson)
£6,000

An etched Italian Infantry half-
armour, comprising Spanish
morion, gorget of two plates
pivoted together at the side,
cuirass with peasecod breast
plate, probably Milanese, circa
1580. (Christie's S. Ken)
£22,000

A composite cuirassier's armour
comprising: close helmet and
large gorget plates, breast and
backplate, mainly 17th century
with Victorian and later elements
(Phillips)
£2,000

A composite Cuirassier's three-
quarter armour, circa 1600,
fingers lacking from gauntlets,
pitted and cleaned overall.
(Phillips)
£2,800

A rare Indian full armour for a
man and horse, all finely
damascened in gold with
scrolling foliage and flower-
heads, partly 17th/18th century.
(Christie's)
£9,900

A composite Continental
armour in mid 16th century
style, with roped borders and
etched decoration, on a wood-
en stand. (Christie's)
£2,000

A well made copy of the Foot-Combat armour of circa 1520 made for King Henry VIII by his Almain armourers, 70in. tall.
(Wallis & Wallis)   £1,800

A composite German full armour, of bright steel, each cuff struck with the Nuremberg mark, the helmet and gauntlets mid-16th century, the remainder in 16th century style, on wooden figure mounted on a wooden plinth.
(Christie's)   £8,800

An armour in 16th century style, comprising close-helmet with two-piece pointed skull, pivoted visor and upper and lower bevors.
(Christie's S. Ken.)   £3,080

An early 17th century suit of armour, the visor with rising peak above fretted eye pieces and fretted front, the breast-plate with period indented test mark, 70in. high.
(Bonhams)   £5,600

A composite Italian armour, comprising close-helmet with one-piece skull, high roped comb, brass plume-holders, comprehensively circa 1570.
(Christie's S. Ken.)   £3,960

17th century infantryman Nuremburg complete suit of armour, stands 70in. high., includes a halberd, mounted on a wood stand.
(Du Mouchelles)   £4,800

A Cromwellian trooper's breast and backplate, breastplate with medial ridge, backplate struck with Commonwealth armourer's mark of helmet over "A". (Wallis & Wallis) £1,000

An English Commonwealth period breastplate, struck with helmet over A (Commonwealth Armourer's Company mark) and maker's initials E.O. (Wallis & Wallis) £550

A breastplate probably adapted in the early 19th century. £350

A breast-plate, early 16th century, probably German, 18$\frac{1}{2}$in. high. (Christie's S. Ken) £1,760

A French Carabinier trooper's breast and backplates of heavy steel overlaid in brass, dated 1832 and adapted for the 2nd Empire period with the addition of the imperial eagle. (Phillips) £550

A breast plate for a Knight of Malta in mid 16th century style, roped neck and articulated arm cusps, vertically ribbed ensuite with two lower plates and first skirt plate. (Wallis & Wallis) £800

An early 19th century officer's steel cuirass of the Household Cavalry, morocco lining and crimped blue velvet edging, leather bound borders and brass studs. (Wallis & Wallis) £1,600

An English Cromwellian period breast and backplate, struck with Commonwealth armourer's company mark of helmet over "A", maker's initials "F.O." (Wallis & Wallis) £600

A Victorian Household Cavalry Officer's breast and backplates, of steel with brass rivets and edging. (Phillips) £900

A 17th century Continental breastplate with twin studs for fastening and shoulder straps. **£225**

An Innsbruck breast-plate from an infantry armour (Harnasch), of bright steel and rounded form, with prominent medial ridge. (Christie's S. Ken) **£1,100**

A Continental articulated breastplate, circa 1700, of swollen form with medial ridge. **£325**

A heavy German cavalry troopers breastplate circa 1800, musket ball proof mark, stamped *Hartkopf*, lugs for strap fastening. (Wallis & Wallis) **£150**

A rare German gothic breast-plate made in two parts (associated) joined by a central screw, late 15th century, 21in. high. (Christie's S. Ken.) **£4,950**

A post-1902 Household Cavalry trooper's plated cuirass, leather lining with blue cloth edging, brass bound borders and studs, leather backed brass scales with ornamental ends. (Wallis & Wallis) **£425**

An English Civil War period breastplate, distinct medial ridge, turned over edges, flared narrow skirt, twin studs for securing straps. (Wallis & Wallis) **£300**

A post-1902 Household Cavalry trooper's plated cuirass, leather lining with blue cloth edging, brass bound borders and studs. (Wallis & Wallis) **£550**

A heavy German cavalry trooper's breastplate circa 1800, musket ball proof mark, lugs for strap fastening, short raised collar, edges pierced with holes for lining attachment. (Wallis & Wallis) **£130**

An English Civil War period breastplate, four brass rosettes to base rim, two buckle fastenings to top, two musket ball proof marks.
(Wallis & Wallis) £430

A good post-1902 major's plated cuirass of the Royal Horse Guards, morocco lining with crimson velvet edging, brass bound borders and studs, shoulder cords and aiguillette.
(Wallis & Wallis) £1,350

A Victorian Royal Horse Guards officer's breast and backplate, burnished finish, brass strip edging, with domed brass studs to borders.
(Wallis & Wallis) £500

A good pair of Cromwellian breast and back plates circa 1640, breastplate with distinct medial ridge, two studs for fastening shoulder straps. Deeply struck with crowned 'I.R.' armourer's mark (James I). £850

A French cuirassier's breastplate, backplate and helmet, steel plates with brass studs, leather backed shoulder chains and buckles, ornamental comb with Medusa head finial.
(Wallis & Wallis) £950

A good French Guard Cuirassier officer's helmet and companion breast and backplate, circa 1870, helmet with plated skull and large gilt comb with Medusa mask. (Wallis & Wallis) £2,500

A good early 17th century Italian breastplate of peascod form, swivel hook fasteners for shoulder scales, simple line pattern, steel studded decoration.
£500

A reinforcing plackart, of great weight and flattened form with low medial ridge, single line border to the arms, supplied in 1673, 11^{1}/$_{2}$in. high.
(Christie's) £550

A French 2nd Empire carabinier officer's brass covered breast and backplate, breast plate skirt engraved 'Manufre Rall de Klingenthal, Avril 1833, 2T Llre No 400 M'.
£700

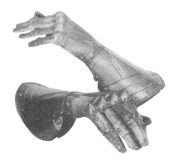

A pair of late 18th century copies of gothic gauntlets, very fine throughout.
(Bonhams) £600

A right handed elbow gauntlet, circa 1640, probably English, 18½in. overall, raised medial ridge, roped turned over border, 6 plate articulated back of hand.
(Wallis & Wallis) £350

A pair of bridle-gauntlets of bright steel, each comprising an elbow-length cuff made in two pieces engraved with two lines and with roped edges, early 17th century, probably English, 20in.
(Christie's) £3,680

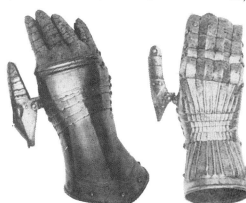

unusual German open ...untlet circa 1600, 13in. overall, single plate arm defence with medial ridge retaining buckles for securing.
(Wallis & Wallis) £375

A pair of German gauntlets, of bright steel, each comprising a flared boxed cuff made in two pieces, roped turned borders with narrow recessed band and central cusp, late 16th century, 11in. (Christie's S. Ken) £2,640

A well made Victorian copy of a Maximilian fluted and articulated right hand gauntlet, cuff with hinged plate. (Wallis & Wallis) £320

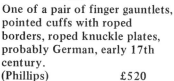

One of a pair of finger gauntlets, pointed cuffs with roped borders, roped knuckle plates, probably German, early 17th century.
(Phillips) £520

A good pair of mid 16th century German mitten gauntlets made for an infantry armour, backs of hand of 11 plates including raised knuckle plate.
(Wallis & Wallis) £400

A Maximilian gauntlet, circa 1520, separate hinged thumb-piece, roped cuff. (Wallis & Wallis) £350

Indo-Persian axe, the head with panels of chiselled strapwork on either side, the flattened peen with chiselled animal combat reserve, length overall 25in.
(Butterfield & Butterfield)   £406

A Saxon miner's guild axe with iron head comprising angular head pierced with a slipped trefoil and triangular front spike with brass finial, and small block-shaped peen, the wooden handle inlaid with staghorn dots and plaques, 18th century, 31in.
(Christie's)   £977

Indo-Persian axe, the watered steel head decorated on the sides and on the flattened peen with gold koftgari borders, the haft sheathed in repoussé silver decorated with flowering plants and spiral bands, length overall 23in.
(Butterfield & Butterfield)   £589

Indian axe, the broad head with lappet-shaped reserve containing chiselled inscription, the peen in the form of a gilt lion's head, hollow iron haft, length overall 29$\frac{1}{2}$in.
(Butterfield & Butterfield)   £331

A massive and rare 19th century Hindu sacrificial axe, probably from Chota Nagpur, 41in., moustache shaped blade 23in., central column applied with brass device of trisula upon mound with flag.
(Wallis & Wallis)   £52

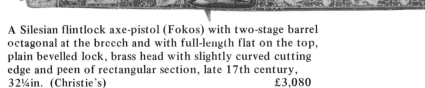

A Silesian flintlock axe-pistol (Fokos) with two-stage barrel octagonal at the breech and with full-length flat on the top, plain bevelled lock, brass head with slightly curved cutting edge and peen of rectangular section, late 17th century, 32¼in. (Christie's)   £3,080

A 19th century Persian Qjar all steel axe, 27³/₄in., crescent head 8in. chiselled with Islamic inscriptions and some damascened embellishment, steel haft of part faceted part spiral section.
(Wallis & Wallis) £180

A good and unusual 19th century Indian axe zaghnal, 25in., thick heavy steel head 10³/₄in. including pagoda finial, pierced with foliate sides and a little silver damascened ornament.
(Wallis & Wallis) £160

A 19th century Persian qjar etched steel axe, 34in., crescent head 8¼in., etched with two mounted horsemen clashing with shamshirs, dhals, axes, severed limbs. Square section top spike, hollow zoomorphic backpiece, steel haft with swollen pommel. £150

A 19th century Persian steel axe, 30in., crescent head 6½in., steel haft filed with facets and spiral lines in alternate sections.
£200

A fine 19th century Indian steel axe, 30in., blade of elephant's ear form 10in. finely pierced with a tiger springing onto two elephants in silhouette, thickly silver damascened overall with foliate and geometric ornaments.
(Wallis & Wallis) £200

An all steel Indian axe Bhuj, 28in., recurved swollen watered blade 11in., chiselled with palmette at forte, steel haft.
(Wallis & Wallis) £120

A brass martingale badge of the 5th Punjab Cavalry, KC, size 2⁵/₈ x 1³/₈in.
(Wallis & Wallis) £100

A good officer's die struck gilt metal badge of the 7th Carnatic Infantry, with lugs and interesting slot-in backing plate.
(Wallis & Wallis) £140

A good and unusual post 1902 darkened Maltese Cross badge of the 2nd A.B. Shropshire Royal Volunteers.
(Wallis & Wallis) £75

A German World War I Navy observer airman's badge, in silver gilt, rayed back panel stamped with crown and crescent mark.
(Wallis & Wallis) £360

An officer's gilt and silver plated badge of the United Provinces Horse, brooch pin, by J. R. Gaunt, London.
(Wallis & Wallis) £35

An officer's dead and bright gilt star plate of the Warwickshire Yeomanry Cavalry with title on circlet enclosing William IV cypher.
(Christie's S. Ken) £286

A scarce Edward VIII white metal badge of the War Dept. Constabulary.
(Wallis & Wallis) £70

Imperial Russia: badge of the Order of Saint Vladimir in gold and enamels, and issued for 25 years of outstanding military service. (Wallis & Wallis) £390

A Rifle Brigade badge, with additional scroll *Ashantee*, with backing plate.
(Wallis & Wallis) £140

BADGES

A Nazi E Boat war badge, (1st type), by *Schwerin Berlin 66*. (Wallis & Wallis) £270

A fine post 1902 Guards RSM embroidered arm badge, scarlet backing. (Wallis & Wallis) £215

Suffolk Yeomanry tribute medal/lapel badge for South Africa, three coronets within a shield. (Wallis & Wallis) £220

A heavy cast badge of the Scottish Regimental Association of Yorkshire 'The Jocks'. (Wallis & Wallis) £55

A Victorian brass badge, possibly Madras Police, *MP* within curl of crowned French bugle. (Wallis & Wallis) £95

A silver plated wheat sheaf headdress badge of the Rangoon Vol Rifle Corps. (Wallis & Wallis) £70

Order of the Garter breast star in silver and enamels, 85mm. diam., mid Victorian period. (Wallis & Wallis) £2,000

The Royal Guelphic Order, Knight Commander's Civil neck badge in gold, HM 1815, and enamels. (Wallis & Wallis) £950

Spain: Order of Naval Merit, gilt breast star with blue enamelled anchor, 86mm. (Wallis & Wallis) **£70**

CAP BADGES

An officer's cap badge of The Border Regt, hallmarked *Birmingham 1919*, red enamelled centre.
(Wallis & Wallis) £190

A scarce Canadian Militia cap badge of the 99th Manitoba Rangers.
(Wallis & Wallis) £75

A cap badge of The Border Regt., red and white enamelled centre.
(Wallis & Wallis) £75

An officer's cap badge of The Devonshire Regt., gilt centre, marked *Sterling* on back.
(Wallis & Wallis) £120

A good officer's silver cap badge of The Royal Berkshire Regt, hallmarked *Birmingham 1904*.
(Wallis & Wallis) £170

A good post 1902 officer's silver plated, gilt and enamel cap badge of The Royal Hampshire Regt., by Gaunt.
(Wallis & Wallis) £70

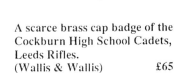

An other rank's white metal cap badge of the 1st Volunteer Bn The Royal Fusiliers.
(Wallis & Wallis) £80

A pre 1947 officer's silver cap badge of the 5th Royal Gurkha Rifles, hallmarked *Birmingham 1944*.
(Wallis & Wallis) £80

A scarce brass cap badge of the Cockburn High School Cadets, Leeds Rifles.
(Wallis & Wallis) £65

CAP BADGES

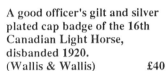

A cap badge of the 4th/7th
Dragoon Guards, marked
Sterling on back.
(Wallis & Wallis)   £75

A good officer's gilt and silver
plated cap badge of the 16th
Canadian Light Horse,
disbanded 1920.
(Wallis & Wallis)   £40

A bi-metal cap badge of the
Punjab Light Horse.
(Wallis & Wallis)   £140

A pre-1903 officer's silver plated
cap badge of the 2nd Bengal
Lancers.
(Wallis & Wallis)   £100

A rare other rank's bi-metal cap
of the 4th–7th Bn The Essex
Regt (1738) with blank *Egypt*
scroll and *S Africa 1900–02*
honour.
(Wallis & Wallis)   £100

An officer's silver cap badge of
the 72nd Punjabis hallmarked
Birmingham 1921.
(Wallis & Wallis)   £155

An officer's silver plated cap
badge of the Leeds Rifles.
(Wallis & Wallis)   £70

An officer's cap badge of the
Herefordshire Regt., gilt scroll,
not hallmarked.
(Wallis & Wallis)   £75

A good Victorian officer's
embroidered forage cap badge
of The Essex Regt.
(Wallis & Wallis)   £85

An officer's silver side cap badge of The Rifle Brigade, hallmarked *Birmingham 1943*.
(Wallis & Wallis) £55

An officer's silver cap badge of The Parachute Regt., hallmarked *Birmingham 1945*.
(Wallis & Wallis) £250

A World War II plastic cap badge of the Army Air Corps.
(Wallis & Wallis) £35

An officer's silver cap badge of the Royal Tank Regt., hallmarked *Birmingham 1940*.
(Wallis & Wallis) £65

A silver cap badge of the Liverpool Pals, hallmarked *London 1914*, as given by the Earl of Derby to each recruit joining before 16.10.14.
(Wallis & Wallis) £75

An officer's silver cap badge of the Wiltshire Yeomanry, hallmarked *Birmingham 1926*.
(Wallis & Wallis) £80

An officer's silver cap badge of the 7th/8th Bn The West Yorks Regt., hallmarked *Birmingham 1940*.
(Wallis & Wallis) £130

An officer's sterling cap badge of The Royal Scots Greys, gilt scroll, marked *Ludlow* and *Sterling*.
(Wallis & Wallis) £100

A pre 1922 officer's cap badge of the 88th Carnatic Infantry, marked *Orr* and *Sil* on the back.
(Wallis & Wallis) £160

CAP BADGES

A good scarce bronzed cap badge of the RNAS Armoured Car Section.
(Wallis & Wallis)   £65

A good pre-1947 officer's silver cap badge of the 1st Madras Pioneers, hallmarked *Birmingham 1926.*
(Wallis & Wallis)   £150

An officer's silver cap badge of the Army Air Corps, hallmarked *Birmingham 1941.*
(Wallis & Wallis)   £220

A good scarce officer's gilt cap badge of the 18th (Princess of Wales's Own) Hussars.
(Wallis & Wallis)   £160

A pre 1922 officer's bronze cap badge of the 1st Duke of York's Own Lancers (Skinner's Horse).
(Wallis & Wallis)   £155

An officer's silver cap of The Suffolk Regt., hallmarked *Birmingham 1903.*
(Wallis & Wallis)   £115

An other rank's white metal cap badge of the 2nd Volunteer Bn Loyal North Lancashire Regt., with *South Africa 1900–02* scroll.
(Wallis & Wallis)   £55

A silver cap badge of The Royal Berkshire Regt., hallmark unclear.
(Wallis & Wallis)   £140

An officer's cap badge of the 3rd Carabiniers, gilt coronet and scroll, by JR Gaunt, London.
(Wallis & Wallis)   £90

GLENGARRY BADGES

A Victorian officer's gilt and silver plated glengarry badge of The Devonshire Regt., original black velvet centre backing.
(Wallis & Wallis) **£85**

A scarce 1908–22 other rank's white metal glengarry badge of the 4th/7th Bns The Black Watch.
(Wallis & Wallis) **£75**

A Victorian officer's gilt and silver plated glengarry badge of The Norfolk Regt., original velvet centre backing.
(Wallis & Wallis) **£85**

A glengarry badge of the 3rd Volunteer Bn The Royal West Kent Regt.
(Wallis & Wallis) **£50**

An other rank's white metal glengarry badge of the 5th Volunteer Bn The Royal Scots.
(Wallis & Wallis) **£50**

A good Victorian other rank's white metal glengarry badge of the 2nd Volunteer Bn The Lincolnshire Regt.
(Wallis & Wallis) **£65**

A glengarry badge of the 1st Volunteer Bn The Shropshire Light Infantry.
(Wallis & Wallis) **£40**

A good officer's silver glengarry badge of The Cameronians, hallmarked *Birmingham 1915*.
(Wallis & Wallis) **£190**

A pre-1881 other rank's brass glengarry badge of The 23 (Royal Welsh Fusiliers) Regt.
(Wallis & Wallis) **£70**

GLENGARRY BADGES

A good officer's silver glengarry badge of The Argyll and Sutherland Highlanders, hallmarked *Edinburgh 1939*.
(Wallis & Wallis)   £180

A Victorian officer's silver plated glengarry badge of a Volunteer Bn. The Royal Warwickshire Regt.
(Wallis & Wallis)   £55

An other rank's white metal glengarry badge of the 4th Aberdeenshire Rifle Volunteer Corps.
(Wallis & Wallis)   £90

An officer's gilt and silver plated glengarry badge of The West Yorks Regt.
(Wallis & Wallis)   £115

An other rank's white metal glengarry badge of the 3rd Aberdeenshire Rifle Volunteer Corps.
(Wallis & Wallis)   £115

A good quality Victorian NCO's brass glengarry badge of The Oxfordshire Light Infantry, traces of gilt wash.
(Wallis & Wallis)   £60

An other rank's blackened glengarry badge of the 38th Dufferin Rifles (Canadian Militia).
(Wallis & Wallis)   £45

A good officer's silver glengarry badge of The Gordon Highlanders, by B&P, hallmarked *Birmingham 1917*.
(Wallis & Wallis)   £50

A good Victorian other rank's white metal glengarry badge of the 10th Lanark Rifle Volunteers (Glasgow Highlanders).
(Wallis & Wallis)   £80

GLENGARRY BADGES

A Victorian other rank's white metal glengarry badge of a Volunteer Bn The Dorsetshire Regt.
(Wallis & Wallis) **£65**

A scarce glengarry of The 36th (Worcestershire) Regt.
(Wallis & Wallis) £190

A Victorian other rank's white metal glengarry badge of The Kings Own Borderers, 1881–87.
(Wallis & Wallis) **£60**

A scarce other rank's white metal glengarry badge of the Scots Company Bombay Volunteer Rifles.
(Wallis & Wallis) £190

A silver glengarry badge of the Highland Brigade, hallmarked *Birmingham 1961*.
(Wallis & Wallis) £120

A good Victorian other rank's glengarry badge of The Hampshire Regt.
(Wallis & Wallis) **£30**

A good Canadian officer's glengarry badge of the Glengarry Fencibles, the back stamped *Sterling*.
(Wallis & Wallis) £65

A good other rank's white metal glengarry badge of the Inverness Highland Rifle Volunteers.
(Wallis & Wallis) **£90**

A good officer's silver glengarry badge of The King's Own Scottish Borderers, hallmarked *Birmingham 1918*.
(Wallis & Wallis) **£205**

GLENGARRY BADGES

A silver glengarry badge of The Gordon Highlanders, hallmarked *Glasgow 1940*.
(Wallis & Wallis) £125

A good quality officer's copper gilt glengarry badge of The 98th Regt.
(Wallis & Wallis) £260

A Victorian officer's silver plated glengarry badge of the Lanarkshire Rifle Volunteers.
(Wallis & Wallis) £70

A scarce 1908–22 other rank's white metal glengarry badge of the 4th to 7th Bns The Black Watch.
(Wallis & Wallis) £85

A Victorian officer's silver plated glengarry badge of the 39th Rifle Volunteers.
(Wallis & Wallis) £45

An other rank's white metal glengarry badge of the Royal Aberdeenshire Highlanders (Militia).
(Wallis & Wallis) £160

A good other rank's white metal glengarry badge of the 1st Argyll Highland Rifle Volunteers.
(Wallis & Wallis) £100

An other rank's white metal glengarry badge of the 1st Aberdeenshire Rifle Volunteers.
(Wallis & Wallis) £210

An other rank's white metal glengarry badge of the 4th Aberdeenshire Rifle Volunteer Corps.
(Wallis & Wallis) £85

A French First Empire officer's gorget of the 17th Light Infantry, of brass with applied silver crowned eagle. (Phillips London) £420

An original Nazi S.A. gorget 'Brutschild der Kornett S.A.', of heart form, blue cloth lined with 2 lugs and central disc marked with large 'RZM'. £250

A rare Nazi political standard bearer's gorget, complete with suspension chain of square links alternating designs of Nazi Eagle and swastika. £225

A good Georgian officer's copper gilt universal pattern gorget, engraved with crowned *GR* cypher and wreath. (Wallis & Wallis) £130

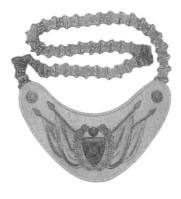

A Nazi old comrades association (Kyffhauserbund) standard bearer's gorget enamelled central shield device bordered by gilt standards. (Wallis & Wallis) £135

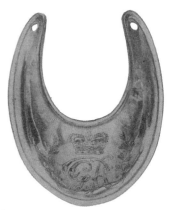

A good Georgian officer's copper gilt universal pattern gorget, engraved with crowned *GR* cypher and wreath. (Wallis & Wallis) £240

A Georgian officer's copper gilt gorget of The Dunfermline Volunteers, engraved with 1801-16 Royal Arms and title scroll. £200

A Nazi Kornett der S.A. standard bearer's gorget, plated finish, NSDAP badge, plated hanging chains. (Wallis & Wallis) £95

A scarce Georgian officer's copper gorget of the Omagh Corps, engraved with crowned *GR*, laurel sprays and *Omagh* and *Corps* within ovals. (Wallis & Wallis) £130

GORGETS

An officer's silver gorget of The 10th (Prince of Wales's Own) Light Dragoons, circa 1785, engraved with the pre-1801 Arms. **£600**

An Imperial German standard bearer's gorget, gilt finish, with applied German silver device of standards, laurel leaves and central crowned device. (Wallis & Wallis) **£110**

A Georgian officer's copper gilt gorget of The Guernsey Royal Artillery, engraved with the badge of the island and title scroll below. **£450**

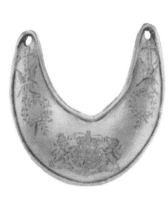

A Georgian officer's gorget of silver, engraved with pre-1801 Royal Arms, the shoulders engraved with a helmet and trophy of arms. (Phillips London) **£420**

A rare French Revolutionary period officer's gorget, of brass with applied silvered trophy of arms and flags, the centre with royalist fleur-de-lys and crown, circa 1789-92. (Phillips London) **£800**

A Georgian officer's universal pattern gilt gorget, engraved with crowned *GR* in wreath, the back scratched with *1949/Wm. Carme.* (Wallis & Wallis) **£120**

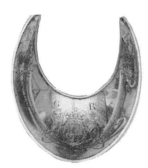

A good scarce Georgian officer's silver gorget of the Sussex Militia, engraved in the centre with pre-1801 Royal Arms surmounted by the letters "G" and "R". (Wallis & Wallis) **£350**

A Nazi Kyfhauserbund standard bearer's gorget, gilt flags around Old Comrades emblem, with Iron Cross devices. (Wallis & Wallis) **£100**

An officer's gorget, possibly for a Sheffield or Hallmashire Militia Unit, late 18th century. **£175**

HELMET PLATES

A Victorian other rank's darkened brass Maltese Cross helmet plate of the Renfrewshire Rifle Volunteers.
(Wallis & Wallis)　　　　£90

A scarce and interesting Victorian other ranks' brass helmet plate of the E Lothian YC or Lothians & Berwick YC.
(Wallis & Wallis)　　　　£70

An officer's gilt and silvered 1878 pattern helmet plate of The 88th (Connaught Rangers) Regt. (Wallis & Wallis)　　　　£135

A good Victorian other rank's white metal helmet plate of the Bombay Volunteer Artillery.
(Wallis & Wallis)　　　　£180

A good post 1902 officer's gilt helmet plate of the East Surrey Regiment.
(Wallis & Wallis)　　　　£120

A good Victorian officer's silver plated and gilt helmet plate of the 4th Volunteer Bn The South Wales Borderers.
(Wallis & Wallis)　　　　£190

A pre-1902 senior officer's gilt helmet plate of the Bedfordshire Regiment.
(Wallis & Wallis)　　　　£200

A good French 2nd Republic officer's gilt eagle helmet plate of the 28th Regt, large single stud fastener with original nut.
(Wallis & Wallis)　　　　£100

A good 1878 pattern Militia officer's helmet plate, gilt plate, silver plated centre bearing Royal Crest.　　　　£110

HELMET PLATES

A scarce Victorian officer's helmet plate of the Ordnance Stores Department.
(Wallis & Wallis)   £150

A good post 1902 officer's hilt helmet plate of The Royal Artillery.
(Wallis & Wallis)   £55

A Victorian OR's darkened Maltese Cross helmet plate of the 5th Ad. Bn. (the Weald of) Kent Rifle Vols. (Wallis & Wallis)   £45

A Victorian officer's gilt and silver plated helmet plate of The Dorsetshire Regiment, in the centre the castle and key with motto scrolls on black velvet.
(Wallis & Wallis)   £180

A scarce Victorian OR's blackened brass helmet plate of the 3rd British Guiana Militia.   £40

A good Victorian other ranks helmet plate of the 3rd Volunteer Bn The Devonshire Regt.
(Wallis & Wallis)   £75

A post 1902 officer's helmet plate of The West Yorkshire Regt.   £80

A Russian Crimean war period OR's helmet plate of the 26th Infantry Regt.
(Wallis & Wallis)   £60

A Victorian officer's darkened helmet plate of the 63rd Rifle Vols, probably Lancashire (Toxteth Park).   £50

HELMET PLATES

BADGES

A Victorian officer's blackened white metal helmet plate of a Volunteer Bn The Royal Irish Rifles.
(Wallis & Wallis) £230

A scarce Victorian helmet plate of the First Aberdeen Engineer Volunteers.
(Wallis & Wallis) £135

A Victorian officer's gilt and silvered helmet plate of The King's (Liverpool Regt.)
(Wallis & Wallis) £95

A scarce Victorian officers gilt helmet plate of the 1st West India Regt, "Dominica" scroll beneath title strap.
(Wallis & Wallis) £130

An OR's brass Maltese Cross helmet plate of the 38th Middlesex (Artists) Rifle Vols.
(Wallis & Wallis) £55

A rare officers 1878 pattern helmet plate of The 26th (Cameronians) Regt, silver mullet.
(Wallis & Wallis) £160

A Victorian other ranks' brass helmet plate of the East Lothian Yeomanry Cavalry.
(Wallis & Wallis) £160

A Vic OR's helmet plate of the 2nd Vol Bn The Manchester Regt.
(Wallis & Wallis) £70

A post 1902 officer's darkened Maltese Cross helmet plate of the 1st Volunteer Bn The R Warwickshire Regt.
(Wallis & Wallis) £55

A scarce Victorian officer's gilt brass helmet plate of the Kingston Volunteer Militia (Jamaica).
(Wallis & Wallis) £100

A post 1902 Canadian OR's brass helmet plate of the 57th Regt (Peterborough Rangers).
(Wallis & Wallis) £35

A good Victorian officer's darkened Maltese Cross helmet plate of the St George's Rifle Volunteer Corps. (Wallis & Wallis) £85

A post 1902 officers gilt and silver plated helmet plate of The Royal Irish Regt.
(Wallis & Wallis) £130

A scarce Vic OR's WM helmet plate of the Second Middlesex Artillery (Vols).
(Wallis & Wallis) £65

A post 1902 officers silver plated helmet plate of the 1st Vol Bn The York & Lancaster Regt.
(Wallis & Wallis) £100

A Vic OR's WM helmet plate of the 8th Lancashire Rifle Vols.
(Wallis & Wallis) £70

A rare Victorian helmet plate of the Tasmanian Local Forces, lion within crowned title strap and wreath on 8 pointed star.
(Wallis & Wallis) £50

A scarce 1902 officers helmet plate of The 7th City of London Regt.
(Wallis & Wallis) £155

PILOT BADGES

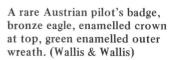

A First Pattern Imperial Austrian Naval pilot's badge (1915). (Wallis & Wallis) £100

A Nazi Luftwaffe pilot observer badge, by C. E. Juncker Berlin. (Wallis & Wallis) £125

A rare Austrian pilot's badge, bronze eagle, enamelled crown at top, green enamelled outer wreath. (Wallis & Wallis) £130

An Imperial Austro-Hungarian pilot's badge. (Wallis & Wallis) £260

A bronze cap badge of The Flying Section, Women's Legion. £85

An Imperial Turkish Empire Air Force pilot's badge. (Wallis & Wallis) £300

An Imperial Austrian pilot's badge, silvered eagle, with enamelled oak-leaf border. (Wallis & Wallis) £320

A silver World War II Free Czech Air Force pilot's badge, with pricker numbering on the reverse '309'. £200

An officer's silver collar badge of the Army Air Corps, hallmarked Birmingham 1942. (Wallis & Wallis) £110

PLAID BROOCHES

A fine officer's silver-coloured plaid brooch of the Scots Company Bombay Volunteer Rifles, with overlaid device of regimental badge.
(Wallis & Wallis)   £600

An officer's silver plaid brooch of The Gordon Highlanders.   £220

A good pre-1881 officer's plaid brooch of The 93rd Sutherland Highlanders, of hollow construction.
(Wallis & Wallis)   £320

A good quality yellow metal plaid brooch of the London Scottish Rifle Volunteers by Morton. (Wallis & Wallis) £140

An officer's gilt and silvered plaid brooch of The Highland Light Infantry. (Wallis & Wallis)   £380

A scarce silver plated plaid brooch of the 1st Citizens Company of Edinburgh.
(Wallis & Wallis)   £60

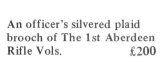

An officer's silvered plaid brooch of The 1st Aberdeen Rifle Vols.   £200

A Victorian hollow-cast gold plaid brooch of the Clan Mackinnon, 1.2oz. Troy.   £250

A silver plated plaid brooch of The 74th (Highlanders) Regt., elephant over *Assaye* on plain circle.
(Wallis & Wallis)   £90

POUCH BELT PLATES

An officer's gilt brass pouch belt badge of the 126th Baluchistan Infantry, with backing plate.
(Wallis & Wallis)   £90

A good Victorian officer's silver plated pouch badge of the West Yorks Rifle Volunteers, crowned ornamental *WYRV* monogram.
(Wallis & Wallis)   £70

A good Vic officers pouch belt badge of the 1st Royal Lancashire Militia.
(Wallis & Wallis)   £75

An officer's white metal pouch belt badge of the Inverness Highland Rifle Volunteers, with backing plate.
(Wallis & Wallis)   £75

An officer's silver Maltese Cross pouch belt badge of The King's Royal Rifle Corps, HM Birmingham 1917.   £80

A scarce blackened brass pouch belt badge of the Lauderdale Rifle Volunteers.
(Wallis & Wallis)   £230

An officer's pouch belt badge of the 4th/5th Bn The Royal Scots, maker's name *Marshall & Aitken Edinburgh.*
(Wallis & Wallis)   £160

A Victorian officer's plated pouch belt badge of the Lincolnshire Rifles Volunteers, with backing plate.
(Wallis & Wallis)   £90

A Victorian officer's silver plated pouch belt badge of the Sussex Rifle Volunteers.
(Wallis & Wallis)   £80

POUCH BELT PLATES

A Victorian Rifle Volunteer officer's silver plated pouch belt badge.
(Wallis & Wallis) £80

A good white metal pouch badge of the 5th Volunteer Bn The Cameronians.
(Wallis & Wallis) £100

A Victorian officer's silver plated pouch belt badge of the 2nd Lancashire Rifles, brass rose in centre.
(Wallis & Wallis) £70

A Victorian officer's silver plated Maltese Cross pouch belt badge of the Dorset Rifle Volunteers, precedence No. 16 in centre.
(Wallis & Wallis) £180

A good and interesting pre-1903 officer's pouch belt badge, whistle and chains and pouch badge of the 4th Bombay Infantry or Rifle Corps.
(Wallis & Wallis) £320

A good scarce Victorian officer's silver plated pouch belt badge of the Huntingdon Rifle Regiment of Militia.
(Wallis & Wallis) £150

A Victorian white metal pouch belt badge of the London Scottish Volunteers.
(Wallis & Wallis) £90

A Victorian officer's pouch belt badge of The Royal Irish Rifles, 17 battle honours to Central India.
(Wallis & Wallis) £230

A Victorian officer's cast silver plated pouch belt badge of the Lanarkshire Rifle Volunteers.
(Wallis & Wallis) £105

217

A good officers silver plated pouch belt of the Cornwall Rifle Volunteers, with backing plate. (Wallis & Wallis) £95

A Victorian officer's silver plated pouch belt badge of the 6th East London Rifle Brigade. (Wallis & Wallis) £60

A scarce post-1902 officer's pouch belt badge of the Huddersfield Rifle Corps. (Wallis & Wallis) £55

An officers silver plated pouch belt badge of the 58th Vaughan's Rifles (Frontier Force), 1903–22. (Wallis & Wallis) £450

A good post 1902 officers silver pouch belt badge of The royal Irish Rifles, battle honours to S. Africa 1899–1902. (Wallis & Wallis) £360

A Vic officers silver plated pouch belt badge of the Central Provinces Police (India). (Wallis & Wallis) £45

A Victorian officer's pouch belt plate of the 4th West York Rifle Volunteers. £140

A pre 1922 officer's heavy cast white metal pouch badge of the 51st Sikhs, (Frontier Force), design as for headdress. (Wallis & Wallis) £20

A scarce Victorian officer's pouch belt badge of the Ripon Rifle Volunteers. (Wallis & Wallis) £80

A post-1902 officer's silver plated pouch belt badge of the 8th Bn. The West Yorkshire Regt. (Leeds Rifles). (Wallis & Wallis) £55

An officer's silvered Rifle Brigade pouch belt badge. (Wallis & Wallis) £65

A pre 1947 officers pouch belt badge of the 2nd Bn (Duke of Cambridge's Own) (Brownlow's) 14th Punjab Regt. (Wallis & Wallis) £80

A Victorian officers pouch belt badge of the Kent Rifle Volunteers. (Wallis & Wallis) £85

A Vic officers silver plated Maltese Cross pouch belt badge of the 4th Lancashire Rifle Vols. (Wallis & Wallis) £115

A post 1902 officers pouch belt badge of the 6th Gurkha Rifles. (Wallis & Wallis) £190

A good officers silver plated pouch belt badge of the East India Railway Regt. (Wallis & Wallis) £90

A Victorian officer's silvered pouch belt plate of the 2nd Vol. Batt. Royal Welsh Fusiliers. (Wallis & Wallis) £80

A fine and interesting officers silver plated pouch belt badge, Maltese Cross with Guelphic crowned wreath. (Wallis & Wallis) £30

PUGGAREE BADGES

A cast silver plated puggaree badge of The 58th (Rutland) Regt., integral flat lugs. (Wallis & Wallis) £50

A good officer's silver plated puggaree badge of the South Indian Railway by Barton. (Wallis & Wallis) £155

A pre-1903 other rank's die struck brass puggaree badge of the 24th Madras Infantry, brooch pin. (Wallis & Wallis) £40

An officer's silver puggaree badge of the Coldstream Guards, gilt garter with blue enamel backing, red enamel to St. George's cross, HM B'ham 1899. (Wallis & Wallis) £210

A good officer's gilt and silver plated puggaree badge of The Dorsetshire Regt., design as for other rank's helmet plate centre. (Wallis & Wallis) £85

A good Geo VI officer's puggaree badge of the Grenadier Guards, red and blue enamel centre, with backing plate and long slide. (Wallis & Wallis) £210

A puggaree badge worn by gun lascars of the Indian Artillery Train. (Wallis & Wallis) £75

An officers puggaree badge of the Natal Carabiniers, brooch pin, by "H&S". (Wallis & Wallis) £30

A good officer's puggaree badge of The 3rd (Prince of Wales's) Dragoon Guards, on a red enamel background. (Wallis & Wallis) £240

220

PUGGAREE BADGES

A good pre 1922 OR's die struck brass puggaree badge of the 3rd Brahmans.
(Wallis & Wallis)   £190

A pre-1922 other rank's cast brass puggaree badge of the 7th Rajputs, brooch pin.
(Wallis & Wallis)   £80

A good pre 1903 heavy quality officer's puggaree badge of the 6th Punjab Infantry, brooch pin.
(Wallis & Wallis)   £150

A heavy quality officers puggaree badge of the 96th Berar Infantry, brooch pin.
(Wallis & Wallis)   £185

A good pre 1903 officer's silver plated puggaree badge of the 30th Punjab Infantry, brooch pin.
(Wallis & Wallis)   £180

An officers heavy quality puggaree badge of the 89th Punjabis, 1903–22, brooch pin.
(Wallis & Wallis)   £130

A good pre-1922 other rank's cast white metal puggaree badge of the 84th Punjabis, brooch pin.
(Wallis & Wallis)   £90

An officer's cap or small puggaree badge of the Burma Signals, brooch pin, not hallmarked.
(Wallis & Wallis)   £60

An officer's cast puggaree badge of The 20th (East Devon) Regt., rose/XX within crowned *Omnia Audax* garter and wreath.
(Wallis & Wallis)   £45

SHAKO PLATES

A good officer's gilt and and silver plated 1861 (Quilted) pattern shako plate of The 9th (East Norfolk) Regt.
(Wallis & Wallis) £280

An officer's gilt shako plate of the South Nottinghamshire Yeomanry Cavalry on title strap enclosing VR cypher.
(Christie's S. Ken) £264

An officer's darkened brass shako plate of the 2nd Hampshire Rifle Volunteers.
(Wallis & Wallis) £80

A scarce Victorian officer's silver plated and gilt Maltese Cross shako plate of the West Somerset Yeomanry.
(Wallis & Wallis) £230

An Imperial Russian Infantry shako-plate with scroll ("For Distinction"), late nineteenth or early twentieth century.
(Christie's S. Ken) £132

A good officer's star shako plate, circa 1825, of the 27th Madras Native Infantry, gilt centre, single battle honour *Mahidpore* on the strap.
(Wallis & Wallis) £170

An officer's gilt 1844 (Albert) pattern shako plate of The 1st (Royal Regiment) of Foot (78).
(Wallis & Wallis) £475

A Victorian officer's 1869 pattern gilt and silver plated shako plate of the 4th Royal Lancashire Light Infantry Militia.
(Wallis & Wallis) £130

An OR's 1869 pattern shako plate of the 27th (Bolton) Lancashire Rifle Vols. (Wallis & Wallis) £55

SHAKO PLATES

A good white metal shako plate
of the 4th Middlesex RVC (West
London Rifles).
(Wallis & Wallis)   £55

A good N.C.O.'s gilt 1869
pattern shako plate of the 77th
(East Middlesex) Regiment.
(Wallis & Wallis)   £65

A scarce officer's 1869 pattern
gilt shako plate of The 74th
(Highlanders) Regt.
(Wallis & Wallis)   £280

An other rank's brass shako
plate of the Royal Dockyard
Battalion 1847–58, with original
soldered loops.
(Wallis & Wallis)   £80

A large Imperial Russian
Artillery shako-plate of circa
1812 (now bearing modern gilt
finish and lacking fixings).
(Christie's S. Ken)   £220

A scarce officer's gilt and silver
plated 1816 (Regency) shako
plate of The 91st (Argyllshire)
Regt.
(Wallis & Wallis)   £180

A scarce Georgian other ranks
thin die struck brass shako plate
of the 4th Hanoverian Infantry.
(Wallis & Wallis)   £100

An officer's white metal and gilt
shako plate of the
Northumberland and Newcastle
Yeomanry with crowned
William IV cypher.
(Christie's S. Ken)   £660

A silver plated brass shako plate
of the 1st Aberdeenshire Rifle
Volunteers.
(Wallis & Wallis)   £85

SHOULDER BELT PLATES

A Georgian other rank's rectangular brass shoulder belt plate of the (39th) Royal Carmarthen Fusiliers, rounded corners.
(Wallis & Wallis) £80

A good pre 1855 officer's gilt rectangular shoulder belt plate of The Royal Artillery (Parkyn 52).
(Wallis & Wallis) £220

A pre-1855 other rank's rectangular brass shoulder belt plate of The 18th (Royal Irish) Regt.
(Wallis & Wallis) £180

A good Georgian officer's rectangular silver shoulder belt plate of the Royal Cheshire Regiment, burnished plate with engraved device of *GR* cypher.
(Wallis & Wallis) £200

A good pre-1881 Militia officer's rectangular shoulder belt plate of the Royal Aberdeenshire Highlanders, silver plated burnished plate with rounded corners.
(Wallis & Wallis) £330

An officer's gilt rectangular shoulder belt plate of the Grenadier Guards, worn 1837–55, large grenade on frosted plate.
(Wallis & Wallis) £180

An officer's gilt and silver plated rectangular shoulder belt plate of the Coldstream Guards, worn 1825–55.
(Wallis & Wallis) £450

A scarce and interesting Indian Army die struck brass shoulder belt plate of the 25th Regt., probably NCO's.
(Wallis & Wallis) £200

A rectangular shoulder belt plate of the 96th Regiment in silver gilt applied with crown over regimental number.
(Phillips) £320

SHOULDER BELT PLATES

A shoulder belt plate of The 41st (Welch) Regt., blue enamel centre backing.
(Wallis & Wallis)   £150

A good officer's rectangular shoulder belt plate of the 2nd West York Militia, 1833–55.
(Wallis & Wallis)   £290

A pre-1855 shoulder belt plate of The 28th (North Gloucestershire) Regt.
(Wallis & Wallis)   £210

A good officer's rectangular gilt shoulder belt plate of the Royal Marines, circa 1850, burnished gilt plate with gilt devices of Royal Crest.
(Wallis & Wallis)   £130

A good post 1902 officer's gilt and silver plated rectangular shoulder belt plate of The King's Own Scottish Borderers, burnished plate bearing Edinburgh Castle within a circle.
(Wallis & Wallis)   £210

A good officer's rectangular shoulder plate of The Royal Regiment of Artillery, worn 1823–33, gilt frosted plate with burnished edges.
(Wallis & Wallis)   £350

A George III officer's rectangular gilt shoulder belt plate of the Grenadier Guards, circa 1815.
(Wallis & Wallis)   £490

A very fine officer's rectangular silver shoulder-belt plate of the 37th (North Hampshire) Regiment, hallmarked Birmingham 1838.
(Wallis & Wallis)   £550

A good scarce George III officer's silver gilt rectangular shoulder belt plate of The 25th (Kings Own Borderers) Regt.
(Wallis & Wallis)   £550

SHOULDER BELT PLATES

A Georgian OR's oval brass shoulder belt plate of The 60th (R. American) Regt, *60* within crowned oval garter.
(Wallis & Wallis) £310

A scarce Georgian Irish other rank's oval brass shoulder belt plate of the Newbliss Cavalry, engraved with Irish harp and scrolls.
(Wallis & Wallis) £210

A good and rare Georgian officer's gilt and silver plated oval shoulder belt plate of the Coldstream Regiment of Foot Guards, circa 1795.
(Wallis & Wallis) £350

A scarce Georgian officer's oval shoulder belt plate of the Renfrewshire Militia, burnished plate with raised silver plated border and centre badge.
(Wallis & Wallis) £110

A rare Georgian other ranks oval brass shoulder belt plate of the New Brunswick Fencible Infantry.
(Wallis & Wallis) £320

A fine Georgian officer's copper gilt oval shoulder belt plate of the Household Cavalry, circa 1795, burnished plate with bright cut border.
(Wallis & Wallis) £280

A good Georgian officer's gilt and silver plated oval shoulder belt plate of The 3rd Foot Guards, circa 1800.
(Wallis & Wallis) £525

A Georgian OR's oval brass shoulder belt plate of the 3rd Bn The 60th Regt circa 1790.
(Wallis & Wallis) £370

A Georgian other rank's oval brass shoulder belt plate of the St. Martin's Loyal Volunteers, raised design.
(Wallis & Wallis) £160

A good iron naval cannon barrel, circa 1800, bore approximately 1¾in., stepped barrel, marked above breech with 'P' and '1.1.15', length overall 37½in., trunnion width 9in. £1,000

A German iron hackbut barrel, octagonal and swamped at the muzzle and breech, early 16th century, 47¼in. barrel.
(Christie's) £1,495

A bronze signal cannon barrel, multi-staged and with turned mouldings, the chase cast with acanthus foliage in relief on a punched ground, 16th century, 24in. long.
(Christie's) £7,700

A 19th century cast iron six pounder carronade, 46in., 16½in. across trunnions, breech cast with Imperial crown and '6pr', reinforcing rings at muzzle and breech with integral loop to cascabel. £1,250

A 19th century Malayan cast bronze swivel cannon lantaka, 48½in., moulded overall with sections of foliage, cylindrical swollen socket mount to rear of breech.
(Wallis & Wallis) £380

A small Continental bronze cannon barrel of tapering multi-stage form decorated with mouldings in relief, those at the muzzle separated by a band of acanthus leaves, finely cast in relief, circa 1750, 18¼in. barrel, 1in. bore.
(Christie's) £1,760

CROSSBOWS AND STONEBOWS

A fine German sporting crossbow with slender steel bow painted black and retained by its original gold painted cords, original green woollen tassels, and original string of twisted cord, walnut full stock, circa 1750, 29in. (Christie's) £10,925

A German sporting crossbow with robust steel bow struck on the inner face with a mark, the top and bottom surfaces covered in horn and engraved on the latter with strapwork and foliage enclosing a heraldic figure in 16th century armour, partly early 17th century, 26½in. (Christie's) £4,180

An English stonebow 'prod' circa 1780, 29½in., span 26¾in., fruit wood stock, four peepholes to hinged rearsight covering lockwork, engraved steel trigger guard. (Wallis & Wallis) £210

A German sporting crossbow with slender steel bow, painted black, except the upper face, original string and gold painted retaining cords, and original purple woollen tassels, early 18th century, 26½in. (Christie's) £1,725

A German stonebow (Schnepper) of characteristic form, with slender steel bow, later string, engraved folding back-sight mounted on the built-in gaffle struck with maker's mark MS over a squirrel in a shield, mid-17th century, 29¾in. (Christie's) £1,092

A German sporting crossbow with slender steel bow, later string and two original green woollen tassels, walnut tiller carved at the front with a lion in the round, with iron tongue, and inlaid with horn lines and plaques engraved with flowerheads and foliage, early 18th century, 28½in. (Christie's) £2,070

A German target crossbow, heavy steel bow of 89.5cm. span, walnut stock with brass mounts including scroll trigger guard, peephole rear sight, double set triggers, 83.5cm. overall. £600

A late 18th century stonebow, span 34in., fold-up 'window' front sight, walnut stock with steel mounts, action and lift-up cocking lever secured by a spring thumb-catch, hinge-up aperture rear peep-sight, chequered small of stock. £1,000

A German sporting crossbow with robust steel bow retained by its original cords, string of twisted cords, angular wooden tiller swelling towards the middle, the top and bottom overlaid with panels of light coloured horn bordered by darker horn, early 17th century, 25½in. (Christie's) £4,370

A German stonebow, the bow struck with a mark, cord strings, built-in gaffle struck with the maker's mark HSB over a bird in a shield, early 17th century, 21¼in. (Christie's) £1,495

DRUMS

A scarce Georgian wooden side-drum of a Kent regiment, painted with the horse of Kent in an eight-pointed star, within an oak wreath.
(Wallis & Wallis) £600

An ERII painted bass drum of the 1st Bn Coldstream Guards, bearing Royal Arms, by George Potter, Aldershot.
(Wallis & Wallis) £600

A painted brass side-drum of the Royal Horse Guards, bearing the Royal Arms, within battle-honour scrolls *Dettingen* to *France and Flanders 1914–18*.
(Wallis & Wallis) £240

A scarce Georgian painted side-drum of the 2nd Regiment, Royal East India Volunteers, painted with Arms and supporters, in the centre a garter inscribed *Royal East India Volunteers*.
(Wallis & Wallis) £525

A fine pair of kettle drums of the Westmoreland and Cumberland Yeomanry, of copper with complex tension mechanism for the vellum skins.
(Christie's) £880

1st Battalion, Irish Guards: rope-tension side-drum by George Potter, 15in. high, the painted brass shell richly embellished with the Royal Arms.
(Christie's) £440

Painted and decorated parade drum, J. & G. Dennison, Freeport, Maine, late 19th century, the green ground decorated in polychrome, 16½in. diam.
(Skinner Inc.) £503

Large painted and decorated parade bass drum, inscribed *William Bridget Maker & Painter, Belfast,* late 19th century, 37in. diam. (Skinner Inc.) £2,515

A mid 19th century Imperial Russian military drum, brass body with large oval plaque embossed with Russian Royal Eagle, cord ties, diameter 14in.
£300

230

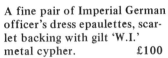

A fine pair of Imperial German officer's dress epaulettes, scarlet backing with gilt 'W.I.' metal cypher. £100

A scarce light company officer's frock coat epaulette of The 92nd (Highland) Regt., circa 1840. (Wallis & Wallis) £100

An extremely fine pair of Victorian full dress bullion epaulettes of The Queen's Bodyguard for Scotland, Royal Company of Archers. £125

An officer's single epaulette of the 1st or the Royal Regt., gilt lace ornamental embroidered scarlet strap, 2½in., GC for age. £500

A fine pair of early Victorian officer's gilt chained full dress epaulettes of the 87th Prince of Wales' Own Irish Fusiliers. £250

One of a pair of Georgian officer's gilt bullion epaulettes of The 6th Dragoon Guards, circa 1825. £300

A pair of Georgian officer's full dress epaulettes of The Royal East India Vol. £70

A Nazi period Field Marshal's epaulette with gold and silver embroidery. £120

A fine pair of George IV officer's full dress embroidered epaulettes of The Coldstream Guards, silver bullion embroidery on yellow cloth. £250

EPROUVETTES

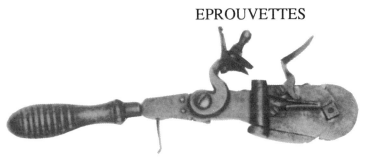

A mid 18th century all steel German flintlock Pulverprufer (powder-tester), 9¼in., exterior action, vertical powder chamber propelling wheel flap downwards, frame side engraved with grades 1-12.   £500

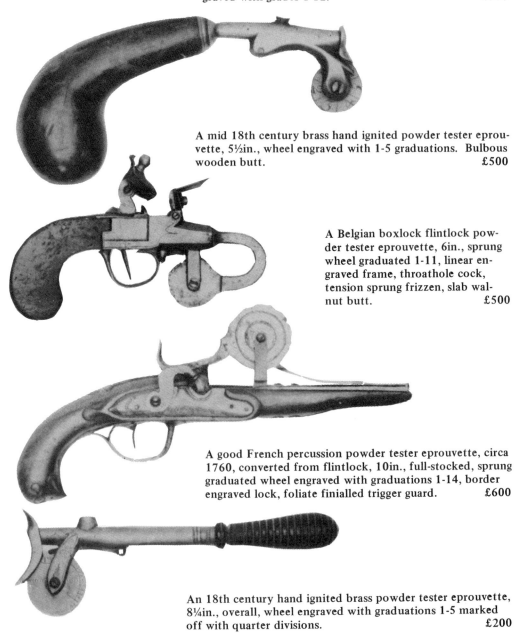

A mid 18th century brass hand ignited powder tester eprouvette, 5½in., wheel engraved with 1-5 graduations. Bulbous wooden butt.   £500

A Belgian boxlock flintlock powder tester eprouvette, 6in., sprung wheel graduated 1-11, linear engraved frame, throathole cock, tension sprung frizzen, slab walnut butt.   £500

A good French percussion powder tester eprouvette, circa 1760, converted from flintlock, 10in., full-stocked, sprung graduated wheel engraved with graduations 1-14, border engraved lock, foliate finialled trigger guard.   £600

An 18th century hand ignited brass powder tester eprouvette, 8¼in., overall, wheel engraved with graduations 1-5 marked off with quarter divisions.   £200

A scarce detached Scandinavian flintlock lock, circa 1650, 7 in. engraved with perched bird and foliage. (Wallis & Wallis) £200

A scarce English detached matchlock lock from a musket, circa 1680, slightly rounded lockplate. (Wallis & Wallis) £255

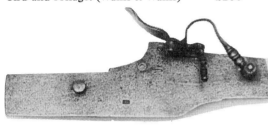

A rare detached snap matchlock lock, circa 1600, plate 8 in., struck with maker's initials "H.M." within rectangle. (Wallis & Wallis) £230

A rare Continental military style detached self priming pill lock from a musket, 6¼in., pill reservoir with screw on stopper. (Wallis & Wallis) £220

A detached Scandinavian flintlock lock, circa 1650, 7¾in., mainspring acts on toe of hammer. (Wallis & Wallis) £200

A detached Italian snaphaunce gun lock, circa 1675, 6¼in., plate chiselled with figure, scrollwork and stylised face on tail in relief. (Wallis & Wallis) £160

An unusual detached flintlock lock, probably provincial Italian, circa 1700, 6¾in., tail chiselled with animal's head, plate with reclining figure. (Wallis & Wallis) £180

A scarce detached English dog lock from a flintlock musket, circa 1650, 8½in. horizontally acting scear, swivel dog safety catch, (Wallis & Wallis) £210

An unusual detached double flintlock lock, for use on a gun with 2 charges in the same barrel, probably early 18th century. (Wallis & Wallis) £190

A good detached flintlock lock by Brooks, circa 1825 with patent enclosed pan, 4¾in. (Wallis & Wallis) £190

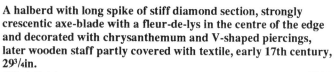

A halberd with long spike of stiff diamond section, strongly crescentic axe-blade with a fleur-de-lys in the centre of the edge and decorated with chrysanthemum and V-shaped piercings, later wooden staff partly covered with textile, early 17th century, 29³/₄in.
(Christie's) £805

A Swiss halberd with slender spike of stiff diamond section, crescent-shaped axe-blade pierced with three shaped radiating slots and with convex edge, wooden octagonal staff, late 17th century, probably Bern, 20¹/₄in. head.
(Christie's) £690

A Swiss halberd with waved spear-head shaped spike and turned mouldings at its base, the axe-head and fluke pierced with scrollwork, wooden staff (probably original) reinforced at the end with a ring and a short spike, late 17th century, probably Swiss, 22¹/₄in. head.
(Christie's) £977

A halberd, the axe-blade cusped at the back and pierced with a trefoil, flat beak-shaped fluke, cusped above and below and struck on one face with a mark, on original wooden staff, German or Swiss, early 16th century, 20in. head.
(Christie's) £977

A halberd with associated spear-head shaped spike, crescent axe-blade, the points of the crescents reinforced, with V- and cross-bottonée shaped piercings, and octagonal wooden staff, late 16th/early 17th century, 23³/₄in. head.
(Christie's) £483

A halberd, with very long tapering spike of stiff diamond section, flat crescentic axe-blade pierced with key-hole shaped holes, two long straps, and wooden staff, late 16th century, probably German or Swiss, 34in. head. £330

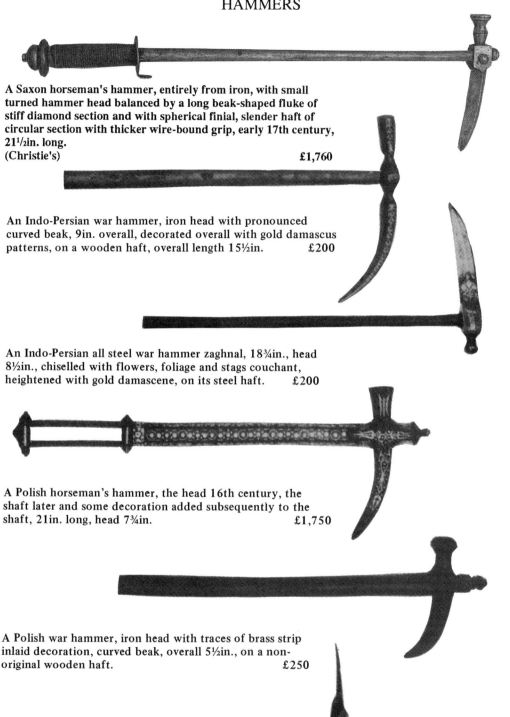

A Saxon horseman's hammer, entirely from iron, with small turned hammer head balanced by a long beak-shaped fluke of stiff diamond section and with spherical finial, slender haft of circular section with thicker wire-bound grip, early 17th century, 21½in. long.
(Christie's) £1,760

An Indo-Persian war hammer, iron head with pronounced curved beak, 9in. overall, decorated overall with gold damascus patterns, on a wooden haft, overall length 15½in. £200

An Indo-Persian all steel war hammer zaghnal, 18¾in., head 8½in., chiselled with flowers, foliage and stags couchant, heightened with gold damascene, on its steel haft. £200

A Polish horseman's hammer, the head 16th century, the shaft later and some decoration added subsequently to the shaft, 21in. long, head 7¾in. £1,750

A Polish war hammer, iron head with traces of brass strip inlaid decoration, curved beak, overall 5½in., on a non-original wooden haft. £250

A 16th century Lucerne hammer, tapering diamond section spike, 15in., long back beak, 4½in., of diamond section, spike head 3½in., long straps with domed studs. £650

HEADDRESS

BALL TOPPED HELMETS

A Victorian officer's blue cloth ball topped helmet of The R. Artillery, gilt mounts, velvet backed chinchain and ear rosettes.
(Wallis & Wallis) £210

An officer's blue cloth helmet of the Royal Army Medical Corps by J. B. Johnstone, Sackville Street London.
(Christie's) £187

A post-1902 officer's blue cloth ball-topped helmet of The Royal Army Medical Corps. (Wallis & Wallis) £180

A Volunteer Artillery Officer's blue cloth ball topped helmet, silver plated mounts. (Wallis & Wallis) £150

Blue cloth ball-topped helmet, silver mounts and badge with scarlet backing, bearing title 'First London Artillery Volunteers'. £800

A post 1902 RAMC Captain's uniform, comprising blue cloth ball topped helmet, shoulder belt and pouch; full dress blue tunic, mess jacket with matching dull cherry waistcoat and pair breeches.
(Wallis & Wallis) £600

BEARSKINS

A good officer's bearskin of the Irish Guards, St. Patrick's blue feather plume, velvet backed graduated link gilt chinchain.
(Wallis & Wallis) £415

An officer's bearskin cap of the Royal Welsh Fusiliers with fine white metal mounted gilt grenade. (Christie's) £260

5th (Northumberland Fusiliers): officer's bearskin cap with regimental gilt grenade, inside is marked H.W. Archer, Esq., 5th Fusiliers.
(Christie's) £385

A peaked burgonet, circa 1620, with high comb and hinged ear flaps embossed with rosettes, traces of later etched decoration overall, plume holder at base of comb. (Wallis & Wallis)   £850

An unusual French closed burgonet of bright steel, with tall two-piece fluted skull of conical form with prominent ogival comb, circa 1630, 19in. high.
(Christie's)   £7,475

A German burgonet of bright steel, the one-piece skull with prominent comb and fixed fall pierced for a nasal secured by a wing screw, late 16th century, 11in. high.
(Christie's)   £3,680

A close burgonet, the heavy two-piece rounded skull with low rolled-over comb with iron plume-pipe at the base containing an iron candlestick nozzle, circa 1630, probably Dutch, 15in. high.
(Christie's)   £1,320

A closed burgonet, the rounded two-piece skull joined along the low finely roped comb with a rolled overlap, early 17th century, probably French, 12in. high.
(Christie's)   £3,300

A burgonet, the two-piece skull with roped comb, riveted pointed fall, single riveted neck-plate and deep hinged cheek-pieces, painted inside *SO 87*, mid-17th century, German or Dutch, 10$^{1}/_{2}$in. high.
(Christie's)   £660

A German closed burgonet from a black and white armour (polished bright), comprising one-piece skull with prominent roped comb, mid-16th century, 10$^{1}/_{2}$in. high.
(Christie's S. Ken.)   £2,420

A closed cuirassier's Savoyard type burgonet with raised comb and pointed peak.
(Christie's)   £1,155

A rare French burgonet, of blackened steel, the robust two-piece skull with high roped comb, third quarter of the 16th century, 11$^{3}/_{4}$in. high.
(Christie's S. Ken.)   £4,180

BUSBIES

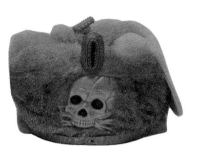

An Imperial German officer's busby of the 1st Leib Hussars, with applied silver skull and crossbones badge to the front. (Phillips London) £950

An Artillery officer's busby by Hawkes & Co., the metal case inscribed Earl of Chester's Rifles. £300

An Imperial German Hussar officer's busby of The 2nd Leib Hussar Regt. (Queen Victoria of Prussia). (Wallis & Wallis) £1,750

A good officers busby of the 15th (The King's) Hussars, scarlet bag with gilt braid trim and purl button. (Wallis & Wallis) £390

An officer's fur busby of The Royal Corps. of Signals, with leather lining. (Wallis & Wallis) £95

A good R.H.A. officers brown fur busby circa 1900, scarlet bag, 15in. white ostrich feather plume with white vulture feather base. (Wallis & Wallis) £210

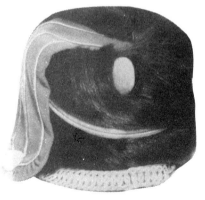

A good Royal Horse Artillery other rank's busby, scarlet cloth bag, yellow cords and acorns, white hair plume in flame socket.
(Wallis & Wallis) £125

An officer's fur busby of The 20th Hussars. (Wallis & Wallis) £340

An officer's busby of The Alexandra, Princess of Wales's Own Yorkshire Hussars. £500

BUSBIES

A good scarce post 1902 other rank's sealskin busby of the 8th Royal Rifles (Canadian Militia), black cord and plaited loop. (Wallis & Wallis) £70

A fine Imperial German officer's busby of the Leib Garde Hussar Regt., silvered Guard star badge plate with enamelled centre. (Wallis & Wallis) £700

A scarce 1902–8 other rank's grey cloth busby of the Queen's Westminster Rifle Volunteers, scarlet piping to top, grey cord and plaited loop trim. (Wallis & Wallis) £190

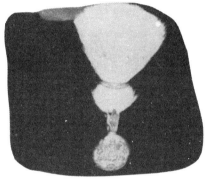

An officer's fur busby of the 19th (Queen Alexandra's Own) Royal Hussars, triple gilt cord, gilt gimp cockade, white busby bag with gilt braid trim and purl button. (Wallis & Wallis) £950

A good post 1902 Royal Artillery Officer's busby, scarlet bag, gilt grenade plume holder, white goatshair plume. (Wallis & Wallis) £130

A Rifles officer's Astrakhan busby, a tunic with scarlet facings and a composite pouch-belt with a whistle, chin-boss and badge. (Christie's) £240

An officer's busby of the Royal Gloucestershire Hussars circa 1880 by Hawkes, 14 Piccadilly with scarlet bag and with crimson and gold cord lines around busby. (Christie's) £462

A fine Imperial German officer's busby of the 17th (Brunswick) Hussars, bearskin covered body, silver plated skull and crossbones badge plate. (Wallis & Wallis) £950

An officer's busby of the Yorkshire Hussars by Hawkes, Piccadilly, embroidered with large Prince of Wales's plumes. (Christie's) £495

239

CLOSE HELMETS

A French close-helmet, the one-piece skull with high roped comb, brass plume holder, pointed visor with single vision slit, circa 1570, 12in. high.
(Christie's) £3,960

A Cuirassier's close helmet of light construction, the two-piece skull with low comb, the visor with small peak and attached bevor, 17th century.
(Phillips) £650

A cuirassier close-helmet, the rounded two-piece skull joined along the low comb with a rolled overlap, English or Dutch, circa 1630, 13in. high.
(Christie's) £2,640

A close-helmet, the rounded skull with low roped comb made in two pieces joined across the back of the neck, the main edges throughout bordered by pairs of engraved lines, English or Flemish, circa 1530–40, 13in.
(Christie's S. Ken) £2,860

A visored bascinet (Hounskull) in 14th century style, the one-piece skull drawn up to a point to the rear of centre and the edges bordered by holes for the lining and vervels for an aventail, 10¼in. high.
(Christie's S. Ken) £3,520

A German foot-combat close-helmet with one-piece skull with low file-roped comb, brass plume-holder, bluntly pointed visor and upper and lower bevors pivoted at the same points on either side, circa 1630, 12½in. high.
(Christie's) £6,600

A cuirassier helmet with rounded one-piece skull and low file-roped comb, domed steel lining rivets throughout, circa 1600, probably Italian, 11in. high.
(Christie's) £2,530

A composite German ('Maximilian') close helmet with one-piece globular fluted skull cut out at the back for one plain and two fluted neck-plates, early 16th century, 12in. high.
(Christie's) £3,740

A cuirassier helmet, of bright steel, with fluted ovoidal two-piece skull rising to a ring finial on star-shaped rosette, early 17th century, probably German, 12in. high.
(Christie's) £2,090

CLOSE HELMETS

A good early 17th century European Horseman's close helmet of 'Savoyard' type, skull with small raised comb, peaked hinged visor with pierced vent holes. £1,000

A cuirassier helmet, the rounded two-piece skull with piped comb, bevor and pointed fall, circa 1630, 13in. high. (Christie's) £3,450

A Civil War steel helmet, with peaked hinged visor applied with large brass rivets, a single ridge to the skull extending down to a single socket plume holder. (Spencer's) £820

A well made modern copy of an English close helmet from a Greenwich armour, of good form and weight. (Wallis & Wallis) £280

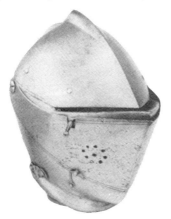

A close helmet for the tilt, the one-piece skull with low roped comb, two-piece visor with single sight aperture, possibly Italian, 16th century. (Phillips) £3,200

An interesting composite close helmet made up for the Pisan Bridge Festival, the skull from a very rare Milanese armet circa 1440-1450. (Wallis & Wallis) £1,500

A close-helmet with one-piece skull with high roped comb, pointed visor with single vision-slit and lifting peg, circa 1560, probably Italian, 11¾in. high. (Christie's) £8,250

An early 17th century European Horseman's close helmet of 'Savoyard' type, peaked hinged visor. £1,200

A 4-plate folding buff, top plate with roped border and pierced sights, circa 1600. £850

HELMETS

An officer's helmet of the Hertfordshire Yeomanry, silvered skull with gilt fittings, circa 1870. (Phillips London) £950

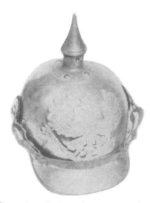

A Prussian Cuirassier trooper's helmet with grey metal helmet plate and spike. (Wallis & Wallis) £360

A Vic Officer's helmet of the Royal Horse Guards, plated brass skull, gilt peak binding. (Wallis & Wallis) £1,250

A post 1902 officer's silver plated helmet of The Life Guards, gilt peak bindings and ornaments, silver plated spike, gilt and silver plated helmet plate with good red and blue enamelled centre. (Wallis & Wallis) £1,350

A fine and rare Imperial German officer's helmet of the Saxon Guard Reiter Regiment, tombak skull with fine helmet plate of silvered rayed star.(Wallis & Wallis) £10,000

An OR's white metal helmet of the Royal Horse Guards, brass peak binding, ornaments, leather backed graduated link chinchain and ear rosettes, brass and white metal helmet plate. (Wallis & Wallis) £600

An Albert pattern officer's helmet of the 2nd Dragoon Guards, gilt brass skull and fittings, including front plate with *VR* cypher. (Phillips London) £700

A Prussian Mounted Rifles other ranks helmet, a wartime issue in grey metal, skull fitted with eagle plate, top spike, roundels, leather chinstrap, dated 1916. (Phillips) £360

A good other ranks helmet of the 1st Dragoon Guards, brass skull and fittings, brass and white metal helmet plate, red horse hair plume. (Phillips) £500

HELMETS

An Other Rank's brass 1871 pattern helmet of The 1st King's Dragoon Guards. (James Norwich Auctions) £325

A good Imperial German Cuirassier officer's helmet, gilt Line Eagle helmet plate and mounts. (Wallis & Wallis) £1,000

A post-1902 Royal Horse Guards Officer's helmet, silver plated skull with copper gilt plate applied with garter star in silver. (Phillips) £1,400

A French 3rd Republic Cuirassier officer's helmet, the silver plated skull with gilt fittings including front plate embossed with foliage and flaming grenade. (Phillips) £700

A very scarce Royal Artillery officers trial pattern dress helmet, c. 1850, German silver skull of unusual one piece form. (Wallis & Wallis) £850

An officer's 1817 pattern steel helmet of the Household Cavalry, brass binding to front and rear peaks, skull embellished with acanthus foliage. (Wallis & Wallis) £4,000

A post-1902 royal Horse Guards trooper's helmet, plated steel skull with brass plate applied with garter star, plume holder with red horsehair plume. (Phillips) £520

A rare Imperial German Garde du Corps Parade helmet, tombak skull with German silver mounts. (Wallis & Wallis) £5,800

An 1871 pattern officer's helmet of the 2nd Dragoon Guards, gilt brass skull, silver, gilt and enamel front plate, rosette bosses. (Phillips London) £850

HELMETS

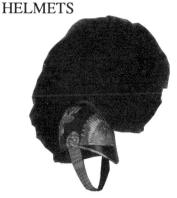

An 1818–34 officer's pattern helmet of the Royal Dragoons with black japanned skull of 'Roman' form decorated with gilt laurel leaf ornaments.
(Christie's) £4,400

A 19th century Austrian cavalry troopers black leather helmet, raised ribs to skull, black and white wool comb.
(Wallis & Wallis) £2,600

A trooper's brass 1843 pattern helmet of the 2nd The Queen's Dragoon Guards with ornate brass comb and mounted helmet plate.
(Christie's) £1,375

An officer's 1847 (Albert) pattern helmet of The 5th (Princess Charlotte of Wales's) Dragoon Guards, gilt skull with oak and acanthus ornaments and top mount.
(Wallis & Wallis) £1,000

An Austrian Dragoons officer's helmet circa 1860 of black finished metal with gilt ornaments including the front plate mounted with Franz-Josef I cypher.
(Christie's) £825

An Imperial Bavarian trooper's M 1842–79 helmet as worn by the Kurassier Regiment No. 2, steel skull, brass raised comb with black horsehair crest.
(Wallis & Wallis) £800

A Victorian black cloth plumed helmet of the 3rd Devon Light Horse, having Queens Crown badge with garter and oak leaf border.
(Bearne's) £1,300

An extremely fine 1843 pattern officer's helmet of the 3rd Dragoon Guards, plain burnished gilt skull, ornate rayed plate mounted with Royal Arms and the battle-honours.
(Christie's) £3,300

A trooper's helmet of French Cuirassiers circa 1870, steel skull with brass front plate and comb and ear bosses with slightly defective chin-chain.
(Christie's) £715

Coldstream Military Antiques

Fine 19th Century Head-dress and Badges of the British Army

Steven Bosley

POSTAL ADDRESS
55A High Street,
Marlow, Bucks.
SL7 1BA

LAPADA
MEMBER

Telephone
and
Facsimile
0628 822503

London And Provincial Antique Dealers Association

Valuations for Insurance and Probate

JAPANESE HELMETS

HEADDRESS

An 18-plate oboshi-hoshibachi, the rear plate signed Myochin Munenaga, 17th century. £1,750

An 18th/19th century Japanese folding helmet tatami, the bowl of 4 laced plates, red lacquered ensuite with 5 plate shikoro, retained by a wing nut on sprung steel top bar. £550

A black and gold lacquered jingasa decorated with a coiled dragon around a circular mon, gold lacquer interior, 14in. wide. (Christie's) £480

KABUTO

A kabuto, the fine russet-iron thirty-two plate sujibachi with a copper-gilt six-stage tehen-kanamono, the russet iron mabizashi and black-lacquered fukigaeshi, signed *Kayo*, 1770–1835.
(Christie's) £4,180

An unusual Hoshi-Bashi kabuto of conical form constructed of thirty-two plates each with ten upstanding rivets, late Momoyama or early Edo Period.
(Phillips) £6,800

A kabuto comprising a russet-iron thirty-two-plate sujibachi with iron mabizashi, copper-gilt five-stage tehen kanamono, the engraved bottom stage of yukimochi form, unsigned, 17th century.
(Christie's) £2,750

A 17th century kabuto with russet-iron hoshi-bachi, unsigned. (Christie's) £1,760

A 62-plate Japanese helmet, kabuto, signed Iye Mushi, with two feather gilt mon and printed doe skin cover-ing. £2,000

Early 19th century kabuto with a russet-iron sixty-two plate hoshi-bachi, rear plate signed Nagamichi. (Christie's) £1,760

KEPI

A Victorian officer's kepi style shako of The 1st Lanarkshire Rifle Vols., elcho grey cloth, blue piping, white and blue diced headband. £125

A scarce American Civil War Officers dark blue kepi, black lace edge trim and side welts. (Wallis & Wallis) £270

An officer's 'floppy' kepi in the American style, probably 3rd Norfolk Rifle Volunteers, grey cloth, with three narrow bands of red braid, leather peak. £125

A scarce American Civil War Union Cavalry O.R.'s kepi known as the 'Bummers Cap'. (Wallis & Wallis) £100

A French grey cloth kepi of the Swiss police, Bern maker's mark inside. £25

A late 19th century French officer's kepi of a 'General De Brigade', in its original wooden box. £185

KULAH KHUD

A good Indian kulah khud circa 1800, one piece bowl chiselled overall with flowering foliage having gold damascened borders, reserves and cartouches. (Wallis & Wallis) £800

A Persian chiselled and damascened steel kulah khud, the skull cut with twelve petal shaped panels and fitted with three plume holders, 19th century, 10in. high. (Christie's S. Ken) £3,520

A good attractive 19th century Persian Qjar helmet Kulah khud, steel bowl gold damascened overall with arabesques and 4 cartouches of inscription. (Wallis & Wallis) £650

LANCE CAPS

A fine Saxony officer's Tschapka, fine gilt rayed star badge plate with silvered state badge to centre. (Wallis & Wallis) £875

A Bavarian M.1915 Uhlan ORs Tschapska, grey painted helmet plate and mounts. (Wallis & Wallis) £180

A fine Prussian Uhlan officer's Tschapka with gilt Line eagle badge plate and black and white horsehair parade plume. (Wallis & Wallis) £675

An officer's lance-cap (chapka) of the Bedfordshire Yeomanry with patent leather body bearing ornamental gilt metal fittings including rosette with plain gilt half-ball button. (Christie's S. Ken) £2,860

A Prussian other rank's lance cap as worn by The 1st and 2nd Uhlan Regt. (Wallis & Wallis) £500

An Edward VII officer's lance-cap of The 5th (Royal Irish) Lancers, black patent leather skull, scarlet cloth top and sides. (Wallis & Wallis) £2,050

A fine Guard Uhlan officer's Tschapka (Lance Cap) fine silvered badge plate with enamelled centre to Guard Star. (Wallis & Wallis) £925

A scarce Imperial Prussian other rank's lance cap (Tschapka), silvered line eagle helmet plate, leather backed chinscales, leather lining. (Wallis & Wallis) £400

An Edward VII officer's lance-cap of the East Riding of Yorkshire Imperial Yeomanry, black patent leather skull and top. (Wallis & Wallis) £1,500

LANCE CAPS

An Edward VII officer's lance cap of The 12th (Prince of Wales's Royal) Lancers, with scarlet cloth sides and top. (Wallis & Wallis) £2,800

A Victorian officer's lance cap of the 16th (The Queen's) Lancers, black patent leather skull, blue cloth sides and top, embroidered peak, gilt lace trim and cords. (Wallis & Wallis) £1,400

A composite lance-cap (chapka) as for 16th Lancers with Q.V.C. white metal mounted gilt chapka-plate bearing honours to Aliwal and Sobraon. (Christie's S. Ken) £1,320

An extremely rare 1830–55 pattern Russian chapka of an officer of the 18th Serpoukhoff Regiment of Lancers with gilt numerals mounted on the white metal double-headed eagle plate. (Christie's S. Ken) £4,400

An Edward VII officer's lance-cap of The 12th (Prince of Wales's Royal) Lancers black patent leather skull and embroidered peak, gilt lace bands, scarlet cloth sides. (Wallis & Wallis) £2,000

A trooper's Victorian lance cap of the 9th (Queen's Royal) Lancers, of black patent leather with black/dark blue cloth sides. (Christie's S. Ken) £308

An officer's fine scarlet topped Victorian lance cap (chapka) of the 12th (Prince of Wales's Royal) Lancers, with scarlet feather plume with gilt socket. (Christie's S. Ken) £1,980

A Prussian NCO's lance cap of The 1st Guard Uhlan Regt. (Wallis & Wallis) £650

An officer's very rare lance-cap of the Bedfordshire Yeomanry with black cloth sides bearing ornamental gilt metal fittings. (Christie's) £3,300

LOBSTER TAIL HELMETS

A Cromwellian lobster tail helmet, ribbed skull with suspension loop, the peak with traces of armourer's mark and initial *F*, sliding nasal bar. (Wallis & Wallis) £650

A Cromwellian trooper's 'lobster tailed' helmet, two piece skull with low raised comb, pierced ear flaps, hinged visor with triple bar face guard. (Wallis & Wallis) £1,025

A Cromwellian period trooper's lobster tailed helmet "pot", one piece skull embossed with 6 radial flutes, small hanging ring finial. (Wallis & Wallis) £570

A lobster tailed pot, the one piece hemispherical ribbed skull with separate ring shaped finial, probably German, second quarter of the 17th century, 11in. high. (Christie's S. Ken) £605

An East European lobster-tailed pot (Zischägge) with one-piece fluted skull studded at the base of the flutes with brass rosettes and fitted at the rear with a brass plume-holder, third quarter of the 17th century, 12in. high. (Christie's S. Ken) £2,420

A Cromwellian trooper's lobster tail helmet, the skull formed in two halves with overlapping join, hinged peak stamped with initials *IH*. (Wallis & Wallis) £1,550

An East European lobster-tailed pot (Zischägge) with one-piece ribbed and fluted skull with separate ring-shaped finial on rosette-shaped washer, the peak formed as a separate piece, mid-17th century, 11½in. high. (Christie's) £1,650

An English lobster tailed Civil War period helmet, two piece siege weight skull, hinged visor with good quality triple bar face guard. (Wallis & Wallis) £900

A Cromwellian lobster tail steel helmet, the skull with six flutes, four piece articulated neck lames with large steel rivets. (Spencer's) £770

MORIONS

A good late 16th century Spanish morion, forged from one piece, of classic form with tall comb. (Wallis & Wallis) £900

A 17th century German black and white morion of Town Guard type, formed in two-pieces, plume holder. £500

A North Italian 'Spanish' morion, in one piece, with skull rising to a stalk, the base encircled by a row of brass lining rivets with rosette-shaped washers, late 16th century, 11¹/₂in. high. (Christie's) £5,280

A rare Saxon Electoral Guard comb-morion of one piece with roped comb and brim, the base of the skull encircled by sixteen gilt-brass lion-masks capping the lining rivets, struck on the brim with the Nuremberg mark, circa 1580, 11¹/₂in. high. (Christie's S. Ken) £8.800

An Italian 'Spanish Morion', of one piece, with tall pointed skull, etched throughout in the 'Pisan' manner with bands and borders of trophies, circa 1570, 10³/₄in. high. (Christie's S. Ken) £880

A Saxon Electoral Guard comb morion, of one piece, with roped comb and brim, the base of the skull encircled by sixteen gilt-brass lion-masks capping the lining rivets, the brim struck with the Nuremberg mark, circa 1580, 11³/₄in. high. (Christie's) £12,100

A good German late 16th century morion, made for a town guard, two piece skull with tall roped comb, turned over ribbed borders. (Wallis & Wallis) £550

An Italian 'Spanish morion' of one piece, with tall pointed skull surmounted by a stalk, encircled at the base by holes for lining rivets, circa 1580, 7¹/₂in. high. (Christie's) £1,100

A good morion circa 1580, formed in one piece, roped comb, retaining a few brass rosettes around base, roped edges. (Wallis & Wallis) £550

PEAKED CAPS

A Nazi army officer's peaked cap, white piping, metal badges, silver braided chin cords.
(Wallis & Wallis) £100

A good Victorian officer's blue cloth peaked forage cap of The Bedfordshire Regiment, black patent leather peak with gilt embroidery.
(Wallis & Wallis) £380

A World War I officer's khaki peaked SD cap of the 11th Hussars, 'floppy' top, blue headband, bronze badge.
(Wallis & Wallis) £40

An Imperial German officer's, Colonial Troops, tropical peaked cap with grey crown and blue cap band. £100

An officer's peaked cap of the Scots Guards, embroidered peak, red, white and blue silk headband, gilt and silver plated badge.
(Wallis & Wallis) £85

A Victorian officer's rifle green peaked drill cap of the 4th Berkshire Rifle Volunteers, embroidered badge, silver wire embroidered peak.
(Wallis & Wallis) £200

A scarce RAF officer's barathea SD cap of Air Rank, gilt bullion embroidery badge with gilt eagle, peak heavily gilt embroidered.
(Wallis & Wallis) £70

A post-1902 R.N. Flag officer's dark blue peaked cap. (Wallis & Wallis) £220

A scarce WWI R Naval Volunteers Captains uniform, comprising: peaked cap, 2 double breasted tunics and frock coat.
(Wallis & Wallis) £130

PICKELHAUBEN

A good Wurttemberg Reservist Artillery officer's Pickelhaube, gilt helmet plate, gilt leather backed chinscales and mounts. (Wallis & Wallis) £425

A good Imperial German Hesse Reservist Infantry officer's Pickelhaube, gilt helmet plate with Landwehr cross. (Wallis & Wallis) £700

A 1915 pattern infantryman's Pickelhaube of Mecklenburg Schwerin, as worn by the 1st or 3rd Battalions of the 89th Grenadier Regiment. (Wallis & Wallis) £290

A scarce Imperial German Saxony General officer's Pickelhaube gilt star helmet plate with superimposed silver star with gilt and enamelled centre. (Wallis & Wallis) £1,275

A fine and rare officer's Pickelhaube of the 1st Grand Ducal Hessian (Leibgarde) Infantry No. 115. (Wallis & Wallis) £2,500

A rare Imperial German officer's Pickelhaube as worn by the 1st and 2nd Battalion of the 92nd Brunswick Infantry Regiment, enamelled cross of the Order of Henry the Lion on breast. (Wallis & Wallis) £1,000

An Imperial German Prussian M 1897 Pickelhaube as worn by Guard Infantry or Railway Battalions, removeable spike and mounts. (Wallis & Wallis) £260

A fine Imperial German officer's Pickelhaube of the 109th Baden Leib Regiment. (Wallis & Wallis) £700

A Prussian infantryman's ersatz pressed tin Pickelhaube, brass helmet plate, spike and mounts, leather lining and chinstrap. (Wallis & Wallis) £260

PICKELHAUBEN

A Prussian M.1915 Ersatz (Pressed Felt) O.R's Pickelhaube of a Pioneer Battalion. (Wallis & Wallis) £140

A fine Prussian General Staff officer's Pickelhaube, silvered Guard helmet plate, with enamelled centre to Guard star. (Wallis & Wallis) £1,200

A fine Prussian Telegraph Company officer's Pickelhaube, fine gilt helmet plate of Line Eagle. (Wallis & Wallis) £350

A fine Prussian General officer's Pickelhaube, gilt Guard Eagle helmet plate with silver and enamelled Garde Star. (Wallis & Wallis) £950

A good, scarce 1842 pattern Prussian Reservist Infantry officer's Pickelhaube, gilt helmet plate with Landwehr cross. (Wallis & Wallis) £850

A fine Bavarian Chevauleger Reservist officer's Pickelhaube, fine gilt helmet plate, leather backed chinscales and mounts. (Wallis & Wallis) £550

A scarce Imperial German Wurttemburg General officer's Pickelhaube, gilt helmet plate with superimposed star and enamelled centre, gilt fluted spike. (Wallis & Wallis) £1,000

A Wurttemberg infantryman's ersatz (pressed tin) Pickelhaube gilt helmet plate, brass mounts with traces of gilt. (Wallis & Wallis) £230

An Imperial German Hesse Infantry officer's Pickelhaube gilt helmet plate, leather backed chinscales and mounts, fluted spike, both cockades, leather and silk lining. (Wallis & Wallis) £460

PICKELHAUBEN

A Prussian Infantryman's ersatz (pressed felt) Pickelhaube of The 87th Infantry Regt. (Wallis & Wallis)
£270

A Prussian Artillery officer's Pickelhaube of The 10th Field Artillery Regt. (Wallis & Wallis)
£310

A fine Imperial German officer's Pickelhaube of an Adjutant of the Lippe Detmold Infantry Regt. (Wallis & Wallis)
£1,700

A fine Baden Artillery officer's Pickelhaube, fine gilt helmet plate, leather backed chinscales and mounts. (Wallis & Wallis)
£675

A good Prussian military official's Pickelhaube, fine gilt Line Eagle helmet plate, gilt leather backed chinscales and mounts. (Wallis & Wallis)
£375

A fine Bavarian General's Pickelhaube, fine silvered helmet plate with enamelled state arms. (Wallis & Wallis)
£1,200

A fine officer's Pickelhaube of the Mecklenburg-Schwerin infantry with black parade plume on tall fluted stem, flat gilt chinscales with strap ends. (Christie's S. Ken)
£1,100

A fine Imperial German Reservist officer's Pickelhaube of the 2nd Battalion of the 96th Infantry Regt. (Wallis & Wallis)
£1,700

An Imperial German Infantry officer's Pickelhaube as worn by the 3rd Battalion of the 96th Infantry Regiment, brass helmet plate with German silver Schwarzburg arms. (Wallis & Wallis)
£510

255

PIKEMAN'S POTS

An English Civil War period pikeman's pot, two piece skull with raised comb, rivetted border.
(Wallis & Wallis)   £575

A 17th century pikeman's helmet "pot", two piece skull with shallow raised comb, turned over rivetted brim, deeply struck with I.R. armourer's mark.
(Wallis & Wallis)   £575

A mid 17th century pikeman's pot, the skull formed in two halves with raised comb and recessed border to brim.
(Wallis & Wallis)   £1,200

PILL BOX HATS

A scarce floppy pill box hat of the Eton Volunteer Rifle Corps, Elcho grey cloth, triple lace headband, leather chinstrap.
(Wallis & Wallis)   £100

An officer's pattern blue pillbox cap circa 1880 of the East Lothian Yeomanry Cavalry, and a scarlet jacket of the same.
(Christie's)   £220

A good officers pillbox hat of The royal Artillery, gilt lace and braided top ornament, in its tin case.
(Wallis & Wallis)   £135

SALLETS

A sallet of great weight, made from a single piece, the rounded skull with low keel-shaped comb pierced for a crest-holder, perhaps 15th century Italian, 9in. high.
(Christie's)   £3,300

A very rare Milanese sallet, of one piece, the rounded skull arched over the face, with low-keel-shaped comb, short pointed tail and narrow outward turn along the lower edge, late 15th century, 10³/₄in. high.
(Christie's)   £22,000

A German gothic sallet and bevor in late 15th century style, the sallet, of one piece, the bevor of two plates pivoted together.
(Christie's)   £4,600

SHAKOS

U.S. Army dress shako, circa 1850, complete with cockade and light infantry plate. (Butterfield & Butterfield) £809

An interesting Italian Marines shako, circa 1910, black cloth, leather top, headband and peak, red plaited loop and braid trim. (Wallis & Wallis) £130

An Imperial German Prussian Landwehr OR's shako (re issued M 1866 pattern) oval metal badge in state colours with Landwehr cross. (Wallis & Wallis) £190

An Imperial Austrian army officer's shako, gilt Imperial eagle helmet plate, bullion cockade with *FJI* cypher, bullion cloth band. (Wallis & Wallis) £110

An officer's shako, circa 1855, of the 10th (The Prince of Wales's Own Royal) Light Dragoons (Hussars), black velvet body, black patent leather front peak. (Wallis & Wallis) £1,700

A good 1869 pattern officer's blue cloth shako of the 2nd Royal Cheshire Militia, patent leather peak, silver braid trim, velvet backed silver plated chinchain. (Wallis & Wallis) £450

A scarce officer's shako, circa 1850, of the Royal Dock Yard Battalion, black felt sides and top, silver lace top band. (Wallis & Wallis) £550

An officer's 1869 pattern shako of The 15th (York East Riding) Regt., two narrow gilt lace bands to top, one to headband, velvet backed gilt chinchain and ear rosettes. (Wallis & Wallis) £390

A Nazi Police officer's shako with bullion cockade and silk and leather lining. £350

SHAKOS

A Victorian officer's shako of the 31st Regiment, blue cloth body with two gold lace bands to top. (Phillips London) £340

A good Prussian Reservist Jager officer's shako, gilt shako plate with Landwehr cross. (Wallis & Wallis) £400

An officer's 1869 pattern blue cloth shako of the Worcestershire Militia trimmed with silver lace. (Christie's S. Ken) £286

An officer's 1855 pattern shako bearing gilt plate of the 82nd Regiment with VR cypher on the gilt ball, upper lining missing. (Christie's) £400

A scarce Prussian foul weather shako circa 1840, black oil skin covered overall, state metal cockade, black cloth lining. (Wallis & Wallis) £150

A good Spanish Officers shako, fawn cloth, leather peak and headband, simulated leather top. (Wallis & Wallis) £210

A good Imperial German officer's shako of the 14th Jager Battalion, silvered state arms upon gilt rayed star shako plate. (Wallis & Wallis) £500

An Imperial Austrian army officers shako, black patent leather crown and peak, black cloth covered body with yellow cloth band, gilt brass Imperial eagle. (Wallis & Wallis) £190

An officer's very rare Waterloo pattern shako bearing the gilt plate of the Kent Militia and with crimson and gold plaited cord with tassels. (Christie's) £3,850

SHAKOS

A Nazi Police shako, field green cloth covered body, black fibre imitation leather crown, neck guard and peak, leather lining stamped 'Pol 1937'. (Wallis & Wallis) £145

A post-1902 officer's shako of The Highland Light Infantry. (Wallis & Wallis) £210

A good Imperial German officer's shako as worn by the Guard Jager and Guard Schutzen Battalions. (Wallis & Wallis) £850

A good Victorian Officer's 1855 (French) Pattern shako of The 4th West York Militia. black beaver body, leather top and peaks, in its tin case. (Wallis & Wallis) £690

A very rare Other Rank's red shako circa 1830 of the 15th Hussars of heavy construction entirely covered in red cloth trimmed with yellow worsted braid around top. (Christie's S. Ken) £990

A good officer's 1869 pattern shako of The 76th Regiment, blue cloth, gilt braid trim including 2 lines around the top, gilt mounts. (Wallis & Wallis) £500

An officer's Albert pattern shako of the 90th Regiment, rifle green felt skull with leather top and peaks, dark green ball tufts. (Phillips) £700

A French 2nd Empire other ranks leather shako of the 47th Regt, brass eagle helmet plate with stencilled "47" on the ball, red, white and blue tin rosette. (Wallis & Wallis) £330

A French Second Republic shako, with copper front plate, painted tricolour cockade, silver lace top band. (Phillips London) £260

HEADDRESS

An interesting Victorian officer's blue cloth spiked helmet of The Cheshire Regt., gilt mounts, velvet backed chinchain and ear rosettes. (Wallis & Wallis) £400

A Victorian officer's blue cloth spike helmet of The Bedfordshire Regt., gilt mounts, velvet backed chinchain and ear rosettes. (Wallis & Wallis) £340

An officer's Victorian blue cloth helmet of the Cheshire Regiment by Cater & Co., Pall Mall. (Christie's) £176

A scarce officer's 1878 pattern blue cloth spiked helmet of The 59th (2nd Nottingham-shire) Regiment. (Wallis & Wallis) £380

A very good post-1902 officer's blue cloth spiked helmet of The North Staffordshire Regiment, gilt mounts, velvet backed chinchain. (Wallis & Wallis) £470

A Victorian officer's blue cloth spiked helmet of the 5th Volunteer Battalion, The Royal Scots. (Wallis & Wallis) £625

A scarce officer's 1878 pattern blue cloth spiked helmet of The 108th (Madras Infantry) Regiment. (Wallis & Wallis) £320

A good Victorian officer's blue cloth spiked helmet of the 4th Volunteer Bn The Royal West Kent Regt, silver plated mounts. (Wallis & Wallis) £360

A very fine Victorian officer's blue cloth spiked helmet of the 1st Gloucester Volunteer Engineers, silver plated mounts. (Wallis & Wallis) £360

A Victorian officer's green cloth spiked helmet of The Prince Albert's (Somersetshire Light Infantry), gilt mounts and white leather backed chinchain and ear rosettes.
(Wallis & Wallis) £500

A post 1902 officer's blue cloth spike helmet of The Worcestershire Regt., gilt mounts, velvet backed chinchain and ear rosettes.
(Wallis & Wallis) £380

A post 1902 officer's full dress uniform of a Territorial Bn. The Queen's (R. West Surrey) Regt., comprising: blue cloth spiked helmet, scarlet tunic, and pair overalls.
(Wallis & Wallis) £360

A Victorian officer's green cloth spiked helmet of the 1st Fifeshire Rifle Volunteer Corps.
(Wallis & Wallis) £300

An officer's blue cloth spiked helmet of The Royal Warwickshire Regt. (Wallis & Wallis) £310

An officer's dark green cloth helmet with white metal plate of the Lanarkshire Rifle Volunteers. (Christie's)
£308

Helmet from the uniform of Col. Pilkington, 4th Vol. Bn. The King's Regt. (Wallis & Wallis) £800

A good Victorian officer's blue cloth spiked helmet of the 1st Volunteer Battalion The Bedfordshire Regiment, silver plated mounts.
(Wallis & Wallis) £525

A Victorian officer's blue cloth spiked helmet of the 3rd Lanarkshire Rifle Volunteers, silver plated mounts, leather backed chinchain and ear rosettes.
(Wallis & Wallis) £420

A Goto school kozuka, Edo period (circa 1600, attested to Goto Eijo by Goto Hojo, signed *Mon Eijo Mitsuaki* with kao, length 9.6cm.
(Christie's) £1,637

A Goto style kozuka, Edo period (circa 1750), inlaid in high relief with three fans, in gold, silver and shakudo, the frame made of wood with a strong red and black grain, length 9.7cm.
(Christie's) £205

A Hamano school style kozuka, Edo period (circa 1750), signed *Gyokuunsai*, carved and inlaid with Kwan Yu and his attendant who holds his halberd, width 1.4cm.
(Christie's) £546

An Edo Kinko kozuka, Edo period (circa 1850), the shibuichi plate carved with swirling water around rocks and fish in shakudo with gold accents, length 9.7cm.
(Christie's) £546

A Yokoya school kozuka, late Edo period (circa 1825), signed *Somin* with kao (Yokoya Somin III), the shakudo shishi in very high relief with traditional gold inlay spots, length 9.7cm.
(Christie's) £2,046

A Tanaka school kozuka, Edo period, dated *Ansei 6* (1859) *Nanro* (eighth month), signed Katsumi Tosai with kao, the polished shibuichi plate with a South Sea islander pulling a large coral log by a golden rope, length 9.7cm.
(Christie's) £375

An Uchida family kozuka, Edo period (circa 1750), signed *Uchida Masachika* with kao, the shibuichi plate carved in very high relief and decorated with a tiger in shibuichi with shakudo stripes, on a rocky promontory, length 9.8cm.
(Christie's) £648

An Edo Kinko kozuka, Edo period (circa 1800), the shakudo plate with a gold dragon entwined among the clouds, length 9.7cm.
(Christie's) £409

A Yokoya school kozuka, Edo period (circa 1825), signed *Somin* with kao, a shibuichi plate carved in brushstroke style (katakiribori) with a design of heron in a pine tree, length 9.6cm.
(Christie's) £239

A Hamano school kozuka, Edo period (circa 1800), signed *Hokusai Naoteru* with kao, carved in deep and high relief with a design of Endo Morito under the waterfall, width 1.5cm.
(Christie's) £887

A Hamano school kozuka, Edo period (circa 1850), signed *Mitsuyoshi* with kao, carved and inlaid with a design of a street performer and two children at play, width 1.4cm.
(Christie's) £682

An Edo Kinko kozuka, Edo period (circa 1800), the polished shibuichi plate carved in relief with a dragonfly on churning waves and water, length 9.6cm.
(Christie's) £307

An Edo Kinko kozuka, Edo period (circa 1800), the shakudo plate decorated with a large pine tree of copper, and a plum branch in shakudo with two silver blooms and a silver bud, length 9.6cm.
(Christie's) £443

A Tsuchiya style kozuka, Edo period (circa 1850), the copper plate mixed on the surface with gold to give the effect of water, with silver inlay moon and grasses carved in brushstroke style (katakiribori), length 9.7cm.
(Christie's) £579

A Kaga school kozuka, Edo period (circa 1800), inlaid with flush shakudo in a vine pattern with three sedge hats, width 1.4cm. (Christie's) £205

An Otsuki school kozuka, Edo period (circa 1800), signed *Motohiro* with kao, carved and inlaid with a shakudo bridge that has gold supports , length 9.7cm. (Christie's) £750

A Yanagawa school kozuka, Edo period (circa 1825), signed *Nakajima Haruhide* with kao, decorated with two tatebina dolls in relief of gold, silver and shakudo, length 9.7cm. (Christie's) £750

A Goto school kozuka, Muromachi period (circa 1550), inscribed *Mon Sojo Saku Teijo* with kao, with a shakudo design of shinto-miya objects in relief, width 1.3cm. (Christie's) £273

A Hamano school kozuka, Edo period (circa 1800), signed *Hamano Morihide*, the copper plate carved with the sage Shinno holding a gold plant stem in his mouth, width 1.5cm. (Christie's) £1,364

An Edo Kinko kozuka, Edo period (circa 1850), the polished copper plate with relief design of a large bottom fish in shibuichi and shakudo, near shakudo rocks and gold seaweed, length 9.9cm. (Christie's) £327

An Iwamoto school kozuka, Edo period (circa 1700), carved in very high relief with a copper crayfish and several copper lines representing water, the eyes inlaid in shakudo, length 9.6cm. (Christie's) £443

An Edo Kinko kozuka, Edo period, dated *Manen Kanoe Saru Naka Aki* (mid autumn 1860), the copper plate carved with a figure of Hotei, length 9.7cm. (Christie's) £1,637

A Mito school kozuka, Edo period (circa 1750), decorated in high relief with the theme of Aritoshi Myojin, inlaid in shakudo, gold, silver and shibuichi, length 9.8cm. (Christie's) £546

A Yokoya school kozuka, Edo period (circa 1825), signed *Somin* with kao, the plate of polished copper with the head and arm of the Daruma inlaid in relief, height 9.7cm. (Christie's) £2,182

A Mito style kozuka, Edo period (circa 1750), signed *Kenseido Katsutoshi Koku* (Horo), decorated in high relief with the theme of Aritoshi Myojin, inlaid in shakudo, gold, silver and shibuichi, length 9.8cm. (Christie's) £1,227

An Omori school kozuka, Edo period (circa 1775), signed *Tekkosai Morita Terutoshi* with kao, carved and inlaid with a silver stream and gold plants, with silver moon behind nanako clouds, length 9.7cm. (Christie's) £511

An Edo Kinko kozuka, Edo period (circa 1850), the polished shibuichi plate carved and inlaid with a landscape design of rocky pine-covered island and two men in a boat in shakudo, gold, silver and copper, length 9.7cm. (Christie's) £750

An Omori school kozuka, Edo period (circa 1800), inscribed *Omori Eishu* (Teruhide) with kao, deeply cut with crashing waves and two fish, one in copper and the other in shakudo, with a shakudo octopus between them, length 9.7cm. (Christie's) £546

A Waki Goto kogai, Edo period (circa 1700), of shakudo plate with nanako ground and low relief design of a gold dragon among shakudo clouds.
(Christie's) £286

A Goto school kogai and kozuka, Edo period (circa 1650), attested to Goto Teijo by Goto Hojo (Mitsuaki), decorated with swallows in bamboo branches, kogai, length 21.0cm., kozuka, length 9.7cm.
(Christie's) £8,184

A Goto school mitokoromono, early Edo period (circa 1625), attested to Goto Sokujo by Goto Keijo, the kogai with two figures in gold from the No drama Yuya, on a 'cod roe' pattern ground, the gold grips (menuki) with a scene from a No drama, kogai: length 21.2cm.
(Christie's) £8,316

A Waki Goto kogai, Edo period (circa 1650), decorated with a large radish (daikon), the leaves in shakudo and gold and the radish in silver, length 21cm.
(Christie's) £286

A Yanagawa school kogai and kozuka, Edo period (circa 1775), both pieces signed *Yanagawa Naomitsu* with kao, the kogai decorated with a gold shishi with a peony branch in its mouth, the kozuka decorated with a mother shishi with a peony branch in her mouth and a young shishi playing near the mouth end of the kozuka, kogai length 21.4cm.
(Christie's) £4,092

A Goto school mitokoromono, early Edo period (circa 1675), attested to Goto Renjo by Goto Hojo, with unusual design of uprooted young pine, representing a New Year's court tradition dating back to the Heian period, kogai: length 21.3cm., kozuka: length 9.7cm.
(Christie's) £6,583

A mace, the head with eight lobed-shaped flanges each pierced with seven circular holes, octagonal haft with bulbous capital and central and basal moulding brass and iron wire-bound grip, 16th century, 23¹/₄in. long.
(Christie's)   £1,100

A Polish or Hungarian mace (buzdygan), the iron head with six flanges and long tubular socket, brass haft ribbed longitudinally, the head 17th century, 24in.
(Christie's)   £8,250

An impressive embossed and chased brass Indo Persian ceremonial mace, 28in. overall, lion's head pommel embossed with finely stylised features and applied glass eyes.
(Wallis & Wallis)   £200

A German mace, with dolphin-shaped flanges each with small lug at the bottom inlaid with circular copper dots, button finial, and three-stage tubular haft, mid-16th century, 22in.
(Christie's)   £2,990

A very rare German combined four-barrelled matchlock gun, mace and spear with wooden cylindrical head stained black and containing four iron barrels, bound on the outside with three iron bands, circa 1600, 34in. long.
(Christie's)   £5,500

A German mace, entirely of iron, the head with six pierced pointed flanges (finial missing), tubular haft lined with wood, the handle indicated by upper and lower mouldings, mid-16th century, 21¹/₂in.
(Christie's)   £2,415

Saxony: Order of Albert the Valorous, 1st class knight's cross with swords, in silver gilt and enamels, marked on edges of cross *Sharpenberg Dresden.* (Wallis & Wallis) £90

Four: MC, Geo V issue, BWM, Victory with MID leaf (A. Major R.E. Heaslip); Colonial Auxiliary Forces Decoration (reverse crown engraved *Lt Col R.E. Heaslip, MC, Hald Rif*). (Wallis & Wallis) £430

B.E.M. military, George VI issue for Meritorious service (Aus 20750 Cpl Alfred Edward Woodnutt, R.A.A.F). (Wallis & Wallis) £290

South Atlantic Medal 1982 "with rosette", and 2 additional rosettes (Sailor Wong Tam Yuen RFA Sir Galahad). (Wallis & Wallis) £210

Six medals, Order of St John officers (Brothers) badge, BWM, Victory, Defence, Coronation 1911, St John service medal with 7 additional bars (50 years service). (Wallis & Wallis) £75

Q.S.A. 4 bars C.c., Wepener, Trans, Witte. (3408 Pte E A Hulseberg Cape M.R.), and details of the siege of Wepener are included. (Wallis & Wallis) £215

Indian Mutiny 1857–58, no bar (John Ashworth, 53rd Regt). (Wallis & Wallis) £100

Five: D.F.M. George VI, 1939–45 star, Air Crew Europe star, Defence, War (1311804 Sgt W.C. White R.A.F). (Wallis & Wallis) £460

East and West Africa Medal 1887, 4 bars 1887–8, 1892, 1893–94, Sierra Leone 1898–99 (2739 Pte N Waddle 1/W.I. Rgt). (Wallis & Wallis) £140

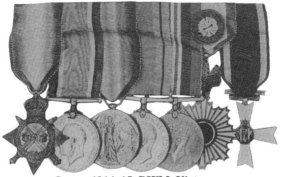

An interesting silver Fire Brigade medal, obverse fireman's helmet over crossed axes above "Valour" and motorised appliance. (Wallis & Wallis) £55

Seven: 1914–15, BWM, Victory, Defence, War, Japan Order of the Rising Sun (4th Class), Norway Freedom Cross, (1st 3 only named, Lt Commr and Commr R.D.F. Forbes RN). (Wallis & Wallis) £410

Order of St John: Life Saving medal, 2nd type, in silver with black watered ribbon 1¹/₂in. wide (pre 1950 issue). (Wallis & Wallis) £115

German group of eleven, Prussia, Iron Cross, 1914, Bavaria, Order of Military Merit, Germany, Cross of Honour, Bavaria, Army Jubilee Medal, 1905, Third Reich, Armed Forces L.S. Decoration, Third Reich, Armed Forces L.S. Medal, Saxony, Military Cross of Merit, 1915, Austria, Order of the Iron Crown, Austria, Military Merit Cross, Hungary, War Medal, 1914–18, Bulgaria, Order of Military Merit. (Spink) £550

Natal Medal, with bar 1906, (Tpr C E Duncan, Zululand Mtd Rifles). (Wallis & Wallis) £85

Four: D.C.M. George V military bust, 1914–15 star, BWM, Victory with MID (2076 Pte D Cresty 1/7 Lanc Fus T.F.). (Wallis & Wallis) £260

South Africa 1853 (impressed Chas Hogg 74th Regt). (Wallis & Wallis) £145

267

MEDALS

Pair: South Africa 1877-9, bar 1879; I.G.S. 1854, 1 bar Burma 1885-7, (981 Pte A. McCulloch, 2-21st Foot). (Wallis & Wallis).   £135

Four: Military Medal George VI first type (2031262 Spr I. Stokes, R.E.), 1939-45 star, Defence and War, VF London Gazette 27.8.1940. (Wallis & Wallis)   £200

Seven: Queen's Sudan, Q.S.A. 6 bars Bel, Mod. River, Paarde, Drief, O.F.S, Trans; K.S.A. both date bars; 1914-15 star trio; Khedive's Sudan 1 bar Khartoum, (3988 Pte H. Miller North'd Fus, WWI as 12381 Pte H. Miller Leic R), VF (some Q.S.A. rivets replaced) together with a civic "Victory" medal of Loughborough, un-named. (Wallis & Wallis)   £140

Punjab medal 1849, 2 bars Chilianwala, Goojerat (Richard Calcutt 9th Lancers). (Wallis & Wallis)   £160

M.G.S. 1793, 5 bars Vittoria, Pyr., Nive, Orthes, Toulouse (J. Taylor, R. Arty Drivers). (Wallis & Wallis)   £160

Group of six to Wing Commander O.C. Cassels, R.A.F.V.R., comprising O.B.E. 2nd type military; D.F.C. George V issue; B.W.M. and Victory (Lieut. R.A.F.); Defence and War. (Wallis & Wallis)   £550

Four: Crimea, 1 bar Sebastopol; Indian Mutiny 2 bars Relief of Lucknow, Lucknow; I.G.S. 1854, 1 bar Umbeyla; Turkish Crimea British issue. (Wallis & Wallis) £210

Pair: Egypt 1882, 3 bars Alexandria 11th July, Suakin 1885, Tofrek; Khedive's star 1882 (A. Carter, Pte R. M. H.M.S. Penelope). (Wallis & Wallis) £120

I.G.S. 1854, 1 bar Umbeyla, (Lieut. E. C. Davidson, 71st Highlrs), VF, with Hunt and Roskill suspender; and a miniature I.G.S. 1854 without bar. (Wallis & Wallis) £140

Group of eleven to Lt. Col. C.G.R. Sydney-Turner, R.A.S.C., comprising D.S.O. George V issue; O.B.E. military first type; Order of St John of Jerusalem Serving Brother badge of skeleton (WWII) issue; Mons Star (Capt), B.W.M., Victory with M.I.D. (both Lt. Col.); Defence; France, Legion of Honour 4th class (1916); Italy Order of the Crown 4th class, (1919); Belgium Order of the Crown 4th class, (1916); Belgium Croix de Guerre. (Wallis & Wallis) £575

Five: Egypt 1882 no bar, (22978 Corpl T. Munro 4/1st Lon Div R.A.) NVF pitted; B.W.M. and Victory (Major T. Munro), Coronation 1911 (engraved Major T. Munro RA); Khedive's Star 1882 (engraved Corpl Munro 4/1 L.D. R.A.)(Wallis & Wallis) £65

South Africa 1877-79, with bar 1877-8-9 (1445 Pte C. Bryson, 90th Foot). (Wallis & Wallis) £90

Pair; China 1900 no bar (Pte W Burns, Shanghai Vols); Shanghai Volunteer Corps Long Service medal.
(Wallis & Wallis) £310

Group of three: Queen's Sudan (3736 Pte C. Rose 21/L/cers); Imperial Service Medal; Khedive's Sudan, 1 bar Khartoum.
(Wallis & Wallis) £775

Pair: Arctic Medal 1818-1855 (engraved Henry P Bance Assistance), Baltic medal (unnamed, suspender reaffixed to Baltic), with extensive research material.
(Wallis & Wallis) £320

Six: BWM, Victory (Lieut G. L. Lushington), Defence and War, Efficiency Decoration George V issue with bar Ceylon sewn to riband, reverse engraved "Capt G. L. Lushington C.P.R.C." Colonial Auxiliary Forces LS medal, George V military bust.
(Wallis & Wallis) £300

The King's Police Medal, Geo V issue, (Edward Victor Collins, Commr of Police, Gold Coast).
(Wallis & Wallis) £155

Pair: M.V.O. 4th Class, Territorial Decoration Geo V issue (reverse engraved Lieut Col Donald A Matheson T.D.)
(Wallis & Wallis) £155

Pair: The Hong Kong Plague medal 1894, silver issue, Queen Victoria Diamond Jubilee medal 1897.
(Wallis & Wallis) £775

Pair: Indian Mutiny, 2 bars Defence of Lucknow, Lucknow; Army LS & GC Victorian issue with scroll suspender. (Wallis & Wallis) £320

Pair: Transport medal, no bar (E. Drakeford); Mercantile Marine (Ernest E Drakeford). (Wallis & Wallis) £150

Four: D.C.M. Geo V military bust second type, MM Geo V military bust, BWM and Victory, D.C.M. London Gazette 16.1.1919. (Wallis & Wallis) £430

Pair: Indian Mutiny, bar Central India, (I, Merrill 14th Lgt Drgns); Army LS & GC, Vic issue. (Wallis & Wallis) £210

Army of India medal, 1 bar Nepaul (engraved Lieut. H. F. Caley 1st Grenr. Bn). (Wallis & Wallis) £420

Group of Five to Lt. Col. N. Coates, Welsh Regiment, comprising Military Cross George V issue; 1914-15 star (Lieut.); B.W.M. and Victory with M.I.D. emblem (Lt. Col.); mounted as worn; Imperial Russian Order of St. Anne, 2nd class neck badge with swords, in gilt and enamels (50mm). (Wallis & Wallis) £575

Military Medal, George VI first issue, (2716717 L. Sjt E. Walsh, Ir. Gds), GEF, in original card carton dated 31.8.44. (Wallis & Wallis) £500

Three: D.C.M., Vic issue (Colour Sergt S. Smith, 90th Foot), South Africa 1877–9 with bar, Army L.S. & G.C., D.C.M. 1878 for operations against the Gaikas. (Wallis & Wallis) £2,900

Iraq, Order of the Hashemites Grand Cross set by Garrard & Co. Ltd. consisting of a breast star 111mm. diameter, in silver, gold and enamel. (Spink) £1,400

An interesting Volunteer medal, enamelled in four colours with oval bearing *To perpetuate the memory of Wm Morris as a Voluntary Defender of his Country 1803.*
(Wallis & Wallis) £80

Pair of Colour Sergt. John Burgess 97th Foot (later 2nd Batt. R. West Kents), Distinguished Conduct Medal, Crimea, 1 bar Sebastopol.
(James Norwich Auctions) £360

A gold medal by Wyon, obverse uniformed bust right with legend *Labore Et Constantia,* reverse view of building, legend *Opened 1 March 1836, La Martiniere Prize Medal.*
(Wallis & Wallis) £100

D.S.O., George VI issue, 1938–48 type, reverse of suspender bar engraved *1944*, in its Garrard's case of issue.
(Wallis & Wallis) £420

Four medals: South Africa 1877–79, bar 1879, Egypt 1882, China 1900 no bar, Khedives Star 1882.
(Wallis & Wallis) £525

Kaiser-i-Hind medal, George V 2nd solid issue, in its Calcutta Mint case.
(Wallis & Wallis) £105

A Nazi War Order of the German Cross in silver.
(Wallis & Wallis) £260

Pair: G.S.M. 1962, 1 bar N. Ireland, South Atlantic medal with rosette, together with an H.M.S. Ambuscade cap tally.
(Wallis & Wallis) £170

Venezuelan silver and blue enamel pin in star form, central medallion depicting Simon Bolivar, the liberator, 3in. long.
(Eldred's) £140

A silver medal from HRH Albert Edward, Prince of Wales's Visit to India 1875–6, crowned oval medallion. (Wallis & Wallis) £160

Three: Crimea 3 bars Alma, Bal, Seb; Indian Mutiny 1 bar Lucknow; Turkish Crimea Sardinian issue. (Wallis & Wallis) £360

Canadian General Service medal, 1 bar Fenian Raid 1866 (impressed upper and lower case Pte W. Armstrong 13th Bn). (Wallis & Wallis) £80

Waterloo medal 1815, (William McCoane, 2nd Bn 73rd Regt Foot). (Wallis & Wallis) £290

Four: M.C. Geo V (reverse engraved Lieut F.W. Rivett R.G.A. 3.6.19), Mons Star, BWM, Victory. (Wallis & Wallis) £190

Military General Service medal 1793, 5 bars Pyrenees, Nivelle, Nive, Orthes, Toulouse. (Wallis & Wallis) £310

A fine and attractive 15ct. gold medal, obverse *Sigillum Commne Burgi de Lewys*, enamelled with the town crest of Lewes, Sussex. (Wallis & Wallis) £200

Pair of F. Frost, 9th Lancers: Punjab 2 bars; Indian Mutiny, 3 bars. (James Norwich Auctions) £380

African Chiefs Badge of Honour, a circular silver badge, 77mm. diameter, bearing the crowned bust of George V, surrounded by the legend *GEORGE V REX ET IMP.* (Spink) £400

A post 1902 heavy gilt crown Household Cavalry standard top, 4¹/₄in., with base screw stud.
(Wallis & Wallis) £60

A late 18th century model of a bronze barrelled field gun, 21in. overall, bronze barrel 9in. with turned reinforces, swollen muzzle and cascabel.
(Wallis & Wallis) £370

Civil War Ketcham hand grenade, marked *Patented Aug. 20, 1861*, mounted on a wood plaque.
(Butterfield & Butterfield) £294

A German cartridge-holder, comprising wooden body drilled for five cartridges and inlaid on either side, blackened iron frame with bright lines, circa 1570, 4¹/₄in. high.
(Christie's) £977

The embroidered devices from an early Victorian Household Cavalry trumpet banner, double sided, laid down on pink damask, with original gilt cords and tassels, 26 x 24in.
(Wallis & Wallis) £35

A massive brass shell case, 16 x 31in., engraved *Jokobynessen Battery (Deutschland)* headstamped *Polte Magdeburg X–17–1679*.
(Wallis & Wallis) £210

A leather, brass & steel MacArthur & Prain 1905 patent 'Gannochy rapid load' cartridge-dispenser, for one hundred 12-bore cartridges.
(Christie's) £418

A silver bugle of the London Rifle Brigade, engraved with Regimental Badge, and, around the mouth, *Presented by Captain G. R. Reeve, M.C., and Lieutenant R. R. Reeve 6th May 1935*.
(Wallis & Wallis) £400

A rare Accles Positive feed magazine, for the Model 1883 Gatling gun, the hollow drum with internal spiral guides and rotating cartridge propeller.
(Christie's) £632

A massive brass shell case, 48in. in length, engraved *Knocke Battery (Kaiser Wilhelm II)* on wooden stand.
(Wallis & Wallis) £360

A good .56in. Colt bullet mould for the percussion revolving rifle, 8in., for ball and bullet, body stamped *.56 S*, cut off stamped *Colts Patent*.
(Wallis & Wallis) £150

A scarce Victorian embroidered buff silk pipe banner of the 1st Bn The Seaforth Highlanders, gilt tasselled border.
(Wallis & Wallis) £300

A remarkable 1890 halfpenny coin, the obverse stamped *Oakley*, the edge deformed by shot or bullet strike.
(Christie's) £1,380

An Imperial Chemical Industries Eley & Kynoch cartridge-board with metallic and paper dummy-cartridges and components arranged radially around an *I.C.I* medallion, 31 x 25in. overall.
(Christie's) £1,320

An interesting 18th century turned wood ramrod head, for a 32pr gun, diameter 6in., stamped on rear flat *32*.
(Wallis & Wallis) £115

A large, well produced Italian Fascist Party calendar for 1933 bearing a portrait of Mussolini, in unused state.
(Wallis & Wallis) £135

A rare Imperial German Leib Gendarmerie helmet Parade Eagle, gilt finish, screw-nut attachment, 7in. high.
(Wallis & Wallis) £650

An interesting 18th century gunpowder barrel, height 21in., diameter 18in., bound with four copper bands and remains of split willow binding.
(Wallis & Wallis) £50

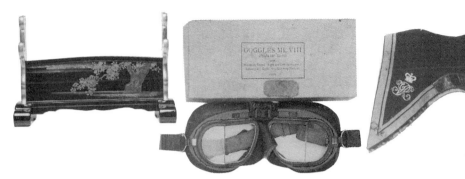

A lacquer katana stand for a daisho, Meiji period (circa 1900), raised on two rolled feet, and decorated with gilt lacquer on the leading edges of the supports, width 59cm.
(Christie's) £2,633

A pair of R.A.F. goggles, Mk. VIII, with spare reflective pattern lenses, dated *1940*, in their original cardboard carton.
(Wallis & Wallis) £70

The shabraque of an officer of the Long Melford Troop of the Suffolk Yeomanry Cavalry of dark blue cloth with scarlet cloth borders.
(Christie's) £660

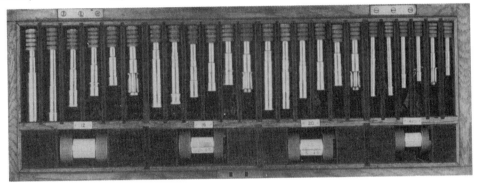

A rare set of gunmaker's master pattern chamber-gauges, for $2^9/_{16}$in. chambers, 28 gauges in total, possibly made by Charles Osborne & Co., in their oak velvet-lined and fitted case.
(Christie's) £715

A miniature armour in the Maximilian style, the helmet with one-piece fluted skull and bellows visor, mounted on a wood stand, 68cm. high, 19th century. (Phillips) £1,250

A good pair of officer's gilt chain link shoulder scales of the East Lothian Yeomanry, on scarlet cloth with gilt embroidered edging.
(Wallis & Wallis) £50

A lacquer tachi stand, Meiji period (late 19th century), on a rectangular base with indented corners, fitted with shaped neck terminating in a leaf-form upper support, 62.5cm. high.
(Christie's) £2,911

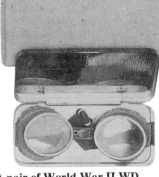

A lacquer katana stand, Meiji period (late 19th century), raised on two rolled feet and fitted with three vertical supports and a cross-bar, width 66.3cm.
(Christie's) £3,326

A pair of World War II WD dispatch rider's goggles in original issue packet and tin dated *1944*.
(Wallis & Wallis) £30

A large heavy dark green velour table cover 64 x 68in., bearing the richly embroidered ornaments from one side of an officer's shabraque of the 14th Light Dragoons.
(Christie's) £308

A good 18 cavity brass gang mould c. 1800 for casting graduated balls from 120 bore to 12 bore.
(Wallis & Wallis) £75

A well made 19th century miniature copy of a full suit of 16th century Maximilian armour, comprising fluted breast and backplate, helmet with fluted and pierced visor, overall height 23in.
(Wallis & Wallis) £1,150

A rare World War I R.A.F. part chamois lined leather enclosed flying helmet, original printed linen label *Adastra. Supplied by Geo. H. Leavey 1918*.
(Wallis & Wallis) £120

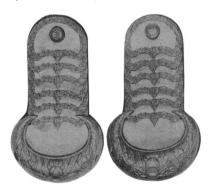

A pair of pre 1855 officer's gilt shoulder scales of the Bengal Artillery, padded scarlet cloth backing and original lace ties.
(Wallis & Wallis) £160

An officer's full dress waistbelt of the 6th (Inniskilling) Dragoons, gilt regimental lace on red morocco.
(Wallis & Wallis) £150

A pair of officer's gilt greatcoat shoulder scales of The Royal Regt of Artillery 1840–55, bearing silver plated crown/ Bath star/badge.
(Wallis & Wallis) £260

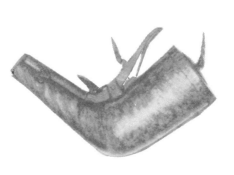

A 17th century Continental flattened cow horn powder flask for a wheel-lock rifle, 11¼in., with shaped brass aprons. (Wallis & Wallis) £250

A 17th/18th century Persian Circassian walnut powder flask, 6in., sprung steel lever charger with shaped top. £350

A horn powder flask of flattened form, the body engraved with flowers and geometric patterns, 29.5cm. overall, 17th century. (Phillips) £320

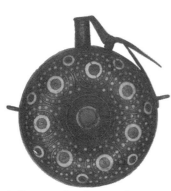

A German circular powder-flask, of wood with a horn-lined hole in the centre, iron nozzle and tap, and two rings for suspension, 17th century, 5½in. (Christie's) £1,092

A triangular musketeer's powder-flask with cloth-covered wooden body mounted in iron, the back with a pierced design, late 16th/early 17th century, probably German, 10in. high. (Christie's) £1,265

A German circular powder-flask with turned wooden body encircled by a thin steel band carrying the nozzle, late 17th century, 5¾in. diameter. (Christie's) £825

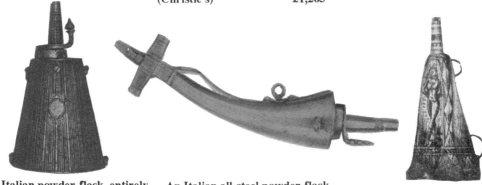

An Italian powder-flask, entirely of steel, with fluted triangular body of plano-convex section engraved with bands of running foliage, 17th century, 7¾in. high. (Christie's) £632

An Italian all-steel powder-flask of curved faceted conical form with tapering two-stage nozzle octagonal at the base, curved into belt hook, early 17th century, 9¾in. long. (Christie's) £715

An engraved bone Continental powder flask, circa 1600, 6¾in. tall. £400

17TH CENTURY

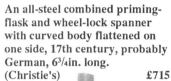

A 17th century Italian fluted steel powder flask, 7in. over-all. £500

An all-steel combined priming-flask and wheel-lock spanner with curved body flattened on one side, 17th century, probably German, 6³/₄in. long. (Christie's) £715

A 17th century Italian brass mounted steel powder flask, 7in. overall, with belt hook. £500

A German powder-flask in the manner of Johann Michael Maucher of Schwäbish-Gmünd, carved in high relief with two hounds attacking a boar, late 17th century, 4¹/₄in. diameter. (Christie's) £8,800

A 17th century staghorn powder flask, 8in., body engraved with a man and woman standing together in contemporary costume. (Wallis & Wallis) £400

A German circular powder-flask in the manner of Hans Schmidt of Ferlach, with turned rootwood body inlaid on the front with scenes of the chase in engraved silver sheet, third quarter of the 17th century, 5¹/₂in. diameter. (Christie's) £4,620

A German staghorn powder-flask with forked body of natural horn, the outer-face carved in low relief with the Temptation of Adam and Eve, 7³/₄in. (Christie's S. Ken) £715

A German powder-flask of flattened cow-horn incised on the front with three figures in a procession, and on the back with patterns of concentric circles and semi-circles, early 17th century, 12¹/₄in. (Christie's) £462

A German combined powder-flask, wheel-lock spanner and turnscrew, with tapering reeded horn body of circular section with wooden base-plate, second half of the 17th century, 8¹/₄in. (Christie's) £550

18TH CENTURY

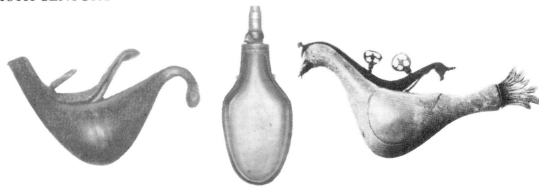

An 18th century Persian all steel powder flask, of swollen boat or swan form. £100

A late 18th century pressed lant-horn powder flask, 7½in., two piece translucent body with ribbed brass edges. (Wallis & Wallis) £105

An 18th century Persian priming powder flask, 5in. overall. £800

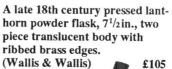

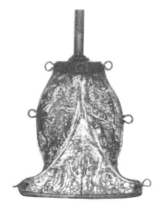

An 18th century staghorn powder flask, 7½in. overall, with small down turned nozzle and iron hanging loops. (Wallis & Wallis) £30

A Continental silver-mounted priming-flask, with brass mounts, and four rings for suspension, early 18th century, possibly Dutch, 4¼in. long. (Christie's) £660

An 18th century engraved bone powder flask, 8¼in. overall, with six hanging rings. (Wallis & Wallis) £105

An early 18th century Arab silver mounted powder flask Barutdan, 8in., of iron in coiled horn form. £100

A Spanish 18th century powder flask, made from a section of Ibex or similar horn, 10½in. overall. (Wallis & Wallis) £80

An 18th century staghorn powder flask, 10½in. overall, with two horn hanging loops. (Wallis & Wallis) £125

An engraved map powderhorn, inscribed and dated *Joseph Clayton, 1761*, decorated with British arms above the inscription *New Yorke*, 11³/₄in. long.
(Christie's) £2,957

A scarce 18th century Persian silver mounted brass powder flask of swollen form, 5½in., engraved overall with flowers and foliage. (Wallis & Wallis) £160

An interesting American powder horn inscribed with scrimshaw work depicting an Indian hunting an officer on horseback, inscribed *Made in Hez'ah, Calvin Aitchpillake AD 1785*, 12½in. wide.
(Bearne's) £2,700

A brass mounted circular Scandinavian flask, dated 1787, 3¾in. diameter, body of 'bird's eye' maple, central bosses engraved 1787 within foliage. £300

An 18th century staghorn powder flask, 9in. overall, wooden charger and iron hanging loops. (Wallis & Wallis) £80

A late 18th century European horn bodied common topped gun sized powder flask, brass adjustable charger. £50

An eastern European powderflask with forked body of natural staghorn, the outer side engraved with geometric designs, Carpathian Basin, 18th century, 13¼in.
(Christie's) £920

An early 18th century Scandinavian carved powder horn, 8½in. overall.
(Wallis & Wallis) £590

A good 18th/19th century Transylvanian stag horn powder flask, 6in. decorated overall with geometric devices.
(Wallis & Wallis) £100

19TH CENTURY

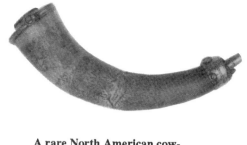

A rare shaped copper powder flask circa 1800, 6¹/₂in., body of flattened waisted form with flat bottom, ribbed top with common charger and fixed nozzle.
(Wallis & Wallis)   £85

A rare North American cow-horn powder-flask incised with scrimshaw-work depicting in great detail the area of the Great Lakes, and **Powder And Ball Will Conquer All. Confusion Upon The Foe. A Pox On Them All'**, circa 1812, 12in.
(Christie's S. Ken)   £825

An embossed copper powder flask, 8¹/₂in., with net design and foliage overall, common brass top stamped *G & JW Hawksley*.
(Wallis & Wallis)   £95

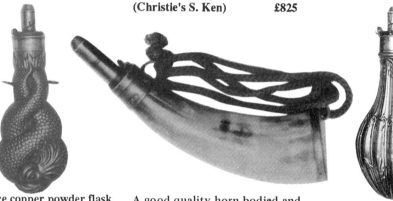

A scarce copper powder flask embossed as entwined dolphins, 8¹/₄in. long, twin steel hanging rings, common brass top stamped *Bartram & Co.*, nozzle graduated from 2–2¹/₂ drams.
(Wallis & Wallis)   £300

A good quality horn bodied and brass mounted powder flask of the type carried for use with the Baker rifle, circa 1800, the body of round form with circular brass base engraved "G 57".   £200

An embossed copper powder flask, 8¹/₄in., embossed with swollen fluting, common brass top stamped *G&JW Hawksley Sheffield.*
(Wallis & Wallis)   £85

An embossed copper 3 way powder flask, 5in., fixed nozzle with common lever charger, base cap with 2 swivel covers.
(Wallis & Wallis)   £115

An engraved rifle horn with carved horntip powder measure, Midwest, dated 1843, in cartouche, 4¹/₂in. long. (Robt. W. Skinner Inc.)   £714

An embossed circular brass powder flask, 6in., body with beaded edge, graduated nozzle stamped *Sykes patent.*
(Wallis & Wallis)   £95

19TH CENTURY

A copper bodied 3 way flask, 4³/₄in. overall, fixed nozzle, blued spring, hinged cover for balls, screw on base cap.
(Wallis & Wallis)   £85

A brass mounted military gunner's priming horn circa 1820, 9¹/₂in., sprung brass charger with lever, brass end cap with unscrewable base for filling.
(Wallis & Wallis)   £135

An embossed copper powder flask, 8¹/₄in., body embossed with woven design and foliage, common brass top with adjustable nozzle.
(Wallis & Wallis)   £70

An embossed copper powder flask, 8¹/₄in., embossed with a design of hanging game above *James Dixon & Sons.*
(Wallis & Wallis)   £105

A fine mid 19th century Afridi tribe powder horn from the North West Frontier, 9in. of polished horn.   £250

An embossed copper powder flask, 8¹/₄in., embossed with dog and stag, patent top stamped *G&JW Hawksley Sheffield.*
(Wallis & Wallis)   £120

A scarce embossed copper powder flask 8¹/₄in., embossed with foliage and geometric devices within flutes, with graduated nozzle.
(Wallis & Wallis)   £125

A good white metal mounted scrimshaw engraved cow horn powder flask, circa 1840, 8¹/₂in. overall, nicely engraved with very early steam train, line engraved with adjustable nozzle.
(Wallis & Wallis)   £145

A good bag shaped copper pistol flask, 5³/₄in., lacquered body and common brass top stamped *James Dixon & Sons*, unusually long nozzle.
(Wallis & Wallis)   £165

A Bizen Yokoyama naginata, Edo period, dated *Genroku 10* (1697), signed *Bishu Osafune [No] Ju Nin Yokoyama Kozuke Daijo Sukesada*, naginata; length 40.2cm.
(Christie's) £3,118

An Italian glaive, with large cleaver-shaped blade with convex main edge, back-edged towards the point with, at the bottom, a small projection formed as the outline of a dolphin's head, later velvet-covered wooden staff partly set with nails, the heads formed as bronze masks, circa 1587, probably Brescian, 36in. head.
(Christie's) £862

An early 18th century partizan, head 9¼in. with slightly thickened tip, baluster socket, on later brass studded wooden haft with elaborate silk tassels woven around gilt octagonal ferrule.
(Wallis & Wallis) £130

A 16th century ceremonial polearm, broad blade 28in. etched with portrait busts in medallions, crouching dogs breathing stylised flames and *IHS Mara, Vyve Le Roy 1588*.
(Wallis & Wallis) £1,200

A 17th century polearm partizan, head 9¾in. including baluster turned socket, side wings with shaped edges, raised central rib and swollen tip.
(Wallis & Wallis) £110

A Partizan head, circa 1600, of plain form, raised central rib, small projecting side lugs, overall 23in. £200

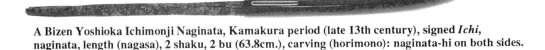

A Bizen Yoshioka Ichimonji Naginata, Kamakura period (late 13th century), signed *Ichi*, naginata, length (nagasa), 2 shaku, 2 bu (63.8cm.), carving (horimono): naginata-hi on both sides.
(Christie's) £23,870

POLEARMS

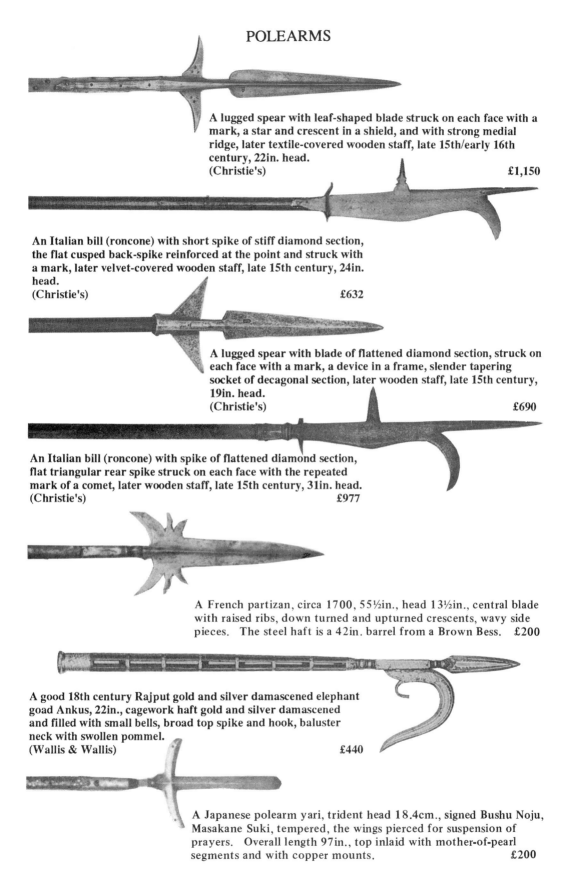

A lugged spear with leaf-shaped blade struck on each face with a mark, a star and crescent in a shield, and with strong medial ridge, later textile-covered wooden staff, late 15th/early 16th century, 22in. head.
(Christie's) £1,150

An Italian bill (roncone) with short spike of stiff diamond section, the flat cusped back-spike reinforced at the point and struck with a mark, later velvet-covered wooden staff, late 15th century, 24in. head.
(Christie's) £632

A lugged spear with blade of flattened diamond section, struck on each face with a mark, a device in a frame, slender tapering socket of decagonal section, later wooden staff, late 15th century, 19in. head.
(Christie's) £690

An Italian bill (roncone) with spike of flattened diamond section, flat triangular rear spike struck on each face with the repeated mark of a comet, later wooden staff, late 15th century, 31in. head.
(Christie's) £977

A French partizan, circa 1700, 55½in., head 13½in., central blade with raised ribs, down turned and upturned crescents, wavy side pieces. The steel haft is a 42in. barrel from a Brown Bess. £200

A good 18th century Rajput gold and silver damascened elephant goad Ankus, 22in., cagework haft gold and silver damascened and filled with small bells, broad top spike and hook, baluster neck with swollen pommel.
(Wallis & Wallis) £440

A Japanese polearm yari, trident head 18.4cm., signed Bushu Noju, Masakane Suki, tempered, the wings pierced for suspension of prayers. Overall length 97in., top inlaid with mother-of-pearl segments and with copper mounts. £200

SABRETACHES

An officer's full dress sabretache of the Madras Light Cavalry, the pocket of blue Russia leather with light blue cloth face. (Christie's) £1,980

A Prussian officer's full dress sabretache of The 12th Hussars, circa 1890. £350

An officer's fine very early Victorian sabretache of the 10th Prince of Wales Own Hussars, embroidered with *VR* cypher. (Christie's) £1,705

An officer's sabretache flap of the 9th Queen's Royal Lancers with blue cloth face edged with regimental lace and richly embroidered with St. Edward's crown. (Christie's) £1,485

An Imperial German Cavalry officer's full dress sabretache of The 2nd Hanoverian Hussars, circa 1850. £400

An officer's full dress sabretache of the 16th (The Queen's) Light Dragoons (Lancers) circa 1847, bearing the *VR* cypher in gold embroidery superimposed on crossed lances. (Christie's) £1,485

An officer's full dress sabretache of the Scots Greys circa 1850, 13½in. high, embroidered with *VR* cypher beneath a Guelphic crown. (Christie's) £1,595

An officer's Victorian full dress sabretache of the 7th Queen's Own Hussars 11¾in. high, bearing the *QO* cypher in gold embroidery. (Christie's) £990

An officer's fine Victorian sabretache of the 11th (Prince Albert's Own) Hussars circa 1850, embroidered with *VR* cypher. (Christie's) £2,530

A Victorian officer's full dress
embroidered pouch of The 4th
Royal Irish Dragoon Guards,
blue velvet on morocco leather.
(Wallis & Wallis)   £180

A good officer's tan leather
pouch of the B(ombay?) Light
Horse, silver plated mounts and
ornamental *BLH* monogram
flap badge.
(Wallis & Wallis)   £260

A scarce Victorian officer's
black leather pouch of the
British German Light Cavalry
Legion, brass bound edge to the
flap.
(Wallis & Wallis)   £250

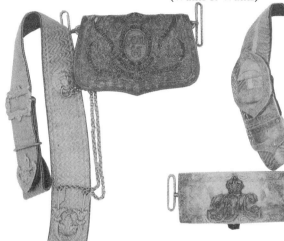

A George V officer's full dress
shoulder belt and pouch of the
18th (Victoria Mary Princess of
Wales's Own) Hussars.
(Wallis & Wallis)   £200

A good pre-1922 officer's full
dress lace shoulder belt and
pouch of the 19th Lancers
(Fane's Horse), silver lace with
French grey central stripe.
(Wallis & Wallis)   £1,750

A fine and desirable pre 1903
officer's shoulder belt and silver
mounted pouch of the Central
India Horse, silver lace belt on
blue morocco.
(Wallis & Wallis)   £725

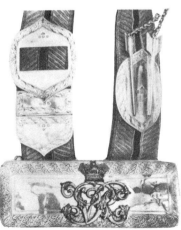

A Victorian officer's silver
mounted shoulder belt and
pouch of The 19th Hussars, gilt
lace belt with white central
stripe.
(Wallis & Wallis)   £310

A Victorian Cavalry officer's
silver mounted full dress
shoulder belt and pouch of
The 20th Hussars.   £325

A Victorian Lancer officer's
silver mounted full dress
shoulder belt and pouch, gilt
lace belt with crimson central
stripe.
(Wallis & Wallis)   £210

A rare, 18th century tinder box, 4½ins. overall, with an oval pan with a hinged lid. £150

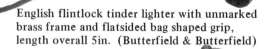

English flintlock tinder lighter with unmarked brass frame and flatsided bag shaped grip, length overall 5in. (Butterfield & Butterfield) £441

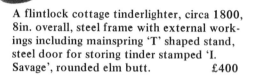

A flintlock cottage tinderlighter, circa 1800, 8in. overall, steel frame with external workings including mainspring 'T' shaped stand, steel door for storing tinder stamped 'I. Savage', rounded elm butt. £400

A late 18th century flintlock cottage tinder lighter, 7in., slab wooden chequered butt, external action, candle sconce and side door revealing compartment for storing spare flints, tinder and tapers. £350

A scarce French flintlock tinder pistol, circa 1770, 8in., overall, barrel 4½in. engraved with trophies of arms and acanthus leaves, flat stepped lock with unbridled frizzen, the plate engraved with stand of flags. (Wallis & Wallis) £450

Scottish flintlock tinder lighter, the brass frame engraved with draped banners and marked Ross on left side and Edinburgh on the obverse, flat sided bag shaped grip. (Butterfield & Butterfield) £552

A very good brass-framed boxlock flintlock tinder lighter candlestick, 7in., frame engraved with military trophies. £750

A charming French gentleman's pocket boxlock flintlock tinder lighter, circa 1800, 3½in., throathole cock. £400

15TH CENTURY

A Kamakura-Bori style tsuba, Muromachi period, circa 1450, the rounded diamond-form (otofuku mokko) iron plate pierced with three stylized banners.
(Christie's) £2,875

An Onin style tsuba, Muromachi period (circa 1400), inlaid with brass dots (tenzogan) and brass wire lines, width 7.1cm.
(Christie's) £1,909

A Kamakura-Bori tsuba, Muromachi period, circa 1450, the round iron plate pierced with an openwork design of a paulownia crest, height 7.8cm.
(Christie's) £1,200

A Kamakura style tsuba, Muromachi period, circa 1450, the round iron plate carved in both broad and thin lines with a dragon design, height and width 8.4cm. (Christie's) £475

An Onin style tsuba, Muromachi period (circa 1400), decorated on both sides in brass dot (tenzogan) and thin wire inlay, width 7.6cm.
(Christie's) £887

A Katchushi tsuba, Muromachi period, circa 1450, the round iron plate has a surface which has been hammered and polished it has a delicately raised edge (uchikaeshi) with many strong iron bones, height and width 8.6cm. (Christie's) £1,100

A Katchushi school tsuba, Muromachi period (circa 1400), the iron-plate has an open-cornered, four-lobed shape (inome kirikime mokko), width 8.2cm.
(Christie's) £818

A Kamakurabori type tsuba, Muromachi period (circa 1400), thin thin, six-lobed iron plate carved on each side with a wide groove, and with six scroll lines, width 8.6cm.
(Christie's) £578

A classic Onin brass inlay tsuba, Muromachi period (circa 1450), inlaid with brass wire depicting a mandarin orange and the crest (mon) of the Sakuma daimyo of Owari, width 8.4cm.
(Christie's) £3,751

15TH CENTURY

An Onin style tsuba, Muromachi period (circa 1450), the flat plate areas decorated in brass with family crests and floral designs, width 8.5cm. (Christie's) £554

An Onin style tsuba, Muromachi period (circa 1450), both sides inlaid with four rows of brass dots and a circle of brass wire, width 8.1cm. (Christie's) £381

A Kamakurabori style tsuba, Muromachi period (circa 1450), carved in low relief with a Shinto shrine and landscape design on one side, width 8.4cm. (Christie's) £614

A rare Muromachi Period oval yamagane ko-kinko tsuba, the plate with a simple punched pattern, late 15th/early 16th century, 6.7cm., in wood box with descriptive hakogati by Sasano Masayuki. (Christie's) £770

An Onin sukashi tsuba, Muromachi period (circa 1450), pierced with four handle-shaped (kan) pierced areas which are outlined in brass wire on both sides, width 7.3cm. (Christie's) £887

A rare Muromachi Period circular bronze kagamishi (mirror-makers) tsuba, with kozuka-hitsu, early 15th century, 7.2cm., in wood box with descriptive hakogati by Sasano Masayuki. (Christie's) £1,760

A Kamakura-Bori style tsuba, Muromachi period (circa 1450), the iron plate carved on the face with two fans, a half plum flower and a cherry tree branch, width 8.5cm. (Christie's) £312

A Kamakura-Bori style tsuba, Muromachi period (circa 1400), carved on the face with a design of plum flowers, bracken and leaves, width 8.7cm. (Christie's) £277

A Kamakura-Bori style tsuba, Muromachi period (circa 1400), carved with a design of a five-level pagoda, mountains, torii, house and plum branch, width 9.1cm. (Christie's) £3,811

16TH CENTURY

A Heianjo tsuba, Muromachi period (circa 1575), carved and pierced with six petals of a chrysanthemum bloom, width 6.3cm.
(Christie's) £208

Late 16th century Momo-yama period tsuba decorated with two men towing a boat, 8.6cm. (Christie's) £715

A Ko-Kinko tsuba, Momoyama period (circa 1575), inlaid with gold ivy leaves and shakudo tendrils, width 5.2cm.
(Christie's) £277

A Heianjo tsuba, Muromachi period (circa 1550), the iron plate pierced with a design of cloud forms, decorated with brass Onin style inlay of leaves and clove buds, width 8cm.
(Christie's) £693

A Ko-Shoami school tsuba, Momoyama period (circa 1573–1600), pierced with a design of a diagonal wide and narrow bands and a kiri mon on the upper right, width 7.5cm.
(Christie's) £589

A Kamakurabori sukashi tsuba, Muromachi period (circa 1500), pierced with a design of a stone lantern, a fern frond bud, hanabishi flower and Genji chapter crests (mon), width 8cm.
(Christie's) £1,909

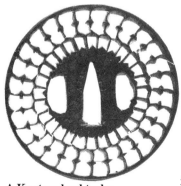

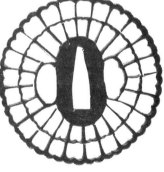

A Kyoto school tsuba, Momoyama period (circa 1575), carved in an openwork design of birds in flight and chrysanthemum petals around the central area, width 8.2cm.
(Christie's) £580

A Ko-Mino Goto school tsuba, Momoyama period (circa 1575), the shakudo nanako plate decorated with a raised design of autumn flowers, the details covered in gold uttori-zogan, width 6.3cm.
(Christie's) £1,386

A Kyoto school tsuba, Momoyama period (circa 1550), carved in an openwork design of a double row of chrysanthemum petals within a petal-form rim, width 7.8cm.
(Christie's) £477

16TH CENTURY

A Heianjo tsuba, Muromachi period (circa 1500), decorated on both sides in brass inlays of peony blooms, leaves and tendrils, width 10cm.
(Christie's) £1,091

A Kamakurabori style tsuba, Muromachi period (circa 1500), carved on both sides in low relief with a mountain landscape, width 8.5cm.
(Christie's) £1,091

A Ko Shoami school tsuba, Muromachi period (circa 1500), the lower right area decorated with a large openwork design of three kiri leaves, width 8.4cm.
(Christie's) £750

A Heianjo style tsuba, Momoyama period (circa 1575), the outer edge and rim formed as a twenty-eight petal chrysanthemum bloom, width 6.8cm.
(Christie's) £273

An early Owari sukashi tsuba, Muromachi period (circa 1500), pierced with a symmetrical design of chrysanthemum leaves and buds, width 8.2cm.
(Christie's) £2,864

A Proto-Koike Yoshiro tsuba, Momoyama period (circa 1575), pierced and inset with eight reticulated roundels and decorated with vine leaves and tendrils.
(Christie's) £1,091

A Hirata style tsuba, Muromachi period (circa 1575), inscribed *Donin* with kao, formed as a double wisteria bloom crest (fuji mon) with flower buds in gold wire outline, width 6.4cm.
(Christie's) £2,864

An Onin style tsuba, Muromachi period (circa 1550), of openwork design, with three bars in circles (kiki maru), the family crest of the Abe and other daimyo families, width 8.1cm.
(Christie's) £1,091

An Owari sukashi tsuba, Momoyama period (circa 1575), pierced with a symmetrical quadrant design of scrolls beside pointed arches centred with ancient sword blade, width 8.1cm.
(Christie's) £1,909

17TH CENTURY

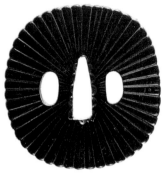

A Kaga style inlaid tsuba, Edo period (circa 1675), the face and reverse inlaid with designs of kiri crests, leaves and vine tendrils, width 7.7cm.
(Christie's) £682

A tachikanagushi tsuba, Edo period (circa 1650), carved as a forty-seven petal chrysanthemum, width 7.7cm.
(Christie's) £818

A Mino Goto tsuba, Momoyama period (circa 1600), with overall raised design of a cherry tree with hanging branches and many gold blooms, width 7.1cm.
(Christie's) £3,751

A nine luminaries Hosokawa crest (Kyuyo mon) tsuba, early Edo period (circa 1650), attributed to Hayashi Matashichi (1613–1699), decorated in gold damascene (nunome), width 8cm.
(Christie's) £4,910

A Canton-style tsuba, Momoyama period (circa 1600), the web carved with an interlocking undercut scroll design that entangles and suspends a dragon, fish, waves, pavilions and clouds, width 7.7cm.
(Christie's) £409

A Kawaji school tsuba, Edo period (circa 1675), signed *Choshu Ju Kawaji Sahyoe no jo Tomotsune*, pierced and carved with four water plantain leaves (omodaka), width 7.8cm.
(Christie's) £1,637

A Higo style tsuba, Edo period (circa 1650), of rectangular, uneven petal-form shape with an openwork design of informal kiri leaves and blooms, width 7.1cm.
(Christie's) £259

A Kyoto Shoami school tsuba, Edo period (circa 1650), the plate with openwork design of two bows, three arrows, and a saihai (general's baton), width 10.9cm.
(Christie's) £5,115

A Goto school tsuba, Edo period (circa 1675), signed *Goto Senjo* with kao, the rim and edge carved in high relief with crashing waves and two dragons positioned head to tail, width 6.6cm.
(Christie's) £955

A Kyoto school tsuba, Edo period (circa 1650), carved with an openwork design of a band of pine-river-diamond crests, width 7.5cm.
(Christie's)   £375

A circular iron Heianjo Tsuba decorated in Shinchu takazogan with children's toys, unsigned, 17th century, 8.2cm.
(Christie's)   £495

A circular iron heianjozogan tsuba with brass inlay forming a circle of chrysanthemum clumps, 17th century, 8.6cm.
(Christie's)   £330

A tsuba in the style of Koike Yoshiro, Edo period (circa 1625), pierced and inset with eight openwork brass crests and decorated with vines, leaves and tendrils, width 7.5cm.
(Christie's)   £346

An Umetada School tsuba, Edo period, circa 1650, signed Umetada, the rectangular brass plate tanto guard composed of four gourds joined by their tops to the seppa-dai.
(Christie's)   £5,100

A circular iron migakiji tsuba with cherry blossom, kiri and joined circles in kosukashi, signed *Tadatsugu*, Umetada school, late 17th/early 18th century, 8.7cm.
(Christie's)   £605

A Shonai area tsuba, Edo period (mid-17th century), the copper plate guard decorated on the ishime ground with sprays of chrysanthemums, width 6.3cm.
(Christie's)   £554

A Kaga brass inlay tsuba, Edo period (circa 1650), the whole surface of both sides, and the edge, inlaid in brass wire of intricate meander pattern, width 7.3cm.
(Christie's)   £139

A Katchushi school tsuba, Momoyama period (circa 1600), decorated with two swallows in stylised negative sukashi, width 7cm.
(Christie's)   £579

17TH CENTURY

A Kyoto Shoami school tsuba, Edo period (circa 1600), the plate of openwork design with two dragons pursuing the flaming jewel between them, width 7.6cm.
(Christie's) £327

A large kyo-sukashi tsuba of stylised chrysanthemum form, 17th century, 8.8cm.
(Christie's) £715

A Shoami School Kenjo tsuba, Edo period, circa 1690, the round iron plate decorated with a gold nunome design which extends over the entire surface.
(Christie's) £1,100

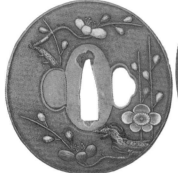

A circular santoku hari-ishimeji tsuba, blossoming plum branches in gilt, silver, shakudo and copper takazogan, probably Shonai Shoami school, second half 17th century, 8cm.
(Christie's) £660

A circular shakudo-nanakoji tsuba, the face with six sunk roundels containing flowers in shishiaibori, decorated in similar style on the reverse, unsigned, Goto school, 17th century, 7.4cm.
(Christie's) £1,320

A circular shinchu tsuchimeji tsuba decorated in shakudo hirazogan and silver with two hats and a staff, bars and circles on the reverse, Umetada school, early 17th century.
(Christie's) £4,950

A tsuba in the style of Koike Yoshiro Naomasa (Edo period (circa 1625), the plate pierced and decorated with a ground of brass-inlaid vine leaves and tendrils, width 8.3cm.
(Christie's) £1,500

A shakudo-nanakoji gilt rimmed aoigata tsuba decorated in iroe takazogan with aki-no-nanakusa, unsigned, Mino-Goto school, 17th century, 6.7cm.
(Christie's London) £462

A 17th/18th century circular iron tsuba decorated with the takaramono in cloisonne enamels, unsigned, 8.5cm. diam.
(Christie's) £1,210

295

A Suruga tsuba, Edo period, circa 1650, the round iron plate pierced with a design of a catfish (namazu) leaping over a wave, height and width 7.5cm. (Christie's)   £950

A Miyamoto Musashi-type tsuba, Edo period, circa 1650, the iron plate formed as two rings joined at the top and bottom of the seppa-dai.
(Christie's)   £2,000

An Owari Sukashi tsuba, Edo period, circa 1650, the oval iron plate pierced with a design of a clock gear (tokei), the rounded square rim has strong iron bones. (Christie's) £385

A Higo tsuba, Edo period, circa 1650, the oval copper plate decorated with a dragon carved from the face and another matching dragon inlaid in shakudo.
(Christie's)   £1,150

An Awa-Shoami tsuba, Edo period, circa 1650, attributed to Hirata Ujinao, the brass plate with copper coloured patination decorated with gold damascene.
(Christie's)   £3,200

An iron tsuba, Edo period, circa 1625, the round iron plate carved on the surface with vertical lines, there are five pierced apertures which are formed by interlocking sangaibishi crests.
(Christie's)   £350

A Higo style tsuba, Edo period (circa 1650), the iron plate of four interlocking rings joining in a four-lobed shape (mokko), width 8.2cm.
(Christie's)   £818

A swordsmith's tsuba, Edo period, circa 1625, signed Kuniyasu, the surface decorated with cloud-like tiny hammer marks, mainly in the centre, 9.4cm. high.
(Christie's)   £1,800

A Kinai school tsuba, Edo period (circa 1675), pierced and carved with four maple leaves on a stream of dots of dew in brass inlay, width 7.8cm.
(Christie's)   £150

A Shoami School tsuba, Momoyama period, circa 1600, the elongated four-lobed brass plate dished from the edge to the centre of the plate. (Christie's) £325

A Higo Hirata School tsuba, Edo period, circa 1625, the rounded oval copper plate well hammered with three large cloud-like apertures. (Christie's) £1,150

A Kyoto Shoami school design, Edo period (circa 1600), the centre is carved with three groups of crashing waves, width 7.7cm. (Christie's) £614

A Jingo School tsuba, early Edo period, circa 1650, the rounded square iron plate with a well-hammered surface texture decorated in heavy brass inlay. (Christie's) £5,750

An Iyo Shoami tsuba, Edo period, dated eighth month Jokyo 1 (1684), signed Yoshu Ju Shoami Hidenaga, the round brass plate pierced and carved in the round with three comma motifs (mitsutomoe), (Christie's) £4,785

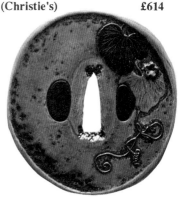

A Shonai School tsuba, Edo period, (Genroku Era 1688-1704), signed Arichika, the oval brass (shinchu) plate carved and inlaid in gilt. (Christie's) £32,000

A Heianjo style tsuba, Edo period (circa 1650), plate formed as two ginger plant buds, width 7.9cm. (Christie's) £341

A Koike School tsuba, Edo period, circa 1625, signed Koike Yoshiro, the iron four-lobed plate decorated with sheet-brass flush inlay of cloud forms and wire inlay creating the same shapes. (Christie's) £380

A Kaga style inlaid tsuba, Edo period (circa 1650), pierced with a twenty-three petal chrysanthemum bloom design, width 8.4cm. (Christie's) £511

Late 18th century ju-mokko-
gata migakiji iron tsuba, Awa
Shoami style. (Christie's)
£440

An iron higo tsuba formed
as a blossoming plum tree,
circa 1725, 7.8cm. diam.
(Christie's)   £330

An 18th century gilt rimmed
shakudo mokkogata tsuba,
unsigned, 7.6cm. (Christie's)
£660

A fine aorigata iron tsuba, a
dancing crane (tsuru-maru)
above breaking waves in yosukashi, unsigned, Higo school,
style of Nishigaki Kanshiro,
18th century, 6.7cm. (Christie's
London)   £462

A futatsu-mokkogata tsuba,
sentoku with leaves inlaid in gilt
and shakudo hirazogan, applied
shibuichi rim, signed *Kataoka
Tachibana Tadayoshi* (Shoami
school), worked in Kyoto, circa
1716–35, 7.5cm.
(Christie's)   £4,180

An irregular shaped iron tsuba,
flowering plum tree in yosukashi with slight engraved and
gilt detail, unsigned, Hayashi
school of Higo, early 18th century, 8.1cm. (Christie's
London)   £550

A mokkogata shakudo-nanakoji
tsuba, horses and autumn
plants in copper, gilt and
shakudo takazogan, inscribed
Ganshoshi Nagatsune, late 18th
century, 6.8cm. (Christie's
London)   £902

A fine circular iron tsuba,
circa 1748, signed Kato
Shigemitsu, decorated in
nikubori and iroe takazogan,
with an octopus and varieties
of fish trapped in a large net,
7.5cm. (Christie's)   £330

A rare Namban tsuba based on
the shape of a European smallsword guard, carved and pierced
with interlaced tendrils,
unsigned, Nagasaki work, 18th
century, 7.5cm.
(Christie's)   £1,320

18TH CENTURY

An 18th century mokkogata shakudo-nanakoji tsuba, Mino-Goto style, 7.1cm. (Christie's) £506

An 18th century oval iron tsuchimeji tsuba, Nara school, 7.7cm. (Christie's) £220

Late 18th century oval iron tsuba, signed Chosu ju Masa-asada, 7.5cm. (Christie's) £300

A circular iron tsuba decorated in hikone-bori with men cutting scouring-rush, signed Kofu Hikone ju Soheishi Nyudo Soten sei, 18th century, 8.1cm. (Christie's) £1,320

A Hamano School tsuba, mid-Edo period, circa 1750, signed Rifudo Shozui, the oval brass plate carved and inlaid with soft metals with a design of five tengu peeking out from behind pine trees on Mt. Kurama. (Christie's) £27,000

Mid 18th century circular iron tsuba formed as the madogiri or paulownia and window design in yosukashi and kebori, 8.5cm. (Christie's) £1,100

A circular iron tsuba decorated in brass inlay with water-weed fronds and mon-sukashi in yoshiro-zogan style, signed *Saburodaiyu Kore-o Saku*, 18th century, 7.3cm. (Christie's) £2,860

A tsuba of irregular outline, sentoku formed as two lobes filled with iron intricate interlacing tendrils and dragon's heads, unsigned, Canton style, 18th century, 7.8cm. (Christie's) £638

An oval iron hikone-bori tsuba depicting the Chinese military servant Yojo stabbing the cloak of Prince Cho Bujutsu, signed *Goshu Hikone ju Soheishi Nyudo Soten sei*, 18th century, 7.6cm. (Christie's) £528

299

A Nara school tsuba, Edo period (circa 1700), signed *Kaneshige*, the right half of the face carved and inlaid in gold with a design of Fudo Myo-o under a waterfall, width 7.3cm. (Christie's) £511

A Shonai style tsuba, Edo period (circa 1775), the face inlaid in high relief with a shakudo centipede with gold eyes and feelers, and another centipede, width 6.2cm. (Christie's) £1,773

A Nara school tsuba, Edo period (circa 1700), the plate hammered and punched to create the appearance of a rock face, inlaid in gold, silver and shibuichi, width 6.8cm. (Christie's) £477

A Shingen style tsuba, Edo period (circa 1700), the plate of spoked-wheel, chrysanthemum shape, bound with brass, copper and silver wire in classic Shingen style, width 10.5cm. (Christie's) £3,275

A Bushu Ito school tsuba, Edo period (circa 1725), signed *Gyonen Hachijuichi Masatsune*, carved and pierced as two bunches of noshi with gold accents, width 7.1cm. (Christie's) £750

A Shingen style tsuba, Edo period (circa 1700), originally carved with a series of open circles around the rim, now filled with a copper, rope-form wire pattern, width 8.4cm. (Christie's) £546

A Shingen style tsuba, Edo period (circa 1700), the rim area is woven wire of iron and brass in a basketweave pattern, width 7.8cm. (Christie's) £818

A Mito-style tsuba, Edo period (circa 1700), signed *Eihan Yoshimitsu*, overlaid with a brass dragon in high relief, width 6.7cm. (Christie's) £286

A Mito school tsuba, Edo period (circa 1750), carved in the web with a dragon in the round, the eyes and teeth in gold, width 7.7cm. (Christie's) £1,023

18TH CENTURY

A Yokoya school tsuba, Edo period (circa 1775), signed *Soyo* with kao, decorated with a tiger by a large bamboo tree trunk, width 5.9cm.
(Christie's) £546

A Mino school tsuba, Edo period (circa 1750), signed *Mino ju Nakanaga*, decorated with flowers and insects in high relief and finished in gold and silver, width 6.6cm.
(Christie's) £1,705

A Mito Shoami school tsuba, Edo period (circa 1750), carved and inlaid with a Dutchman and his dog under a pine tree, width 9.9cm.
(Christie's) £2,182

A Shonai Shoami school tsuba, Edo period (circa 1700), the face inlaid with two large and three small family crests of the oxalis bloom (katabami mon), width 7.2cm.
(Christie's) £1,296

An Owari Nobuie tsuba, Edo period (circa 1750), signed *Nobuie*, the thick iron plate with nearly tubular rim carved in a wide rope pattern over the outer edge, width 7.8cm.
(Christie's) £579

An Akasaka Nobuie tsuba, Edo period (circa 1750), slightly dished to the centre with openwork design of an adze, a plum blossom, and a melon, width 7.6cm.
(Christie's) £546

A Tadatsugu style tsuba, Edo period (circa 1700), signed *Tadatsugu*, pierced with three oars and two dots representing water spray, width 7.8cm.
(Christie's) £682

A Hizen school tsuba, Edo period (circa 1750), the web decorated in scroll work with two dragons pursuing the celestial pearl, width 6.8cm.
(Christie's) £177

An Okamoto school tsuba, Edo period (circa 1700), gold seal, carved in the round as a dragon, depicted head to tail, around the seppa-dai area, width 7.2cm.
(Christie's) £579

18TH CENTURY

An oval iron tsuba, a coiled dragon in ikizukashi with gilt detail, signed *Echizen ju Kinai saku*, 18th century, 7.4cm. (Christie's) £605

A Sendai Katchushi style tsuba, Edo period (circa 1700), the centre right pierced with large peony bloom, width 7.8cm. (Christie's) £139

A mokkogata iron hikone-bori tsuba depicting warriors outside a temple among pines, signed *Goshu Hikone ju Soheishi Nyudo Soten sei*, 18th century, 7.8cm. (Christie's) £550

A circular iron tsuba, yosukashi and nikubori, a crab, seaweed, sea-urchin and assorted shells, signed *Echizen ju Kinai saku*, 18th century, 8.5cm. (Christie's) £352

A circular iron tsuchimeji tsuba with stylised cherry-blossom in kosukashi, the plate thinning towards the narrow shakudo pipe-rim, signed Tadatsugu, 18th century. (Christie's) £220

A broad oval sentoku tsuchimeji tsuba, marumimi, grapevine and trellis in shakudo hirazogan, signed *Hisanori*, 18th century, 8.4cm. (Christie's) £6,600

A Heianjo style tsuba, Edo period (circa 1750), carved on the face with cloud forms and inlaid with a dragon in copper gilt, width 7.3cm. (Christie's) £173

Late 18th century iron tsuba, signed Bushu ju Masakata, 7.7cm. diam., and another, early Echizen school, 7cm. diam. (Christie's) £330

An oval iron tsuba, a coiled dragon in marubori chasing a flaming tama, unsigned, Echizen Kinai school, 18th century, 7.3cm. (Christie's) £550

18TH CENTURY

An 18th century iron tsuba, signed Choshu Hagi ju Kawaji, 7.4cm. diam. (Christie's)   £220

A mokko sentoku tsuba, the ishimeji cushioned plate decorated with a bell cricket and gilt vine leaves in takazogan, 18th century, 7.2cm. (Christie's)   £660

An 18th century iron soten tsuba depicting Kyoyu and Sofu in hikone-bori, 8.3cm. diam. (Christie's)   £506

A Nagoya-Mono tsuba, Edo period (circa 1750), the oval nigurome plate with overall nanako ground, the rim with sprays of gilt flowers, width 6.5cm. (Christie's)   £277

A double dragon brass inlay tsuba, Edo period, circa 1750, the oval iron plate deeply carved on both sides with a whirlpool design which covers most of the plate area, height 8.6cm. (Christie's)   £2,250

A Nagoya-Mono tsuba, Edo period (circa 1700), the four-lobed, nigurome plate with nanako ground and sprays of chrysanthemums carved in relief, width 6.7cm. (Christie's)   £554

A circular iron tsuba, tree peony seedlings in yosukashi, signed *Inshu ju Suruga saku*, 18th century, 8cm. (Christie's London)   £990

An otafukumokkogata tsuba, a hat and bag in shinchu takazogan, signed *Yatsushiro Jingo saku*, 1746–1823, 7.4cm. (Christie's)   £495

Late 18th/early 19th century oval shakudo migakiji tsuba, Shoki in shishiaibori with gilt and silver detail, 7cm. (Christie's)   £1,045

18TH CENTURY

A Higo style tsuba, Edo period (circa 1700), pierced on either side of the central opening with large, fan-shaped apertures, width 7.7cm.
(Christie's) £286

A Goto style tsuba, Edo period (circa 1700), the raised rim decorated in high relief design of spring flowers and grasses, width 7.3cm.
(Christie's) £1,091

A Kyoto Shoami school tsuba, Edo period (circa 1700), carved in an openwork design of poppy buds, leaves and stems, width 7.9cm.
(Christie's) £327

An Edo Kinko school tsuba, Edo period (circa 1775), carved in relief and openwork with the figure of Hotei in a punt, with a child at his feet next to his sack, width 7.5cm.
(Christie's) £1,296

A Kinai school tsuba, Edo period (circa 1750), signed *Echizen ju Kinai saku*, pierced and finely carved with large leaves branching from one stem on either side of the central opening, width 8cm.
(Christie's) £818

A Goto style tsuba, Edo period (circa 1700), the oval nigurome plate decorated in a high relief of spring flowers and insects in two tones of gold and copper, width 7.1cm.
(Christie's) £887

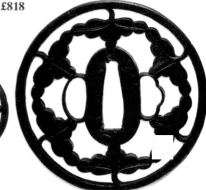

A Higo school tsuba, Edo period (circa 1750), with pierced and carved design of a three-level pine tree (sangai matsu), width 7.6cm.
(Christie's) £477

A Higo school tsuba, Edo period (circa 1700), with openwork design of four family crests, width 7cm.
(Christie's) £818

A Kyoto school tsuba, Edo period (circa 1700), carved in an openwork design of six triple-branch pine boughs, width 8.1cm.
(Christie's) £375

18TH CENTURY

A Higo style tsuba, Edo period (circa 1700), the pipe-form rim enclosing an openwork area with pine branches above, width 7.1cm.
(Christie's) £1,023

A Hirati style tsuba, Edo period (circa 1750), inlaid on the face with two heart-shaped gold cloisonné, clear glass inlays, width 7.2cm.
(Christie's) £1,296

A Sendai inlay tsuba, Edo period (circa 1750), the thick solid shakudo plate formed as a polearm, in Chinese style, width 6.5cm.
(Christie's) £2,182

A Kyoto school tsuba, Edo period (circa 1700), carved in an openwork design of boar's-eyes and 'T' bars, width 7.5cm.
(Christie's) £443

A Myochin school tsuba, Edo period (circa 1700), signed *Tsugaru no ju Shinto go tetsu ren Myochin*, the oval plate with fine woodgrain (mokume) surface, carved with two leaves, width 7.4cm.
(Christie's) £682

A Kyoto school tsuba, Edo period (circa 1725), carved in an openwork design of birds and pine-river-diamond crest (matsukawabishi mon), width 7cm.
(Christie's) £546

A Kyoto school tsuba, Edo period (circa 1700), carved in an openwork design of linked scrolls (karakusa), width 8.2cm.
(Christie's) £887

A Kaga school inlay tsuba, Edo period (circa 1700), the round, polished, shakudo plate inlaid in two tones of sheet gold with a bamboo plant, width 7.1cm.
(Christie's) £1,159

A Goto style tsuba, Edo period (circa 1750), decorated on the rim with a deeply carved relief of flowers and crickets in gold, silver and shakudo, width 6cm.
(Christie's) £1,296

An iron tsuba, Edo period (circa 1700), signed *Shushin Saku*, pierced to form two interlocking jewels (tama), width 7.3cm. (Christie's) £1,159

An 18th century mokkogata shakudo-nanakoji tsuba, Mino-Goto style, 7.1cm. (Christie's) £506

A Nagoya-Mono tsuba, Edo period (circa 1750), the plate of nanako ground covered with high relief sprays of large spring flowers, width 6.3cm. (Christie's) £450

A cloisonné inlay tsuba, Edo period (circa 1700), carved on the face with two dragons, the wide border with keyfret pattern filled with turquoise opaque glass, width 7.7cm. (Christie's) £416

A rare Iyo Shoami tsuba, mid-Edo period (circa 1750), signed *Yoshu Matsuyama ju Shoami Hidetsugu* (Shoami Hidetsugu [fl. circa 1750]), the plate with heart-shaped (inome-bori) openings at the indentations, width 7.8cm. (Christie's) £4,433

A tsuba in the style of Koike Yoshiro, Edo period (circa 1700), pierced and inset with six openwork brass crests and decorated with vines and tendrils, width 8.1cm. (Christie's) £381

A Choshu style tsuba, Edo period (circa 1750), pierced in a design of two peony blooms and a bud caught in a web of scrolling stems, width 7.8cm. (Christie's) £477

A Myochin school tsuba, Edo period (circa 1750), of squared four-lobed shape, the top lobe with two scrolls in sukashi, width 6.4cm. (Christie's) £194

A Shonai style tsuba, Edo period (circa 1750), inscribed *Tsuchiya Tasuchika*, carved and inlaid with a tiger with gold stripes, width 7.3cm. (Christie's) £1,317

19TH CENTURY

A Tokyo Art School tsuba, Meiji era (circa 1875), the left half carved as rocky hills with a clump of shakudo pine trees and a silver moon, width 7.7cm.
(Christie's) £194

A Kamiyoshi school tsuba, Edo period (circa 1865), attributed to Kamiyoshi Rakuju, pierced with a design of two conch shells and decorated with inlaid gold wire whorls, width 7.3cm.
(Christie's) £2,218

A Kano Natsuo school tsuba, Meiji era (circa 1900), inscribed *Iwamoto Konkan*, the iron plate with two carp carved in high relief from the plate, width 8cm.
(Christie's) £1,732

A Yoshioka style tsuba, Edo period (circa 1800), inscribed *Yoshioka Inaba No Suke*, the right side decorated with chrysanthemums on water, in gold, shakudo and silver inlay, width 6.7cm.
(Christie's) £1,525

A Yokoya school tsuba, Edo period (circa 1800), inscribed *Yokoya Tomotsune* with kao, the shakudo plate decorated in gold carved with a shishi, two peony blooms, three buds and two leaves, width 6.7cm.
(Christie's) £3,465

A Kinko tsuba, Edo period (circa 1800), inscribed *Iwamoto Konkan* with kao, the shakudo nanako plate inlaid with a bonsai plant in a shakudo and gold large rectangular tub, width 7cm.
(Christie's) £1,802

A Tanaka school tsuba, Meiji era (circa 1875), signed *Hoshisai Toshikage*, the iron plate inlaid with a bird in a plum tree over a stream, all with gold accents, width 7.4cm.
(Christie's) £312

A Teimei school tsuba, Edo period (circa 1800), signed on the face *Kishu Ju Teimei* and on the reverse *Goshu Ju Namitoshi*, decorated with a pierced design of eggplants, width 7.8cm.
(Christie's) £832

A Hirata school tsuba, Edo period (circa 1800), signed *Hirata Naritsuke* with kao, the face inlaid with three butterflies in clear and opaque (white) cloisonné, width 7.2cm.
(Christie's) £2,633

A Kamiyoshi school tsuba, Edo period (circa 1825), pierced and carved with cherry blooms on water, width 7.3cm.
(Christie's) £327

An Edo Kinko tsuba, Edo period (circa 1880), inlaid in high relief with a silver dragon and gold accents, width 6cm.
(Christie's) £750

A Kamiyoshi tsuba, Edo period (circa 1825), pierced and carved in an openwork design of a bamboo branch, width 7.3cm.
(Christie's) £682

An Uchikoshi school tsuba, Edo period (circa 1800), signed *Hirotoshi* with kao, decorated in very high relief with two herons, wading in a stream beside plants of gold and shakudo, width 7.1cm.
(Christie's) £1,364

A Satsuma-style tsuba, Edo period (circa 1850), pierced with four crests (juji mon) of a cross within a circle and four individual crosses, width 6.9cm.
(Christie's) £327

An Uchikoshi school tsuba, Edo period (circa 1825), signed *Jogetsusai Hiroyoshi* with kao, inlaid with a design of a large flowering plum tree, width 7.2cm.
(Christie's) £1,023

An Edo Higo tsuba, Edo period (circa 1850), carved with a ginko leaf, cherry blooms, petals and pine needles, width 7.8cm.
(Christie's) £750

A tachikanagushi type tsuba, Edo period (circa 1850), the nanako overlaid in relief with five family crests on the face, width 8.9cm.
(Christie's) £1,227

A Bushu school style tsuba, Edo period (circa 1800), pierced with a design of snowflakes and a cherry bloom, width 7.2cm.
(Christie's) £150

A Sunagawa style tsuba, Edo period (circa 1850), carved overall as chrysanthemum blooms, width 7.4cm. (Christie's) £955

An Edo Kinko tsuba, Edo period (circa 1800), inlaid in high relief with a deer in copper, with gold spots and antlers, width 4.7cm. (Christie's) £614

An Edo Kinko tsuba, Edo period (circa 1800), decorated with a shakudo willow tree with gold and silver leaves, width 6.5cm. (Christie's) £1,023

A swordsmith school tsuba, late Edo/early Meiji period (circa 1865–75), signed *Yoshitane*, the oval plate carved in low relief with a Chinese-style landscape on the face, width 6.7cm. (Christie's) £477

A Nakai school tsuba, Edo period (circa 1800), signed *Choshu ju Tomotsune*, carved in deep, rounded relief with a chrysanthemum bloom and leaves, width 6.8cm. (Christie's) £273

An Uchikoshi school tsuba, Edo period (circa 1825), signed *Hiroyoshi* with kao, pierced and carved in a design of a tiger guarding the entrance to a cave, width 6.1cm. (Christie's) £1,091

A Kamiyoshi school tsuba, Edo period (circa 1825), pierced with a design of a plum branch and cloud forms, width 8.2cm. (Christie's) £511

A Sunagawa style tsuba, Edo period (circa 1850), carved in low relief with an overall pattern of cherry blooms and leaves, width 8.1cm. (Christie's) £477

A Tachikanagushi style tsuba, Edo period (circa 1850), hot stamped on the face with seven paulownia crests, width 6.4cm. (Christie's) £832

TSUBAS

19TH CENTURY

A fine aorigata copper migakiji tsuba with inome piercings and a shakudo rim, the plate delicately inlaid in silver, unsigned, 19th century, 7.8cm. (Christie's) £440

A 19th century iron migakiji tsuba decorated in takabori and iroe takazogan with Chinnan and Gama sennin, 7.6cm. diam. (Christie's) £748

A fine shakudo hari-ishime aorigata tsuba, a Bodhisattva in a precipitous landscape, gilt detail, unsigned, 19th century, 6.3cm. (Christie's London) £550

  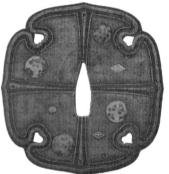

A circular shinchu tsuba decorated in shakudo, silver and copper with two fans and a rat nibbling at the cords, signed *Sadamasa* and *Kao*, circa 1800, 7.6cm. (Christie's) £770

A 19th century sentoku and copper tsuba formed as the eight-headed snake, signed Katsuchika, 8.8cm. (Christie's) £2,860

An iron aoigata tsuba with inomebori (boar's-eyes piercings) at the four corners, 18th century, the enamels later, possibly by Hirata Harunari, first half 19th century, 9.3cm. (Christie's) £935

An aorigata iron tsuba, decorated in takabori and iroe takazogan with the Chinese Emperor Meiko watching his ghostly protector Shoki, signed *Katsunobu*, late 19th century, 9.1cm. (Christie's) £1,100

A fine circular iron migakiji tsuba decorated in nikubori with a group of Tartar hunters near a pine forest, signed Choshu Toyoura ju Torino Mobe Tomoshige saku, 19th century, 8cm. (Christie's) £413

A lacquer tsuba decorated in Shibayama style and gold and silver hiramakie on a kinji ground with birds among tree peony and a fallen fisherman losing his eels, late 19th century, 10cm. wide. (Christie's) £2,750

Late 19th century hari-ishimeji tsuba decorated with Emma-O and a demonic attendant, inscribed Hamano Noriyuki, 9.6cm. (Christie's) £3,080

Late 19th century otafuku-mokko sentoku hari-ishimeji tsuba decorated with two carp, signed Nagamasa. (Christie's) £5,500

An oval Sentoku Migakiji Tsuba decorated in iroe takazogan with a part of a rats procession, signed Jogetsusai Hiroyoshi, first half 19th century, 6.7cm. (Christie's) £550

A fine circular iron migakiji tsuba decorated in shakudo takazogan and nikubori with a wild boar breaking cover near a rocky rivulet, signed Ichiryusai Masamitsu, 19th century, 7.9cm. (Christie's) £352

A rounded rectangular iron tsuba decorated in copper and gilt takazogan with Tenaga seated stretching beneath a pine tree, signed Ichiyoken Nagatsugu, late 19th century. (Christie's) £935

An oval shakudo-nanakoji tsuba, 19th century, signed Sekisaido Hiroyuki, decorated in silver, gilt and shakudo takazogan with flowering plum branches, 6.6cm. (Christie's) £440

An otafuku-mokkogata shakudo migakiji tsuba on omote, shibuichi on ura, copper, gilt and silver hirazogan and takazogan, signed Kakusensai Yoshimune and Kao, late 19th century, 7cm. (Christie's) £2,200

A large rounded square mi-parti tsuba of iron and rogin, iroe hirazogan and takazogan, the migakiji iron plate decorated with the ceremony of Setsubun on the eve of Risshun, late 19th century, wood box, 8.5cm. (Christie's) £3,410

An oval dark shibuichi migakiji tsuba, takabori and iroe takazogan, Yoritomo hiding in a hollow tree and Kagetoki driving out two wood pigeons, signed Shojuken Hamano Haruteru, 19th century, 6.9cm. (Christie's) £880

A Hamano school tsuba, Edo period (circa 1800), signed *Hiroyuki*, decorated in high relief with the 'Red Cliff' theme, with inlay of copper, shakudo, silver and gold, width 5.7cm. (Christie's) £955

An Uchikoshi school tsuba, Edo period (circa 1800), signed *Masayoshi* with kao, carved with a rock cave entrance and a hawk in shakudo and gold accents, width 5.8cm. (Christie's) £955

A Sunagawa school tsuba, Edo period (circa 1800), signed *Sunagawa Masanori Saku*, carved with an overall pattern of overlapping maple leaves, width 7.3cm. (Christie's) £1,023

A Kato school tsuba, Edo period, dated *Sei* (Ansei) *Kinoe Tora Moshun* (early spring 1859), decorated with lily flowers in shakudo and gold relief, width 7.5cm. (Christie's) £648

A Hagiya school tsuba, Edo period (circa 1875), signed *Hagiya Katsuhira*, inlaid with two finely carved gold dragons, width 7.8cm. (Christie's) £3,751

A Jingo school tsuba, Edo period (circa 1825), the web carved in a design of a water dragon executed in silver damascene (nunome), width 7.7cm. (Christie's) £205

An Iwata school tsuba, Edo period (circa 1850), with slightly raised design on a gourd vine and leaves with tendrils, width 7.7cm. (Christie's) £286

A Tanaka school tsuba, Edo period (circa 1850), with kao, carved and hammered in a stone finish, the edge carved with a tortoise-shell pattern, width 4cm. (Christie's) £171

A Goto style tsuba, Edo period (circa 1800), carved in an openwork design and inlaid with flush gold chrysanthemum blooms, landscape scenes, geometric patterns and poem cards, width 6.9cm. (Christie's) £1,159

19TH CENTURY

A Sendai style tsuba, Edo period (circa 1850), the rounded, trapezoidal-shaped iron plate with an overall gold nunome pattern of pine trees, width 5.5cm.
(Christie's) £614

A Tanaka school tsuba, Edo period (circa 1850), signed *Kagetoshi* with kao, carved with rain lines and inlaid with a relief sea turtle (minogame) in silver, width 6.2cm.
(Christie's) £682

A Bushu Ito school tsuba, Edo period (circa 1800), signed *Bushu Ju Masanobu*, carved and pierced with a melon vine and leaves, almost in the round, width 7.3cm.
(Christie's) £682

A Sendai style tsuba, Edo period (circa 1800), the thin, irregularly shaped iron plate with a delicate, raised rim, the web overlaid with gold damascene, width 6cm.
(Christie's) £443

A Jingo school tsuba, Edo period (circa 1825), the face inlaid with a sedge hat in copper with silver tie cords and a money bag in brass, width 7.6cm.
(Christie's) £375

A Tanaka style tsuba, Meiji era (circa 1870), signed *Yoshitsugu Tsukuru Kore*, decorated in high relief with large iron rocks and two pine trees with gold needles, width 7.7cm.
(Christie's) £818

An Oyama school tsuba, Edo period (circa 1800), signed *Tankasai Motoaki*, inlaid in very high relief shibuichi with Kanzan and Jitoku holding a silver scroll, width 7.9cm.
(Christie's) £1,773

An Edo Kinko tsuba, Edo period (circa 1850), signed *Senga Masamitsu* with kao, carved in low relief with the wind god, Futen Myo-o, accented in gold, width 8cm.
(Christie's) £580

A swordsmith's tsuba, Edo period (circa 1800), signed *Sadayuki Saku*, acid-etched in low relief, with a design of a dragon in swirling clouds, width 8.3cm.
(Christie's) £887

A circular iron tsuba decorated with mixed diaper patterns in gilt sujizogan and with a shakudo ropework rim, signed with a kao, Kenji style, 19th century, 7.6cm.
(Christie's) £660

A Choshu area tsuba, Edo period (circa 1800), formed as a branch of chrysanthemum with the stem and leaves at the base and two blooms above, width 7.6cm.
(Christie's) £277

An Edo Kinko tsuba, Meiji era (circa 1880), inscribed *Iwamoto Konkan* with kao, inlaid with a large copper octopus holding two large waterlily leaves as an umbrella, width 7.6cm.
(Christie's) £2,772

An Edo Kinko tsuba, Edo period (circa 1800), inscribed *Nampo*, inlaid with a farm house with a gold thatched roof and one behind it in shakudo, with a shakudo and copper tree between them, width 5.8cm.
(Christie's) £832

A Hamano style tsuba, Meiji era (circa 1875), signed *Sanin Inaba Masahiro* and inscribed *Shozui*, the plate carved with clouds touched with gold nunome and inlaid with the arhat Handaka Sonja in shibuichi and gold, width 7.3cm.
(Christie's) £1,802

A Bamen Tsunemasa school tsuba, Edo perod (circa 1800), pierced forming a thin-line diamond with eight stylised birds connecting the diamond to the seppa-dai and the hitsu-ana, width 6.7cm.
(Christie's) £194

An aorigata copper ishimeji tsuba decorated with Emma-o the King of Hell holding a shaku, 9.1cm. (Christie's) £2,750

A Kofu school tsuba, Edo period (circa 1800), signed *Kofu ju Toshimasa*, carved in an openwork design in the shape of a water dragon, width 6.3cm.
(Christie's) £273

An oval iron migakiji tsuba decorated with branches of bamboo in kosukashi, circa 1875, 8.5cm. (Christie's) £1,210

TSUBAS

A Hamano school tsuba, Edo period (circa 1800), inscribed *Hamano Naoyuki*, carved and inlaid with Kanyu and his attendant, who is reading a scroll under a pine tree, width 6.4cm.
(Christie's) £485

An Edo tsuba, Edo period (circa 1800), the plate (mokko) carved with an overall openwork (sukashi) pattern of interlocking rings (shippo), width 7.2cm.
(Christie's) £580

An Edo Kinko tsuba, Edo period (circa 1825), inscribed *Yasuchika*, dated *1717*, carved and inlaid with a torii with a squirrel on top and a shrine attendant looking at it through a torn umbrella, width 5.8cm.
(Christie's) £589

An Edo Kinko tsuba, Edo period (circa 1850), inscribed *Echizen No Daijo Fujiwara Nagatsune* with kao, carved as a waterfall with a very high relief shakudo and an inlaid gold striped tiger, width 6.5cm.
(Christie's) £693

An Akasaka school tsuba, Edo period (circa 1800), carved in an openwork design as a flight of geese, width 7.3cm.
(Christie's) £614

An Ishiguro style tsuba, Edo period (circa 1800), the oval shakudo nanako plate decorated with a gold peahen under a blooming cherry tree, width 6.5cm.
(Christie's) £832

An Edo Kinko tsuba, Edo period (circa 1800), inscribed *Otsu Mitsuoki* with kao, carved on the face with a pine tree in front of a waterfall and a silver hawk inlaid above, width 6cm.
(Christie's) £901

An oval sentoku tsuba, ishimeji, shakudo and gold inlay of a crag above billowing waves, the reverse with a poem, inscribed *Kaze Haruaki* and *Tou zu*, 19th century, wood box 6.3cm.
(Christie's) £1,595

An Ichinomiya school tsuba, Edo period (circa 1800), inscribed *Tsunenao* with kao, carved and inlaid with two grooms and a horse between them, width 6.8cm.
(Christie's) £589

An Edo Kinko school tsuba, Edo period (circa 1800), carved in deep relief with a gold dragon in high relief within waves, width 6.2cm.
(Christie's)   £1,637

A Kinai school tsuba, Edo period (circa 1800), pierced and carved as five arrow points, nearly in the round, width 7.3cm.
(Christie's)   £682

An Edo Kinko tsuba, Edo period (circa 1800), inscribed *Hamano Noriyuki*, inlaid with mandarin ducks in shakudo and gold, width 6.3cm.
(Christie's)   £1,296

A Nara school tsuba, Edo period (circa 1800), carved with a stone surface and depicting Shoki carved in very low relief, width 6.9cm.
(Christie's)   £1,023

A Goto Ichijo school tsuba, Edo period (circa 1850), carved and inlaid with a plum tree, the flowers in copper, silver and gold, width 5.7cm.
(Christie's)   £818

A Hirati school tsuba attributed to Haruyuki, Edo period (circa 1875), the face inlaid with two roundels in clear glass with gold cloisonné frames and several cherry blooms and petals in opaque glass (doro shippo) width 8cm.
(Christie's)   £5,115

A Jingo school tsuba, Edo period (circa 1850), the face carved with a kiri leaf in silver nunome and a kiri bloom in gold nunome, width 7.6cm.
(Christie's)   £273

An Ishiguro style tsuba, Edo period (circa 1875), with a hawk in shibuichi, shakudo, silver and gold, perched on the stump of a large oak tree, width 7.9cm.
(Christie's)   £3,069

A Kamiyoshi school tsuba, Edo period (circa 1825), pierced to resemble the inside of two overlapping clam shell halves, width 7.6cm.
(Christie's)   £955

TSUBAS

An Edo Higo tsuba, Meiji era (circa 1900), finely carved in an openwork design of the New Year's fern and rope (uzuriha), width 6.7cm.
(Christie's) £443

A Kamiyoshi school tsuba, Edo period (circa 1825), pierced with two water plantain leaves (omodaka) on either side of the central bar, width 7.3cm.
(Christie's) £546

A Mito school tsuba, Edo period (circa 1850), signed *Seiunsai Yukimitsu* with kao, carved in very high relief depicting a dragon in clouds, width 6.4cm.
(Christie's) £1,023

An Umetada school tsuba, Edo period (circa 1850), the sunken web carved in relief with an old plum tree, one bloom with gold centre, width 7.6cm.
(Christie's) £375

An Ishiguro school tsuba, Edo period (circa 1800), inscribed *Jugakusai Ishiguro Masayoshi* with kao, inlaid in low relief with a rooster in shakudo, copper and gold, near a gold chick, width 6.9cm.
(Christie's) £2,728

A Saotome style tsuba, Edo period (circa 1850), carved on both sides with wide radiating grooves, width 7.9cm.
(Christie's) £191

An Edo Kinko tsuba, Edo period (circa 1850), signature *Shibui Yoshimasa Hori*, inlaid with a praying mantis in nigurome with gilt wings, width 8.1cm.
(Christie's) £1,773

An Edo Kinko tsuba, Edo period (circa 1800), inlaid in relief with vines, leaves and blooms in shakudo, gold and silver, width 7cm.
(Christie's) £818

A Kamiyoshi school tsuba, Edo period (circa 1825), the plate with two wide bars with openwork above and below the central opening, width 7.5cm.
(Christie's) £273

A Mokkogata Nerikawa tsuba decorated in roironuri and gold hiramakie with two swallows flying above waterfalls, inscribed *Zeshin*, 7.8cm. (Christie's London) £1,100

A kakumokko-gata shibuichi tsuba, migakiji, inlaid in iroe takazogan with a fox in human clothing, the reverse with a fox trap, 19th century, 7cm. (Christie's) £440

A rounded-rectangular iron tsuba decorated with silver sujizogan and gilt nunomezogan in the style of Nakane Heilachiro of Higo, circa 1850, 8.6cm. (Christie's) £605

A fine rounded square copper ishimeji tsuba decorated in nikubori with a dragon concealed in vapour ascending Mount Fuji, on the reverse a toy dragon suspended from a branch of bamboo, signed Tsuneyuki, early 19th century, 7cm. (Christie's) £550

A gomokkogata iron tsuba decorated in shinchu takazogan with scrolling karakusa and family mon, signed *Oizumi Yuzenkio Mitsuchika*, mid 19th century, 9cm. (Christie's) £4,950

An oval iron migakiji tsuba decorated in takabori and takazogan with the Paragon of Filial Piety Taishun, on the reverse an elephant and two birds tilling and weeding the ground, signed Ukoku Oizumi Mitsuchika and dated 1849. (Christie's) £1,320

A rich shakudo elongated octagonal tsuba, chrysanthemums on a bamboo trellis, gilt detail, unsigned, 19th century, 6.7cm. (Christie's) £495

An iron tsuba with maple leaves and pine needles in ikizukashi, signed Suruga Takayoshi saku, circa 1850, 7.8cm. diam. (Christie's) £550

An irregularly shaped tsuba formed as a coiled snake in sentoku marubori, the eye gilt, signed *Unpo shujin koku*, 19th century, 8cm. (Christie's) £682

A broad oval iron migakiji tsuba, kirimon scattered inside a scrolling ropework border in gilt nunomezogan, unsigned, Edo Higo style, circa 1850. (Christie's) £550

A copper tsuba of squared form, 6.1cm., signed Masachika, katakiri engraving of a boy playing a flute, some wear and a little distressing. (Wallis & Wallis) £100

An inome-ni aoigata migakiji tsuba, cherryblossom and clouds in gilt nunomezogan, unsigned, Awa Shoami or Sendai school, 19th century, 8cm. (Christie's) £880

A rounded-rectangular iron yakite-shitate tsuba with radiating spokes and bekko pattern, the wide shallow rim with a long-eared rabbit, bird and paulownia designs, signed Naoaki, mid 19th century, 8.6cm. (Christie's) £770

A hachimokkogata iron migakiji tsuba decorated in silver and gilt nunomezogan with chrysanthemum flowers, unsigned, Awa Shoami or Sendai style, 19th century, 7.5cm. (Christie's) £770

A circular iron tsuba, ikizukashi with copper and gilt detail, a peasant loaded with brushwood holding two oxen by their tethers, signed *Nagato Hagi ju Kawaji Gon-nojo Tomokane saku,* early 19th century, 8.3cm. (Christie's London) £4,180

A flat shitogigata iron migakiji tsuba, coiled dragons and clouds in gilt nunomezogan, signed *Goto Seijo* and *Kao,* 19th century, 6.8cm. (Christie's) £605

A shallow mokkogata tsuba decorated with Susano-o no Mikoto attacking the monster Yamata no orochi, Meiji period, 8.9cm. (Christie's) £1,045

A superb oval shakudo-nanakoji tsuba decorated with karashishi, rocks and free-peonies, signed *Egawa Toshimasa,* first third 19th century, 7.9cm. (Christie's) £10,450

319

A Mito school tsuba, Edo period (circa 1800), carved in the web with two dragons in the round, positioned head to tail, width 5.9cm.
(Christie's)   £443

A Tanaka school sukashi tsuba, late Edo period (circa 1850), signed *Ikkanshiki Ryuso Hogen* (Tanaka Kiyotoshi [1804–1876]), width 7.5cm.
(Christie's)   £8,866

An Akao school tsuba, Edo period (circa 1825), the oval shakudo plate pierced in an openwork design of five broken fans, width 6.8cm.
(Christie's)   £1,023

A Shonai school tsuba, Edo period (circa 1800), the plate decorated with gold-stemmed bamboo leaves, and inlaid with a large copper crab, width 8.2cm.
(Christie's)   £1,091

An Edo Kinko tsuba, Edo period (circa 1850), decorated in high relief with two gold crests of hanging wisteria and one shakudo crest of a pine tree, width 7.7cm.
(Christie's)   £818

A Mito school tsuba, Edo period (circa 1800), signed *Koenshi Joei*, carved in high relief with a dragon writhing amongst the clouds, width 7.9cm.
(Christie's)   £3,751

A Bushu school tsuba, Edo period (circa 1800), pierced and carved with a design of peony blooms and a butterfly, width 7.4cm.
(Christie's)   £150

An Akao school tsuba, Edo period (circa 1850), carved in an openwork design of a praying mantis, width 6.9cm.
(Christie's)   £259

A Kinai school tsuba, Edo period (circa 1800), signed *Echizen ju Kinai Saku*, pierced and carved as a design of orchids, width 7.4cm.
(Christie's)   £818

A Higo style tsuba, Edo period (circa 1800), pierced and carved with a branch of chrysanthemum, width 7.1cm. (Christie's) £239

Japanese inlaid shakudo tsuba, 19th century, of oval form, each hitsu with gold plug, decorated in relief, 3¼ x 3in. (Du Mouchelles) £138

A 19th century iron tsuba with a crayfish in marubori, with gilt hirazogan seal of Munenori, 6.9cm. diam. (Christie's) £506

An Edo Kinko tsuba, Edo period (circa 1850), inscribed 'This copy made to order', Iwamoto Konkan, the shakudo plate carved with waves and wave heads, width 7.2cm. (Christie's) £1,940

A rounded rectangular sentoku tsuba, nikubori and iroe takazogan, Susano-o no Mikoto recuing Inada-hime from a serpent with eight heads, unsigned, 19th century, 7.6cm. (Christie's) £715

A very shallow mokkogata iron migakiji tsuba, nikubori and takazogan, a fish-eagle on a rocky outcrop above breaking waves, signed Hashimoto Isshi and Kao, 19th century, 8.6cm. (Christie's) £3,300

An oval iron migakiji tsuba, Haichu no Fuji or Fuji reflected in a sake cup representing the elixir of life, signed Shinoda Hisakatsu, 19th century. (Christie's London) £2,640

A Hamano style tsuba, Edo period (circa 1800), inscribed Otsuryuken Miboku, the stone surface carved with Chokaro in an openwork cave releasing the horse from his gourd, width 6.1cm. (Christie's) £450

A circular iron tsuba with a stylised thundercloud pattern in silver sujizogan, the iron plate 18th century, the shippo 19th century, Hirata school, possibly by Harunari, 8.1cm. (Christie's) £1,100

UNIFORMS

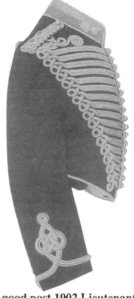

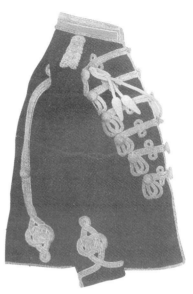

A Victorian Colonels full dress scarlet tunic of the 16th Lucknow Regt, white facings, lightweight cloth, gilt lace and braid trim, shoulder cords, fine gilt buttons.
(Wallis & Wallis) £200

A good post 1902 Lieutenant's full dress blue jacket of The Royal Horse Artillery, scarlet collar, gilt cord and lace trim, including 17 loops with ball buttons to chest.
(Wallis & Wallis) £360

A good Captain's full dress blue tunic of the 3rd (Kings Own) Hussars, scarlet collar, gilt lace, braid and gimp trim, including 6 loops with purl buttons and olivets to chest.
(Wallis & Wallis) £975

A rare WWI Lieutenants khaki uniform of the Womens Royal Air Force, comprising peaked soft cap, tunic, ankle length skirt with twin pockets.
(Wallis & Wallis) £530

A Victorian Colour Sergeants full dress scarlet tunic of the 1st Volunteer Bn The R. West Kent Regt, blue facings, shoulder straps embroidered 1/V/W. Kent, enbroidered crown/ crossed standards and 3 silver chevrons to right sleeve, 3 stars to cuff.
(Wallis & Wallis) £130

A Lieutenant's full dress scarlet tunic of The Queen's Royal Regt (West Surrey) circa 1925, blue facings, gilt lace and braid trim, shoulder cords, gilt collar badges.
(Wallis & Wallis) £120

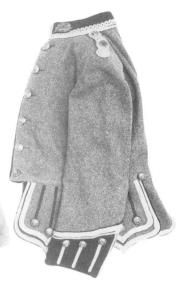

A good rare Captain's khaki tropical uniform of the Calcutta Scottish, comprising glengarry with red and green diced headband, linen doublet, Calcutta Scottish shoulder titles, pair linen spats.
(Wallis & Wallis)   £105

A Captains full dress khaki tunic of the Indian Frontier Force, light brown cord trim, including 5 loops with olivets and purl buttons to chest, gimp shoulder cords.
(Wallis & Wallis)   £500

A good scarce Victorian Lieutenants full dress elcho doublet of the London Scottish Volunteers, blue facings, white lace, cord and braid trim, shoulder cords, embroidered collar badges.
(Wallis & Wallis)   £280

A good Major's full dress scarlet tunic of the 5th Mahratta Light Infantry, black facings, gilt lace and braid trim, shoulder cords, silver collar badges. (Wallis & Wallis)   £175

A pre 1922 officer's full dress drab tunic of the 124th Baluchistan Infantry, scarlet facings, gilt lace and braid trim, shoulder cords.
(Wallis & Wallis)   £50

A Lt Colonel's full dress blue tunic of the 17th Cavalry, white facings and semi plastron, gilt lace, cord and gimp trim, shoulder cords, large gilt buttons.
(Wallis & Wallis)   £1,200

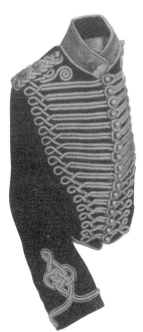

A post 1902 Lieutenant's full dress blue jacket of The Royal Horse Artillery, with scarlet collar, gilt cord and lace trim including 17 loops to chest. (Wallis & Wallis) £260

An officer's uniform of the 2nd Life Guards comprising full dress scarlet tunic with Field officer's ornate gold embroidery and blue velvet collar and cuffs. (Christie's) £1,540

A pre 1855 officer's scarlet coatee of The 19th (1st York, N Riding) Regt, good gilt buttons and embroidered skirt ornaments. (Wallis & Wallis) £410

A good Victorian Captain's full dress uniform of the 1st Volunteer Bn The Queens Own Cameron Highlanders, comprising scarlet doublet, silver plated buttons, pair tartan trews, pair Wellington boots, in a tin case. (Wallis & Wallis) £575

A yellow Skinner's kurta with plain shoulder chains, a fine pouchbelt and its Skinner's Horse title scroll. (Christie's) £3,000

A post-1902 Lieutenant's full dress scarlet tunic of The Lancashire Fusiliers, white facings, gilt lace and braid trim, shoulder cords, large embroidered grenade collar badges; pair overalls; crimson waistsash and tassels. (Wallis & Wallis) £60

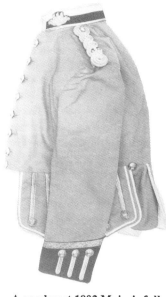

A good complete WWII Subaltern's khaki SD uniform of the Auxiliary Training Service, comprising: baize cloth peaked cap, tunic and belt, 2 ties, skirt, together with details of the wearer's service.
(Wallis & Wallis) £480

A Prussian Rittmeister's dress tunic of the 14th Uhlan Regt., dark blue with maroon piping and cuffs. (Wallis & Wallis) £172

A good post 1902 Major's full dress scarlet doublet of The Kings Own Scottish Borderers, blue facings, white piping, gilt lace and braid trim, shoulder cords, embroidered collar badges, gilt buttons.
(Wallis & Wallis) £230

An officer's blue full dress tunic of the Staffordshire Yeomanry (Queens Own Royal Regiment) with scarlet facings and trimmed with silver cord.
(Christie's) £352

An other rank's full dress tunic probably of Bengal Light Cavalry circa 1857 of heavy blue-grey cloth with facings light red and white cord loops. (Christie's) £330

A Lancashire Hussars officer's magnificent full dress blue jacket and pélisse both heavily embellished with gold cord. (Christie's) £990

An officer's scarlet short-tailed coatee with blue facings of the Royal Flintshire Militia, trimmed with gold lace and bearing fine gilt buttons. (Christie's) £990

A good Lieutenant's full dress scarlet tunic circa 1865 of the 18th (Royal Irish) Regt., with its crimson silk shoulder sash. (Wallis & Wallis) £250

A rare Georgian officer's blue short coatee of The 12th (The Prince of Wales's) Light Dragoons, buff facings, edging and plastron. (Wallis & Wallis) £1,150

An officer's green frock coat of the 1st Scinde Horse, worn 1861–85, black facings, black gimp trim including 5 loops with purl buttons and olivets to chest. (Wallis & Wallis) £800

An officer's dark blue full dress coatee circa 1825 of the Kings Cheshire Yeomanry with scarlet facings and white metal buttons. (Christie's)   £275

A scarce Victorian Royal Navy midshipman's coatee, circa 1840, nine buttons with narrow silk cord lines to chest. (Wallis & Wallis)   £490

An officer's short-tailed scarlet coatee with blue facings and gilt buttons with letters LEV and with gold-laced scarlet cloth shoulder-wings. (Christie's)   £418

A fine Colonel's full dress scarlet tunic of The Royal Warwickshire Regt., with a crimson silk waistsash and tassels. (Wallis & Wallis)   £220

United States Coast Guard uniform, late 19th/early 20th century, consisting of jacket, pants, hat, small flag, belt and two leashes. (Eldred's)   £123

A complete Civil Service levée dress uniform, circa 1900, worn by a member of the Indian Civil Service, comprising: cocked hat; tailcoat; courtsword; pair Wellington boots; pair court shoes and buckles. (Wallis & Wallis)   £310

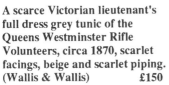

A scarce Victorian lieutenant's full dress grey tunic of the Queens Westminster Rifle Volunteers, circa 1870, scarlet facings, beige and scarlet piping. (Wallis & Wallis) £150

A good scarce Victorian lieutenant's full dress uniform of the Royal Naval Artillery Volunteers 1887–91, comprising: cocked hat, tail coat and gilt epaulettes. (Wallis & Wallis) £600

A Lewes Home Guard blouse, rank Private, (factory label missing). (Wallis & Wallis) £35

An officer's blue full dress jacket of the Royal Maylor Cavalry circa 1830 with scarlet facings, silver Russia braid trimming and white metal curb-chain wings. (Christie's) £1,210

A Victorian Lieutenant-Colonel's uniform of the Second West York Artillery Volunteers, blue full dress tunic, good embroidered sabretache, bearing Royal Arms and scrolls *Second West York Artillery Volunteers*. (Wallis & Wallis) £1,200

A Captain's dress uniform of the 6th Duke of Connaught's Royal Canadian Hussars, comprising brown fur busby, in its japanned tin, dark blue tunic with gold bullion frogging and decoration. (Phillips) £880

A scarce and interesting World War II Corporal's khaki BD blouse of the 23rd (Lewes) Sussex Home Guard, with *Home Guard/Sx/23* shoulder titles.
(Wallis & Wallis)   £70

A good pre-1855 officer's scarlet long tailed coatee of the 18th Bengal Native Infantry, yellow facings, two gilt lace loops with buttons to collar.
(Wallis & Wallis)   £190

A Captain's full dress blue tunic of a Bengal Lancers Regt., scarlet facings and semi plastron, gilt lace and gimp trim.
(Wallis & Wallis)   £240

A good Victorian Major's full dress scarlet tunic, circa 1885, of a Militia Battalion, The Devonshire Regiment, white facings, gilt lace and braid ornamentation to cuffs.
(Wallis & Wallis)   £80

An impressive full life representation of a Corporal, 20th (Service) Bn The King's Liverpool Regt. (the 'Liverpool Pals') as serving with the 30th Division in France, 1916.
(Wallis & Wallis)   £1,000

A good Coldstream Guards officer's full dress scarlet tunic with blue facings, white piping, heavy gilt embroidered collar, cuffs, skirts and shoulder straps.
(Wallis & Wallis)   £230

A scarce other ranks' Zouave style light blue jacket of the Algerian Turcos, yellow lace trim, with its matching vest. (Wallis & Wallis) £40

Pre-1914 Major's blue tunic of The Royal Regt. of Artillery. (James Norwich Auctions) £25

A Georgian officer's scarlet coatee of the 1st Somerset Regiment of Militia, circa 1815. (Wallis & Wallis) £750

A post 1902 Lieutenants full dress scarlet tunic of the 16th (The Queens) Lancers, blue facings and plastron, collar badges, gilt lace trim, shoulder cords. (Wallis & Wallis) £710

A good Leicestershire Yeomanry Squadron Quarter Master Sergeants uniform, c. 1910 comprising: blue peaked cap, blue jacket with scarlet facings, pair of blue overalls, pair of Wellington boots, pair of gloves, and a scarlet mess waistcoat. (Wallis & Wallis) £370

Civil uniform items of a Privy Councillor as follows: the full dress blue coatee, the levée coatee, cocked hat with white feather border and court sword. (Christie's) £495

A good Major's full dress scarlet tunic of the 6th Bn The Royal Welsh Fusiliers, blue facings, silver lace and braid trim, shoulder cords with "T" below crown.
(Wallis & Wallis)   £140

An Edward VII blue mess jacket and waistcoat of The King's Own Norfolk Yeomanry, worn by Regt. Sgt. Major Hudgell. (James Norwich Auctions)
                                £75

An officer's full dress rifle green tunic 1903–22 of the 130th (King George's Own) Baluchis (Jacobs Rifles), crimson facings, cord and lace trim, including 5 loops with purl buttons.
(Wallis & Wallis)   £450

A Captain's full dress scarlet tunic of The Norfolk Regt., yellow facings, gilt lace and braid trim, shoulder cords, gilt collar badges, name inside "GB Northcote". (Wallis & Wallis)   £80

A complete Vic 1876 Pattern uniform of a Lieutenant of the City of London comprising: cocked hat, peaked cap, scarlet tunic, court sword, pair shoes with box spurs and trees.
(Wallis & Wallis)   £600

The elaborate full state style livery of a Footman to the Earls of Shrewsbury consisting of heavy maroon cloth coat, skirted waistcoat and knee-breeches of red plush.
(Christie's)   £132

331

An Edward VII Lieutenant's full dress uniform of The 5th (Princess Charlotte of Wales's) Dragoon Guards, comprising scarlet tunic, gilt lace shoulder belt, silver mounted pouch. (Wallis & Wallis) £575

An officer's short-tailed scarlet coatee of Napoleonic Wars period, presumably Cinque Ports Volunteers with yellow facings and white metal buttons. (Christie's) £715

A Vic Major's full dress blue tunic of the 1st Punjab Cavalry, scarlet facings, gilt lace, cord and braid trim, including heavy cuff ornaments. (Wallis & Wallis) £750

A post-1902 Lieutenant's full dress scarlet tunic of the 16th (The Queens) Lancers, blue facings and plastron, collar badges, gilt lace trim, shoulder cords; gilt cap lines; good gilt and crimson girdle. (Wallis & Wallis) £400

A good Egyptian officer's full dress uniform, circa 1910, comprising blue frock coat, integral waistbelt, gilt waist belt plate with applied silver Egyptian arms. (Wallis & Wallis) £120

A scarce Victorian officer's short scarlet coatee of The 93rd Highlanders, circa 1850, white facings, two lines of ten buttons to chest. (Wallis & Wallis) £650

A scarce Algerian Spahi officer's full dress red jacket, finely worked overall with purple embroidery, open sleeves, studs to chest.
(Wallis & Wallis)   £240

The Victorian coatee and epaulettes of an officer of the Yeomen of the Guard, the coatee scarlet with rich gold embroidery. (Christie's S. Ken)
£462

A good, rare officers uniform, c. 1835, of the Royal Perthshire Militia comprising scarlet coatee, double breasted with 2 lines of 10 buttons in pairs, pair epaulettes, blue cloth with silver thistle embroidery solid crescents.
(Wallis & Wallis)   £610

A good post 1902 Colonel's full dress scarlet doublet of The Royal Scots Fusiliers, blue facings, gilt lace and braid trim, shoulder cords, embroidered collar grenades with solid thistles.
(Wallis & Wallis)   £540

A white Wolseley helmet with gilt chin-chain, a dark blue tunic with black velvet facings and with General's buttons, white leather gloves.
(Christie's)   £350

A good post 1902 Lt. Colonel's full dress scarlet doublet of The Gordon Highlanders, and a pair of tartan trews. (Wallis & Wallis)   £200

A scarce other rank's white metal waist belt clasp of the 5th Battn Cheshire Rifle Volunteers. (Wallis & Wallis) £50

A good Victorian officer's silver plated waist belt clasp of the Ayrshire Rifle Volunteers. (Wallis & Wallis) £70

A scarce other rank's blackened brass waist belt clasp of the Melrose Rifle Volunteers. (Wallis & Wallis) £220

An officer's silvered waist belt clasp of The 2nd Volunteer Bn. The Welsh Regt. Dragon device in centre. £150

An officer's gilt and silvered waist belt clasp of The 97th (The Earl of Ulster's) Regt. £100

A Victorian officer's gilt and silver waist belt clasp of The 4th Royal South Middlesex Militia. Title in old English style in circle and crowned Roman IV numeral. £100

A good other rank's white metal waist belt plate of the Dumbartonshire Volunteers. (Wallis & Wallis) £70

An officer's gilt and silver plated waist belt plate of The Royal Scots Fusiliers. (Wallis & Wallis) £50

A good Victorian officer's gilt and silvered waist belt clasp of The Royal Irish Fusiliers. (Wallis & Wallis) £200

A good officer's gilt and silver plated waist belt plate of The Dorsetshire Regt. (Wallis & Wallis) £65

A good bronzed waist belt plate of the Fifeshire Volunteer Rifles. (Wallis & Wallis) £90

A fine officer's gilt and silver plated waist belt plate of The 39th (Dorsetshire) Regt. (Wallis & Wallis) £110

French combination cane/revolver, the angular staghorn handle removing to reveal a six shot fluted .22 calibre cylinder, the action, with folding trigger, marked *Paris/Brevette*, length overall 35in.
(Butterfield & Butterfield)   £1,652

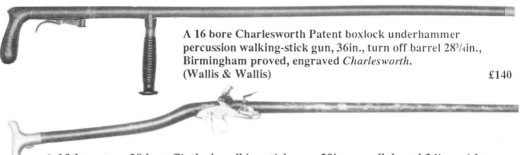

A 16 bore Charlesworth Patent boxlock underhammer percussion walking-stick gun, 36in., turn off barrel 28¾in., Birmingham proved, engraved *Charlesworth*.
(Wallis & Wallis)   £140

A 19th century 28-bore flintlock walking stick gun, 50in. overall, barrel 34in., with traces of brown painted finish. (Wallis & Wallis)   £500

A good .36 pump-up air-cane walking stick-rifle, 37¼in., brass liner barrel assembly 21in., with wooden barrel rod and brass cap, the steel construction painted to simulate bamboo, small wooden screw-on handle which is removed to screw on a well figured walnut skeleton stock with foliate engraved steel end piece.   £250

An interesting S.S. 9mm. walking stick shot gun, 31¼in., barrel 23in., stamped: "J.G. Barnes Regd. 27th Dec. 1879", scalloped horn handle fixed to cane by means of white metal ferrule which also serves to conceal the trigger, black cane covered barrel terminating in brass end piece into which screws a steel muzzle protector.   £300

A good .380 all-steel walking-stick air cane rifle, 38in., screw-on barrel section with brass barrel liner 20in., black lacquer overall, screw-on horn handle, with small loading port with lever access, fixed sights, in its oak case, trade label of 'Edward-London', green felt-lined, with compartments, a 'T' piece barrel key.   £300

PISTOLS

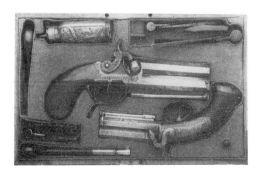

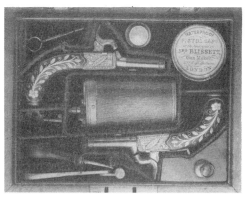

Interesting cased set of Irish double barrel percussion pistols, the first, with heavy 5in. octagon barrels marked *W & I Rigby Dublin*, the chequered bag shaped grip with silver escutcheon engraved *R. Bateson/Esq.* and hinged butt compartment. **£1,472**

Cased pair of English percussion muff pistols, having 1¹/₈in. round screw barrels, the engraved frames marked *Clark* on the left side and *London* on the obverse, the bag shaped grips inlaid with leafy plants in silver wire and with silver escutcheons. **£1,288**

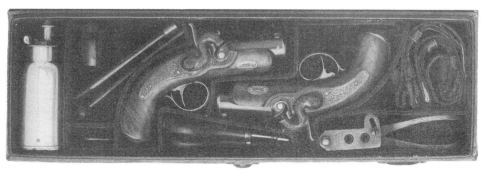

Exceptional cased pair of Nimschke engraved percussion Deringers by A. G. Genez, calibre .44, 1⁵/₈in. barrels, with platinum blowout plugs, marked *A.G. Genez, Maker, No. 9 Chambers St. N.Y.*, ³/₄in. breeches, the finely scroll engraved locks marked *A.G. Genez*, hammers and breech sections decorated en suite. **£20,133**

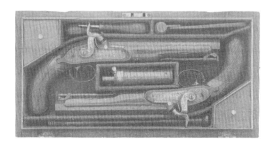

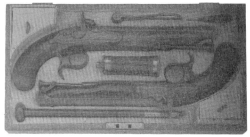

A pair of percussion officer's pistols with browned octagonal sighted barrels signed on the top flats, engraved case-hardened breeches with platinum line and plug, engraved case-hardened tangs, signed engraved case-hardened bolted locks, by Westley Richards, Birmingham proof marks, circa 1850, 13¹/₂in. long. **£1,870**

A pair of percussion officer's pistols, converted from flintlock, with browned twist sighted barrels each engraved *London* on the top flat, platinum line, engraved case-hardened tangs, signed case-hardened bolted locks engraved with a trophy of arms on the tails, by Beckwith, London, Birmingham proof marks, early 19th century, 14¹/₂in. long. **£1,430**

PISTOLS

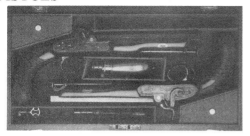

Cased pair of English percussion officer's pistols, .75 calibre 8in. octagon barrels engraved *Westley Richards 170 New Bond St. London*, platinum line at the breeches, scroll engraved locks with push-on safeties, platinum blow-out plugs. £3,661

Rare cased Dumonthier-type percussion knife-pistol, having a straight 9in. blade with central fuller mounted with a 4in. round barrel on either side and marked *Dumonthier/Brevette*, ribbed ivory grips with flat German silver buttcap.

£3,679

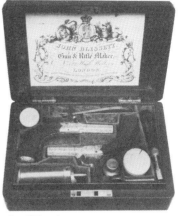

A rare cased Borchardt 1893 patent 7.65mm. self-loading pistol by Waffenfabrik Loewe, Berlin, retaining virtually all of its original finish, with vertical sliding thumb-safe, V-notched fixed-backsight, pyramidal frontsight, chequered walnut grips, with original 'Patent' magazine, 7^1/2in. barrel, in its original black leather case with white-metal mounts. £14,300

Cased pair of English percussion screwbarrel muff pistols, having 1^1/4in. octagonal German silver barrels scroll engraved and marked *John Blisset/316 & 321 High Holborn/London*, scroll engraved German silver frames, chequered grips with German silver buttcaps and iron compartment lids. £2,023

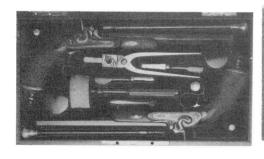

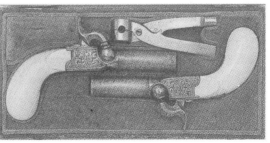

Cased pair of Belgian percussion target pistols, the 10in. octagon barrels engraved *Y Boussart a Liege*, engraved and casehardened locks, trigger guards and breeches, ebony stocks with chequered forends and grips. £2,391

A pair of small Belgian box-lock percussion pocket pistols with etched twist turn-off barrels, bright actions engraved with scrolling foliage, folding triggers, and swelling ivory butts, Liège proof, mid-19th century, 4^1/4in.

£1,100

PISTOLS

Rare cased pair of English patch lock percussion pistols 1810–1815, the 10in. octagon barrels, with gilt maker's stamp and gold line at breech, engraved *Samuel Nock Regent Circus*, the barrel ribs with two thimbles retaining brass tipped ramrods.
(Butterfield & Butterfield)   £4,783

Cased engraved Volcanic lever action pistol, serial No. 1059, .31 calibre, 3½in. barrel marked *New Haven Conn. Patent Feb. 14, 1854*, scroll engraved silver plated brass frame, blued barrel and lever, casehardened hammer, varnished walnut grips.
(Butterfield & Butterfield)   £8,785

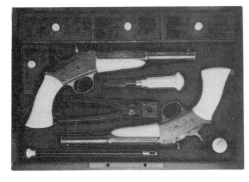

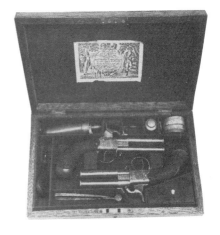

Deluxe cased pair of Exhibition Remington model 1871 single shot cartridge pistols, serial numbers 2 and 3, .50 calibre, 8½in. part-round/part-octagon cannon turned barrels marked in gold inlay *E. Remington & Sons Ilion New York U.S.A.*, Liège proofed under the forearms, the breeches gold inlaid with an American Eagle, shield and *E. Pluribus Unum* riband motifs.
(Butterfield & Butterfield)   £29,285

Cased pair of English swivel breech double barrel percussion pistols, 2½in. barrels with British proofs, chequered bag shaped grips with diamond shaped German silver escutcheons.
(Butterfield & Butterfield)   £1,324

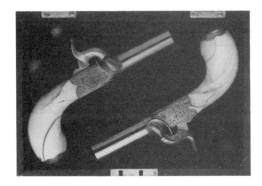

Cased pair of Belgian screwbarrel percussion pistols, having 1¾in. round barrels, scroll engraved frames with Liège proofs, ivory grips, engraved buttcaps with compartments.
(Butterfield & Butterfield)   £809

Cased pair of Continental screwbarrel percussion pistols, Belgian or French, each with 2⅛in. round barrel, fluted grips with floral relief carving.
(Butterfield & Butterfield)   £1,104

PISTOLS

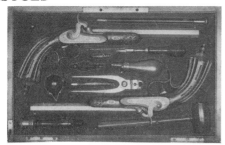

A pair of 42 bore Belgian percussion duelling pistols circa 1850, No. 6382, 15³/₄in., octagonal twist barrels 9¹/₂in., Liège proved, numbered *1* and *2* at breeches, foliate engraved locks and steel furniture.
(Wallis & Wallis)   £2,600

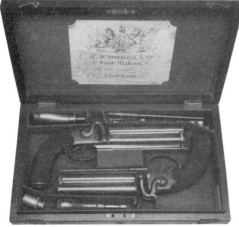

Cased pair of English double barrel percussion belt pistols, the 5¹/₂in. over/under barrels marked *R. B. Rodda & Co. London & Calcutta*, swivel ramrods, finely chequered grips with butt compartments.
(Butterfield & Butterfield)   £2,943

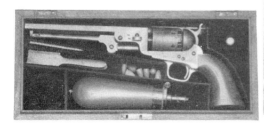

A good 6 shot .36 inch London single action Colt Navy percussion revolver No. 25724, 13 inches, octagonal barrel 7½ inches, stamped "Address Col Colt London", London proved. Underlever rammer, cylinder roll engraved with naval engagement scene, hardened frame stamped "Colts Patent". (Wallis & Wallis)   £2,100

A scarce 20-shot pinfire revolver, 13cm. sighted barrel, frame engraved with foliage against a stippled ground and signed J. Chaineux.
(Phillips)   £2,100

A good scarce 5 shot 54 bore Reeve's Patent self cocking percussion revolver no. 1869, 11½in., octagonal barrel 6in., Birmingham proved. (Wallis & Wallis)
                                     £1,550

A five-shot 54 bore percussion revolver, 13cm. octagonal sighted barrel signed *Willmer, Grantham*, rammer mounted on the left side, plain open top frame, plain blued cylinder, two-piece chequered wood grips, contained in a baize lined mahogany case with some accessories.
(Phillips)   £480

BELT PISTOLS

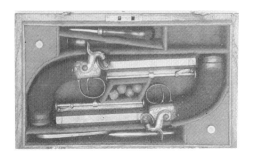

A pair of percussion box lock belt pistols with octagonal sighted barrels signed in full on the top flat and rifled with eight grooves, foliate engraved breeches and tangs, foliate engraved bolted actions, by E. & W. Bond, 45 Cornhill, London, London proof marks, circa 1840, 9¼in. (Christie's S. Ken) £1,320

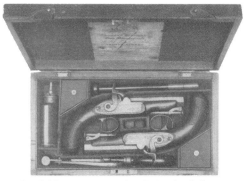

A pair of 16 bore percussion belt pistols by Westley Richards, 9in., octagonal twist barrels 4½in., platinum inlaid breech line and safety plugs, fullstocked, foliate engraved bolted locks. (Wallis & Wallis) £2,100

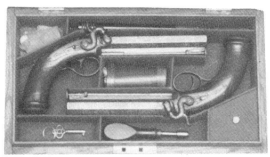

A good pair of 18 bore back action percussion belt pistols by Manton & Son, 10½ inches, browned octagonal twist barrels 6 inches. London proved, engraved "London". Colour hardened foliate and border engraved locks with Manton & Sons, sliding safety bolts, dolphin hammers. Swivel ramrods. (Wallis & Wallis) £2,300

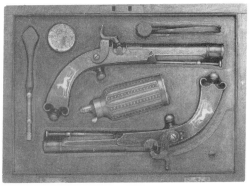

A pair of Highland all-metal percussion belt pistols with reblued three-stage barrels engraved with thistles, engraved faceted breeches, engraved flat locks, engraved stocks inlaid with an engraved silver panel on each side of the fore-end, Birmingham proof marks, mid-19th century, 10in. long. (Christie's) £1,870

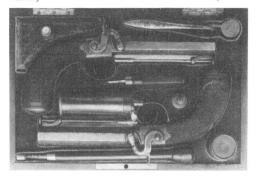

Cased pair of English percussion belt pistols, the 4½in. large calibre octagon barrels engraved *C & H Egg London*, rib mounted swivel ramrods, scroll engraved fittings, finely chequered grips with hinged butt compartments and German silver escutcheons. (Butterfield & Butterfield) £1,398

A pair of 24 bore percussion belt pistols by Wogdon circa 1790, drum converted from flintlock 15in., swamped octagonal barrels engraved *Wogdon London*, stepped bolted locks foliate engraved, detented actions, set triggers, breech drums with platinum safety plugs. (Wallis & Wallis) £1,800

TARGET PISTOLS

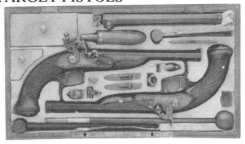

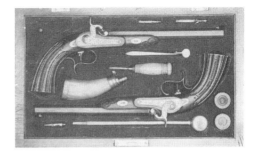

An unusual pair of German target pistols, the locks with interchangeable flint and percussion parts, the interchangeable smooth and rifled rebrowned octagonal sighted barrels signed in full and dated in silver on the top flats, by Franz Ulrich In Stuttgart, dated *1828*, 14¹/₂in. long.
£3,520

A pair of Belgian percussion rifled target pistols with browned octagonal sighted barrels inscribed *A cier* on the top flats, adjustable back sights, foliate engraved tangs, the locks and mounts decorated en suite, Liege proof marks, circa 1850, 15½in.
£1,760

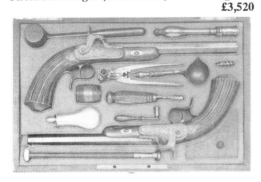

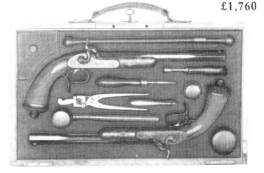

A pair of percussion target or duelling pistols, 26.5cm. octagonal rifled sighted damascus barrels signed in gold on the top flat against a blued ground Lassence-Rongé a Liege, contained in their brass mounted baize lined close fitted mahogany case complete with all accessories.
£3,800

A good pair of percussion target or duelling pistols, 27.5cm. sighted rifled blued octagonal barrels with fluted central sections signed Gastinne Renette à Paris, the finely chequered butts inlaid 1 and 2 in gold, contained in their baize lined close fitted oak case complete with all accessories.
£5,000

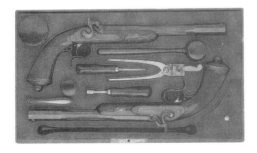

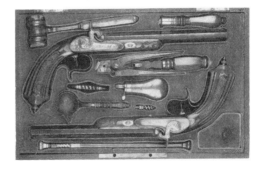

A pair of French percussion target pistols with minor differences, the three-stage partly fluted blued octagonal sighted barrels of hog's back form and rifled with twelve grooves, signed *Fni Par Gastinne Renette à Paris* and numbered 1 and 2 at the case-hardened scroll engraved faceted breeches, second half of the 19th century, 16¹/₂in. long.
£3,300

A pair of Belgian percussion rifled target pistols with signed rebrowned octagonal sighted barrels, scroll engraved case-hardened breeches and tangs, the latter each fitted with adjustable back-sight, figured walnut half-stocks carved with scrolling foliage in relief, in original fitted mahogany case lined in plum velvet, by Charles Lenders, Liège, circa 1860, 16in.
£3,520

PEPPERBOX REVOLVERS

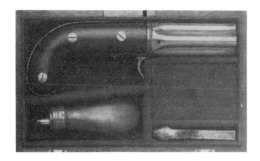

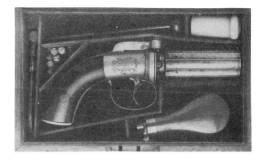

Rare cased English percussion pepperbox pistol, 3¼in. brass five barrel cluster featuring interior nipples with numbered vents, the extended bag-shaped grip with brass frame marked *Budding/Maker*.
(Butterfield & Butterfield) £3,679

Cased English percussion pepperbox pistol, having 3½in. fluted barrels in six shot configuration, scroll engraved German silver frame and grip straps, engraved steel trigger guard, wood grips.
(Butterfield & Butterfield) £589

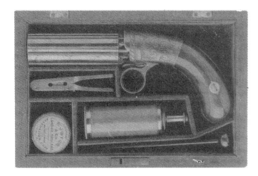

A Blunt & Syms under-hammer six-shot percussion pepperbox revolver with blued fluted barrels, blued rounded action engraved with open scrolling foliage, ring-trigger, figured walnut grips, and much original finish, unsigned, mid-19th century, 7¾in. long.
(Christie's) £1,100

A self cocking six shot percussion pepperbox revolver with case hardened fluted barrels, in original lined and fitted brass bound mahogany case with trade label and accessories including three way copper flask, by B. Cogswell, 224 Strand, London, London proof marks, circa 1850, 9½in. (Christie's S. Ken) £3,300

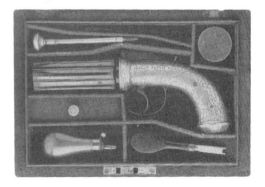

Cased English percussion pepperbox pistol, having a 3½in. six shot fluted barrel cluster, the engraved action marked *John Blissett/321 High Holborn/London*, finely chequered bag shaped grip with brass escutcheon, length overall of gun 9in.
(Butterfield & Butterfield) £809

An unusual self-cocking six-shot percussion pepperbox revolver with reblued fluted barrels engraved at the muzzles and numbered from 1 to 6, by Joseph Wood, Lewes, London proof marks, mid-19th century, 8¾in. long.
(Christie's) £1,870

POCKET REVOLVERS

Cased Colt model 1849 Wells Fargo pocket revolver, serial No. 48234, 3in. barrel without loading lever and marked with two line New York address, varnished walnut grips.
(Butterfield & Butterfield)   £29,431

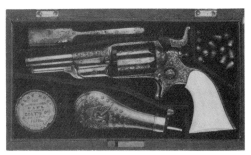

Cased factory engraved Colt Root model 1855 sidehammer pocket pistol, serial No. 7902 IE, .31 calibre, scroll engraved on frame, loading lever, hammer, cylinder and backstrap, ivory grips.
(Butterfield & Butterfield)   £3,679

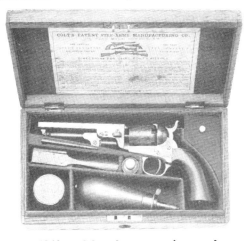

A Colt 1849 model pocket percussion revolver, with blued octagonal sighted barrel stamped with New York address, cylinder with roll engraved stagecoach hold-up scene, case-hardened frame and loading lever, silvered trigger-guard and back-strap, 9½in.
(Christie's)   £1,650

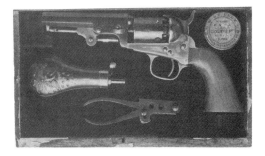

Rare presentation book casing of Colt model 1849 pocket model percussion revolver, serial No. 198066, .31 calibre, 4in. barrel marked *Address Col. Sam'l Colt New York U.S. America*, varnished oak grip, believed to be from the Charter Oak, blue and casehardened finish, six-shot cylinder bearing stagecoach hold-up scene.
(Butterfield & Butterfield)   £25,624

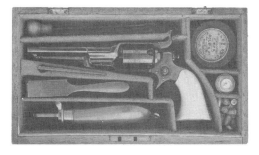

A Colt-Root 1855 model .31 percussion pocket revolver, No. 12864E for 1868, with blued two-stage sighted barrel engraved with London address, in original lined and fitted oak case with full accessories, London proof marks, 9in. long.
(Christie's)   £4,950

A Colt 1849 model pocket percussion revolver, the blued sighted barrel engraved *Sam Colt* in gothic script on the top flat, in original American mahogany case lined in blued velvet with accessories including 'eagle and shield' flask, 9in. (Christie's S. Ken)
          £2,860

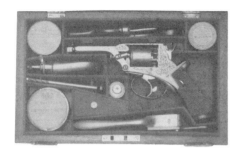

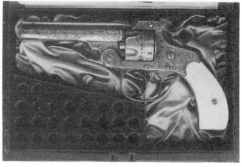

A good 5 shot 120 bore Tranter's patent self cocking percussion revolver, 8in., barrel 3³/₄in., Birmingham proved, engraved with retailer *Thos Williams, South Castle St. Liverpool,* spring stud retains arbour pin, sliding safety bolt locks cylinder.
(Wallis & Wallis)   £1,550

Cased Nimschke engraved presentation Smith & Wesson Second model double action revolver, serial No. 15362, .32 calibre, 3¹/₂in. barrel, profusely scroll engraved on barrel, frame and cylinder, the backstrap engraved *L.V. Sone/ From/N.Y. Rifle Club,* mother-of-pearl grips.
(Butterfield & Butterfield)   £4,393

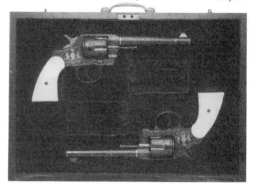

Cased Colt second model 1855 Root sidehammer percussion revolver, factory engraved and presentation inscribed, serial No. 6707, .265 calibre, 3¹/₂in. octagon barrel marked *Colt's Pt. 1855 and Address Col Colt Hartford, Ct. U.S.A.,* finely scroll engraved frame, hammer, barrel and loading lever.
(Butterfield & Butterfield)   £11,714

Deluxe cased presentation pair of Colt model 1895 double action revolvers gold and silver inlaid and engraved by Cuno Helfricht, serial numbers 88566 and 88567 hand engraved, .38 calibre, 6in. barrels with gold band inlays at breech and muzzle, engraved overall in tight floral-scroll motifs.
(Butterfield & Butterfield)   £29,285

Cased Colt Bisley flattop single action army revolver, engraved with pearl grips, serial No. 326568, .44 Russian calibre, 7¹/₂in. barrel stamped on left side *Bisley Model 44 Russian Ctg,* engraved by Cuno Helfricht with scroll engraved frame, barrel, gripstraps and both cylinders on a punched ground.
(Butterfield & Butterfield)   £47,587

Cased Colt factory engraved single action army revolver, English proofed, serial No. 53441, .450 Eley calibre, 5¹/₂in. barrel marked *Colt's Pt. Mfg. Co. Hartford Ct. U.S.A. Depot 14 Pall Mall London,* profusely factory scroll engraved with nickel plated finish, blued screws and mother-of-pearl grips.
(Butterfield & Butterfield)   £32,945

REVOLVERS

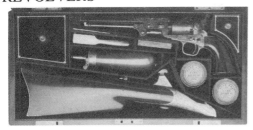

Deluxe cased and engraved Colt model 1851 navy percussion revolver with attachable shoulder stock, serial No. 90140, .36 calibre, 7¹/₂in. barrel marked *Address Col. Colt London*.
(Butterfield & Butterfield) £80,532

Cased Colt model 1851 navy revolver, serial No. 198817, .36 calibre, standard model, the modern red velvet lined case containing *Colt's Patent* flask and mould and two cap tins.
(Butterfield & Butterfield) £1,656

A rare 6-shot 54-bore Pennell's patent open-frame self-cocking percussion revolver, 13¹/₂in. overall, detachable barrel 7in. engraved *Clark, Lynn*, Birmingham proved, totally enclosed action with half-cock button on left of scroll-engraved frame.
(Wallis & Wallis) £1,600

A 5-shot .31in. Colt model 1849 pocket percussion revolver, 10in. overall, barrel 5in., number *6347* on all parts, London address and proofs, stage coach scene on cylinder, steel trigger guard with traces of plating, plain polished walnut grips.
(Wallis & Wallis) £1,300

Special issue Buffalo Bill Historical Center Winchester Museum 1 of 250 Colt Frontier revolver, serial No. 1BB, 44–40 calibre, 7¹/₂in. barrel marked *Colt's P.T.F.A. Mfg. Co. Hartford, Ct. U.S.A.* and at the muzzle *Buffalo Bill Historical Center/Winchester Museum/1 of 250* with scroll engraving featuring panel of Buffalo Bill as a Pony Express rider.
(Butterfield & Butterfield) £5,857

Unique deluxe cased engraved and inscribed pair of Colt model 1851 navy percussion revolvers with attachable shoulder stock, serial numbers 88066 and 88067, .36 calibre, 7¹/₂in. barrels marked *Address Sam's Colt Hartford Ct.*, frames, hammers, recoil shields, loading levers and iron grip straps profusely scroll engraved by the shop of Gustave Young.
(Butterfield & Butterfield) £109,817

A 5 shot 120 bore model 1851 Adam's patent self cocking percussion revolver made under licence by Francotte of Liege, No. 16851, 8in., octagonal barrel 3¼in. engraved *A. Francotte a Liege.*
(Wallis & Wallis)   £575

A scarce 6-shot .455in. Cordite Webley Fosbery automatic cocking revolver number 3159, 10¾in. overall, barrel 6in., Birmingham proofs, side of top strap stamped *Webley Fosbery.*
(Wallis & Wallis)   £1,200

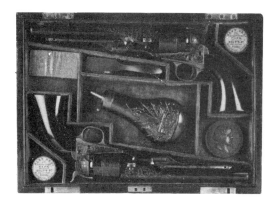

Deluxe engraved cased pair Colt model 1860 army percussion revolvers, .44 calibre, serial numbers 151388 and 151389, 7½in. barrels, marked *Address Col. Saml. Colt New York, U.S. America.*
(Butterfield & Butterfield)   £161,581

A rare Colt Hartford-English dragoon percussion revolver, No. 477 for 1853, the blued barrel with New York address, blued cylinder with traces of roll-engraved Texas Ranger and Indian scene, case-hardened frame and rammer, the lid with trade label of *I. Murcott, 68 Haymarket, London,* London proof marks, 14¼in. long.
(Christie's)   £7,150

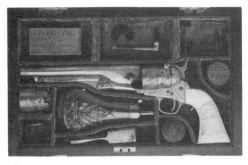

Elaborate deluxe cased Colt model 1860 army Thuer conversion revolver engraved by Gustave Young, serial No. 185326 I.E., 44 calibre, 8in. barrel marked Address Col. Sam'l Colt New York U.S. America.
                                                      £212,313

A 120-bore Beaumont-Adams double action percussion revolver, with blued octagonal sighted rifled barrel stamped *L.A.C.,* in original lined and fitted oak case with accessories including bullet mould, London proof marks, 10in. (Christie's S. Ken)   £990

REVOLVERS

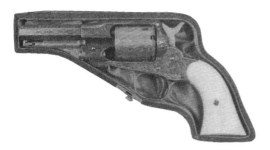

Cased Remington New Model police revolver, serial number 7168, factory converted to .38 rimfire calibre, 3½in. octagon barrel marked with Remington address, patent dates and *New Model*.
(Butterfield & Butterfield)   £4,971

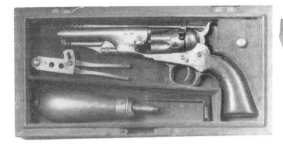

A cased Colt percussion new model Police pistol, single action, 4½in. round barrel signed *address Col. Colt London*, .38 calibre, 5-shot half-fluted cylinder, plain cylinder with London black powder proof marks, plain varnished wooden grips, 10in. overall, in lined and fitted wooden case with accessories.
(Bonhams)   £480

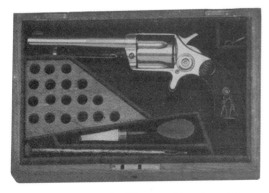

Cased Colt new police 'Cop and Thug' model revolver, British proofed, 4½in. barrel with two line Pall Mall address, 38 CF calibre, rare nickel finish with blued hammer, chequered hard rubber grips, serial No. 17879.
(Butterfield & Butterfield)   £3,450

A 120-bore Adams patent double-action five-shot percussion revolver, with blued octagonal sighted rifled barrel, the top strap engraved 'Calderwood & Son, 14, North Earl St, Dublin', in lined and fitted oak case with some accessories including Hawksley flask and bullet mould, 10½in.
(Christie's S. Ken)   £825

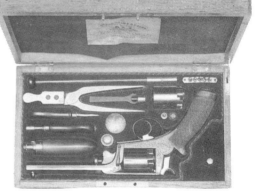

A 5 shot 54 bore Continental copy of a Beaumont Adams double action percussion revolver, 12½ inches, octagonal barrel 6½ in.
(Wallis & Wallis)   £1,100

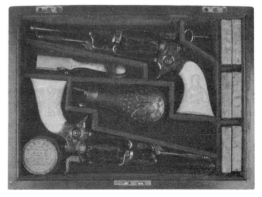

Outstanding cased pair of engraved presentation Colt Root model 1855 percussion revolvers, circa 1863, .31 calibre, 4½in. barrels marked *Address Col. Colt New York, U.S.A.*
(Butterfield & Butterfield)   £124,293

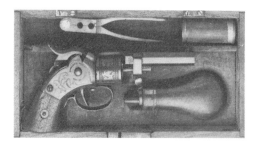

Cased Massachusetts Arms Co. Maynard primed pocket revolver, serial No. 153, .28 calibre, 2½in. octagon barrel, manually revolved cylinder, the Maynard primer reservoir retaining a roll of caps. **£1,177**

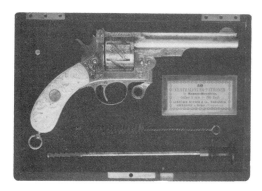

Rare cased engraved Mauser model 1878 zig-zag revolver, serial No. S 2379, 9mm. 5⅜in. barrel, scroll engraved frame and cylinder, gilt and nickel plated finish, the ivory grips finely carved with a dragon and a stork amid scrolling vines. **£5,857**

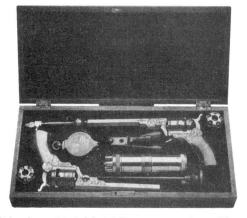

Pair of cased belt Model Paterson revolvers (No. 2), Patent Arms Manufacturing Company, circa 1837–40, serial No. 626 and 678, in untouched condition, engraved *Abraham Bininger*, barrel 5½in. long. **£142,350**

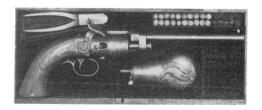

Cased Massachusetts Arms Co. Wesson & Leavitt Dragoon revolver, serial No. 223/53, .40 calibre, 6in. round barrel, standard model with loading lever, the blue velour lined case containing Massachusetts Arms Co. marked bullet mould and copper eagle flask. **£4,047**

Special Tiffany cased and gripped Colt single action army custom gun shop revolver, serial No. SAA1 gold inlaid on frame and cylinder, .45 Long Colt calibre, 8in. barrel marked *Colt's Pt. F.A. Mfg. Co. Hartford, Ct. U.S.A.* in two lines, the scroll engraved barrel adorned on the left side with gold inlaid model designation *Colt Custom Gun Shop/SAA.45/Special* and relief gold inlaid rampant lion. **£31,115**

A good scarce 5 shot 60 bore single action second model Webley Longspur percussion revolver, retailed by Bales of Ipswich and Colchester, 10in., octagonal barrel 4¾in. **£2,400**

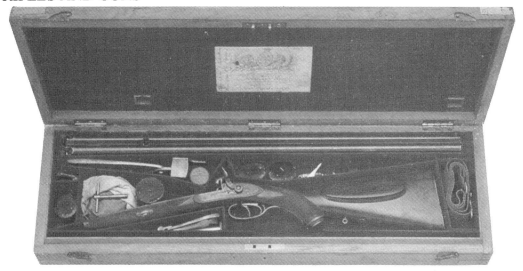

A fine 40-bore D.B. percussion sporting rifle with browned twist barrels leaf sighted to 250 yards and rifled for a belted ball, in original fitted oak case lined with red felt with trade label and accessories, by J. Purdey, 314½ Oxford Street, London, London proof marks, 30in. barrels.   £5,170

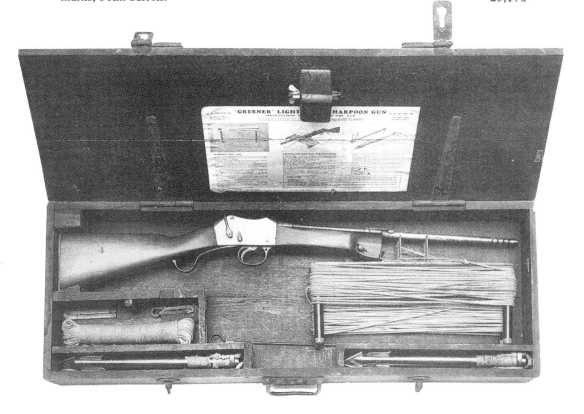

A Greener 'light model' martini-action harpoon-gun by W. W. Greener, nickel-plated finish, manual lever-safe, cocking-indicator, stock with butt-plate, the forestock with brass mounting for a line-release frame, 20in. barrel, nitro proof, in its wooden case with instruction label, five stainless-steel barbed-harpoons.   £770

RIFLES AND GUNS

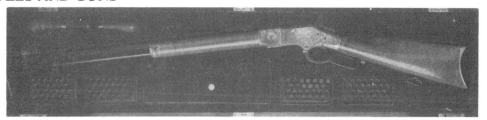

Rare cased Ulrich engraved Winchester model 1866 rifle stocked in select maple, serial No. 79862, .44 calibre, 24in. barrel marked *Winchester's Repeating Arms, New Haven Ct. King's Improvement Patented-March 29, 1866, October 16, 1860*, gold plated and scroll engraved frame, buttplate and forend cap.   £183,028

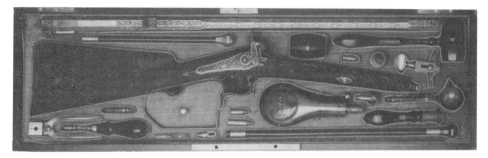

Cased Exhibition grade single shot percussion rifle, German circa 1840, the $27^{1}/_{2}$in. barrel of octagonal and polygonal sections decorated in etched foliate patterns against a grey ground, and marked *Klett & Sohne Zella* in gold inlay, the barrel fitted with folding leaf rear sight.   £14,642

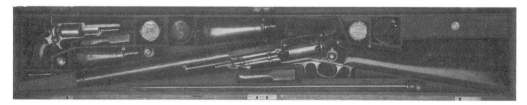

Rare cased combination Colt Root model 1855 percussion revolver and Colt Root model 1855 percussion rifle, Colt 1st model Root Sporting rifle, serial No. 465, .36 calibre, 18in. barrel marked *Colt Pt. 1856 and Address Col. Colt Hartford Ct. U.S.A.*, blued frame, cylinder, trigger guard and buttplate.   £27,454

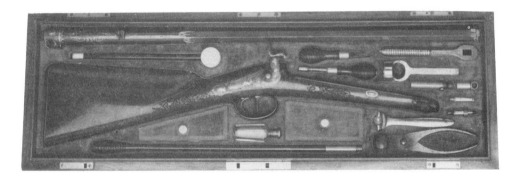

Elaborate cased and gold inlaid percussion sporting rifle, German, 19th century, the 28in. .56 calibre part-round/part-octagon barrel gold inlaid at muzzle, barrel stage and breech with lines, bands and reposing stag, inscribed in gold near breech *Schneevoigt in Lahr 1841*.   £7,321

RIFLES AND GUNS

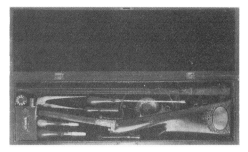

A 12-bore double-barrelled side-lock ejector shot gun by James Purdey & Sons, No. 1554, with 30in. Sir Joseph Whitworth fluid press steel barrels. £5,956

A fine and ornate single-barrelled hammerless target rifle by T. Läuger (Lörrach), rotary underlever with slide-and-tilt action, double set-triggers, the action and furniture with profuse decoration of relief-engraved and silver-inlaid birds, 28³/₄in. barrel, in its mahogany case, with all accessories and the winning target. £2,185

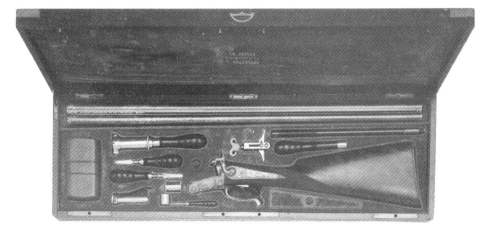

A fine Belgian double barrelled 12-bore pin-fire presentation sporting gun with browned damascus barrels encrusted in gold with lines and symmetrical scrolls at the muzzle and breech, by Adolph Jansen Arquebusier du Roi à Bruxelles, the barrels by Eugéne Bernard of Liège, circa 1866, 29¹/₂in. barrels. £12,100

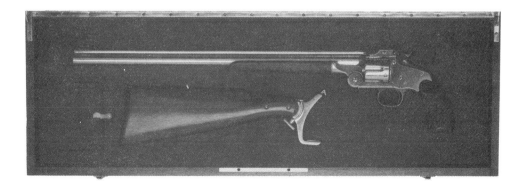

Rare cased Smith & Wesson model 320 revolving rifle, serial No. 358, .32 calibre, rare 16in. barrel marked *Smith & Wesson Springfield, Mass. U.S.A.* with patent dates, full nickel finish with blued sights and casehardened hammer and trigger guard. £10,301

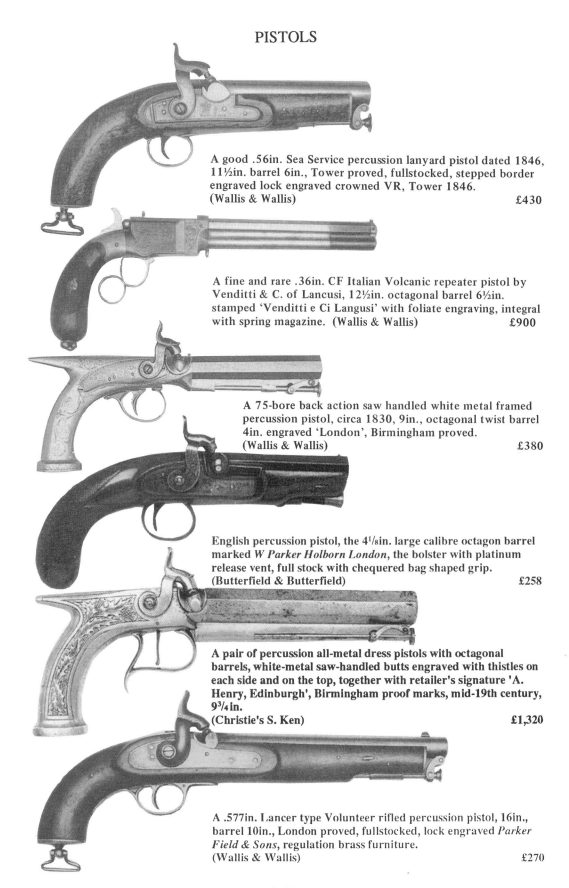

A good .56in. Sea Service percussion lanyard pistol dated 1846, 11½in. barrel 6in., Tower proved, fullstocked, stepped border engraved lock engraved crowned VR, Tower 1846.
(Wallis & Wallis) £430

A fine and rare .36in. CF Italian Volcanic repeater pistol by Venditti & C. of Lancusi, 12½in. octagonal barrel 6½in. stamped 'Venditti e Ci Langusi' with foliate engraving, integral with spring magazine. (Wallis & Wallis) £900

A 75-bore back action saw handled white metal framed percussion pistol, circa 1830, 9in., octagonal twist barrel 4in. engraved 'London', Birmingham proved.
(Wallis & Wallis) £380

English percussion pistol, the 4¹/₈in. large calibre octagon barrel marked *W Parker Holborn London*, the bolster with platinum release vent, full stock with chequered bag shaped grip.
(Butterfield & Butterfield) £258

A pair of percussion all-metal dress pistols with octagonal barrels, white-metal saw-handled butts engraved with thistles on each side and on the top, together with retailer's signature 'A. Henry, Edinburgh', Birmingham proof marks, mid-19th century, 9³/₄in.
(Christie's S. Ken) £1,320

A .577in. Lancer type Volunteer rifled percussion pistol, 16in., barrel 10in., London proved, fullstocked, lock engraved *Parker Field & Sons*, regulation brass furniture.
(Wallis & Wallis) £270

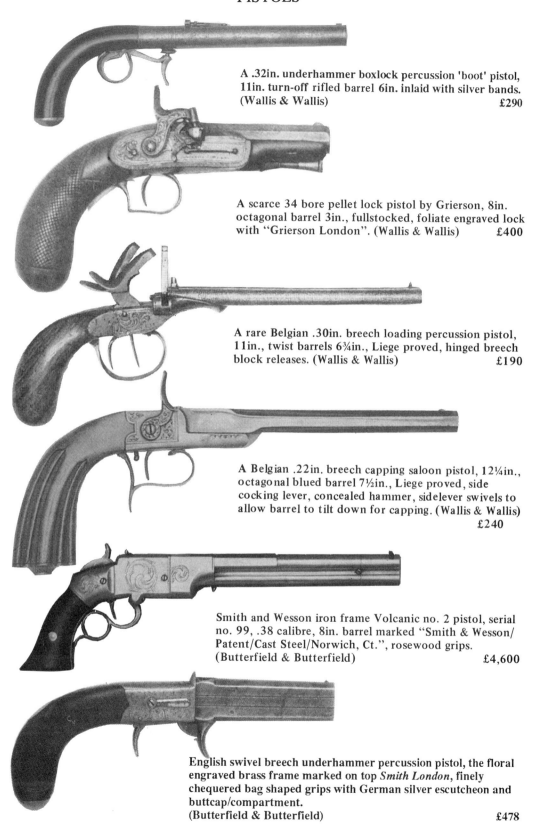

A .32in. underhammer boxlock percussion 'boot' pistol, 11in. turn-off rifled barrel 6in. inlaid with silver bands. (Wallis & Wallis) £290

A scarce 34 bore pellet lock pistol by Grierson, 8in. octagonal barrel 3in., fullstocked, foliate engraved lock with "Grierson London". (Wallis & Wallis) £400

A rare Belgian .30in. breech loading percussion pistol, 11in., twist barrels 6¾in., Liege proved, hinged breech block releases. (Wallis & Wallis) £190

A Belgian .22in. breech capping saloon pistol, 12¼in., octagonal blued barrel 7½in., Liege proved, side cocking lever, concealed hammer, sidelever swivels to allow barrel to tilt down for capping. (Wallis & Wallis) £240

Smith and Wesson iron frame Volcanic no. 2 pistol, serial no. 99, .38 calibre, 8in. barrel marked "Smith & Wesson/ Patent/Cast Steel/Norwich, Ct.", rosewood grips. (Butterfield & Butterfield) £4,600

English swivel breech underhammer percussion pistol, the floral engraved brass frame marked on top *Smith London*, finely chequered bag shaped grips with German silver escutcheon and buttcap/compartment. (Butterfield & Butterfield) £478

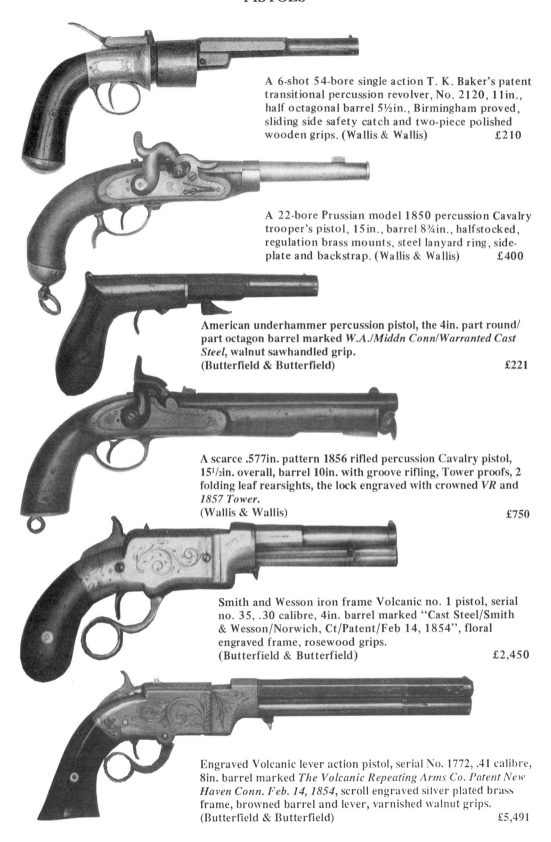

A 6-shot 54-bore single action T. K. Baker's patent transitional percussion revolver, No. 2120, 11in., half octagonal barrel 5½in., Birmingham proved, sliding side safety catch and two-piece polished wooden grips. (Wallis & Wallis) £210

A 22-bore Prussian model 1850 percussion Cavalry trooper's pistol, 15in., barrel 8¾in., halfstocked, regulation brass mounts, steel lanyard ring, side-plate and backstrap. (Wallis & Wallis) £400

American underhammer percussion pistol, the 4in. part round/part octagon barrel marked *W.A./Middn Conn/Warranted Cast Steel*, walnut sawhandled grip.
(Butterfield & Butterfield) £221

A scarce .577in. pattern 1856 rifled percussion Cavalry pistol, 15½in. overall, barrel 10in. with groove rifling, Tower proofs, 2 folding leaf rearsights, the lock engraved with crowned *VR* and *1857 Tower*.
(Wallis & Wallis) £750

Smith and Wesson iron frame Volcanic no. 1 pistol, serial no. 35, .30 calibre, 4in. barrel marked "Cast Steel/Smith & Wesson/Norwich, Ct/Patent/Feb 14, 1854", floral engraved frame, rosewood grips.
(Butterfield & Butterfield) £2,450

Engraved Volcanic lever action pistol, serial No. 1772, .41 calibre, 8in. barrel marked *The Volcanic Repeating Arms Co. Patent New Haven Conn. Feb. 14, 1854*, scroll engraved silver plated brass frame, browned barrel and lever, varnished walnut grips.
(Butterfield & Butterfield) £5,491

AIR PISTOLS

A rare German repeating air pistol on the Girandoni system, with octagonal barrel rifled with six grooves, later folding rear-sight, the breech with sliding transverse breech-block and octagonal steel magazine mounted on the right, Mainz, mid-19th century, 14³/₄in. long.
(Christie's)   £990

A Bohemian crank up air pistol, circa 1850, 15½in., octagonal barrel 7in., inlaid in silver "Rutte in Boh, Leippa", with brass mounted fullstock, steel cylinder, brass mounted wooden butt, set trigger, slotted for shoulder stock.   £1,000

A pre-War .177in. Webley air pistol mark I, 8¼in., rounded frame with patent dates to 1925, with swivel safety to left of frame and plain wood grips inset with brass Webley emblem.
                                                                 £75

A rare Viennese repeating air pistol on the Girandoni system with swamped twist octagonal multigroove rifled sighted barrel signed in silver, the breech inlaid with silver foliage and with sliding transverse breech-block and silver-inlaid tubular steel magazine on the right, signed *Joseph Oesterleinsche Fabrique*, mid-19th century, 14³/₄in. long.
(Christie's)   £1,650

A Dutch strike-pump gallery air pistol with octagonal sighted brass-inlaid barrel pivoting at the breech to allow loading of the cylindrical steel breech-block, action and pivoting cocking aperture cover both engraved with stylised foliage, signed *J. Donaghy, Amsterdam*, mid-19th century, 16in. long.
(Christie's)   £1,100

AUTOMATIC PISTOLS

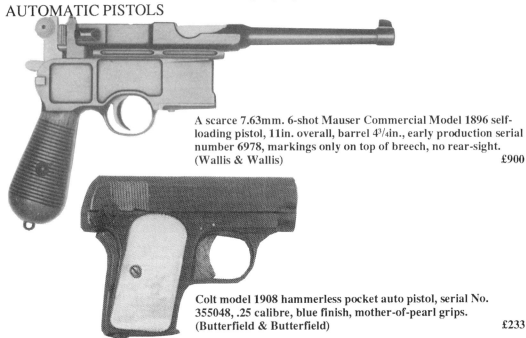

A scarce 7.63mm. 6-shot Mauser Commercial Model 1896 self-loading pistol, 11in. overall, barrel 4³/₄in., early production serial number 6978, markings only on top of breech, no rear-sight. (Wallis & Wallis) £900

Colt model 1908 hammerless pocket auto pistol, serial No. 355048, .25 calibre, blue finish, mother-of-pearl grips. (Butterfield & Butterfield) £233

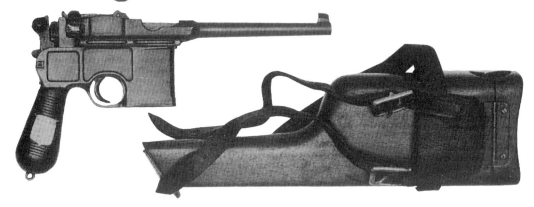

An interesting early 7.63mm. Mauser model 1896 self loading pistol, 11¹/₂in. overall, barrel 5¹/₂in. with address at breech, unmarked frame with recessed panels, cone hammer, the Westley Richards rearsight stamped *Mauser Cartridge 303*. (Wallis & Wallis) £950

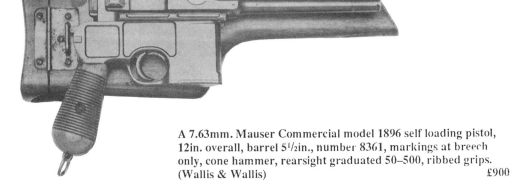

A 7.63mm. Mauser Commercial model 1896 self loading pistol, 12in. overall, barrel 5¹/₂in., number 8361, markings at breech only, cone hammer, rearsight graduated 50–500, ribbed grips. (Wallis & Wallis) £900

AUTOMATIC PISTOLS

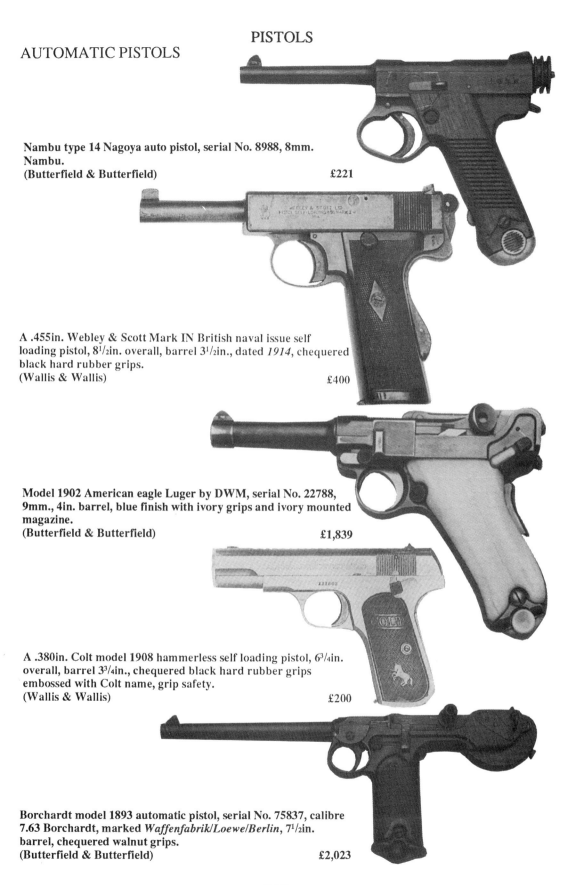

Nambu type 14 Nagoya auto pistol, serial No. 8988, 8mm.
Nambu.
(Butterfield & Butterfield)   £221

A .455in. Webley & Scott Mark IN British naval issue self
loading pistol, 8½in. overall, barrel 3½in., dated *1914*, chequered
black hard rubber grips.
(Wallis & Wallis)   £400

Model 1902 American eagle Luger by DWM, serial No. 22788,
9mm., 4in. barrel, blue finish with ivory grips and ivory mounted
magazine.
(Butterfield & Butterfield)   £1,839

A .380in. Colt model 1908 hammerless self loading pistol, 6¾in.
overall, barrel 3¾in., chequered black hard rubber grips
embossed with Colt name, grip safety.
(Wallis & Wallis)   £200

Borchardt model 1893 automatic pistol, serial No. 75837, calibre
7.63 Borchardt, marked *Waffenfabrik/Loewe/Berlin*, 7½in.
barrel, chequered walnut grips.
(Butterfield & Butterfield)   £2,023

SEMI AUTOMATIC PISTOLS

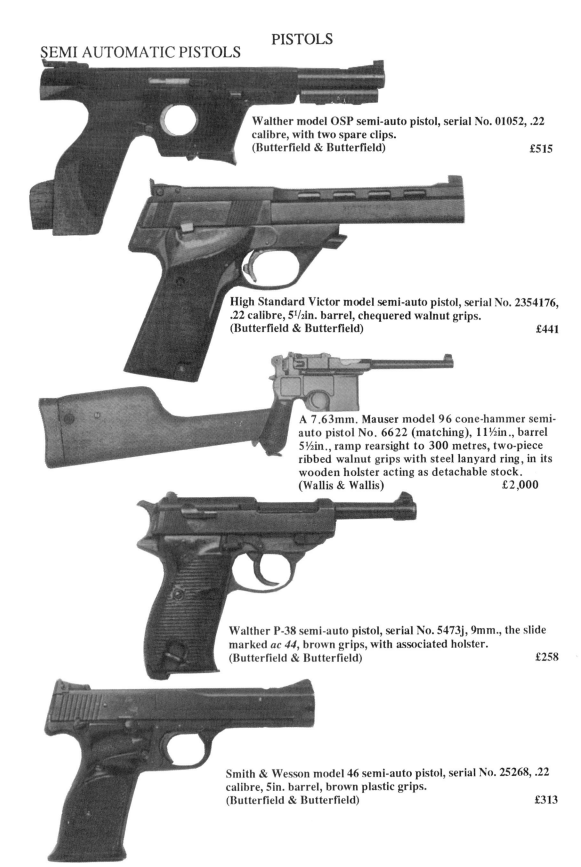

Walther model OSP semi-auto pistol, serial No. 01052, .22 calibre, with two spare clips.
(Butterfield & Butterfield) £515

High Standard Victor model semi-auto pistol, serial No. 2354176, .22 calibre, 5$\frac{1}{2}$in. barrel, chequered walnut grips.
(Butterfield & Butterfield) £441

A 7.63mm. Mauser model 96 cone-hammer semi-auto pistol No. 6622 (matching), 11$\frac{1}{2}$in., barrel 5$\frac{1}{2}$in., ramp rearsight to 300 metres, two-piece ribbed walnut grips with steel lanyard ring, in its wooden holster acting as detachable stock.
(Wallis & Wallis) £2,000

Walther P-38 semi-auto pistol, serial No. 5473j, 9mm., the slide marked *ac 44*, brown grips, with associated holster.
(Butterfield & Butterfield) £258

Smith & Wesson model 46 semi-auto pistol, serial No. 25268, .22 calibre, 5in. barrel, brown plastic grips.
(Butterfield & Butterfield) £313

SEMI AUTOMATIC PISTOLS

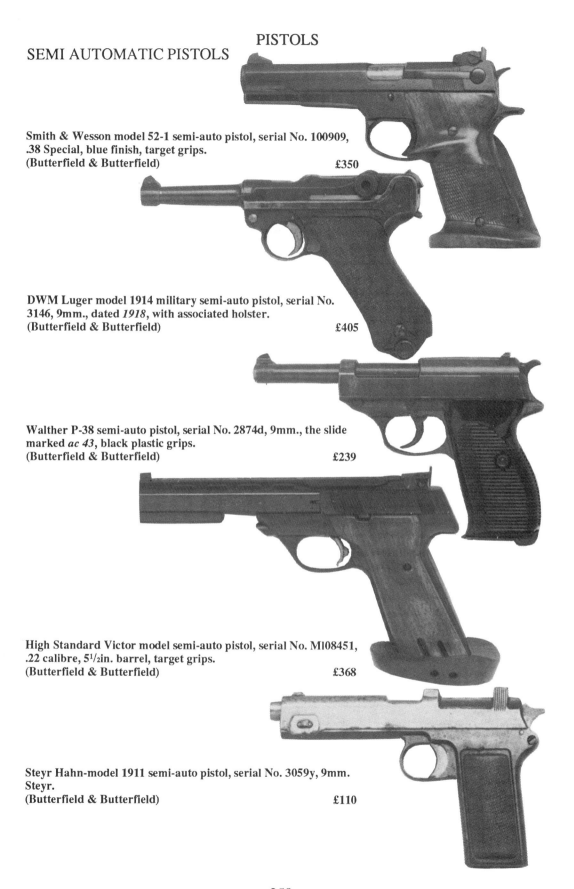

Smith & Wesson model 52-1 semi-auto pistol, serial No. 100909, .38 Special, blue finish, target grips.
(Butterfield & Butterfield)　　　　　　　£350

DWM Luger model 1914 military semi-auto pistol, serial No. 3146, 9mm., dated *1918*, with associated holster.
(Butterfield & Butterfield)　　　　　　　£405

Walther P-38 semi-auto pistol, serial No. 2874d, 9mm., the slide marked *ac 43*, black plastic grips.
(Butterfield & Butterfield)　　　　　　　£239

High Standard Victor model semi-auto pistol, serial No. Ml08451, .22 calibre, $5^{1}/_{2}$in. barrel, target grips.
(Butterfield & Butterfield)　　　　　　　£368

Steyr Hahn-model 1911 semi-auto pistol, serial No. 3059y, 9mm. Steyr.
(Butterfield & Butterfield)　　　　　　　£110

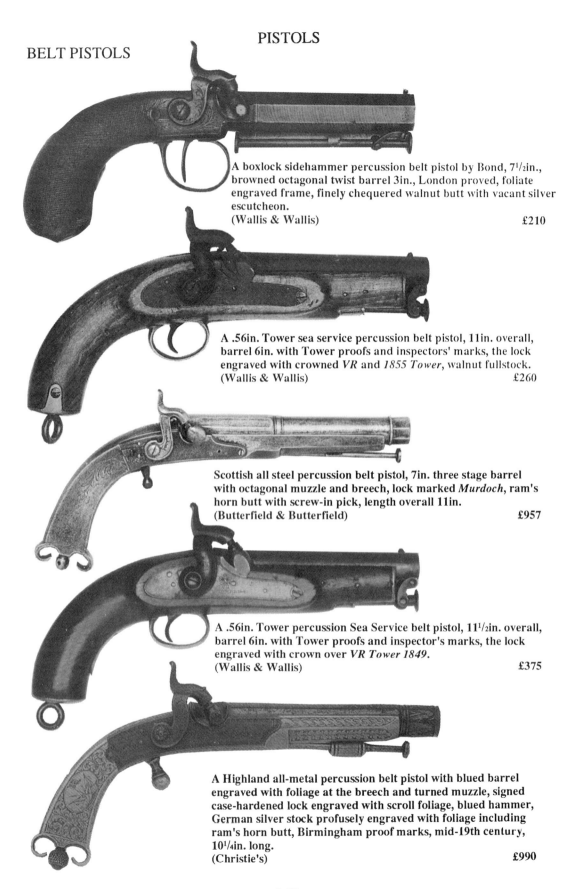

A boxlock sidehammer percussion belt pistol by Bond, 7$^{1}/_{2}$in., browned octagonal twist barrel 3in., London proved, foliate engraved frame, finely chequered walnut butt with vacant silver escutcheon.
(Wallis & Wallis)   £210

A .56in. Tower sea service percussion belt pistol, 11in. overall, barrel 6in. with Tower proofs and inspectors' marks, the lock engraved with crowned *VR* and *1855 Tower*, walnut fullstock.
(Wallis & Wallis)   £260

Scottish all steel percussion belt pistol, 7in. three stage barrel with octagonal muzzle and breech, lock marked *Murdoch*, ram's horn butt with screw-in pick, length overall 11in.
(Butterfield & Butterfield)   £957

A .56in. Tower percussion Sea Service belt pistol, 11$^{1}/_{2}$in. overall, barrel 6in. with Tower proofs and inspector's marks, the lock engraved with crown over *VR Tower 1849*.
(Wallis & Wallis)   £375

A Highland all-metal percussion belt pistol with blued barrel engraved with foliage at the breech and turned muzzle, signed case-hardened lock engraved with scroll foliage, blued hammer, German silver stock profusely engraved with foliage including ram's horn butt, Birmingham proof marks, mid-19th century, 10$^{1}/_{4}$in. long.
(Christie's)   £990

DERRINGERS

A .41in. rimfire Colt no. 3 Derringer, 5in. overall, swing out barrel 2½in., with London proofs, no. 48159, frame and barrel nickel plated overall. £300

A four-barrelled .30in. rimfire Sharp's pepperbox Derringer pistol, No. 2493, wooden grips, bronze frame with spur trigger, fluted barrel group. £225

A .41in. rimfire National Arms Co. Derringer, 5in. overall, barrel 2½in., silver plated scroll engraved brass frame with sheath trigger. £375

A presentation .41in. rimfire Colt No 3 Thuer Derringer, 4½in., barrel 2½, No 26067, two-piece polished ivory grips to bird's head butt, plated bronze factory scroll engraved frame with spur trigger, the barrel sides and muzzle well scroll engraved and nickel plated overall. £400

One of a pair of Philadelphia Derringer pistols, calibre .41, 4in. part-round/part-octagon barrels marked Derringer Phila on bolster, inscribed on escutcheons Col. G. Talcott, early styling in engraved squareback trigger guards, hammers and plain German silver escutcheon plates. (Wallis & Wallis) £10,250

Factory engraved Colt third model Derringer, serial no. 8577 E, .41 calibre, with profuse scroll engraving featuring a wolf's head on left side of barrel, nickel finish with blued hammer, trigger, and screws, checkered ivory grips. (Butterfield & Butterfield) £3,000

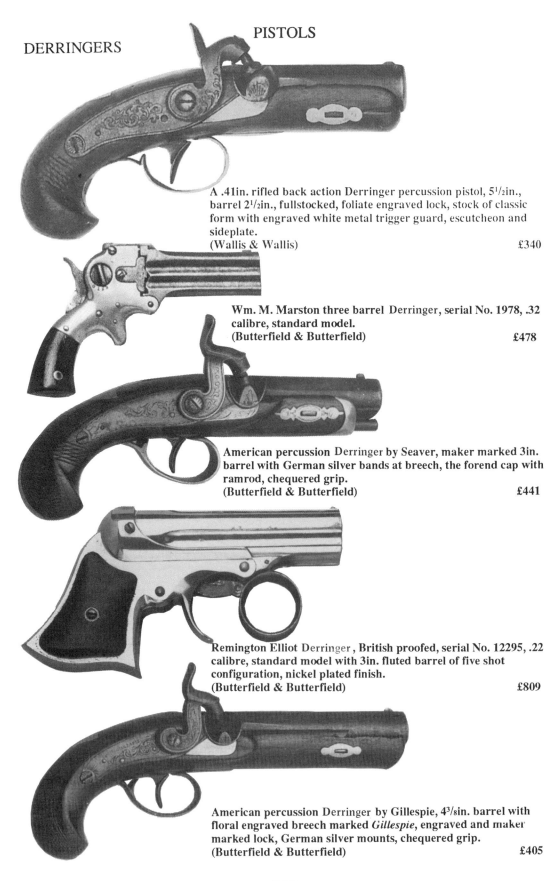

A .41in. rifled back action Derringer percussion pistol, 5½in.,
barrel 2½in., fullstocked, foliate engraved lock, stock of classic
form with engraved white metal trigger guard, escutcheon and
sideplate.
(Wallis & Wallis)   £340

Wm. M. Marston three barrel Derringer, serial No. 1978, .32
calibre, standard model.
(Butterfield & Butterfield)   £478

American percussion Derringer by Seaver, maker marked 3in.
barrel with German silver bands at breech, the forend cap with
ramrod, chequered grip.
(Butterfield & Butterfield)   £441

Remington Elliot Derringer, British proofed, serial No. 12295, .22
calibre, standard model with 3in. fluted barrel of five shot
configuration, nickel plated finish.
(Butterfield & Butterfield)   £809

American percussion Derringer by Gillespie, 4³/₈in. barrel with
floral engraved breech marked *Gillespie*, engraved and maker
marked lock, German silver mounts, chequered grip.
(Butterfield & Butterfield)   £405

DERRINGERS

A 2 shot .41in. rimfire Derringer pistol by Remington No. 721, 4³/₄in., tip up barrels 3in., stamped *Remington Arms Co Ilion NY*, sheathed trigger, chequered extractor knob.
(Wallis & Wallis)   £260

A .41in. rimfire Colt Derringer pistol, 4¹/₂in., barrel 2¹/₂in. deeply stamped *Colt*, London proved, brass framed, sheathed trigger, two piece wooden grips.
(Wallis & Wallis)   £105

Engraved Remington Elliot Derringer, serial no. 4, .22 calibre, the scroll engraved frame with a blank cartouche on grip strap and a grotesque mask on rear of breech.
(Butterfield & Butterfield)   £2,391

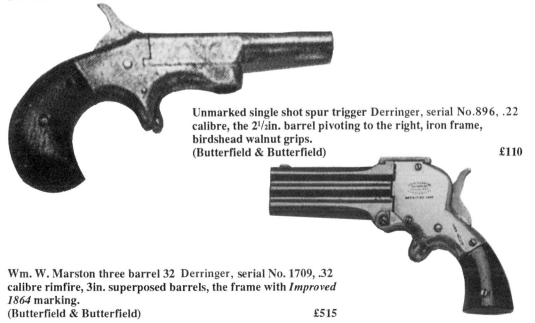

Unmarked single shot spur trigger Derringer, serial No.896, .22 calibre, the 2¹/₂in. barrel pivoting to the right, iron frame, birdshead walnut grips.
(Butterfield & Butterfield)   £110

Wm. W. Marston three barrel 32 Derringer, serial No. 1709, .32 calibre rimfire, 3in. superposed barrels, the frame with *Improved 1864* marking.
(Butterfield & Butterfield)   £515

DOUBLE BARRELLED

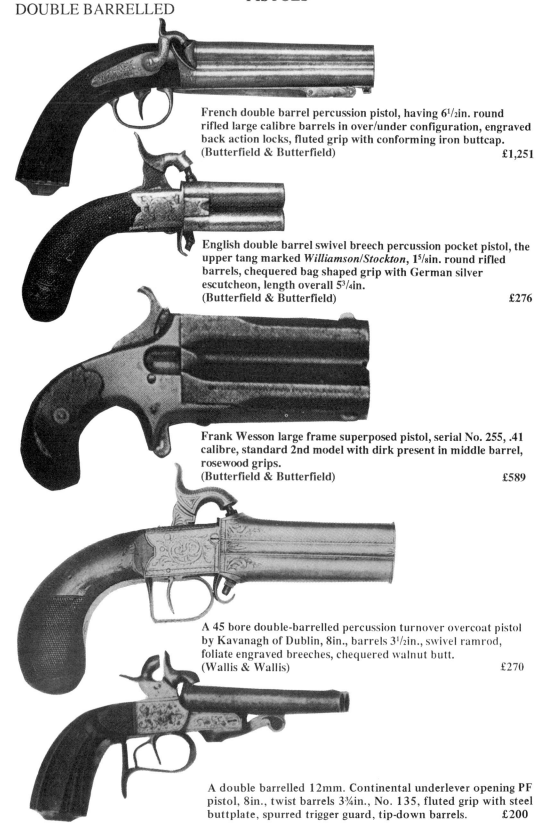

French double barrel percussion pistol, having 6^1/$_2$in. round rifled large calibre barrels in over/under configuration, engraved back action locks, fluted grip with conforming iron buttcap.
(Butterfield & Butterfield)   £1,251

English double barrel swivel breech percussion pocket pistol, the upper tang marked *Williamson/Stockton*, 1^5/$_8$in. round rifled barrels, chequered bag shaped grip with German silver escutcheon, length overall 5^3/$_4$in.
(Butterfield & Butterfield)   £276

Frank Wesson large frame superposed pistol, serial No. 255, .41 calibre, standard 2nd model with dirk present in middle barrel, rosewood grips.
(Butterfield & Butterfield)   £589

A 45 bore double-barrelled percussion turnover overcoat pistol by Kavanagh of Dublin, 8in., barrels 3^1/$_2$in., swivel ramrod, foliate engraved breeches, chequered walnut butt.
(Wallis & Wallis)   £270

A double barrelled 12mm. Continental underlever opening PF pistol, 8in., twist barrels 3¾in., No. 135, fluted grip with steel buttplate, spurred trigger guard, tip-down barrels.   £200

FOUR BARRELLED

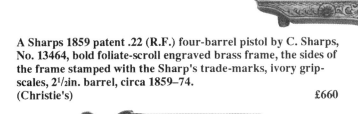

A Sharps 1859 patent .22 (R.F.) four-barrel pistol by C. Sharps, No. 13464, bold foliate-scroll engraved brass frame, the sides of the frame stamped with the Sharp's trade-marks, ivory grip-scales, 2¹/₂in. barrel, circa 1859–74.
(Christie's) £660

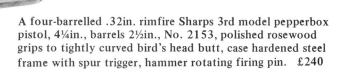

A four-barrelled .32in. rimfire Sharps 3rd model pepperbox pistol, 4¼in., barrels 2½in., No. 2153, polished rosewood grips to tightly curved bird's head butt, case hardened steel frame with spur trigger, hammer rotating firing pin.   £240

An unusual four-barrelled .25in. centre fire Continental pocket pistol, 3¼in. barrels 1¾in., No. 3781, two-piece wooden grips to angular butt, side mounted safety and barrel release catch, the barrels slide vertically down into action body and are removed for loading or extraction. £300

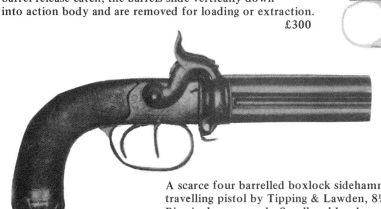

A scarce four barrelled boxlock sidehammer turnover percussion travelling pistol by Tipping & Lawden, 8¼in., fluted barrels 4in., Birmingham proved. Scroll and border engraved frame, dolphin hammers. £400

HARMONICA PISTOL

A very rare 6-shot double action 7mm. pinfire Continental harmonica pistol 5½in., barrel group 2¾in., No. 821, plain wooden grips to bird's head butt. £2,000

A 14 bore Belgian double-barrelled percussion holster pistol, 17in., barrels 10¹/₂in. with raised ribs, foliate engraved locks and steel furniture, chequered grip, steel ramrod.
(Wallis & Wallis) £230

A .56in. Volunteer Lancer's type percussion holster pistol, 15in., barrel 9in., Birmingham proved, fullstocked, regulation lock engraved with crown, regulation brass mounts, swivel ramrod.
(Wallis & Wallis) £200

A 16 bore East India Company percussion holster pistol, 15in., barrel 9in., London proved, fullstocked, lock engraved with lion rampant, regulation brass mounts.
(Wallis & Wallis) £280

A .54in. US martial percussion holster pistol, 14in., barrel 8¹/₂in., halfstocked, lockplate stamped *US Haston, Middtn Conn 1850*, regulation brass mounts, sideplate stipple engraved *G.T.E.*
(Wallis & Wallis) £310

A 16 bore EIG percussion holster pistol dated *1871*, 13¹/₂in., blued barrel 8in. with Tower proofs, fullstocked, colour hardened lock stamped *Birmingham 1871* with crowned *E.I.G.*
(Wallis & Wallis) £350

HOLSTER PISTOLS

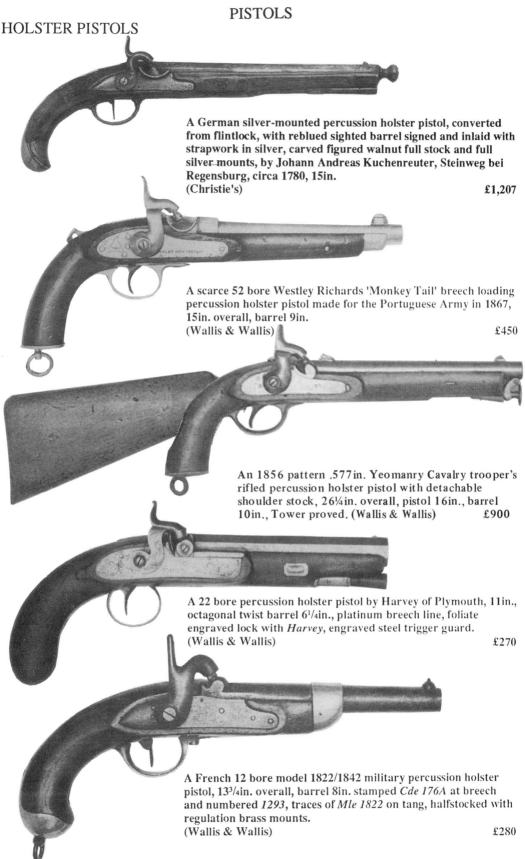

A German silver-mounted percussion holster pistol, converted from flintlock, with reblued sighted barrel signed and inlaid with strapwork in silver, carved figured walnut full stock and full silver mounts, by Johann Andreas Kuchenreuter, Steinweg bei Regensburg, circa 1780, 15in.
(Christie's)   £1,207

A scarce 52 bore Westley Richards 'Monkey Tail' breech loading percussion holster pistol made for the Portuguese Army in 1867, 15in. overall, barrel 9in.
(Wallis & Wallis)   £450

An 1856 pattern .577in. Yeomanry Cavalry trooper's rifled percussion holster pistol with detachable shoulder stock, 26¼in. overall, pistol 16in., barrel 10in., Tower proved. (Wallis & Wallis)   £900

A 22 bore percussion holster pistol by Harvey of Plymouth, 11in., octagonal twist barrel 6¹/₄in., platinum breech line, foliate engraved lock with *Harvey*, engraved steel trigger guard.
(Wallis & Wallis)   £270

A French 12 bore model 1822/1842 military percussion holster pistol, 13³/₄in. overall, barrel 8in. stamped *Cde 176A* at breech and numbered *1293*, traces of *Mle 1822* on tang, halfstocked with regulation brass mounts.
(Wallis & Wallis)   £280

KNUCKLEDUSTER PISTOLS

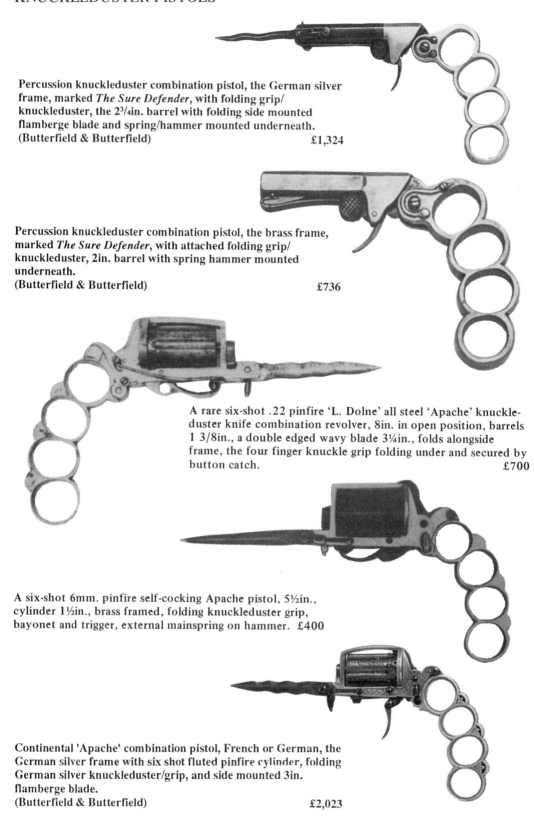

Percussion knuckleduster combination pistol, the German silver frame, marked *The Sure Defender*, with folding grip/ knuckleduster, the 2³/₄in. barrel with folding side mounted flamberge blade and spring/hammer mounted underneath. (Butterfield & Butterfield) £1,324

Percussion knuckleduster combination pistol, the brass frame, marked *The Sure Defender*, with attached folding grip/ knuckleduster, 2in. barrel with spring hammer mounted underneath. (Butterfield & Butterfield) £736

A rare six-shot .22 pinfire 'L. Dolne' all steel 'Apache' knuckleduster knife combination revolver, 8in. in open position, barrels 1 3/8in., a double edged wavy blade 3¼in., folds alongside frame, the four finger knuckle grip folding under and secured by button catch. £700

A six-shot 6mm. pinfire self-cocking Apache pistol, 5½in., cylinder 1½in., brass framed, folding knuckleduster grip, bayonet and trigger, external mainspring on hammer. £400

Continental 'Apache' combination pistol, French or German, the German silver frame with six shot fluted pinfire cylinder, folding German silver knuckleduster/grip, and side mounted 3in. flamberge blade. (Butterfield & Butterfield) £2,023

OVER AND UNDER PISTOLS

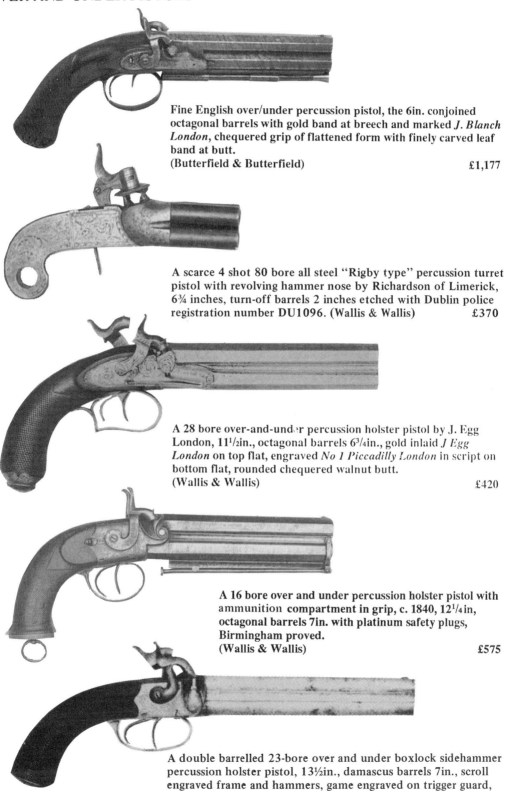

Fine English over/under percussion pistol, the 6in. conjoined octagonal barrels with gold band at breech and marked *J. Blanch London*, chequered grip of flattened form with finely carved leaf band at butt.
(Butterfield & Butterfield)   £1,177

A scarce 4 shot 80 bore all steel "Rigby type" percussion turret pistol with revolving hammer nose by Richardson of Limerick, 6¾ inches, turn-off barrels 2 inches etched with Dublin police registration number DU1096. (Wallis & Wallis)   £370

A 28 bore over-and-under percussion holster pistol by J. Egg London, 11½in., octagonal barrels 6¾in., gold inlaid *J Egg London* on top flat, engraved *No 1 Piccadilly London* in script on bottom flat, rounded chequered walnut butt.
(Wallis & Wallis)   £420

A 16 bore over and under percussion holster pistol with ammunition compartment in grip, c. 1840, 12¼in, octagonal barrels 7in. with platinum safety plugs, Birmingham proved.
(Wallis & Wallis)   £575

A double barrelled 23-bore over and under boxlock sidehammer percussion holster pistol, 13½in., damascus barrels 7in., scroll engraved frame and hammers, game engraved on trigger guard, hinged cap trap to chequered walnut butt.   £400

PALM PISTOLS

A scarce 10-shot .22in. extra short French palm pistol, 4in., part round part octagonal barrel 1½in., No. 6710, round side plates. £300

A scarce 7-shot .32in. centre fire Chicago palm pistol of French manufacture, 4¾in., part octagonal part round barrel 1¾in., No. 603. £200

A scarce 4-shot, .32in. rimfire Elliott Patent Remington, 5in. barrels 3¼in., barrels with patent dates to Oct 1, 1861, two-piece deer antler slab grips to square butt. £300

A rare 5-shot .22in. short Little All Right palm pistol, 4in., barrel 1¾in., No. 124, composition two-piece grips, embossed with "Little All Right, Trade Mark Patented Jany 18 1876" on one side and "All Right Firearms Co. Manufacturers, Mass., U.S.A." £800

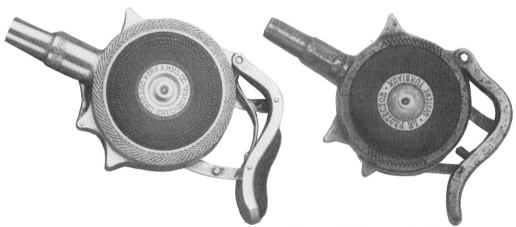

Chicago Firearms Co. protector palm pistol, calibre .32 rimfire, standard model with nickel plated finish and hard rubber inset. (Butterfield & Butterfield) £736

A Continental 'Systeme Turbiaux le Protector' revolving palm-pistol, No. 1454, the iron frame with finger-grips and sliding safety-catch, 1½in. barrel, late 19th century. (Christie's) £198

POCKET PISTOLS

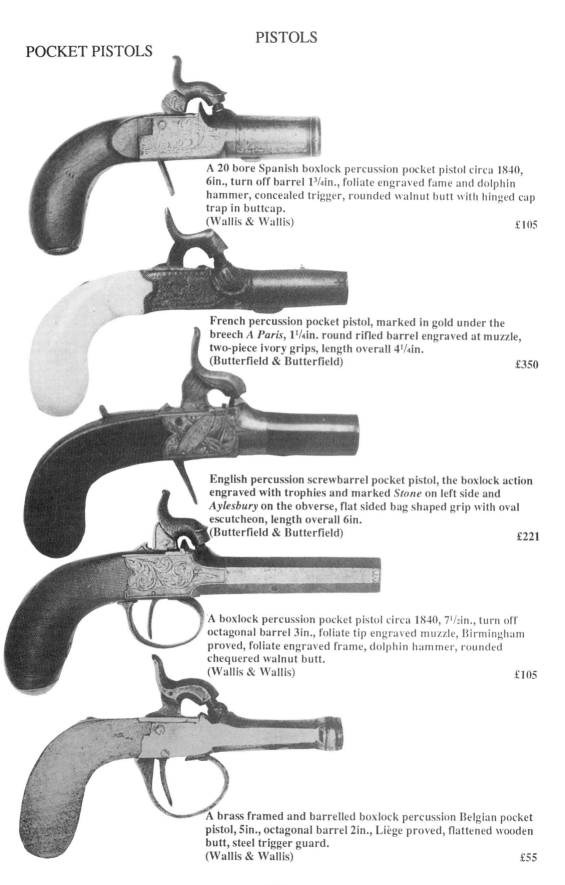

A 20 bore Spanish boxlock percussion pocket pistol circa 1840, 6in., turn off barrel 1³/₄in., foliate engraved fame and dolphin hammer, concealed trigger, rounded walnut butt with hinged cap trap in buttcap.
(Wallis & Wallis)   £105

French percussion pocket pistol, marked in gold under the breech *A Paris*, 1¹/₄in. round rifled barrel engraved at muzzle, two-piece ivory grips, length overall 4¹/₄in.
(Butterfield & Butterfield)   £350

English percussion screwbarrel pocket pistol, the boxlock action engraved with trophies and marked *Stone* on left side and *Aylesbury* on the obverse, flat sided bag shaped grip with oval escutcheon, length overall 6in.
(Butterfield & Butterfield)   £221

A boxlock percussion pocket pistol circa 1840, 7¹/₂in., turn off octagonal barrel 3in., foliate tip engraved muzzle, Birmingham proved, foliate engraved frame, dolphin hammer, rounded chequered walnut butt.
(Wallis & Wallis)   £105

A brass framed and barrelled boxlock percussion Belgian pocket pistol, 5in., octagonal barrel 2in., Liège proved, flattened wooden butt, steel trigger guard.
(Wallis & Wallis)   £55

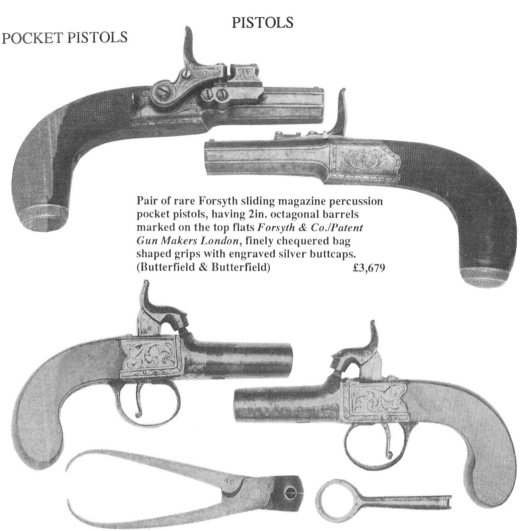

Pair of rare Forsyth sliding magazine percussion
pocket pistols, having 2in. octagonal barrels
marked on the top flats *Forsyth & Co./Patent
Gun Makers London*, finely chequered bag
shaped grips with engraved silver buttcaps.
(Butterfield & Butterfield)   £3,679

A pair of boxlock percussion pocket pistols by S. Huggins circa
1840, 6in., turn off barrels 1³/₄in., foliate engraved frames,
complete with their single cavity steel ball moulds and
combination barrel key and nipple key.
(Wallis & Wallis)   £500

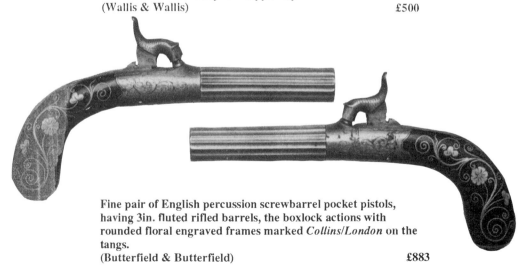

Fine pair of English percussion screwbarrel pocket pistols,
having 3in. fluted rifled barrels, the boxlock actions with
rounded floral engraved frames marked *Collins/London* on the
tangs.
(Butterfield & Butterfield)   £883

SINGLE SHOT PISTOLS

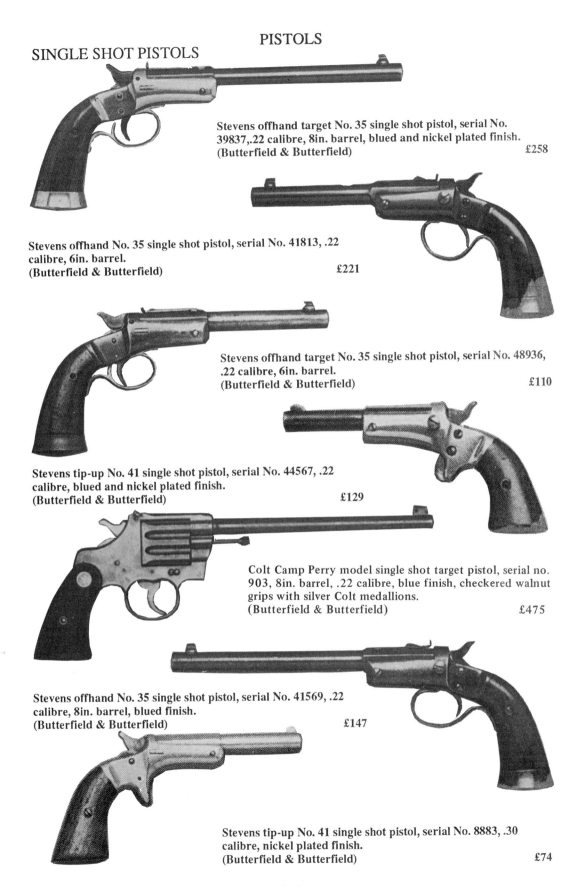

Stevens offhand target No. 35 single shot pistol, serial No. 39837,.22 calibre, 8in. barrel, blued and nickel plated finish. (Butterfield & Butterfield) £258

Stevens offhand No. 35 single shot pistol, serial No. 41813, .22 calibre, 6in. barrel. (Butterfield & Butterfield) £221

Stevens offhand target No. 35 single shot pistol, serial No. 48936, .22 calibre, 6in. barrel. (Butterfield & Butterfield) £110

Stevens tip-up No. 41 single shot pistol, serial No. 44567, .22 calibre, blued and nickel plated finish. (Butterfield & Butterfield) £129

Colt Camp Perry model single shot target pistol, serial no. 903, 8in. barrel, .22 calibre, blue finish, checkered walnut grips with silver Colt medallions. (Butterfield & Butterfield) £475

Stevens offhand No. 35 single shot pistol, serial No. 41569, .22 calibre, 8in. barrel, blued finish. (Butterfield & Butterfield) £147

Stevens tip-up No. 41 single shot pistol, serial No. 8883, .30 calibre, nickel plated finish. (Butterfield & Butterfield) £74

TARGET PISTOLS

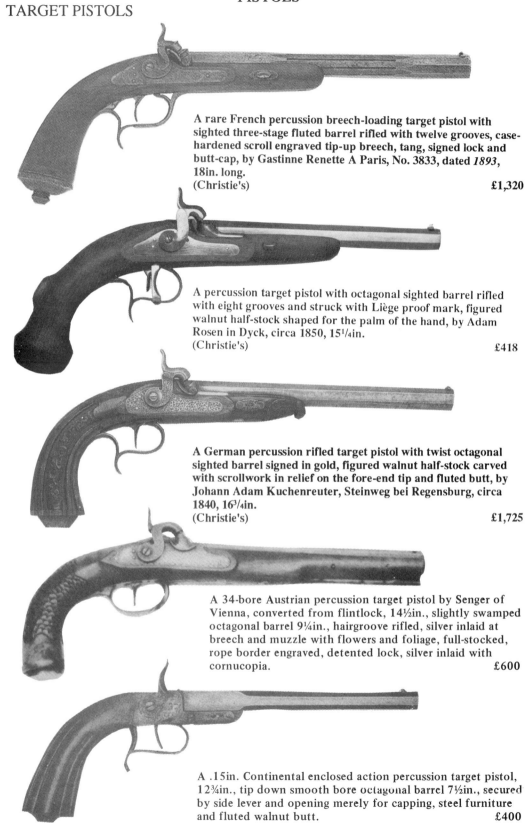

A rare French percussion breech-loading target pistol with sighted three-stage fluted barrel rifled with twelve grooves, case-hardened scroll engraved tip-up breech, tang, signed lock and butt-cap, by Gastinne Renette A Paris, No. 3833, dated *1893*, 18in. long.
(Christie's)   £1,320

A percussion target pistol with octagonal sighted barrel rifled with eight grooves and struck with Liège proof mark, figured walnut half-stock shaped for the palm of the hand, by Adam Rosen in Dyck, circa 1850, 15¼in.
(Christie's)   £418

A German percussion rifled target pistol with twist octagonal sighted barrel signed in gold, figured walnut half-stock carved with scrollwork in relief on the fore-end tip and fluted butt, by Johann Adam Kuchenreuter, Steinweg bei Regensburg, circa 1840, 16¾in.
(Christie's)   £1,725

A 34-bore Austrian percussion target pistol by Senger of Vienna, converted from flintlock, 14½in., slightly swamped octagonal barrel 9¼in., hairgroove rifled, silver inlaid at breech and muzzle with flowers and foliage, full-stocked, rope border engraved, detented lock, silver inlaid with cornucopia.   £600

A .15in. Continental enclosed action percussion target pistol, 12¾in., tip down smooth bore octagonal barrel 7½in., secured by side lever and opening merely for capping, steel furniture and fluted walnut butt.   £400

TRAVELLING PISTOLS

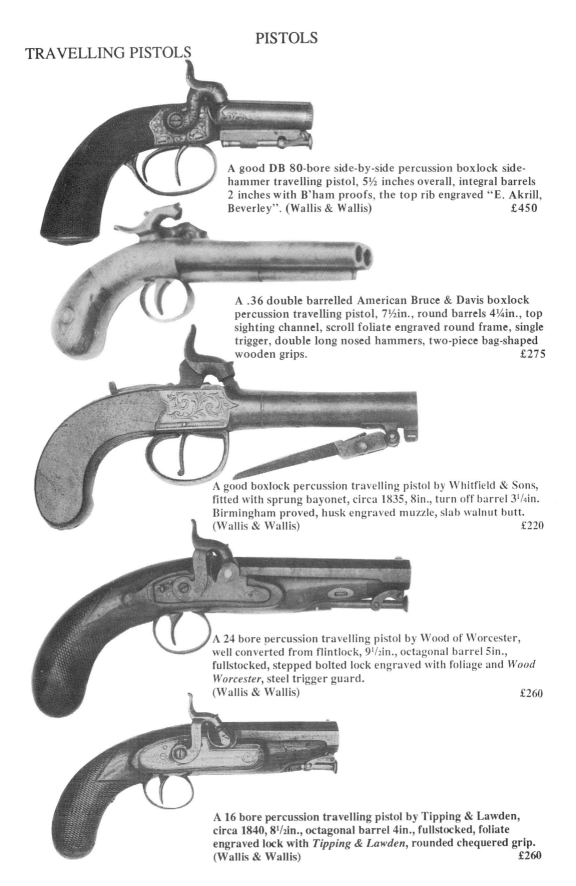

A good DB 80-bore side-by-side percussion boxlock side-hammer travelling pistol, 5½ inches overall, integral barrels 2 inches with B'ham proofs, the top rib engraved "E. Akrill, Beverley". (Wallis & Wallis) £450

A .36 double barrelled American Bruce & Davis boxlock percussion travelling pistol, 7½in., round barrels 4¼in., top sighting channel, scroll foliate engraved round frame, single trigger, double long nosed hammers, two-piece bag-shaped wooden grips. £275

A good boxlock percussion travelling pistol by Whitfield & Sons, fitted with sprung bayonet, circa 1835, 8in., turn off barrel 3¼in. Birmingham proved, husk engraved muzzle, slab walnut butt. (Wallis & Wallis) £220

A 24 bore percussion travelling pistol by Wood of Worcester, well converted from flintlock, 9½in., octagonal barrel 5in., fullstocked, stepped bolted lock engraved with foliage and *Wood Worcester*, steel trigger guard. (Wallis & Wallis) £260

A 16 bore percussion travelling pistol by Tipping & Lawden, circa 1840, 8½in., octagonal barrel 4in., fullstocked, foliate engraved lock with *Tipping & Lawden*, rounded chequered grip. (Wallis & Wallis) £260

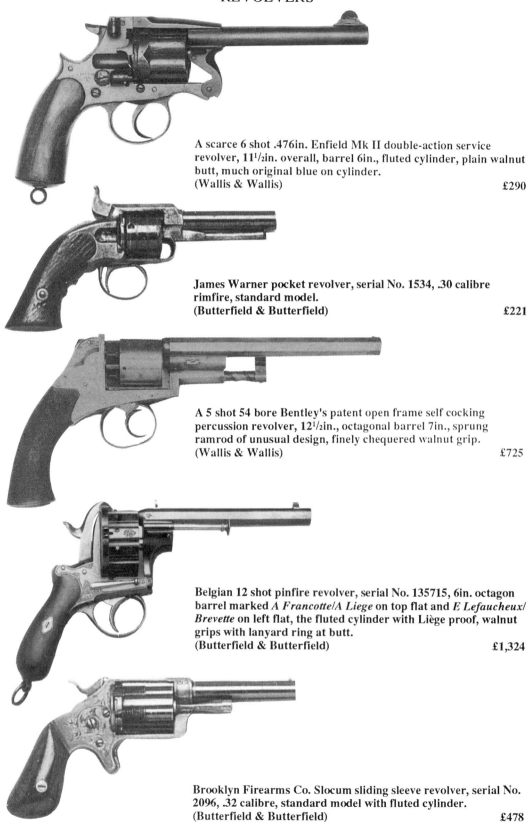

A scarce 6 shot .476in. Enfield Mk II double-action service revolver, 11¹/₂in. overall, barrel 6in., fluted cylinder, plain walnut butt, much original blue on cylinder.
(Wallis & Wallis) £290

James Warner pocket revolver, serial No. 1534, .30 calibre rimfire, standard model.
(Butterfield & Butterfield) £221

A 5 shot 54 bore Bentley's patent open frame self cocking percussion revolver, 12¹/₂in., octagonal barrel 7in., sprung ramrod of unusual design, finely chequered walnut grip.
(Wallis & Wallis) £725

Belgian 12 shot pinfire revolver, serial No. 135715, 6in. octagon barrel marked *A Francotte/A Liege* on top flat and *E Lefaucheux/Brevette* on left flat, the fluted cylinder with Liège proof, walnut grips with lanyard ring at butt.
(Butterfield & Butterfield) £1,324

Brooklyn Firearms Co. Slocum sliding sleeve revolver, serial No. 2096, .32 calibre, standard model with fluted cylinder.
(Butterfield & Butterfield) £478

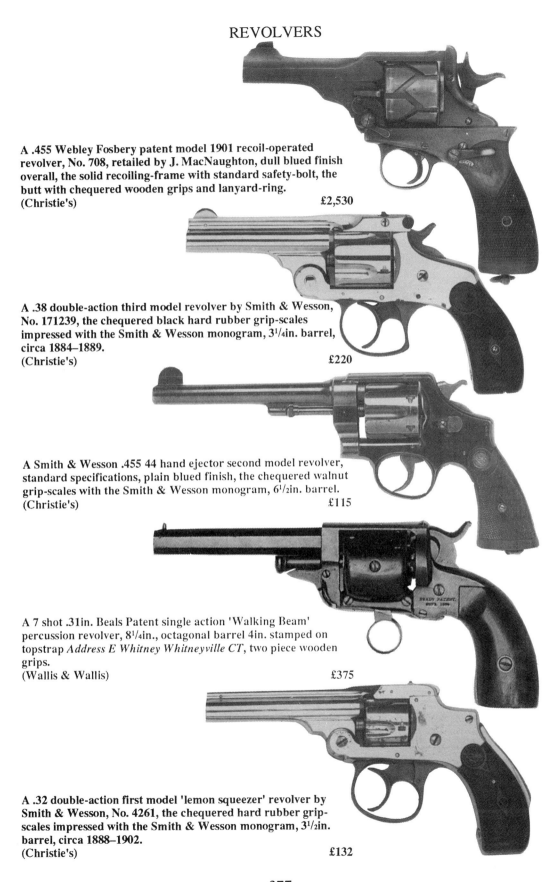

A .455 Webley Fosbery patent model 1901 recoil-operated
revolver, No. 708, retailed by J. MacNaughton, dull blued finish
overall, the solid recoiling-frame with standard safety-bolt, the
butt with chequered wooden grips and lanyard-ring.
(Christie's)   £2,530

A .38 double-action third model revolver by Smith & Wesson,
No. 171239, the chequered black hard rubber grip-scales
impressed with the Smith & Wesson monogram, 3¹/₄in. barrel,
circa 1884–1889.
(Christie's)   £220

A Smith & Wesson .455 44 hand ejector second model revolver,
standard specifications, plain blued finish, the chequered walnut
grip-scales with the Smith & Wesson monogram, 6¹/₂in. barrel.
(Christie's)   £115

A 7 shot .31in. Beals Patent single action 'Walking Beam'
percussion revolver, 8¹/₄in., octagonal barrel 4in. stamped on
topstrap *Address E Whitney Whitneyville CT*, two piece wooden
grips.
(Wallis & Wallis)   £375

A .32 double-action first model 'lemon squeezer' revolver by
Smith & Wesson, No. 4261, the chequered hard rubber grip-
scales impressed with the Smith & Wesson monogram, 3¹/₂in.
barrel, circa 1888–1902.
(Christie's)   £132

A 6 shot 60 bore self cocking transitional percussion revolver, 12in., octagonal barrel 5¹/₂in., London proved, engraved *Smith & Co, London*, foliate engraved round frame.
(Wallis & Wallis)   £185

Massachusetts Arms Co. Maynard primed pocket revolver, serial no. 145/407, .28 calibre, 3in. round barrel, automatically revolved cylinder.
(Butterfield & Butterfield)   £368

Massachusetts Arms Co. Maynard primed pocket revolver, serial No. 242, .28 calibre, 3in. round barrel, automatically revolved cylinder.
(Butterfield & Butterfield)   £1,177

A .38 single-action second model revolver by Smith & Wesson, No. 97634, the chequered hard rubber grip-scales impressed with the Smith & Wesson monogram, sighted rifled barrel, 3¹/₄in. barrel, circa 1877–1891.
(Christie's)   £55

A 6 shot 60 bore self cocking bar hammer transitional percussion revolver, 12in. overall, barrel 5¹/₂in. with Birmingham proofs, engraved *Bentley & Son, Liverpool*, chequered wood grips.
(Wallis & Wallis)   £310

A 6 shot Baker's patent 80 bore single action transitional percussion revolver, 11½in., half octagonal barrel 5½in., Birmingham proved, foliate engraved rounded frame stamped *Registered April 24 1852*, two piece varnished walnut grips.
(Wallis & Wallis)   £270

A .38 double-action fourth model revolver by Smith & Wesson, No. 406863, the backstrap stamped *Am. Ex. Co. 906*, the right-hand side of the frame impressed with the Smith & Wesson monogram, pearl grip-scales, sighted rifled barrel, 3¼in. barrel, circa 1889–1909.
(Christie's)   £77

French model 1892 military revolver, serial No. L13566, 8mm. Lebel, the frame marked *Mre. d'Armes/St. Etienne*, 4½in. barrel marked *Mle 1892* and *S 1922*, chequered grips with lanyard ring in place.
(Butterfield & Butterfield)   £110

Rare factory engraved Smith & Wesson first model 'Baby Russian' revolver, serial No. 8669, .38 calibre, 4in. barrel, scroll engraved on frame and barrel with a circular panel on the left side showing a bearded man in a Roman style helmet.
(Butterfield & Butterfield)   £2,023

A scarce Belgian 4 shot .36in. hammerless ring trigger transitional percussion revolver of Collère type, 11½in. overall, octagonal barrel 5½in. with loading groove below, plain walnut grips.
(Wallis & Wallis)   £250

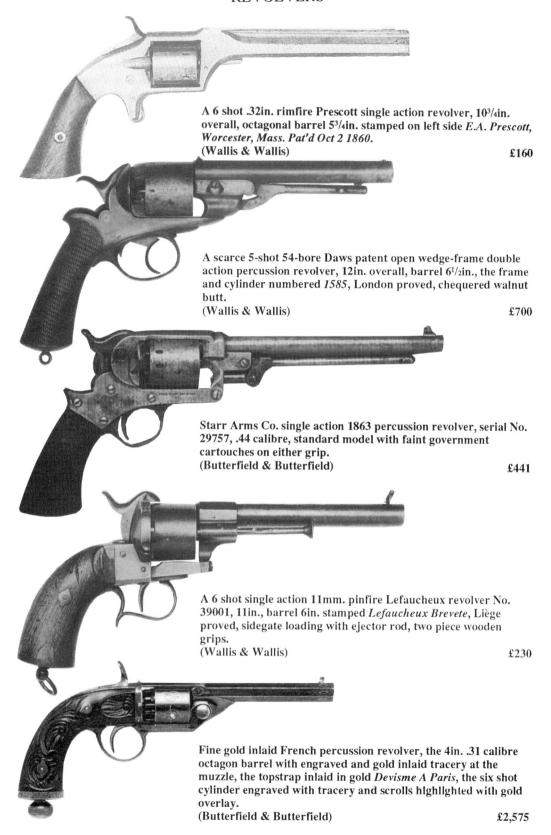

A 6 shot .32in. rimfire Prescott single action revolver, 10³/₄in. overall, octagonal barrel 5³/₄in. stamped on left side *E.A. Prescott, Worcester, Mass. Pat'd Oct 2 1860.*
(Wallis & Wallis)   £160

A scarce 5-shot 54-bore Daws patent open wedge-frame double action percussion revolver, 12in. overall, barrel 6¹/₂in., the frame and cylinder numbered *1585*, London proved, chequered walnut butt.
(Wallis & Wallis)   £700

Starr Arms Co. single action 1863 percussion revolver, serial No. 29757, .44 calibre, standard model with faint government cartouches on either grip.
(Butterfield & Butterfield)   £441

A 6 shot single action 11mm. pinfire Lefaucheux revolver No. 39001, 11in., barrel 6in. stamped *Lefaucheux Brevete*, Liège proved, sidegate loading with ejector rod, two piece wooden grips.
(Wallis & Wallis)   £230

Fine gold inlaid French percussion revolver, the 4in. .31 calibre octagon barrel with engraved and gold inlaid tracery at the muzzle, the topstrap inlaid in gold *Devisme A Paris*, the six shot cylinder engraved with tracery and scrolls highlighted with gold overlay.
(Butterfield & Butterfield)   £2,575

Massachusetts Arms Co. Wesson & Leavitt percussion belt revolver, serial No. 324, .31 calibre, 5in. barrel, standard model and markings.
(Butterfield & Butterfield)   £1,030

A 5-shot 120-bore Third Model Tranters Patent double-trigger percussion revolver, 8½in. overall, barrel 4in. engraved *A. Clayton, High St., Southampton*, the frame numbered *7931T*, scroll engraving to breech, frame, and butt-cap.
(Wallis & Wallis)   £400

A good 5 shot 70 bore double action percussion revolver by E. M. Reilly, 9in., blued octagonal barrel 4½in., Birmingham proved, polished steel side lever rammer, steel frame, grip strap and trigger guard, two piece chequered walnut grips.
(Wallis & Wallis)   £310

Moore's Patent Firearms Co. front loading revolver, serial No. 106, .32 calibre teat-fire, standard model made without hook extractor.
(Butterfield & Butterfield)   £294

Gustav Young engraved Smith & Wesson new model No. 3 revolver, serial No. 11476, .44 calibre, 6½in. barrel, factory exhibition style engraved by Gustav Young on barrel, frame, cylinder, grip straps, hammer and latch.
(Butterfield & Butterfield)   £6,254

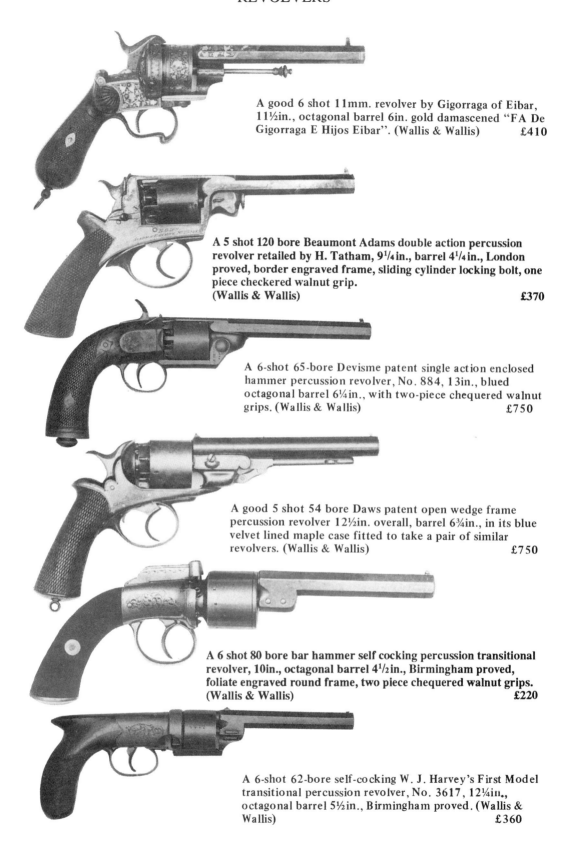

A good 6 shot 11mm. revolver by Gigorraga of Eibar, 11½in., octagonal barrel 6in. gold damascened "FA De Gigorraga E Hijos Eibar". (Wallis & Wallis) £410

A 5 shot 120 bore Beaumont Adams double action percussion revolver retailed by H. Tatham, 9¼in., barrel 4¼in., London proved, border engraved frame, sliding cylinder locking bolt, one piece checkered walnut grip. (Wallis & Wallis) £370

A 6-shot 65-bore Devisme patent single action enclosed hammer percussion revolver, No. 884, 13in., blued octagonal barrel 6¼in., with two-piece chequered walnut grips. (Wallis & Wallis) £750

A good 5 shot 54 bore Daws patent open wedge frame percussion revolver 12½in. overall, barrel 6¾in., in its blue velvet lined maple case fitted to take a pair of similar revolvers. (Wallis & Wallis) £750

A 6 shot 80 bore bar hammer self cocking percussion transitional revolver, 10in., octagonal barrel 4½in., Birmingham proved, foliate engraved round frame, two piece chequered walnut grips. (Wallis & Wallis) £220

A 6-shot 62-bore self-cocking W. J. Harvey's First Model transitional percussion revolver, No. 3617, 12¼in., octagonal barrel 5½in., Birmingham proved. (Wallis & Wallis) £360

ARMY REVOLVERS

A 6 shot .44in. Remington army single action percussion revolver
No. 73082, 13½in., octagonal barrel 8in., underlever rammer,
two piece wooden grips.
(Wallis & Wallis)   £500

Remington new model army percussion revolver, serial No. 6671,
.44 calibre, standard model with government cartouche on left
grip.
(Butterfield & Butterfield)   £1,656

A six-shot Starr army percussion revolver, 15.5cm. sighted
barrel with rammer mounted beneath, plain cylinder, frame
stamped Starr Arms & Co., New York.   £400

Starr Arms Co. double action 1858 percussion army revolver,
serial No. 17875, .44 calibre, standard model with government
cartouche on either side of grip.
(Butterfield & Butterfield)   £625

A six-shot Remington army percussion revolver, 20cm.
sighted octagonal barrel signed Patented Sept 14, 1858
E. Remington & Sons, Ilion, New York, U.S.A., New Model.
                                                                                 £480

A 6-shot 12mm. Dumonthier Military double action pinfire
revolver, 10½in., round barrel 6in., No. 5182, burl walnut
bag-shaped grip with fitted lanyard ring, gate loading and
rod ejection.   £300

COLT REVOLVERS

Colt model 1877 Lightning double action revolver, serial
no. 59549, .38 calibre, 6in. barrel with ejector, nickel
finish, ivory grips.
(Butterfield & Butterfield)   £525

Factory engraved Colt model 1877 Thunderer double
action revolver, serial no. 15979, .41 calibre, 5in. barrel
with ejector, nickel finish, mother-of-pearl grips.
(Butterfield & Butterfield)   £3,000

Colt model 1877 Thunderer double action revolver, serial
no. 3388, .41 calibre, 7½in. barrel without ejector, nickel
finish, checkered rosewood grips.
(Butterfield & Butterfield)   £1,000

Colt presentation grade gold inlaid Metropolitan Museum of Art
single action army revolver, serial No. MMA-I, .45 calibre, 7½in.
barrel marked in flush gold *Colt's Pt. Fa. Mfg. Co. Hartford, Ct.
U.S.A.* and on the left side *Colt's Single Action Army 45*, the
frame, barrel, ejector housing, cylinders, hammer, gripstraps,
sight and buttcap feature high relief and flush gold inlays on a
blued partially scroll engraved ground.
(Butterfield & Butterfield)   £21,963

Rare gold-signatured and engraved Colt officer's model revolver,
serial No. 417169, .38 calibre, 7½in. barrel marked *Colt's Pt. F.A.
Mfg. Co. Hartford Conn. U.S.A. Pat'd. Aug. 5, 1884 July 4, 1905,
Officer's Model 38* on left side, overall engraved by Cuno A.
Helfricht with scrolls on a punched ground.
(Butterfield & Butterfield)   £4,393

COLT REVOLVERS

Colt third model Dragoon percussion revolver cut for
experimental hook-on shoulder stock, serial No. 15826, .44
calibre, 7½in. barrel marked *Address Saml Colt New York City*,
Dragoon and Indian fight scene roll engraved on cylinder.
(Butterfield & Butterfield) £25,624

Colt model 1878 Frontier double action revolver deluxe engraved
and inscribed, serial No. 7336, .45 calibre, 5½in. barrel marked
Colt's Pt. F.A. Mfg. Co. Hartford Ct. U.S.A., overall engraved by
the shop of Cuno A. Helfricht, with elaborate scrolls, ribbons,
wriggle lines, dots, florals, banners and cross-hatching.
(Butterfield & Butterfield) £13,178

Rare Colt Paterson No. 3 belt model percussion revolver
engraved and silver banded, serial No. 754, .34 calibre, 4in.
barrel marked *Patent Arms M'g. Co. Paterson N.J. Colt's Patent*,
floral scrolls engraved on barrel, recoil shield and hammer, silver
plated frame and backstrap.
(Butterfield & Butterfield) £65,890

Colt model 1848 baby Dragoon revolver, serial no. 14287,
.31 calibre, 6in. barrel with loading lever and two line New
York markings, standard late model production with
rectangular stop slots and stagecoach holdup scene.
(Butterfield & Butterfield) £1,100

Rare Colt Whitneyville Walker model 1847 Dragoon percussion
revolver, serial No. 1078, .44 calibre, 9in. half-round/half-octagon
barrel marked *Address Sam'l Colt New York City* and *U.S. 1847*
over wedge, cylinder roll engraved with Dragoon and Indian
fight scene and marked *Model U.S.M.R. Colt's Patent*.
(Butterfield & Butterfield) £95,175

COLT REVOLVERS

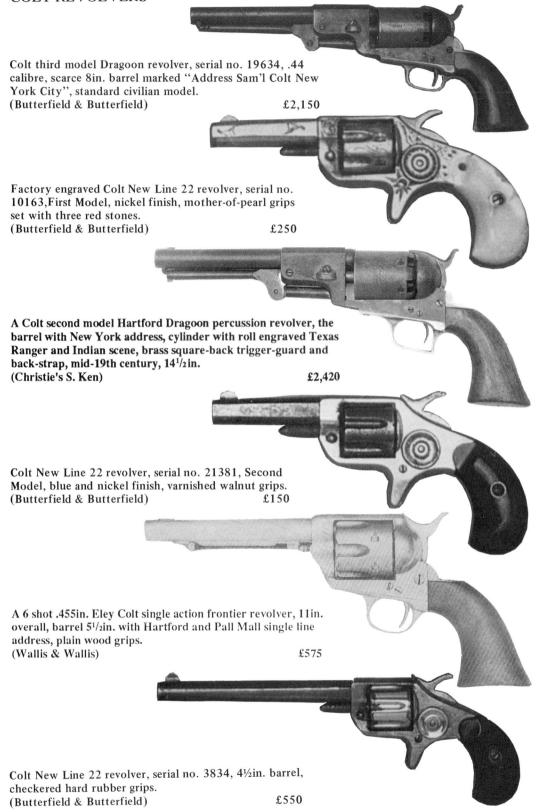

Colt third model Dragoon revolver, serial no. 19634, .44
calibre, scarce 8in. barrel marked "Address Sam'l Colt New
York City", standard civilian model.
(Butterfield & Butterfield)   £2,150

Factory engraved Colt New Line 22 revolver, serial no.
10163,First Model, nickel finish, mother-of-pearl grips
set with three red stones.
(Butterfield & Butterfield)   £250

**A Colt second model Hartford Dragoon percussion revolver, the
barrel with New York address, cylinder with roll engraved Texas
Ranger and Indian scene, brass square-back trigger-guard and
back-strap, mid-19th century, 14½in.**
(Christie's S. Ken)   £2,420

Colt New Line 22 revolver, serial no. 21381, Second
Model, blue and nickel finish, varnished walnut grips.
(Butterfield & Butterfield)   £150

A 6 shot .455in. Eley Colt single action frontier revolver, 11in.
overall, barrel 5½in. with Hartford and Pall Mall single line
address, plain wood grips.
(Wallis & Wallis)   £575

Colt New Line 22 revolver, serial no. 3834, 4½in. barrel,
checkered hard rubber grips.
(Butterfield & Butterfield)   £550

COLT REVOLVERS

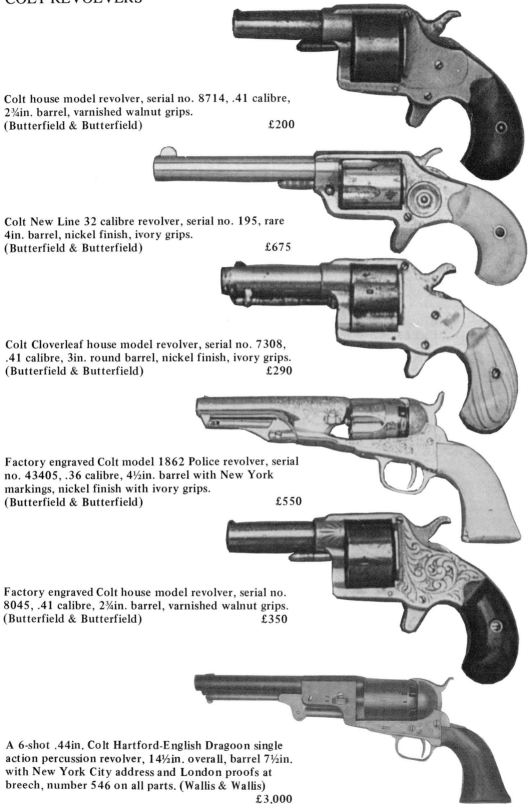

Colt house model revolver, serial no. 8714, .41 calibre, 2¾in. barrel, varnished walnut grips. (Butterfield & Butterfield) £200

Colt New Line 32 calibre revolver, serial no. 195, rare 4in. barrel, nickel finish, ivory grips. (Butterfield & Butterfield) £675

Colt Cloverleaf house model revolver, serial no. 7308, .41 calibre, 3in. round barrel, nickel finish, ivory grips. (Butterfield & Butterfield) £290

Factory engraved Colt model 1862 Police revolver, serial no. 43405, .36 calibre, 4½in. barrel with New York markings, nickel finish with ivory grips. (Butterfield & Butterfield) £550

Factory engraved Colt house model revolver, serial no. 8045, .41 calibre, 2¾in. barrel, varnished walnut grips. (Butterfield & Butterfield) £350

A 6-shot .44in. Colt Hartford-English Dragoon single action percussion revolver, 14½in. overall, barrel 7½in. with New York City address and London proofs at breech, number 546 on all parts. (Wallis & Wallis) £3,000

COLT REVOLVERS

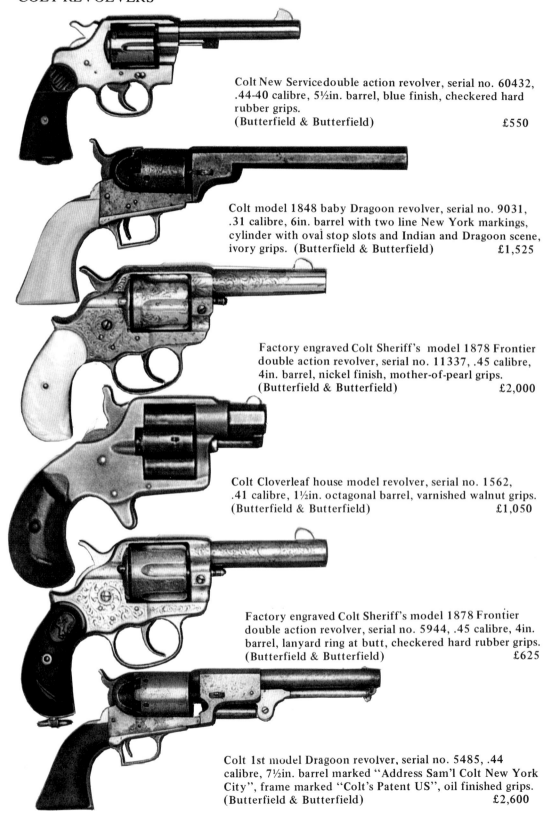

Colt New Service double action revolver, serial no. 60432, .44-40 calibre, 5½in. barrel, blue finish, checkered hard rubber grips.
(Butterfield & Butterfield)   £550

Colt model 1848 baby Dragoon revolver, serial no. 9031, .31 calibre, 6in. barrel with two line New York markings, cylinder with oval stop slots and Indian and Dragoon scene, ivory grips. (Butterfield & Butterfield)   £1,525

Factory engraved Colt Sheriff's model 1878 Frontier double action revolver, serial no. 11337, .45 calibre, 4in. barrel, nickel finish, mother-of-pearl grips.
(Butterfield & Butterfield)   £2,000

Colt Cloverleaf house model revolver, serial no. 1562, .41 calibre, 1½in. octagonal barrel, varnished walnut grips.
(Butterfield & Butterfield)   £1,050

Factory engraved Colt Sheriff's model 1878 Frontier double action revolver, serial no. 5944, .45 calibre, 4in. barrel, lanyard ring at butt, checkered hard rubber grips.
(Butterfield & Butterfield)   £625

Colt 1st model Dragoon revolver, serial no. 5485, .44 calibre, 7½in. barrel marked "Address Sam'l Colt New York City", frame marked "Colt's Patent US", oil finished grips.
(Butterfield & Butterfield)   £2,600

Factory engraved Colt Sheriff's model 1877 Lightning double action revolver, serial no. 43043, .38 calibre, 3½in. barrel without ejector, nickel finish, mother-of-pearl grips. (Butterfield & Butterfield) £675

Colt model 1877 Lightning double action revolver, serial no. 18975, .38 calibre, 4½in. barrel with ejector and London markings, British proofs, blue and case hardened finish, deluxe checkered rosewood grips. (Butterfield & Butterfield) £365

Colt model 1878 Frontier double action revolver, serial no. 855, .45 calibre, 5½in. barrel with London markings, British proofs, blue finish, ivory grips. (Butterfield & Butterfield) £675

Colt Cloverleaf house model revolver, serial no. 3128, .41 calibre, 3in. round barrel, varnished walnut grips. (Butterfield & Butterfield) £400

Colt Sheriff's model 1877 Lightning double action revolver, serial no. 3084, .38 calibre, 3½in. barrel without ejector, nickel finish, checkered hard rubber grips. (Butterfield & Butterfield) £735

Colt Sheriff's model 1877 Lightning double action revolver, serial no. 1061, .38 calibre, 3½in. barrel without ejector, nickel finish, ivory grips. (Butterfield & Butterfield) £525

COLT REVOLVERS

Colt deluxe factory engraved officer's model revolver, serial No. 515559, .38 calibre, 6in. barrel marked *Colt's Pt. F.A. Co. Hartford Ct. U.S.A. Pat'd Aug. 5 1884–July 4, 1905*, floral scroll engraved by Wilbur A. Glahn in Grade B pattern on barrel, frame, crane, gripstraps and cylinder.
(Butterfield & Butterfield) £8,053

A 6 shot .357in. Magnum Colt Python 357 hand ejector target revolver, 11½in. overall, barrel 6in., Pachmayr soft chequered black rubber grips. (Wallis & Wallis) £290

A 6 shot .31 inch Colt single action percussion pocket revolver No. 205952, 10 inches, octagonal barrel 5 inches engraved "Saml Colt" with foliage, foliate engraved underlever rammer. Foliate engraved frame stamped "Colts Patent". (Wallis & Wallis) £650

Rare and unique cased Colt Paterson belt model percussion revolver, engraved and silver banded, .34 calibre, 4⁵/₈in. barrel marked *Patent Arms M'g Co. Paterson N.J. Colts Pt.*
(Butterfield & Butterfield) £435,028

Historic Colt Whitneyville Walker model 1847 Dragoon percussion revolver, .44 calibre, 9in. half round octagon barrel marked *Address Sam'l Colt, New York City* and *U.S. 1847* over wedge.
(Butterfield & Butterfield) £155,367

COLT ARMY REVOLVERS

A 6 shot .44in. Colt Army single action percussion revolver, 14in., round blued barrel 8in. stamped *Address Col Saml Colt New York U.S. America* colour hardened creeping rammer, blued rebated cylinder, one piece wooden grip.
(Wallis & Wallis) **£1,000**

Rare Colt single action army flattop target 'Ejectorless' model revolver, serial No. 1675537, .38 calibre, 7½in. barrel without ejector assembly marked *Colt's Pt. F.A. Mfc. Co. Hartford Ct. U.S.A.* blue finish with casehardened hammer, chequered hard rubber grips with factory letter.
(Butterfield & Butterfield) **£16,473**

Rare Colt single action new army revolver, calibre 41, 6in. barrel marked *Colt D.A. 41* on left side, blued finish, walnut grips, serial No. 1, produced in the 1890s.
(Butterfield & Butterfield) **£5,000**

Historic Colt single action army revolver, serial No. 181419, .45 calibre, 4¾in. barrel, chequered hard rubber Colt grips, the brown leather double loop western rig decorated with punched roundels, rawhide lacing and with leather concho at tip.
(Butterfield & Butterfield) **£2,023**

A Colt 1860 model army percussion revolver of presentation quality, No. 151695E for 1864, with sighted barrel with New York address, rebated cylinder with naval engagement scene, wolf head engraved hammer, frame cut for a shoulder-stock, London proof marks, 14½in. long.
(Christie's) **£4,180**

COLT ARMY REVOLVERS

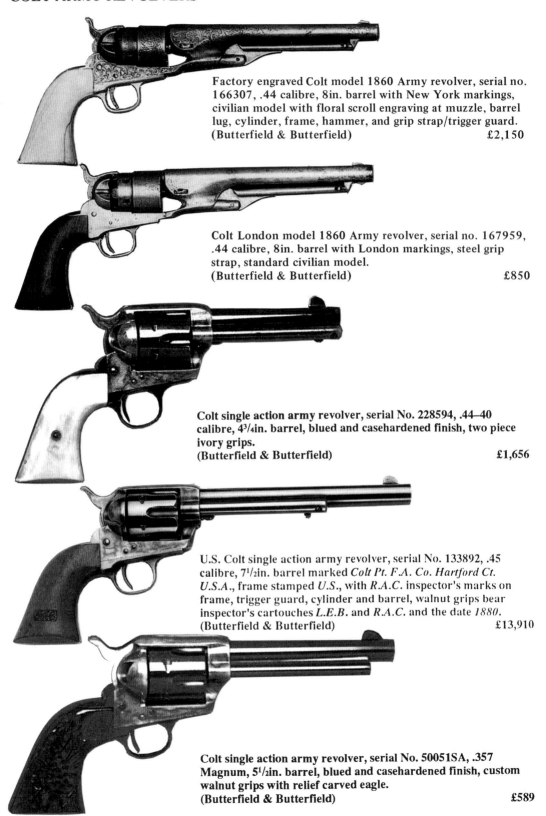

Factory engraved Colt model 1860 Army revolver, serial no. 166307, .44 calibre, 8in. barrel with New York markings, civilian model with floral scroll engraving at muzzle, barrel lug, cylinder, frame, hammer, and grip strap/trigger guard.
(Butterfield & Butterfield) £2,150

Colt London model 1860 Army revolver, serial no. 167959, .44 calibre, 8in. barrel with London markings, steel grip strap, standard civilian model.
(Butterfield & Butterfield) £850

Colt single action army revolver, serial No. 228594, .44–40 calibre, 4³/₄in. barrel, blued and casehardened finish, two piece ivory grips.
(Butterfield & Butterfield) £1,656

U.S. Colt single action army revolver, serial No. 133892, .45 calibre, 7¹/₂in. barrel marked *Colt Pt. F.A. Co. Hartford Ct. U.S.A.*, frame stamped *U.S.*, with *R.A.C.* inspector's marks on frame, trigger guard, cylinder and barrel, walnut grips bear inspector's cartouches *L.E.B.* and *R.A.C.* and the date *1880*.
(Butterfield & Butterfield) £13,910

Colt single action army revolver, serial No. 50051SA, .357 Magnum, 5¹/₂in. barrel, blued and casehardened finish, custom walnut grips with relief carved eagle.
(Butterfield & Butterfield) £589

COLT ARMY REVOLVERS

Colt single action army revolver, serial No. 14475, .45 calibre,
7$^{1}/_{2}$in. barrel, walnut grips.
(Butterfield & Butterfield)

£1,656

Colt single action army revolver, serial No. 28169SA, .38 Special,
5$^{1}/_{2}$in. barrel, blued and casehardened finish, chequered hard
rubber.
(Butterfield & Butterfield)

£552

Colt single action army revolver, serial No. 350035, .45 calibre,
5$^{1}/_{2}$in. barrel, blued and casehardened finish, ivory grips with
raised steerhead motif.
(Butterfield & Butterfield)

£2,759

Colt single action army revolver, serial No. 34196SA, .38 Special,
5$^{1}/_{2}$in. barrel, nickel plated finish, staghorn grips.
(Butterfield & Butterfield)

£625

Colt New Frontier single action army revolver, serial No.
6141NF, .45 calibre, 7$^{1}/_{2}$in. barrel, blued and casehardened finish,
walnut grips with silver Colt medallion.
(Butterfield & Butterfield)

£552

COLT ARMY REVOLVERS

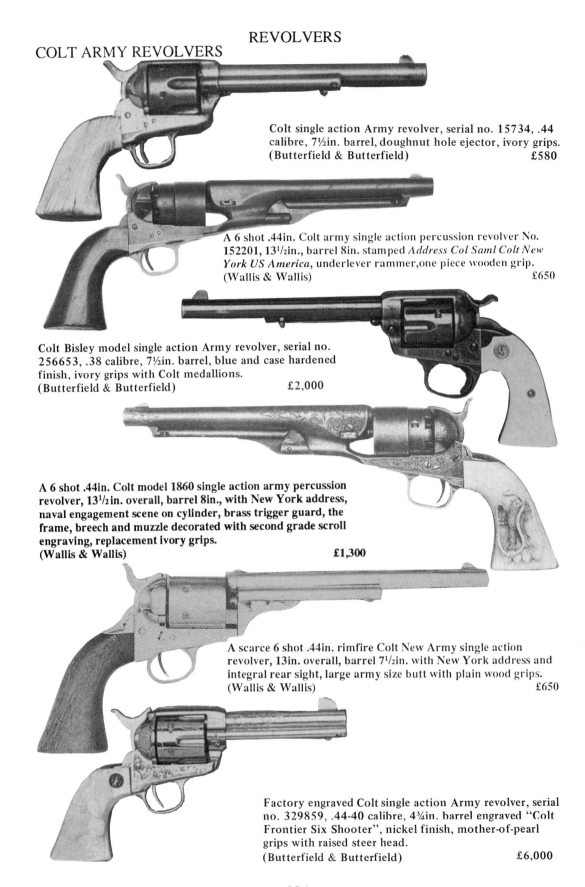

Colt single action Army revolver, serial no. 15734, .44 calibre, 7½in. barrel, doughnut hole ejector, ivory grips. (Butterfield & Butterfield) £580

A 6 shot .44in. Colt army single action percussion revolver No. 152201, 13½in., barrel 8in. stamped *Address Col Saml Colt New York US America*, underlever rammer,one piece wooden grip. (Wallis & Wallis) £650

Colt Bisley model single action Army revolver, serial no. 256653, .38 calibre, 7½in. barrel, blue and case hardened finish, ivory grips with Colt medallions. (Butterfield & Butterfield) £2,000

A 6 shot .44in. Colt model 1860 single action army percussion revolver, 13½in. overall, barrel 8in., with New York address, naval engagement scene on cylinder, brass trigger guard, the frame, breech and muzzle decorated with second grade scroll engraving, replacement ivory grips. (Wallis & Wallis) £1,300

A scarce 6 shot .44in. rimfire Colt New Army single action revolver, 13in. overall, barrel 7½in. with New York address and integral rear sight, large army size butt with plain wood grips. (Wallis & Wallis) £650

Factory engraved Colt single action Army revolver, serial no. 329859, .44-40 calibre, 4¾in. barrel engraved "Colt Frontier Six Shooter", nickel finish, mother-of-pearl grips with raised steer head. (Butterfield & Butterfield) £6,000

COLT NAVY REVOLVERS

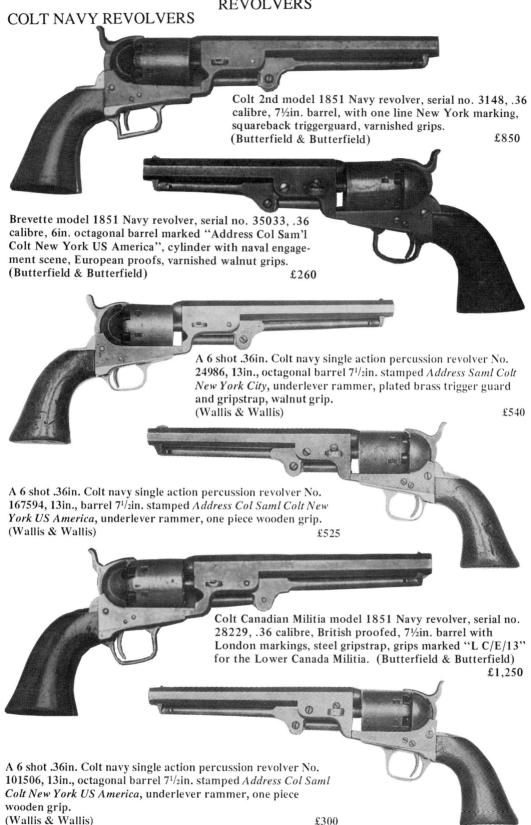

Colt 2nd model 1851 Navy revolver, serial no. 3148, .36 calibre, 7½in. barrel, with one line New York marking, squareback triggerguard, varnished grips. (Butterfield & Butterfield) £850

Brevette model 1851 Navy revolver, serial no. 35033, .36 calibre, 6in. octagonal barrel marked "Address Col Sam'l Colt New York US America", cylinder with naval engagement scene, European proofs, varnished walnut grips. (Butterfield & Butterfield) £260

A 6 shot .36in. Colt navy single action percussion revolver No. 24986, 13in., octagonal barrel 7½in. stamped *Address Saml Colt New York City*, underlever rammer, plated brass trigger guard and gripstrap, walnut grip. (Wallis & Wallis) £540

A 6 shot .36in. Colt navy single action percussion revolver No. 167594, 13in., barrel 7½in. stamped *Address Col Saml Colt New York US America*, underlever rammer, one piece wooden grip. (Wallis & Wallis) £525

Colt Canadian Militia model 1851 Navy revolver, serial no. 28229, .36 calibre, British proofed, 7½in. barrel with London markings, steel gripstrap, grips marked "L C/E/13" for the Lower Canada Militia. (Butterfield & Butterfield) £1,250

A 6 shot .36in. Colt navy single action percussion revolver No. 101506, 13in., octagonal barrel 7½in. stamped *Address Col Saml Colt New York US America*, underlever rammer, one piece wooden grip. (Wallis & Wallis) £300

COLT NAVY REVOLVERS

Colt single action Army revolver, serial no. 66268, .44 calibre, 4¾in. barrel, blue finish overall, varnished walnut grips with silver inlays reading "Colt/44", "JWA" and "1891". (Butterfield & Butterfield)   £1,160

A 6-shot .36in. Colt Model 1851 Navy percussion revolver, 13in. overall, barrel 7½in., number *6371* on all parts, London address and proofs, iron trigger guard, naval scene on cylinder, plain polished wood grips.
(Wallis & Wallis)   £1,100

Colt presentation model 1851 navy percussion revolver with detachable canteen shoulder stock, serial No. 79482, .36 calibre, 7½in. barrel marked *Address Sam's Colt Hartford Ct.*, silver plated brass backstrap cut for stock and bearing the engraved initials *F.W.H.S.*
(Butterfield & Butterfield)   £32,945

Colt single action Army Revolver, serial no. 76803, .455 calibre, 7½in. barrel with Hartford/London markings, British proofs, varnished walnut grips, butt marked "1061". (Butterfield & Butterfield)   £3,000

Colt model 1860 Army Transitional Richards conversion revolver, serial no. 196417, .44 CF calibre, 8in. barrel with New York markings, varnished walnut grips.
(Butterfield & Butterfield)   £1,150

COLT NAVY REVOLVERS

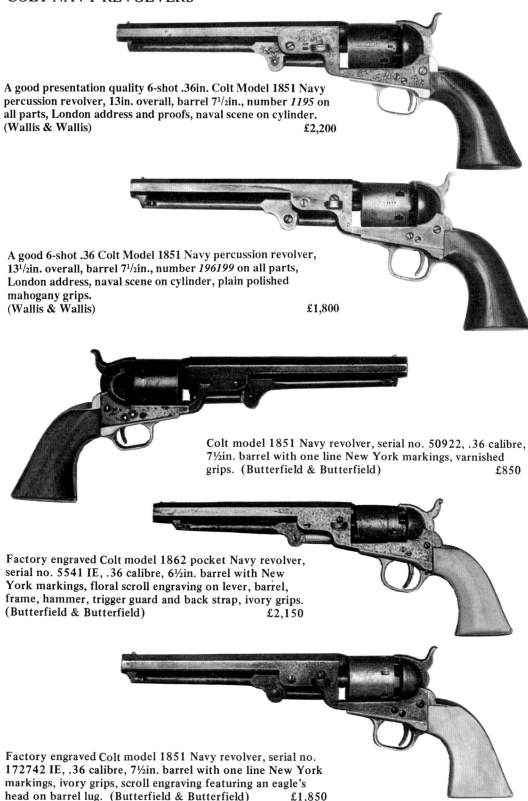

A good presentation quality 6-shot .36in. Colt Model 1851 Navy
percussion revolver, 13in. overall, barrel 7^1/$_2$in., number *1195* on
all parts, London address and proofs, naval scene on cylinder.
(Wallis & Wallis) £2,200

A good 6-shot .36 Colt Model 1851 Navy percussion revolver,
13^1/$_2$in. overall, barrel 7^1/$_2$in., number *196199* on all parts,
London address, naval scene on cylinder, plain polished
mahogany grips.
(Wallis & Wallis) £1,800

Colt model 1851 Navy revolver, serial no. 50922, .36 calibre,
7½in. barrel with one line New York markings, varnished
grips. (Butterfield & Butterfield) £850

Factory engraved Colt model 1862 pocket Navy revolver,
serial no. 5541 IE, .36 calibre, 6½in. barrel with New
York markings, floral scroll engraving on lever, barrel,
frame, hammer, trigger guard and back strap, ivory grips.
(Butterfield & Butterfield) £2,150

Factory engraved Colt model 1851 Navy revolver, serial no.
172742 IE, .36 calibre, 7½in. barrel with one line New York
markings, ivory grips, scroll engraving featuring an eagle's
head on barrel lug. (Butterfield & Butterfield) £1,850

COLT POCKET REVOLVERS

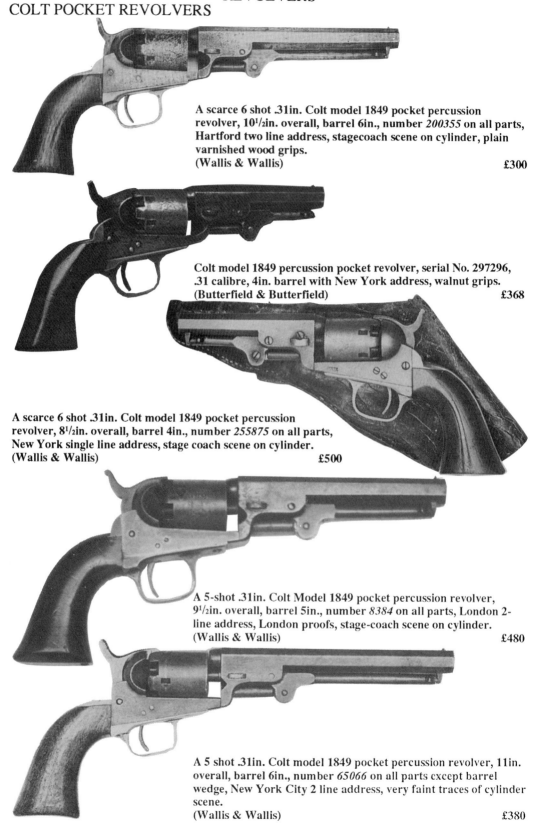

A scarce 6 shot .31in. Colt model 1849 pocket percussion revolver, 10½in. overall, barrel 6in., number *200355* on all parts, Hartford two line address, stagecoach scene on cylinder, plain varnished wood grips.
(Wallis & Wallis)   £300

Colt model 1849 percussion pocket revolver, serial No. 297296, .31 calibre, 4in. barrel with New York address, walnut grips.
(Butterfield & Butterfield)   £368

A scarce 6 shot .31in. Colt model 1849 pocket percussion revolver, 8½in. overall, barrel 4in., number *255875* on all parts, New York single line address, stage coach scene on cylinder.
(Wallis & Wallis)   £500

A 5-shot .31in. Colt Model 1849 pocket percussion revolver, 9½in. overall, barrel 5in., number *8384* on all parts, London 2-line address, London proofs, stage-coach scene on cylinder.
(Wallis & Wallis)   £480

A 5 shot .31in. Colt model 1849 pocket percussion revolver, 11in. overall, barrel 6in., number *65066* on all parts except barrel wedge, New York City 2 line address, very faint traces of cylinder scene.
(Wallis & Wallis)   £380

COLT POCKET REVOLVERS

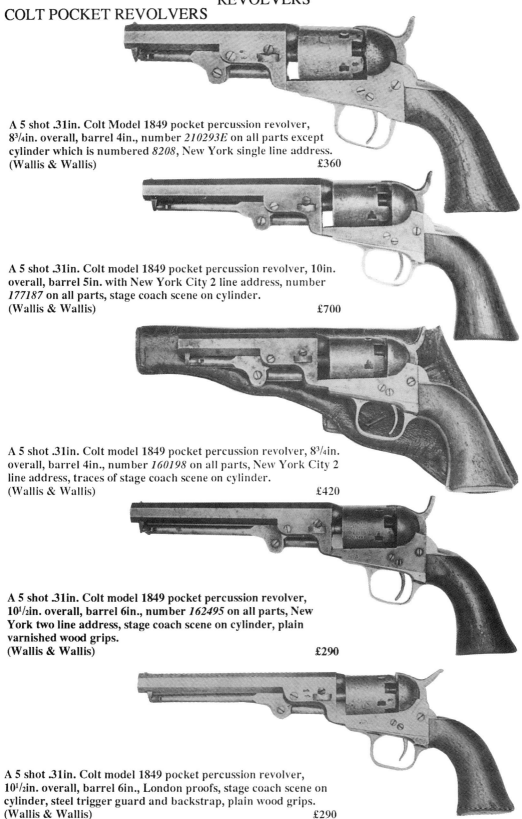

A 5 shot .31in. Colt Model 1849 pocket percussion revolver,
8³/₄in. overall, barrel 4in., number *210293E* on all parts except
cylinder which is numbered *8208*, New York single line address.
(Wallis & Wallis)   £360

A 5 shot .31in. Colt model 1849 pocket percussion revolver, 10in.
overall, barrel 5in. with New York City 2 line address, number
177187 on all parts, stage coach scene on cylinder.
(Wallis & Wallis)   £700

A 5 shot .31in. Colt model 1849 pocket percussion revolver, 8³/₄in.
overall, barrel 4in., number *160198* on all parts, New York City 2
line address, traces of stage coach scene on cylinder.
(Wallis & Wallis)   £420

**A 5 shot .31in. Colt model 1849 pocket percussion revolver,
10¹/₂in. overall, barrel 6in., number *162495* on all parts, New
York two line address, stage coach scene on cylinder, plain
varnished wood grips.
(Wallis & Wallis)   £290**

A 5 shot .31in. Colt model 1849 pocket percussion revolver,
10¹/₂in. overall, barrel 6in., London proofs, stage coach scene on
cylinder, steel trigger guard and backstrap, plain wood grips.
(Wallis & Wallis)   £290

COLT POCKET REVOLVERS

Factory engraved Colt Root model 1855 Sidehammer pocket revolver, serial no. 19469 , .28 calibre, second model, 3½in. barrel with pointing hand and Hartford markings and part round/part octagon loading lever, ivory grips with checkered butt. (Butterfield & Butterfield)   £1,375

Colt model 1849 pocket revolver, serial no. 112775, .31 calibre, 4in. barrel with attached loading lever and two line New York markings, steel gripstraps and varnished walnut grips. (Butterfield & Butterfield)   £675

Colt factory engraved model 1849 pocket revolver, serial no. 105763, .31 calibre, 4in. barrel engraved "Sam'l Colt", standard floral scroll engraving featuring a wolf's head on barrel lug, ivory grips. (Butterfield & Butterfield) £735

Factory engraved Colt Root model 1855 Sidehammer pocket revolver, serial no. 463, .28 calibre, second model, 3½in. barrel with pointing hand and Hartford markings, octagon loading lever. (Butterfield & Butterfield)   £925

Colt factory engraved model 1849 pocket revolver, serial no. 91996, .31 calibre, 5in. barrel engraved "Sam'l Colt", barrel lug, rammer lug, frame, hammer and trigger with floral scroll engraving featuring two eagle heads, ivory grips. (Butterfield & Butterfield)   £1,250

COLT POCKET REVOLVERS

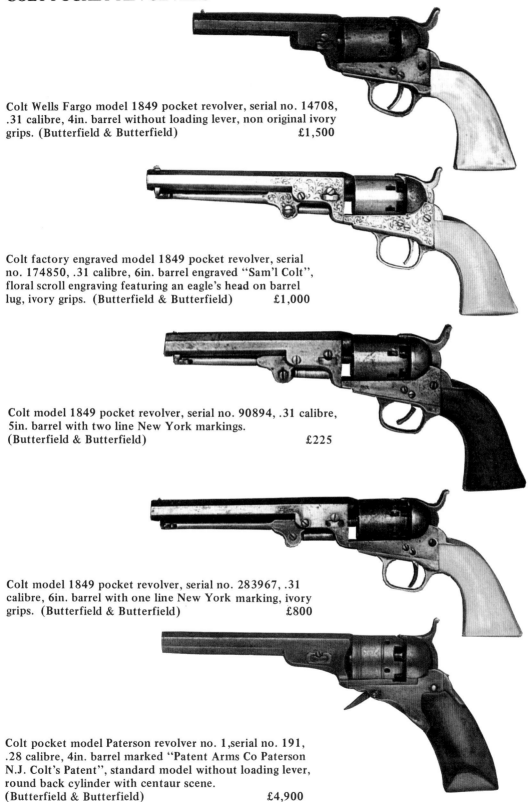

Colt Wells Fargo model 1849 pocket revolver, serial no. 14708, .31 calibre, 4in. barrel without loading lever, non original ivory grips. (Butterfield & Butterfield)   £1,500

Colt factory engraved model 1849 pocket revolver, serial no. 174850, .31 calibre, 6in. barrel engraved "Sam'l Colt", floral scroll engraving featuring an eagle's head on barrel lug, ivory grips. (Butterfield & Butterfield)   £1,000

Colt model 1849 pocket revolver, serial no. 90894, .31 calibre, 5in. barrel with two line New York markings. (Butterfield & Butterfield)   £225

Colt model 1849 pocket revolver, serial no. 283967, .31 calibre, 6in. barrel with one line New York marking, ivory grips. (Butterfield & Butterfield)   £800

Colt pocket model Paterson revolver no. 1, serial no. 191, .28 calibre, 4in. barrel marked "Patent Arms Co Paterson N.J. Colt's Patent", standard model without loading lever, round back cylinder with centaur scene. (Butterfield & Butterfield)   £4,900

NAVY REVOLVERS

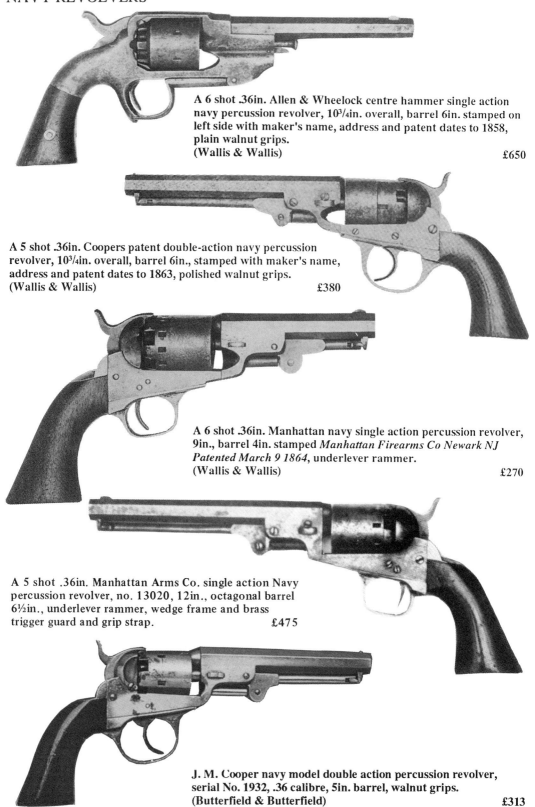

A 6 shot .36in. Allen & Wheelock centre hammer single action navy percussion revolver, 10³/₄in. overall, barrel 6in. stamped on left side with maker's name, address and patent dates to 1858, plain walnut grips.
(Wallis & Wallis)
£650

A 5 shot .36in. Coopers patent double-action navy percussion revolver, 10³/₄in. overall, barrel 6in., stamped with maker's name, address and patent dates to 1863, polished walnut grips.
(Wallis & Wallis)
£380

A 6 shot .36in. Manhattan navy single action percussion revolver, 9in., barrel 4in. stamped *Manhattan Firearms Co Newark NJ Patented March 9 1864*, underlever rammer.
(Wallis & Wallis)
£270

A 5 shot .36in. Manhattan Arms Co. single action Navy percussion revolver, no. 13020, 12in., octagonal barrel 6½in., underlever rammer, wedge frame and brass trigger guard and grip strap.
£475

J. M. Cooper navy model double action percussion revolver, serial No. 1932, .36 calibre, 5in. barrel, walnut grips.
(Butterfield & Butterfield)
£313

PEPPERBOX REVOLVERS

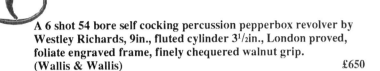

A 6 shot 54 bore self cocking percussion pepperbox revolver by
Westley Richards, 9in., fluted cylinder 3¹/₂in., London proved,
foliate engraved frame, finely chequered walnut grip.
(Wallis & Wallis)   £650

A 4 shot 100 bore Mariette patent ring trigger Belgian percussion
pepperbox revolver, 6¹/₂in., turn off damascus twist barrels 2in.,
two piece bag shaped ivory grips of good colour and patina.
(Wallis & Wallis)   £370

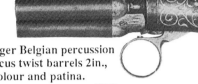

A Belgian six-shot double-action percussion pepperbox revolver
with etched twist turn-off barrels numbered from 0 to 5, ebonised
grips, the back-strap stamped *J.J. Herman Breveté*, Liège proof,
circa 1850, 7¹/₄in.
(Christie's)   £385

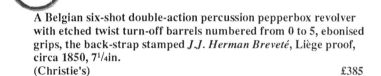

A 46-bore 4-shot ring trigger self-cocking percussion
pepperboxpistol, 7¼in., turn-off fine damascus twist
barrels 2¾in., London proved with two-piece chequered walnut grips. (Wallis & Wallis)   £310

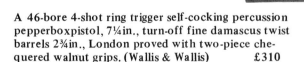

A good 4 shot 45 bore self cocking Mariette patent Belgian
percussion pepperbox by Albert Francotte of Liège, 7¹/₂in., turn
off rifled twist barrels 3in., ring trigger with unusual sliding
safety catch locking trigger.
(Wallis & Wallis)   £320

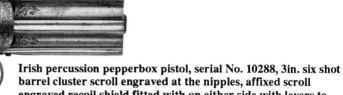

Irish percussion pepperbox pistol, serial No. 10288, 3in. six shot barrel cluster scroll engraved at the nipples, affixed scroll engraved recoil shield fitted with on either side with levers to release the barrel cluster.
(Butterfield & Butterfield)   £2,391

English percussion pepperbox pistol, having 2⁵⁄₈in. fluted barrels in six shot configuration, scroll engraved frame, trigger guard, bar hammer, grip strap and buttcap, walnut grips.
(Butterfield & Butterfield)   £699

Sharps & Hankins four barrel pepperbox pistol, serial No. 11561, .32 calibre rimfire, no sideplate or extractor, wood grips.
(Butterfield & Butterfield)   £313

English percussion pepperbox pistol, having 3in. large calibre barrels in four shot cluster, floral engraved frame, trigger guard and bar hammer, the frame marked *Samuel Nock/London* on the right side.
(Butterfield & Butterfield)   £367

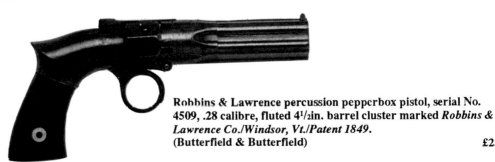

Robbins & Lawrence percussion pepperbox pistol, serial No. 4509, .28 calibre, fluted 4¹⁄₂in. barrel cluster marked *Robbins & Lawrence Co./Windsor, Vt./Patent 1849.*
(Butterfield & Butterfield)   £258

REVOLVERS

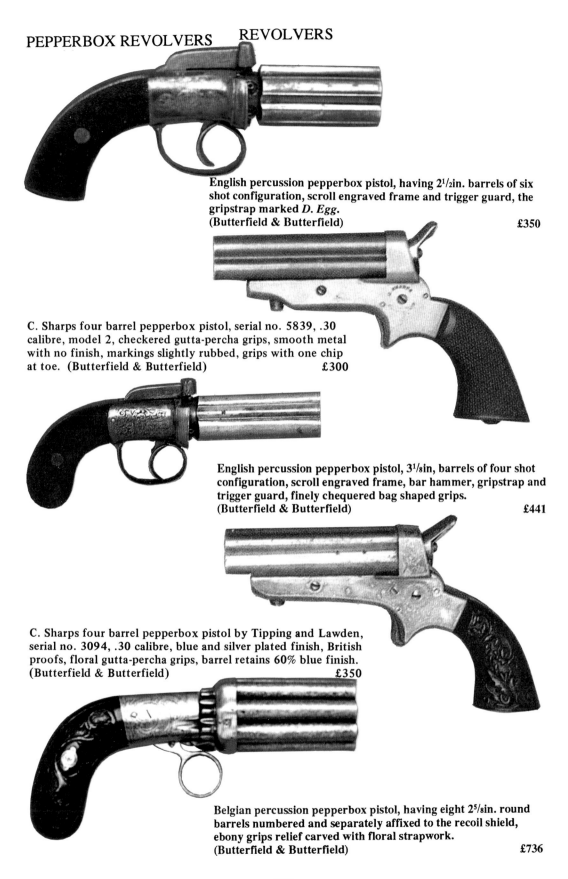

English percussion pepperbox pistol, having 2¹/₂in. barrels of six shot configuration, scroll engraved frame and trigger guard, the gripstrap marked *D. Egg*.
(Butterfield & Butterfield)   £350

C. Sharps four barrel pepperbox pistol, serial no. 5839, .30 calibre, model 2, checkered gutta-percha grips, smooth metal with no finish, markings slightly rubbed, grips with one chip at toe. (Butterfield & Butterfield)   £300

English percussion pepperbox pistol, 3¹/₈in, barrels of four shot configuration, scroll engraved frame, bar hammer, gripstrap and trigger guard, finely chequered bag shaped grips.
(Butterfield & Butterfield)   £441

C. Sharps four barrel pepperbox pistol by Tipping and Lawden, serial no. 3094, .30 calibre, blue and silver plated finish, British proofs, floral gutta-percha grips, barrel retains 60% blue finish.
(Butterfield & Butterfield)   £350

Belgian percussion pepperbox pistol, having eight 2⁵/₈in. round barrels numbered and separately affixed to the recoil shield, ebony grips relief carved with floral strapwork.
(Butterfield & Butterfield)   £736

PEPPERBOX REVOLVERS

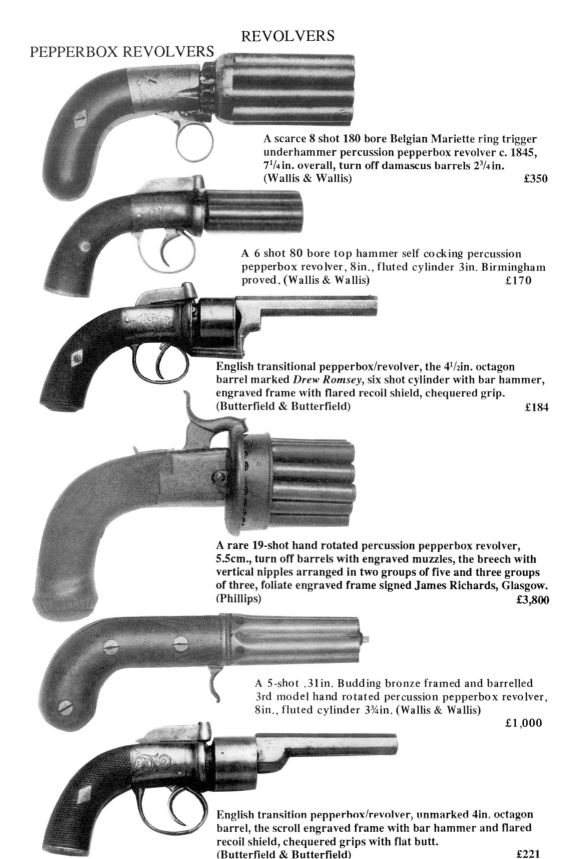

A scarce 8 shot 180 bore Belgian Mariette ring trigger underhammer percussion pepperbox revolver c. 1845, 7¼in. overall, turn off damascus barrels 2¾in. (Wallis & Wallis) £350

A 6 shot 80 bore top hammer self cocking percussion pepperbox revolver, 8in., fluted cylinder 3in. Birmingham proved. (Wallis & Wallis) £170

English transitional pepperbox/revolver, the 4½in. octagon barrel marked *Drew Romsey*, six shot cylinder with bar hammer, engraved frame with flared recoil shield, chequered grip. (Butterfield & Butterfield) £184

A rare 19-shot hand rotated percussion pepperbox revolver, 5.5cm., turn off barrels with engraved muzzles, the breech with vertical nipples arranged in two groups of five and three groups of three, foliate engraved frame signed James Richards, Glasgow. (Phillips) £3,800

A 5-shot .31in. Budding bronze framed and barrelled 3rd model hand rotated percussion pepperbox revolver, 8in., fluted cylinder 3¾in. (Wallis & Wallis) £1,000

English transition pepperbox/revolver, unmarked 4in. octagon barrel, the scroll engraved frame with bar hammer and flared recoil shield, chequered grips with flat butt. (Butterfield & Butterfield) £221

PEPPERBOX REVOLVERS

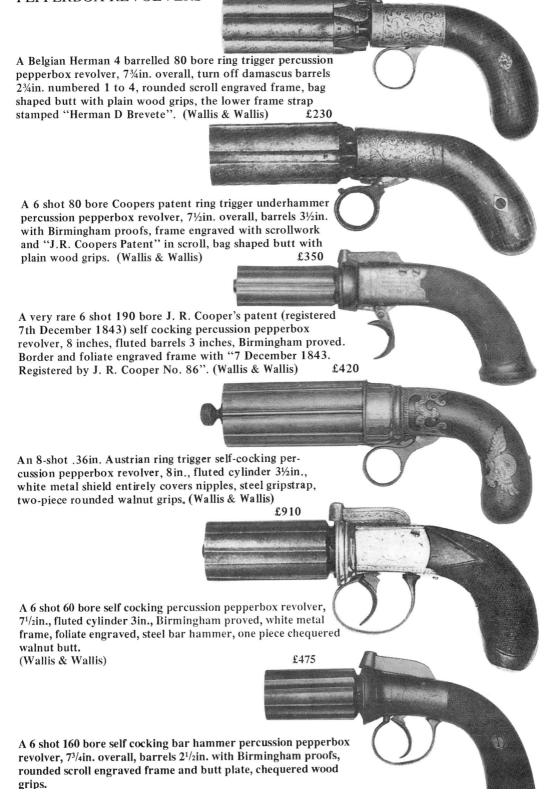

A Belgian Herman 4 barrelled 80 bore ring trigger percussion pepperbox revolver, 7¾in. overall, turn off damascus barrels 2¾in. numbered 1 to 4, rounded scroll engraved frame, bag shaped butt with plain wood grips, the lower frame strap stamped "Herman D Brevete". (Wallis & Wallis) £230

A 6 shot 80 bore Coopers patent ring trigger underhammer percussion pepperbox revolver, 7½in. overall, barrels 3½in. with Birmingham proofs, frame engraved with scrollwork and "J.R. Coopers Patent" in scroll, bag shaped butt with plain wood grips. (Wallis & Wallis) £350

A very rare 6 shot 190 bore J. R. Cooper's patent (registered 7th December 1843) self cocking percussion pepperbox revolver, 8 inches, fluted barrels 3 inches, Birmingham proved. Border and foliate engraved frame with "7 December 1843. Registered by J. R. Cooper No. 86". (Wallis & Wallis) £420

An 8-shot .36in. Austrian ring trigger self-cocking percussion pepperbox revolver, 8in., fluted cylinder 3½in., white metal shield entirely covers nipples, steel gripstrap, two-piece rounded walnut grips. (Wallis & Wallis) £910

A 6 shot 60 bore self cocking percussion pepperbox revolver, 7½in., fluted cylinder 3in., Birmingham proved, white metal frame, foliate engraved, steel bar hammer, one piece chequered walnut butt.
(Wallis & Wallis) £475

A 6 shot 160 bore self cocking bar hammer percussion pepperbox revolver, 7¾in. overall, barrels 2½in. with Birmingham proofs, rounded scroll engraved frame and butt plate, chequered wood grips.
(Wallis & Wallis) £270

CARBINES

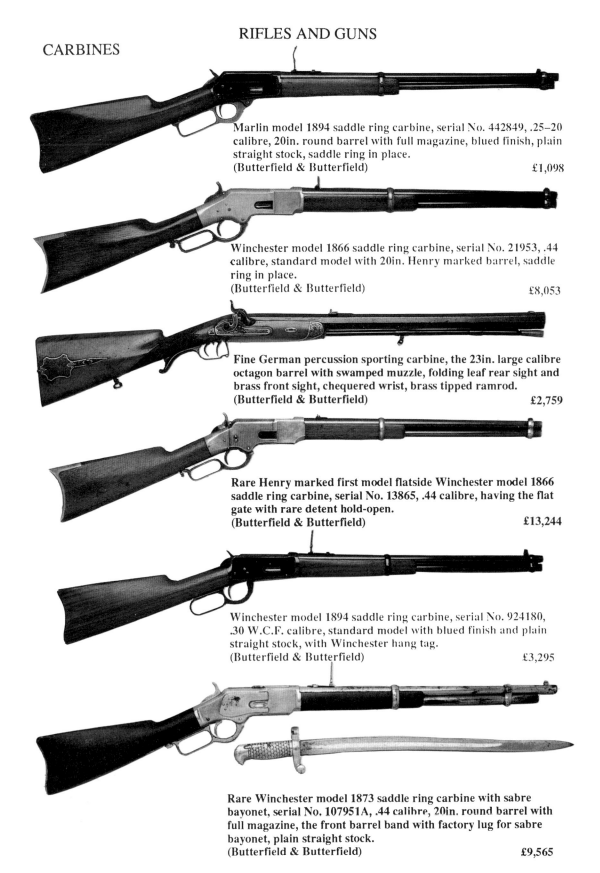

Marlin model 1894 saddle ring carbine, serial No. 442849, .25–20 calibre, 20in. round barrel with full magazine, blued finish, plain straight stock, saddle ring in place.
(Butterfield & Butterfield)   £1,098

Winchester model 1866 saddle ring carbine, serial No. 21953, .44 calibre, standard model with 20in. Henry marked barrel, saddle ring in place.
(Butterfield & Butterfield)   £8,053

Fine German percussion sporting carbine, the 23in. large calibre octagon barrel with swamped muzzle, folding leaf rear sight and brass front sight, chequered wrist, brass tipped ramrod.
(Butterfield & Butterfield)   £2,759

Rare Henry marked first model flatside Winchester model 1866 saddle ring carbine, serial No. 13865, .44 calibre, having the flat gate with rare detent hold-open.
(Butterfield & Butterfield)   £13,244

Winchester model 1894 saddle ring carbine, serial No. 924180, .30 W.C.F. calibre, standard model with blued finish and plain straight stock, with Winchester hang tag.
(Butterfield & Butterfield)   £3,295

Rare Winchester model 1873 saddle ring carbine with sabre bayonet, serial No. 107951A, .44 calibre, 20in. round barrel with full magazine, the front barrel band with factory lug for sabre bayonet, plain straight stock.
(Butterfield & Butterfield)   £9,565

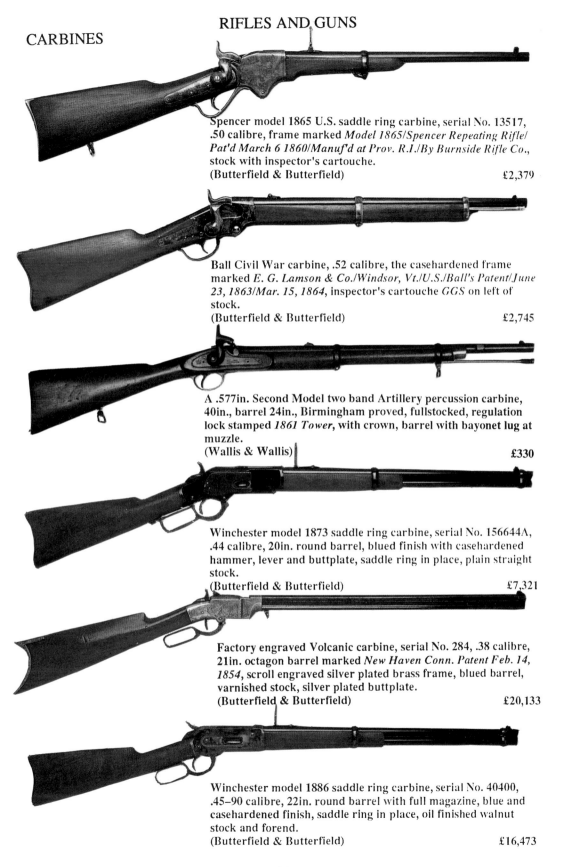

RIFLES AND GUNS

Spencer model 1865 U.S. saddle ring carbine, serial No. 13517,
.50 calibre, frame marked *Model 1865/Spencer Repeating Rifle/
Pat'd March 6 1860/Manuf'd at Prov. R.I./By Burnside Rifle Co.*,
stock with inspector's cartouche.
(Butterfield & Butterfield)   £2,379

Ball Civil War carbine, .52 calibre, the casehardened frame
marked *E. G. Lamson & Co./Windsor, Vt./U.S./Ball's Patent/June
23, 1863/Mar. 15, 1864*, inspector's cartouche *GGS* on left of
stock.
(Butterfield & Butterfield)   £2,745

A .577in. Second Model two band Artillery percussion carbine,
40in., barrel 24in., Birmingham proved, fullstocked, regulation
lock stamped *1861 Tower*, with crown, barrel with bayonet lug at
muzzle.
(Wallis & Wallis)   £330

Winchester model 1873 saddle ring carbine, serial No. 156644A,
.44 calibre, 20in. round barrel, blued finish with casehardened
hammer, lever and buttplate, saddle ring in place, plain straight
stock.
(Butterfield & Butterfield)   £7,321

Factory engraved Volcanic carbine, serial No. 284, .38 calibre,
21in. octagon barrel marked *New Haven Conn. Patent Feb. 14,
1854*, scroll engraved silver plated brass frame, blued barrel,
varnished stock, silver plated buttplate.
(Butterfield & Butterfield)   £20,133

Winchester model 1886 saddle ring carbine, serial No. 40400,
.45–90 calibre, 22in. round barrel with full magazine, blue and
casehardened finish, saddle ring in place, oil finished walnut
stock and forend.
(Butterfield & Butterfield)   £16,473

CARBINES

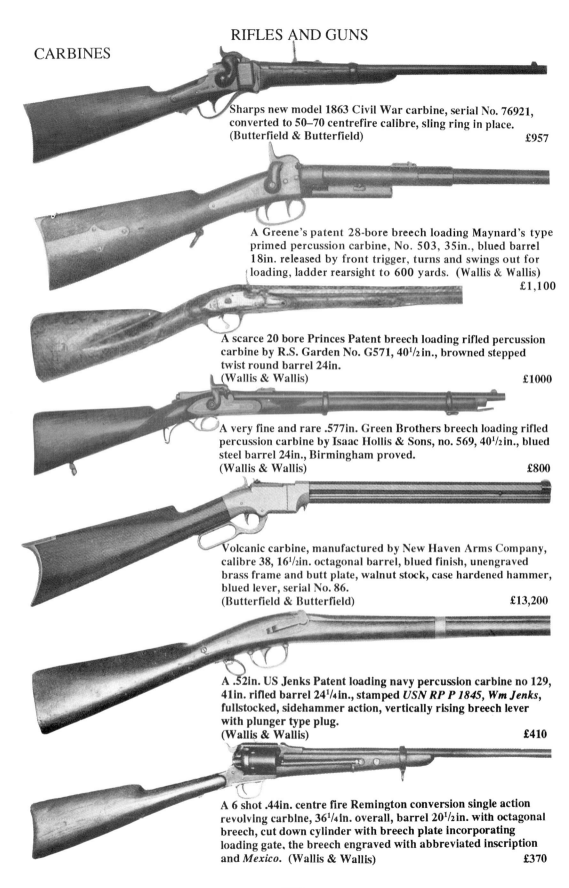

Sharps new model 1863 Civil War carbine, serial No. 76921, converted to 50–70 centrefire calibre, sling ring in place. (Butterfield & Butterfield) £957

A Greene's patent 28-bore breech loading Maynard's type primed percussion carbine, No. 503, 35in., blued barrel 18in. released by front trigger, turns and swings out for loading, ladder rearsight to 600 yards. (Wallis & Wallis) £1,100

A scarce 20 bore Princes Patent breech loading rifled percussion carbine by R.S. Garden No. G571, 40$\frac{1}{2}$in., browned stepped twist round barrel 24in. (Wallis & Wallis) £1000

A very fine and rare .577in. Green Brothers breech loading rifled percussion carbine by Isaac Hollis & Sons, no. 569, 40$\frac{1}{2}$in., blued steel barrel 24in., Birmingham proved. (Wallis & Wallis) £800

Volcanic carbine, manufactured by New Haven Arms Company, calibre 38, 16$\frac{1}{2}$in. octagonal barrel, blued finish, unengraved brass frame and butt plate, walnut stock, case hardened hammer, blued lever, serial No. 86. (Butterfield & Butterfield) £13,200

A .52in. US Jenks Patent loading navy percussion carbine no 129, 41in. rifled barrel 24$\frac{1}{4}$in., stamped *USN RP P 1845, Wm Jenks*, fullstocked, sidehammer action, vertically rising breech lever with plunger type plug. (Wallis & Wallis) £410

A 6 shot .44in. centre fire Remington conversion single action revolving carbine, 36$\frac{1}{4}$in. overall, barrel 20$\frac{1}{2}$in. with octagonal breech, cut down cylinder with breech plate incorporating loading gate, the breech engraved with abbreviated inscription and *Mexico*. (Wallis & Wallis) £370

CARBINES

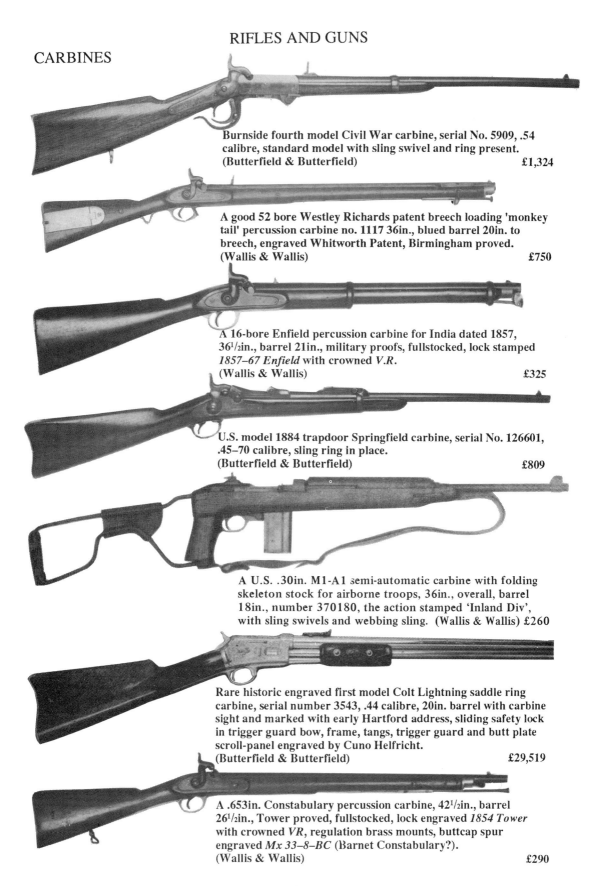

Burnside fourth model Civil War carbine, serial No. 5909, .54 calibre, standard model with sling swivel and ring present. (Butterfield & Butterfield) £1,324

A good 52 bore Westley Richards patent breech loading 'monkey tail' percussion carbine no. 1117 36in., blued barrel 20in. to breech, engraved Whitworth Patent, Birmingham proved. (Wallis & Wallis) £750

A 16-bore Enfield percussion carbine for India dated 1857, 36^1/$_2$in., barrel 21in., military proofs, fullstocked, lock stamped *1857–67 Enfield* with crowned *V.R.* (Wallis & Wallis) £325

U.S. model 1884 trapdoor Springfield carbine, serial No. 126601, .45–70 calibre, sling ring in place. (Butterfield & Butterfield) £809

A U.S. .30in. M1-A1 semi-automatic carbine with folding skeleton stock for airborne troops, 36in., overall, barrel 18in., number 370180, the action stamped 'Inland Div', with sling swivels and webbing sling. (Wallis & Wallis) £260

Rare historic engraved first model Colt Lightning saddle ring carbine, serial number 3543, .44 calibre, 20in. barrel with carbine sight and marked with early Hartford address, sliding safety lock in trigger guard bow, frame, tangs, trigger guard and butt plate scroll-panel engraved by Cuno Helfricht. (Butterfield & Butterfield) £29,519

A .653in. Constabulary percussion carbine, 42^1/$_2$in., barrel 26^1/$_2$in., Tower proved, fullstocked, lock engraved *1854 Tower* with crowned *VR*, regulation brass mounts, buttcap spur engraved *Mx 33–8–BC* (Barnet Constabulary?). (Wallis & Wallis) £290

CARBINES

Rare Remington-Hepburn saddle ring carbine, serial No. 95, .45–70 calibre, 27in. round barrel with adjustable rear sight and secured by a single barrel band, the casehardened frame with bar and saddle ring on left side, plain pistol grip stock.
(Butterfield & Butterfield)   £3,478

Gwyn & Campbell Civil War carbine, serial No. 4351, .52 calibre, type II, 20in. round barrel with octagonal breech, marked *Union Rifle* at forward end of frame.
(Butterfield & Butterfield)   £2,013

Wm. Palmer bolt action Civil War carbine, .50 calibre, 20in. round barrel marked at breech *Wm. Palmer/Patent/Dec 22, 1863*, lockplate marked *U.S./E.G. Lamson & Co./Windsor, Vt.* and at rear dated *1865*.
(Butterfield & Butterfield)   £2,013

Colt model 1855 sidehammer revolving carbine, serial No. 11816, .56 calibre, 21in. round barrel with octagonal breech fitted with double folding leaf sight, breech and fluted cylinder with British proofs.
(Butterfield & Butterfield)   £5,518

Colt model 1839 'Albert Foster' Paterson revolving percussion carbine, serial No. 414, .525 calibre, 24½in. round barrel with bevelled breech, fitted with plain in-the-white cylinder.
(Butterfield & Butterfield)   £6,622

Jenks Mule Ear navy carbine with Maynard tape primer, .54 calibre, 24½in. round barrel marked at breech *W. Jenks/U.S.N/ R.P./P./1847/Cast Steel*, the lockplate marked *Remington's/ Herkimer/N.Y.*, brass fittings.
(Butterfield & Butterfield)   £4,759

Maynard second model Civil War carbine, serial No. 24116, .50 calibre, tang stamped *1865*.
(Butterfield & Butterfield)   £882

CARBINES

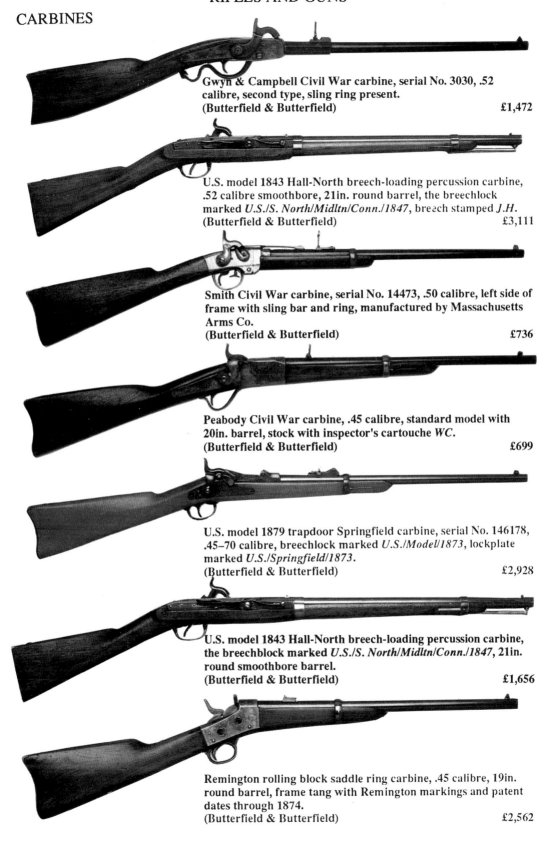

Gwyn & Campbell Civil War carbine, serial No. 3030, .52 calibre, second type, sling ring present.
(Butterfield & Butterfield) £1,472

U.S. model 1843 Hall-North breech-loading percussion carbine, .52 calibre smoothbore, 21in. round barrel, the breechlock marked *U.S./S. North/Midltn/Conn./1847*, breech stamped *J.H.*
(Butterfield & Butterfield) £3,111

Smith Civil War carbine, serial No. 14473, .50 calibre, left side of frame with sling bar and ring, manufactured by Massachusetts Arms Co.
(Butterfield & Butterfield) £736

Peabody Civil War carbine, .45 calibre, standard model with 20in. barrel, stock with inspector's cartouche *WC*.
(Butterfield & Butterfield) £699

U.S. model 1879 trapdoor Springfield carbine, serial No. 146178, .45–70 calibre, breechlock marked *U.S./Model/1873*, lockplate marked *U.S./Springfield/1873*.
(Butterfield & Butterfield) £2,928

U.S. model 1843 Hall-North breech-loading percussion carbine, the breechblock marked *U.S./S. North/Midltn/Conn./1847*, 21in. round smoothbore barrel.
(Butterfield & Butterfield) £1,656

Remington rolling block saddle ring carbine, .45 calibre, 19in. round barrel, frame tang with Remington markings and patent dates through 1874.
(Butterfield & Butterfield) £2,562

HAMMER SHOTGUNS

American Arms Co. double barrel hammer shotgun, serial No. 176, 12 gauge, 27¹/₂in. Damascus barrels, scroll engraved frame, trigger guard and hammers, chequered forend and pistol grip stock.
(Butterfield & Butterfield) **£589**

English double barrel hammer shotgun, serial No. 3835, .410 gauge, 28in. Damascus barrels with matte rib marked *Henry W. Egg No. 1 Picadilly London*, chequered forend and pistol grip stock.
(Butterfield & Butterfield) **£662**

Belgian double barrel percussion shotgun, 12 gauge, the 30in. Damascus barrels with central rib inlaid in gold with an arrow at the front sight and at the breech with gold lines and scrolling florals framing the inscription *Superior Laminated Steel*.
(Butterfield & Butterfield) **£552**

Gold inlaid Remington Exhibition rolling block shotgun, serial No. 1, 16 gauge, 30in. round barrel gold inlaid *E. Remington & Sons Ilion New York, U.S.A.* on the flat sighting ramp, gold filigree at breech and muzzle.
(Butterfield & Butterfield) **£8,053**

Austrian double barrel pinfire shotgun, the 28¹/₂in. Damascus barrels with rib inlaid in gold *Joh. Springer in Wien*, gold lines and florals at breech, chequered straight stock.
(Butterfield & Butterfield) **£368**

Rare gold inlaid Exhibition Sharps model 1853 sporting shotgun, serial No. 18220., 28in. round barrel with brown finish and gold inlay at the breech with scrolling florals framing the Sharps name and address.
(Butterfield & Butterfield) **£16,473**

Colt model 1878 double barrel shotgun, serial No. 18253, 12 gauge, 30in. barrels, standard model with non-engraved frame and plain straight stock.
(Butterfield & Butterfield) **£350**

German double barrel percussion shotgun, the 32¹/₂in. Damascus barrels inlaid with gold lines at breech and *P. Ebert & Sohne In Suhl* in gold on barrel rib, the half stock with finely carved wolf's head forend inlaid with ivory and ebony eyes.
(Butterfield & Butterfield) **£957**

HAMMERLESS SHOTGUNS

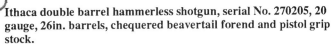

Ithaca double barrel hammerless shotgun, serial No. 270205, 20 gauge, 26in. barrels, chequered beavertail forend and pistol grip stock.
(Butterfield & Butterfield)   £221

Lefever Arms Co. double barrel hammerless shotgun, serial No. 57677, 12 gauge, 30in. Damascus barrels with matte rib, chequered forend and pistol grip stock.
(Butterfield & Butterfield)   £203

Parker VH grade double barrel hammerless shotgun, serial No. 154398, 16 gauge, 26in. barrels marked *Vulcan Steel*, chequered forend and pistol grip stock.
(Butterfield & Butterfield)   £441

Parker D grade double barrel shotgun, serial No. 77172, 16 gauge, 30in. Damascus barrels with ivory front sight, scroll engraved frame with hunting dog and game scenes, chequered forend and pistol grip stock.
(Butterfield & Butterfield)   £276

Winchester model 1887 lever action shotgun, serial No. 31187, 10 gauge, 32in. round barrel, blue and casehardened finish, varnish walnut stock.
(Butterfield & Butterfield)   £3,111

English double barrel hammerless shotgun, 12 gauge, 30in. Damascus barrels, unmarked floral engraved frame, breeches and trigger guard, chequered forend and straight stock.
(Butterfield & Butterfield)   £239

Gold inlaid and engraved Colt model 1883 hammerless shotgun, serial No. 7654, 12 gauge, 30in. and extra 28in. barrels marked *Colts Pt F A Mfg Co Hartford, Ct. U.S.A.* and gold banded at the breech and the breech fences, gold inlaid trigger guard marked *H.S. Kearny*.
(Butterfield & Butterfield)   £12,446

L. C. Smith field grade double barrel hammerless shotgun, serial No. 110929, 12 gauge, 30in. barrels with matte rib and ivory front sight, chequered forend and pistol grip stock.
(Butterfield & Butterfield)   £368

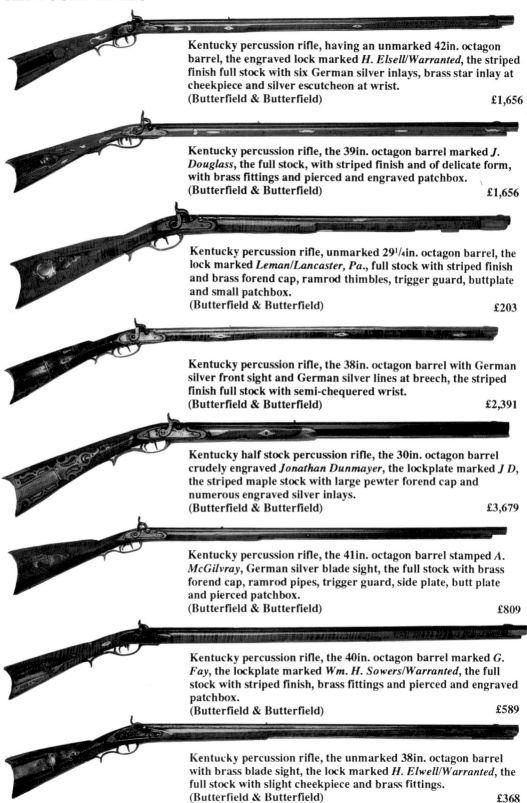

Kentucky percussion rifle, having an unmarked 42in. octagon barrel, the engraved lock marked *H. Elsell/Warranted*, the striped finish full stock with six German silver inlays, brass star inlay at cheekpiece and silver escutcheon at wrist.
(Butterfield & Butterfield)
£1,656

Kentucky percussion rifle, the 39in. octagon barrel marked *J. Douglass*, the full stock, with striped finish and of delicate form, with brass fittings and pierced and engraved patchbox.
(Butterfield & Butterfield)
£1,656

Kentucky percussion rifle, unmarked 29¼in. octagon barrel, the lock marked *Leman/Lancaster, Pa.*, full stock with striped finish and brass forend cap, ramrod thimbles, trigger guard, buttplate and small patchbox.
(Butterfield & Butterfield)
£203

Kentucky percussion rifle, the 38in. octagon barrel with German silver front sight and German silver lines at breech, the striped finish full stock with semi-chequered wrist.
(Butterfield & Butterfield)
£2,391

Kentucky half stock percussion rifle, the 30in. octagon barrel crudely engraved *Jonathan Dunmayer*, the lockplate marked *J D*, the striped maple stock with large pewter forend cap and numerous engraved silver inlays.
(Butterfield & Butterfield)
£3,679

Kentucky percussion rifle, the 41in. octagon barrel stamped *A. McGilvray*, German silver blade sight, the full stock with brass forend cap, ramrod pipes, trigger guard, side plate, butt plate and pierced patchbox.
(Butterfield & Butterfield)
£809

Kentucky percussion rifle, the 40in. octagon barrel marked *G. Fay*, the lockplate marked *Wm. H. Sowers/Warranted*, the full stock with striped finish, brass fittings and pierced and engraved patchbox.
(Butterfield & Butterfield)
£589

Kentucky percussion rifle, the unmarked 38in. octagon barrel with brass blade sight, the lock marked *H. Elwell/Warranted*, the full stock with slight cheekpiece and brass fittings.
(Butterfield & Butterfield)
£368

416

MARLIN RIFLES

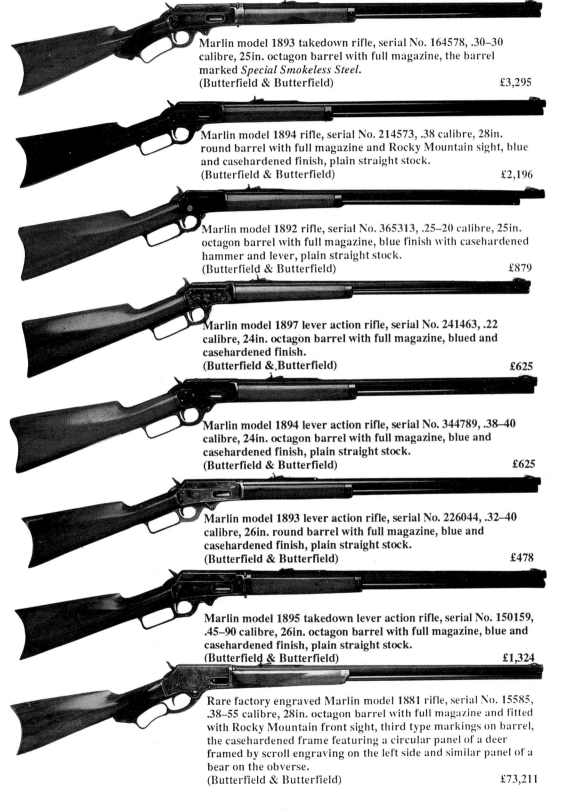

Marlin model 1893 takedown rifle, serial No. 164578, .30–30 calibre, 25in. octagon barrel with full magazine, the barrel marked *Special Smokeless Steel*.
(Butterfield & Butterfield)   £3,295

Marlin model 1894 rifle, serial No. 214573, .38 calibre, 28in. round barrel with full magazine and Rocky Mountain sight, blue and casehardened finish, plain straight stock.
(Butterfield & Butterfield)   £2,196

Marlin model 1892 rifle, serial No. 365313, .25–20 calibre, 25in. octagon barrel with full magazine, blue finish with casehardened hammer and lever, plain straight stock.
(Butterfield & Butterfield)   £879

Marlin model 1897 lever action rifle, serial No. 241463, .22 calibre, 24in. octagon barrel with full magazine, blued and casehardened finish.
(Butterfield & Butterfield)   £625

Marlin model 1894 lever action rifle, serial No. 344789, .38–40 calibre, 24in. octagon barrel with full magazine, blue and casehardened finish, plain straight stock.
(Butterfield & Butterfield)   £625

Marlin model 1893 lever action rifle, serial No. 226044, .32–40 calibre, 26in. round barrel with full magazine, blue and casehardened finish, plain straight stock.
(Butterfield & Butterfield)   £478

Marlin model 1895 takedown lever action rifle, serial No. 150159, .45–90 calibre, 26in. octagon barrel with full magazine, blue and casehardened finish, plain straight stock.
(Butterfield & Butterfield)   £1,324

Rare factory engraved Marlin model 1881 rifle, serial No. 15585, .38–55 calibre, 28in. octagon barrel with full magazine and fitted with Rocky Mountain front sight, third type markings on barrel, the casehardened frame featuring a circular panel of a deer framed by scroll engraving on the left side and similar panel of a bear on the obverse.
(Butterfield & Butterfield)   £73,211

MARLIN RIFLES

Marlin model 1897 rifle, serial no. 203392, .22 calibre, 24in. round barrel with full magazine, plain stock with shotgun buttplate. (Butterfield & Butterfield) **£300**

Marlin model 1893 rifle, serial no. 239387, .32-40 calibre 26in. octagon barrel, standard model. (Butterfield & Butterfield) **£200**

Marlin-Ballard Schuetzen rifle, serial no. 31412, .38-55 calibre, 32in. part round/part octagon barrel, checkered forend, checkered pistol grip stock. (Butterfield & Butterfield) **£1,000**

Marlin model 1894 Takedown rifle, serial no. 173539, 32-20 calibre, 24in. octagonal barrel, plain stock with crescent buttplate and sling swivel. (Butterfield & Butterfield) **£400**

Marlin model 1895 rifle, serial no. 313792, .38-56 calibre, 26in. octagon barrel with full magazine, blue and case hardened finish, plain stock with carbine buttplate. (Butterfield & Butterfield) **£1,100**

Marlin model 1895 carbine, serial no. 167166, .45-70 calibre, 22in. round barrel, saddle ring in place. (Butterfield & Butterfield) **£550**

Factory engraved Marlin model 1894 Takedown rifle, serial no. 191139, .32-20 calibre, 26in. part round/ part octagon barrel drilled for telescopic sight, globe front sight, Marbles rear sight, tang mounted disc peep sight, frame engraved with scroll designs and panels of deer. (Butterfield & Butterfield) **£1,700**

MARLIN RIFLES

Marlin 410 lever action shotgun, serial no. 6412, blue finish, standard model. (Butterfield & Butterfield) £925

Rare Marlin model 1894 musket, serial no. 125487, .38 calibre, 30in. round barrel, no Bureau County markings. (Butterfield & Butterfield) £500

Marlin-Ballard no.9 Union Hill rifle, serial no. 24639, .32-40 calibre, 30in. part round/part octagon barrel, tang peep sight and globe front sight, short pronged offhand buttplate. (Butterfield & Butterfield) £735

Marlin model 1894 Carbine, serial no. 328928, .25-20 calibre, rare 12in. barrel, saddle ring in place. (Butterfield & Butterfield) £1,700

Marlin model 1897 rifle, serial no. 87934, .22 calibre, 24in. round barrel with full magazine, checkered forend and pistol grip stock, crescent buttplate. (Butterfield & Butterfield) £735

Rare Marlin model 1897 bicycle rifle, serial no. 278769, .22 calibre, 16in. round barrel with full magazine, tang peep sight, crescent butt, sling swivels in place. (Butterfield & Butterfield) £735

Marlin-Ballard Schuetzen rifle, serial no. 15055, .22 calibre 30¾in. heavy octagonal barrel, floral engraved frame with animal panels, checkered forend fitted with support, double set triggers, Monte Carlo stock with Schuetzen buttplate. (Butterfield & Butterfield) £1,680

Factory engraved Marlin model 1897 lever action rifle, serial No. 288855, .22 calibre, 26in. octagon barrel with full magazine, chequered forend and pistol grip stock fitted with medium range tang sight.
(Butterfield & Butterfield) £1,656

Marlin model 39 lever action rifle, serial No. S6616, .22 calibre, 24in. octagon barrel with full magazine and Beach combination sight, plain pistol grip stock.
(Butterfield & Butterfield) £294

Marlin model 39A lever action rifle, serial No. 15488, .22 calibre, standard model.
(Butterfield & Butterfield) £184

Marlin model 1892 lever action rifle, serial No. 202198, .22 calibre, 24in. octagon barrel with full magazine, blue finish, plain straight stock.
(Butterfield & Butterfield) £258

Factory engraved Marlin model 1889 lever action rifle, serial No. 58429, .44–40 calibre, 24in. round barrel with full magazine, chequered forend and pistol grip stock.
(Butterfield & Butterfield) £2,391

Factory engraved Marlin model 1893 takedown lever action rifle, serial No. 185043, .30–30 calibre, 26in. octagon barrel with full magazine and fitted with Marble rear sight, chequered forend and pistol grip stock.
(Butterfield & Butterfield) £2,023

Marlin model 1895 rifle, serial No. 141052, .40–65, 28in. octagon barrel with full magazine and Rocky Mountain front sight, blue and casehardened finish, chequered forend and pistol grip stock.
(Butterfield & Butterfield) £2,379

Marlin model 1894 rifle, serial No. 433608, .25–20 calibre, 24in. round barrel with full magazine, plain straight stock, blue and casehardened finish.
(Butterfield & Butterfield) £1,830

MUSKETS

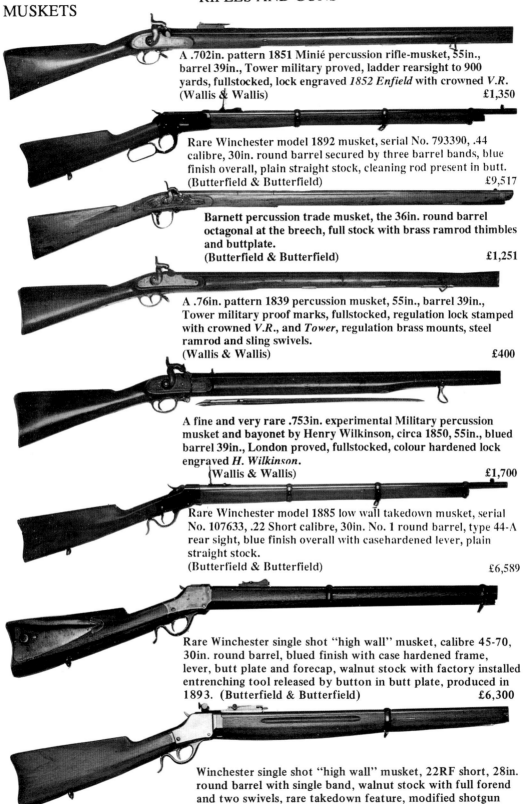

A .702in. pattern 1851 Minié percussion rifle-musket, 55in., barrel 39in., Tower military proved, ladder rearsight to 900 yards, fullstocked, lock engraved *1852 Enfield* with crowned *V.R.* (Wallis & Wallis) £1,350

Rare Winchester model 1892 musket, serial No. 793390, .44 calibre, 30in. round barrel secured by three barrel bands, blue finish overall, plain straight stock, cleaning rod present in butt. (Butterfield & Butterfield) £9,517

Barnett percussion trade musket, the 36in. round barrel octagonal at the breech, full stock with brass ramrod thimbles and buttplate. (Butterfield & Butterfield) £1,251

A .76in. pattern 1839 percussion musket, 55in., barrel 39in., Tower military proof marks, fullstocked, regulation lock stamped with crowned *V.R.*, and *Tower*, regulation brass mounts, steel ramrod and sling swivels. (Wallis & Wallis) £400

A fine and very rare .753in. experimental Military percussion musket and bayonet by Henry Wilkinson, circa 1850, 55in., blued barrel 39in., London proved, fullstocked, colour hardened lock engraved *H. Wilkinson*. (Wallis & Wallis) £1,700

Rare Winchester model 1885 low wall takedown musket, serial No. 107633, .22 Short calibre, 30in. No. 1 round barrel, type 44-A rear sight, blue finish overall with casehardened lever, plain straight stock. (Butterfield & Butterfield) £6,589

Rare Winchester single shot "high wall" musket, calibre 45-70, 30in. round barrel, blued finish with case hardened frame, lever, butt plate and forecap, walnut stock with factory installed entrenching tool released by button in butt plate, produced in 1893. (Butterfield & Butterfield) £6,300

Winchester single shot "high wall" musket, 22RF short, 28in. round barrel with single band, walnut stock with full forend and two swivels, rare takedown feature, modified shotgun style butt plate. (Butterfield & Butterfield) £1,450

A good quality double-barrelled 12 bore pinfire underlever back action sporting gun by H. Tatham, London, circa 1865, 41$^{1}/_{2}$in., browned stub twist barrels 25$^{1}/_{4}$in., London proved, wedge fastened fore-end, horn tip.
(Wallis & Wallis) £300

A double-barrelled 12 bore pinfire underlever sporting gun by Williamson of Bridgnorth, 46$^{1}/_{2}$in., curly twist barrel 30in., engraved *Williamson & Sons Bridgnorth & Ludlow* on top rib, chequered small and wedge fastened fore, finely figured walnut stock.
(Wallis & Wallis) £320

A double-barrelled 12 bore pinfire underlever back action sporting gun by Hook of Tenterden, 46$^{1}/_{2}$in., curly twist barrels 29$^{3}/_{4}$in., foliate engraved action and locks with *H Hook*, chequered small and wedge fastened fore.
(Wallis & Wallis) £300

A good 12 bore double-barrelled underlever pinfire sporting gun by John Lucas, 46in., twist barrels 30in., rotary underlever, rabbit ear hammers, chequered small and fore.
(Wallis & Wallis) £310

A Ghaye patent 15-bore double-barrelled pin-fire sporting gun with browned twist sighted barrels signed in gold on the rib, gold lines and a panel of gold strapwork at the breech, case-hardened long breech tang engraved with scrolling foliage and incorporating an oval gold-encrusted escutcheon with the full arms of Salm within mantling under a crown, signed *Jacob Pilartz in Neuss*, circa 1857–60, 31in. barrels.
(Christie's) £1,540

A 16-bore double-barrelled pin-fire sporting gun with etched twist sighted barrels signed in full in gold and silver on the rib, hinged iron fore-end, pivoting trigger-guard, long tang, signed back-action locks, highly figured walnut butt, by A Rosen Arquebusier de s.a. le Prince de Salm Dyck à Dyck, Liège proof mark, circa 1855, 30in. barrels.
(Christie's) £1,430

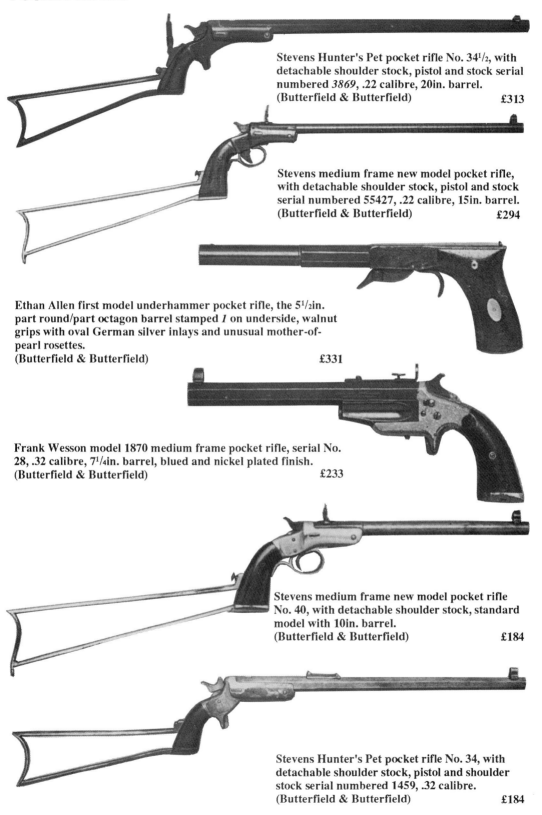

Stevens Hunter's Pet pocket rifle No. 34^1/$_2$, with
detachable shoulder stock, pistol and stock serial
numbered *3869*, .22 calibre, 20in. barrel.
(Butterfield & Butterfield)   £313

Stevens medium frame new model pocket rifle,
with detachable shoulder stock, pistol and stock
serial numbered 55427, .22 calibre, 15in. barrel.
(Butterfield & Butterfield)   £294

Ethan Allen first model underhammer pocket rifle, the 5^1/$_2$in.
part round/part octagon barrel stamped *1* on underside, walnut
grips with oval German silver inlays and unusual mother-of-
pearl rosettes.
(Butterfield & Butterfield)   £331

Frank Wesson model 1870 medium frame pocket rifle, serial No.
28, .32 calibre, 7^1/$_4$in. barrel, blued and nickel plated finish.
(Butterfield & Butterfield)   £233

Stevens medium frame new model pocket rifle
No. 40, with detachable shoulder stock, standard
model with 10in. barrel.
(Butterfield & Butterfield)   £184

Stevens Hunter's Pet pocket rifle No. 34, with
detachable shoulder stock, pistol and shoulder
stock serial numbered 1459, .32 calibre.
(Butterfield & Butterfield)   £184

Rare engraved prototype North and Savage revolving percussion rifle, having a 23^1/$_2$in. part round/part octagon barrel, plain straight stock with engraved brass patchbox.
(Butterfield & Butterfield) £4,415

French pinfire double rifle, the 26in. large calibre Damascus barrels with triple folding leaf rear sight and marked *Leopold Bernard a Paris/G. B. Beecher*, chequered forend and straight stock.
(Butterfield & Butterfield) £478

A .577in. second model 3 band percussion rifle of the Durham University Volunteers, 54in., barrel 39in. Tower proved, ladder rearsight to 900 yards, fullstocked.
(Wallis & Wallis) £475

Unique factory engraved and gold inlaid presentation Marlin model 1881 rifle, serial No. 15731, .45 Government calibre, the 22in. extra heavy octagon barrel with half magazine and fitted with King front sight and buckhorn rear sight, third type barrel markings.
(Butterfield & Butterfield) £29,285

A .577in. pattern 1858 percussion short rifle 'Bar-on-Band' of the Berkshire Volunteers, 49in, barrel 33in., Tower proved with government sale mark, ladder rearsight to 1000 yards, fullstocked, regulation lock stamped *1861 Tower* with crowned *V.R.*
(Wallis & Wallis) £380

Colt model 1855 sidehammer full stock sporting rifle, British proofed, serial No. 384, .50 calibre, 27in. round barrel, the octagonal breech with open rear sight fitted with two folding leaves calibrated to 300 and 600 yards.
(Butterfield & Butterfield) £4,415

A .577in. Snider's patent 3 band Enfield rifle, 55in., barrel 36^1/$_2$in. to breech, London private proofs, breech stamped *Snider's Patent*, ladder rearsight, fullstocked.
(Wallis & Wallis) £200

A scarce double-barrelled oval bore (nominal .450in.) underlever opening back action hammer rifle by Charles Lancaster No. 4584 (for 1873), 45in., damascus twist barrels 28in., chequered buttcap and trigger guard tang, chequered wedge fastened fore-end.
(Wallis & Wallis)   £600

Rare Colt gold inlaid lightning small frame slide action rifle, serial No. 84298, .22 calibre, 24in. octagon barrel with Lyman Hunting front sight, blued finish, chequered forearm, chequered pistol grip stock.
(Butterfield & Butterfield)   £3,295

English breech-loading double rifle, serial No. 19167, .500 Nitro Express calibre, the 28in. barrels with broad matte rib marked *E.M. Reilly & Co. New Oxford St. London. & Rue Scribe Paris* and mounted with floral engraved triple leaf rear sight.
(Butterfield & Butterfield)   £2,207

American half stock percussion rifle, the 29in. octagon barrel marked *D. T. Seeley/Dunkirk/N.Y.*, German silver front sight, the engraved lock marked *Geoe Goulcher*, the half stock with pewter forend cap and German silver wedge plates.
(Butterfield & Butterfield)   £883

Remington-Hepburn no. 3 match rifle, serial No. 8741, .38–55 calibre, 28in. part-round/part-octagon barrel with Globe front sight, finely chequered forend and pistol grip stock with cheekpiece and Schuetzen buttplate, tang mounted flexible peep sight.
(Butterfield & Butterfield)   £1,830

Rare Conrad Ulrich engraved and gold inlaid Marlin model 1893 takedown rifle, serial No. 133416, .38–55 calibre, the 26in. octagon barrel with full magazine and fitted with Lyman front sight and buckhorn rear sight, scroll engraved and inlaid with platinum lines and gold dots at the breech.
(Butterfield & Butterfield)   £43,927

U.S. model 1819 Hall hook lever percussion rifle, converted from flintlock, the lockplate marked *J.H. Hall/H. Ferry – U.S. – 1832*, with associated socket bayonet.
(Butterfield & Butterfield)   £1,251

Stevens Favourite Variant model single shot rifle, serial No.
25691, .22 calibre, 22in. part round/part octagon barrel.
(Butterfield & Butterfield) £239

Rare Colt double rifle, calibre 45–70, 28in. round side by side
barrels, double trigger and double hammer, case hardened
frame, hammers and butt plate with brown damascus finish on
barrels, oil stained chequered walnut stock and forearm, blued
trigger guard, lever and rear and front sight.
(Butterfield & Butterfield) £11,950

Stevens Ideal single shot rifle, serial No. 80054, .25 calibre,
33½in. part round/part octagon barrel, straight stock with
Schuetzen butt.
(Butterfield & Butterfield) £221

A Dreyse 20-bore double-barrelled needle-fire sporting rifle with
browned sighted barrels rifled with seven grooves and signed in
silver on the rib, blued folding back-sight, case-hardened
chambers engraved with scrollwork, the barrels pivoting to the
right for loading, and much original finish, by F. v. Dreyse,
Sömmerda, circa 1870–80, 26¾in. barrels.
(Christie's) £1,980

Remington model 1863 Zouave rifle, the lockplate and barrel
dated *1863*, with brass hilted sword bayonet and scabbard.
(Butterfield & Butterfield) £2,023

A .577in. Volunteer 3 band Enfield percussion rifle, 54in., barrel
39in., ladder rearsight, fullstocked, lock engraved crowned *VR*
with *L.A.Cº 1860*, regulation brass mounts.
(Wallis & Wallis) £540

Rare iron frame Henry rifle, calibre 44 RF, 24in. barrel with
fifteen shot tubular magazine, cleaning rod in butt, blued finish,
walnut stock, serial No. 192.
(Butterfield & Butterfield) £19,500

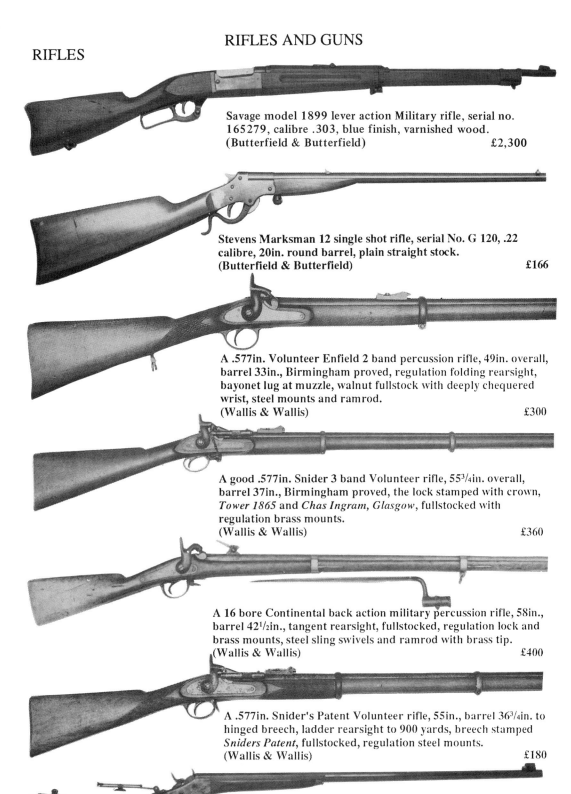

Savage model 1899 lever action Military rifle, serial no.
165279, calibre .303, blue finish, varnished wood.
(Butterfield & Butterfield) £2,300

Stevens Marksman 12 single shot rifle, serial No. G 120, .22
calibre, 20in. round barrel, plain straight stock.
(Butterfield & Butterfield) £166

A .577in. Volunteer Enfield 2 band percussion rifle, 49in. overall,
barrel 33in., Birmingham proved, regulation folding rearsight,
bayonet lug at muzzle, walnut fullstock with deeply chequered
wrist, steel mounts and ramrod.
(Wallis & Wallis) £300

A good .577in. Snider 3 band Volunteer rifle, 55³/₄in. overall,
barrel 37in., Birmingham proved, the lock stamped with crown,
Tower 1865 and *Chas Ingram, Glasgow*, fullstocked with
regulation brass mounts.
(Wallis & Wallis) £360

A 16 bore Continental back action military percussion rifle, 58in.,
barrel 42¹/₂in., tangent rearsight, fullstocked, regulation lock and
brass mounts, steel sling swivels and ramrod with brass tip.
(Wallis & Wallis) £400

A .577in. Snider's Patent Volunteer rifle, 55in., barrel 36³/₄in. to
hinged breech, ladder rearsight to 900 yards, breech stamped
Sniders Patent, fullstocked, regulation steel mounts.
(Wallis & Wallis) £180

Remington longrange Creedmore rifle, serial No. 5290, .44–90
calibre, 34in. part round/part octagon barrel with windgauge/
spirit level sight, chequered pistol grip stock with vernier base
and plate at heel.
(Butterfield & Butterfield) £2,759

RIFLES

Factory engraved Henry model 1860 rifle, serial No. 1443, .44 calibre, 24in. barrel with rear sight blank, silver plated fully scroll engraved frame, early style engraved buttplate, plain straight stock.
(Butterfield & Butterfield)   £29,285

San Francisco half stock percussion rifle, the heavy 30in. octagon barrel with covered front sight and marked *Schneider & Browning San Francisco*, the stock with nicely chequered wrist and iron forend cap.
(Butterfield & Butterfield)   £1,324

Rare factory engraved and gold inlaid Marlin model 1893 takedown rifle, serial No. 134007, .38–55 calibre, the 26in. octagon barrel with half magazine, folding two-leaf rear sight and King front sight, the breech inlaid with platinum lines, scrollwork and two gold dots and with scroll engraving extending five inches up the barrel.
(Butterfield & Butterfield)   £21,963

A German combination 16 bore and 11mm. combined double-barrelled hammer sporting gun/rifle by M. A. Saam of Frankfurt-on-Main, 43^1/4in., barrels 26^3/4in., twist shot barrel, steel rifled barrel, with silver breech lines, numbered *12322*, dated *1892*.
(Wallis & Wallis)   £450

Rare American four barrel swivel breech percussion rifle, the 25in. barrel cluster marked *J. Wurfflein Philada*, the barrels hand rotated with trigger-form locking mechanism forward of trigger guard.
(Butterfield & Butterfield)   £1,398

Henry rifle by New Haven Arms Company, late model, calibre 44 RF, fifteen shot magazine, twenty inch round barrel, walnut stock, blued barrel, brass frame and butt cap, case hardened hammer, blued lever and pointed heel butt plate.
(Butterfield & Butterfield)   £7,000

Rare U.S. Martial Henry rifle, calibre 44 RF, 24in. octagon barrel with fifteen shot tubular magazine, blued barrel, brass frame, cleaning rod in butt, brass frame model with the curved profile on the butt plate. (Butterfield & Butterfield)   £7,000

RIFLES

California half stock percussion rifle, the heavy 32in. octagon barrel with false muzzle, covered front sight, rear sight blank and marked *Kopikus/Sacramento*, the stock fitted with steel forend cap.
(Butterfield & Butterfield)   £2,023

A .700in. Brunswick First Model back action percussion rifle, 46in., twist barrel 30in., one leaf rearsight, military proofs stamped *1842 Enfield*, bayonet bar at muzzle, fullstocked.
(Wallis & Wallis)   £1,450

Remington No. 2 rolling block sporting rifle, serial No. 7690, .40 calibre, 28in. part-round/part-octagon barrel with wind gauge/spirit level front sight, mid-range Vernier tang sight, chequered forend and pistol grip stock with shotgun butt.
(Butterfield & Butterfield)   £2,196

Remington-Hepburn No. 3 sporting rifle, serial No. 10006, .38–55 calibre, the 30in. octagon barrel with Globe windgauge front sight, tang fitted with flexible peep sight, double set triggers, plain forend, chequered pistol grip stock with crescent butt.
(Butterfield & Butterfield)   £2,013

Colt Burgess lever action rifle, serial No. 2389, .44–40 calibre, 25in. barrel with full magazine, plain straight stock, browned barrel with blue frame, crescent buttplate with cleaning rod present.
(Butterfield & Butterfield)   £3,111

Rare Colt double rifle, serial No. 27, .45–70 calibre, 28in. round side by side barrels fitted with adjustable rear sight, casehardened frame and locks marked *Colt's Pt.F.A.Mfg.Co.*, chequered forend and pistol grip stock with shotgun butt.
(Butterfield & Butterfield)   £18,303

Fine Belgian percussion sporting rifle, the 33in. fluted octagonal barrel inlaid in gold at muzzle and breech with floral vines, extending at the breech to a crowned shield framed by laurel wreath, the top flat inlaid in gold *Ancion & Cie a Liege*.
(Butterfield & Butterfield)   £8,053

SPORTING GUNS

A 12 bore single barrelled percussion sporting gun by Isaac Hollis of Cheltenham, No. 5900, 42³/₄in., barrel 26¹/₄in., halfstocked, foliate engraved lock, dolphin hammer, steel furniture, pineapple finialled trigger guard.
(Wallis & Wallis)
£750

A German 11-bore double-barrelled percussion sporting gun with heavy browned twist sighted barrels, case-hardened tang engraved with rococo ornament and flowerheads, signed flat case-hardened locks, by Adam Rosen in Dyck, circa 1830–40, 34in. barrels.
(Christie's)
£1,100

English half stock percussion fowling piece, the 34³/₄in. part-round/part-octagon barrel with German silver lines inlaid at breech and marked *Warranted Twisted*, the breech stamped *London*, the lock marked *Rich & Hollis*.
(Butterfield & Butterfield)
£147

Elaborate silver mounted German or Austrian double barrel tube-lock percussion fowling gun, early 19th century, 30in. two stage 20 gauge barrels with gilt muzzles, sight rib and polygonal breech section, balance blued.
(Butterfield & Butterfield)
£9,943

A German 22-bore double-barrelled percussion sporting gun with rebrowned twist sighted barrels with gilt bands at the muzzles and breeches, case-hardened engraved tang, highly figured walnut half-stock carved at the base of the grip with a Chinese dragon's head in the round, by Adam Rosen in Dyck, circa 1830–40, 31in. barrels.
(Christie's)
£2,860

A single barrelled 12 bore percussion sporting gun by Barbar, converted from flintlock with breech drum, originally circa 1770, 49in. overall, barrel 33³/₄in. with raised teardrop panel engraved with maker's name, plain walnut stock with steel mounts.
(Wallis & Wallis)
£145

SPORTING GUNS

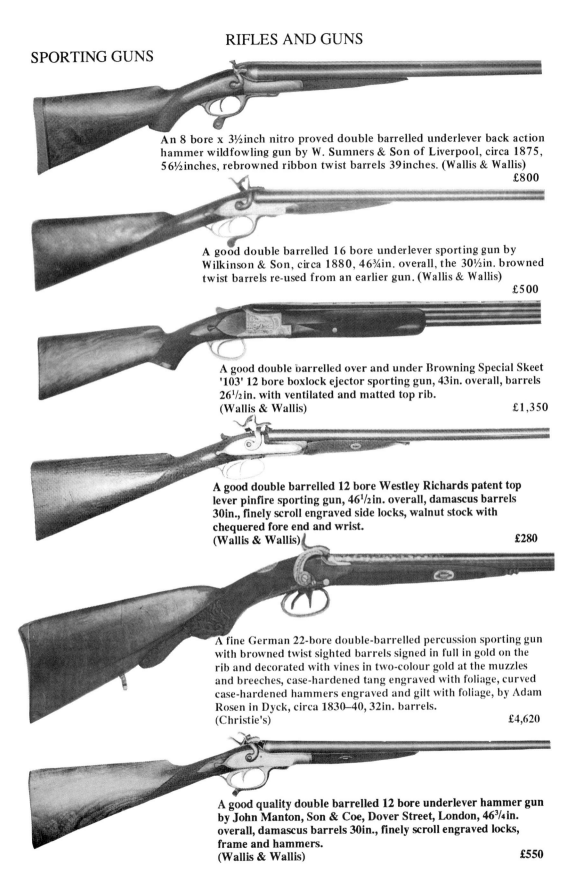

An 8 bore x 3½inch nitro proved double barrelled underlever back action hammer wildfowling gun by W. Sumners & Son of Liverpool, circa 1875, 56½inches, rebrowned ribbon twist barrels 39inches. (Wallis & Wallis)
£800

A good double barrelled 16 bore underlever sporting gun by Wilkinson & Son, circa 1880, 46¾in. overall, the 30½in. browned twist barrels re-used from an earlier gun. (Wallis & Wallis)
£500

A good double barrelled over and under Browning Special Skeet '103' 12 bore boxlock ejector sporting gun, 43in. overall, barrels 26½in. with ventilated and matted top rib.
(Wallis & Wallis)
£1,350

A good double barrelled 12 bore Westley Richards patent top lever pinfire sporting gun, 46½in. overall, damascus barrels 30in., finely scroll engraved side locks, walnut stock with chequered fore end and wrist.
(Wallis & Wallis)
£280

A fine German 22-bore double-barrelled percussion sporting gun with browned twist sighted barrels signed in full in gold on the rib and decorated with vines in two-colour gold at the muzzles and breeches, case-hardened tang engraved with foliage, curved case-hardened hammers engraved and gilt with foliage, by Adam Rosen in Dyck, circa 1830–40, 32in. barrels.
(Christie's)
£4,620

A good quality double barrelled 12 bore underlever hammer gun by John Manton, Son & Coe, Dover Street, London, 46¾in. overall, damascus barrels 30in., finely scroll engraved locks, frame and hammers.
(Wallis & Wallis)
£550

SPORTING GUNS

A 12-bore self-opening sidelock, ejector gun by J. Purdey, best bouquet and scroll engraving, brushed bright and reblued finish, boldly-figured stock, 30in. barrels. (Christie's) £5,720

A lightweight 12-bore self-opening sidelock ejector gun by Edwinson Green, patent self-opening action, best close foliate-scroll engraving with much hardening-colour, well-figured stock, 28in. barrels. (Christie's) £2,860

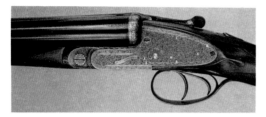

A pair of lightweight 12-bore 'Premiere XXV' assisted-opening sidelock ejector guns by E.J. Churchill, Baker patent assisted-opening action, double rolled-edge triggerguards, 25in. barrels, circa 1936. (Christie's) £15,400

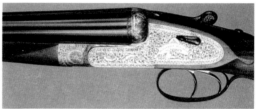

A pair of light 12-bore 'Royal Brevis Self-Opener' sidelock ejector guns by Holland & Holland, hand-detachable locks, rolled-edge triggerguards, well-figured stocks, 28in. barrels, circa 1936. (Christie's) £16,500

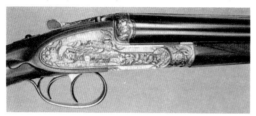

A Kelly-engraved 12-bore (2¾in.) self-opening sidelock ejector gun by J. Purdey, treble-grip action with side-clips, rolled-edge triggerguard, gold-plated triggers, articulated front-trigger, boldly-figured stock, 28in. barrels, circa 1985. (Christie's) £14,850

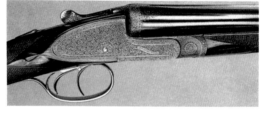

A 12-bore (2¾in.) single-double trigger 'Premiere XXV' sidelock ejector gun by E.J. Churchill, patent single-double trigger action, gold-plated triggers with double rolled-edge triggerguard, boldly figured stock with buttplate, 25in. barrels, circa 1932. (Christie's) £7,150

A pair of 12-bore self-opening sidelock ejector guns by J. Purdey, rounded bars, rolled-edge triggerguards, well figured stocks, chopper-lump barrels with semi-raised game-ribs, 28in. barrels, circa 1976. (Christie's) £30,800

A matched pair of 12-bore (2¾in.) 'Royal Modele De Luxe Self-Opener' sidelock ejector guns by Holland & Holland, hand-detachable locks, rolled-edge triggerguards, the fences chiselled in relief with acanthus leaves, 27in. barrels, circa 1976. (Christie's) £28,600

SPORTING GUNS

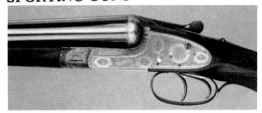

A pair of 12-bore sidelock ejector guns by Boss, standard easy-opening action, rolled-edge triggerguards, best bouquet and scroll engraving, well-figured stocks, 30in. barrels. (Christie's)
£12,100

A matched pair of 12-bore self-opening sidelock ejector guns by J. Purdey, best bouquet and scroll engraving, well-figured stocks, 28in. barrels, circa 1933. (Christie's)
£9,900

A pair of 12-bore sidelock ejector guns by Harrison & Hussey, best bouquet and scroll engraving with much hardening-colour, well-figured stocks with extensions, 28in. barrels. (Christie's)
£6,600

A pair of 12-bore (2¾in.) self-opening sidelock ejector guns by J. Purdey, rolled-edge trigger-guards, best bouquet and scroll engraving with full hardening-colour, well-figured stocks, 28in. barrels, circa 1986. (Christie's) £28,600

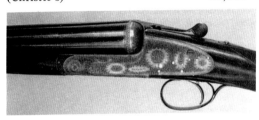

A pair of lightweight 12-bore round-body single-trigger self-opening sidelock ejector guns by Boss, Boss patent single-triggers with rolled-edge triggerguards, best bouquet and scroll engraving with some hardening-colour, well-figured stocks with semi-pistol grips, 27in. barrels, circa 1938. (Christie's)
£33,000

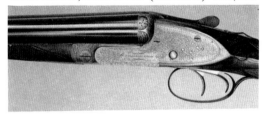

A matched pair of 12-bore sidelock ejector guns by J. Woodward, arcaded fences, pro-truding tumbler-pivots, best foliate-scroll engraving with traces of hardening-colour, well-figured stocks with buttplates, 29in. barrels, circa 1898 and 1904. (Christie's)
£6,600

A 12-bore (2¾in.) self-opening sidelock ejector gun by J. Purdey, best bouquet and scroll engraving with full hardening-colour and blueing, boldly-figured stock, chopper-lump barrels with Churchill-style rib, 28in. barrels, circa 1981. (Christie's)   £13,200

A pair of light 12-bore sidelock ejector guns by F. Beesley, the fences chiselled in relief with an acanthus-leaf motif, highly-figured stocks, chopper-lump barrels with game-ribs and scroll-engraved breech-ends, 28in. barrels, circa 1937. (Christie's)   £22,000

RIFLES AND GUNS

A .450in. Westley Richards 'monkey-tail' breech loading percussion sporting rifle, No. 5550.C, 42½in., octagonal barrel 25in., Birmingham proved, five-leaf rearsights to 500 yards, ladder rearsight to 1000 yards. **£700**

A German percussion sporting rifle with browned twist octagonal sighted barrel rifled with seven grooves and signed in full in gold Gothic script at the breech, figured walnut full stock, the butt carved with a flowerhead behind the cheek-piece and with oak leaves and a scallop shell behind the chequered grip, by Adam Rosen in Dyck, circa 1850, 30¾in. barrel. **£1,210**

A German royal presentation percussion sporting rifle with earlier sighted barrel octagonal changing to polygonal and rifled for a belted ball, decorated with flowerheads and bands of waved lines against a punched fishroe ground, shield-shaped German silver escutcheon engraved with initials *F.S.* for Prince Friedrich Salm-Dyck (1812–1848), 30½in. barrel. (Christie's) **£1,650**

A German 28-bore double-barrelled percussion sporting rifle with multigroove rifled sighted barrels with raised longitudinal ribs over their entire length, long case-hardened tang engraved with scrolling foliage, by Adam Rosen in Dyck, circa 1830–40, 25¼in. barrels. (Christie's) **£880**

A very fine German percussion sporting rifle with blued octagonal sighted barrel rifled with eight grooves and decorated with running scrollwork in encrusted gold at the muzzle and breech, shaped adjustable back-sight engraved with strapwork, highly figured walnut full stock profusely carved in relief with scrolling foliage inhabited by birds and animals, by Adam Rosen in Dyck, circa 1850, 28in. barrel. (Christie's) **£22,000**

TARGET RIFLES

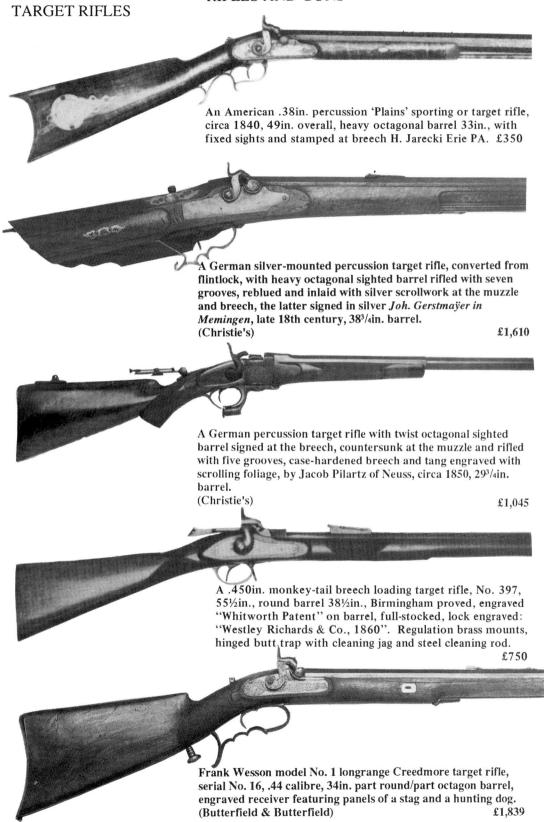

An American .38in. percussion 'Plains' sporting or target rifle,
circa 1840, 49in. overall, heavy octagonal barrel 33in., with
fixed sights and stamped at breech H. Jarecki Erie PA. £350

A German silver-mounted percussion target rifle, converted from
flintlock, with heavy octagonal sighted barrel rifled with seven
grooves, reblued and inlaid with silver scrollwork at the muzzle
and breech, the latter signed in silver *Joh. Gerstmaÿer in
Memingen*, late 18th century, 38³/₄in. barrel.
(Christie's)   £1,610

A German percussion target rifle with twist octagonal sighted
barrel signed at the breech, countersunk at the muzzle and rifled
with five grooves, case-hardened breech and tang engraved with
scrolling foliage, by Jacob Pilartz of Neuss, circa 1850, 29³/₄in.
barrel.
(Christie's)   £1,045

A .450in. monkey-tail breech loading target rifle, No. 397,
55½in., round barrel 38½in., Birmingham proved, engraved
"Whitworth Patent" on barrel, full-stocked, lock engraved:
"Westley Richards & Co., 1860". Regulation brass mounts,
hinged butt trap with cleaning jag and steel cleaning rod.
                                                                £750

Frank Wesson model No. 1 longrange Creedmore target rifle,
serial No. 16, .44 calibre, 34in. part round/part octagon barrel,
engraved receiver featuring panels of a stag and a hunting dog.
(Butterfield & Butterfield)   £1,839

Ulrich engraved Winchester model 1866 rifle, serial No. 80361, .44 calibre, 24in. barrel with full magazine, scroll engraved with large panel scenes, the left side depicting a hunter firing into a herd of buffalo as his companion holds their horses.
(Butterfield & Butterfield) £32,945

Engraved Winchester model 1873 rifle, British proofed, serial No. 6304, .44 calibre, late 1st model with thumbprint dust cover, 24in. round barrel with full magazine.
(Butterfield & Butterfield) £3,679

A rare Winchester .44 W.C.F. 'Model 1873' lever-action repeating smoothbore rifle, the body of the stock inset with a steel presentation plaque inscribed *Presented by Annie Oakley to W.R.C. Clarke, 1891*, the blued round smoothbore barrel with full-length magazine and non-standard rear-and-fore-sights, 20in. barrel.
(Christie's) £84,000

Winchester model 1886 extra lightweight takedown rifle, serial No. 136270, .33 W.C.F. calibre, 24in. Rapid Taper barrel with Lyman Hunting front sight and half magazine, blue finish with casehardened lever and hammer, deluxe wood and forend and pistol grip stock chequered in H pattern.
(Butterfield & Butterfield) £3,295

Rare Ulrich engraved Winchester model 1873 One of One Thousand rifle, serial No. 35298, .44, first model with thumbprint dust cover, 26in. octagon barrel scroll engraved at breech and muzzle, and at breech with the legend *One of One Thousand*, platinum barrel bands.
(Butterfield & Butterfield) £109,817

Winchester model 1885 high wall rifle, serial No. 97506, .32–40 calibre, 30in. No. 3 octagon barrel with Beach front sight, tang mounted Mid-Range Vernier peep sight, plain straight stock with crescent butt.
(Butterfield & Butterfield) £1,171

Rare Winchester model 1873 One of One Thousand rifle, serial No. 18322, .44 calibre, 24in. octagon barrel with platinum lines and scroll engraving at muzzle and breech, the breech top flat engraved *One of One Thousand*.
(Butterfield & Butterfield) £23,913

WINCHESTER RIFLES

Factory engraved Winchester first model 'opentop' 1876 rifle, serial No. 966, .45 calibre, 28in. octagon barrel with Beach combination sight and scroll engraving at breech, full magazine, full nickel finish, the frame, including carrier block, profusely scroll engraved with semi-deep relief panels of stags on either side.
(Butterfield & Butterfield)   £27,454

Factory engraved and gold inlaid Winchester model 1894 takedown rifle, serial No. 502304, .32 W.S. calibre, 24in. octagon barrel with half magazine and Lyman front sight, blue finish with casehardened hammer and lever, frame engraved in style No. 9 with panels of stags on either side.
(Butterfield & Butterfield)   £13,178

Factory engraved Winchester model 1873 rifle, serial No. 148088A, .32 calibre, 24in. round barrel with full magazine and Beach combination front sight, gilt and nickel plated finish, scroll engraved frame with panel of stag on left side and panel of bear on right.
(Butterfield & Butterfield)   £45,757

Winchester model 1873 deluxe rifle, serial No. 654955, .38 W.C.F. calibre, 24in. octagon nickel steel barrel with full magazine and standard sights, blued finish with casehardened hammer, lever and buttplate, tang mounted flexible peep sight, deluxe chequered pistol grip stock and forend.
(Butterfield & Butterfield)   £13,178

Winchester model 1873 rifle, serial No. 497783B, .32 calibre, 24in. octagon barrel with full magazine, blue finish with casehardened lever, hammer and buttplate, plain straight stock.
(Butterfield & Butterfield)   £1,647

Factory engraved Winchester model 1886 rifle, serial No. 78427, .45–90 W.C.F. caliber, 26in. octagon barrel with full magazine, nickel plated and gilt finish, frame scroll engraved with panel scene of stag and doe on the left side, single set trigger, deluxe wood with pistol grip stock chequered in style H.
(Butterfield & Butterfield)   £11,714

Engraved Winchester model 1907 self loading rifle, serial No. 48690, .351 calibre, 20in. barrel scroll engraved at breech, the frame engraved with scrolling florals framing a panel of a stag on the left side and a pronghorn antelope on the right.
(Butterfield & Butterfield)   £2,391

WINCHESTER RIFLES

Rare Winchester model 1873 cutaway rifle, no serial number, .44 calibre, Third model, 24in. octagon barrel dovetailed for front and rear sights, the barrel with standard markings and additional stamping at breech *From W.F. Sheard/Tacoma. Wash. Tacoma, Wash.*
(Butterfield & Butterfield)   £5,125

Rare and important engraved Winchester model 1866 saddle ring carbine with raised carved ivory stock, serial No. 21921, .44 calibre, 20in. round barrel marked *Henry's Patent Oct. 16, 1866*, profuse Nimschke style scroll engraving on frame, barrel and buttplate, silver and blued finish, elephant ivory forearm and buttstock.
(Butterfield & Butterfield)   £248,918

Rare Ulrich engraved and inscribed Winchester model 1866 rifle, serial No. 96020A, .44 calibre, 24in. octagon barrel with full magazine and Globe front sight, scroll engraved and gold washed forend cap and buttplate, Ulrich scroll engraved gold washed frame featuring a hound on the left front and a rabbit on the obverse.
(Butterfield & Butterfield)   £27,454

Rare important factory engraved presentation Henry model 1860 rifle, serial No. 1978, .44 calibre, 24in. barrel marked *Henry's Patent Oct. 16, 1860/Manufactured by the New Haven Arms Co. New Haven, Ct.*, the silver plated frame inscribed on the left side *Presented to/Capt J. R. Burton/1st Conn. Artillery/By/O.F. Winchester/Oct. 23rd, 1863* and framed by scroll engraving.
(Butterfield & Butterfield)   £135,441

Rare factory engraved Henry marked Winchester model 1866 rifle, serial No. 19668, .44 calibre, 24in. Henry marked octagon barrel with full magazine, the silver plated frame scroll engraved, forend cap and buttplate also scroll engraved, deluxe wood with straight stock.
(Butterfield & Butterfield)   £21,963

Nimschke engraved Winchester model 1866 saddle ring carbine, serial No. 97876, .44 calibre, third model, 20in. round barrel with full magazine and standard sights, the scroll engraved silver plated frame featuring the coat of arms of Chilé on the left side.
(Butterfield & Butterfield)   £14,642

WINCHESTER RIFLES

Fine Nimschke engraved Winchester model 1866 deluxe sporting rifle, serial No. 105533, .44 calibre, the 24in. octagonal, nickel plated barrel with rare scroll engraving at muzzle and breech.
(Butterfield & Butterfield)   £7,358

Winchester model 1873 deluxe rifle, serial No. 18313, .44 calibre, late First model with thumbprint dust cover, 24in. octagon barrel, full nickel plated finish, single set trigger, fitted with sling swivels, deluxe wood with chequered forend and straight stock.
(Butterfield & Butterfield)   £11,714

Winchester model 1885 single shot high wall Schuetzen rifle, serial No. 108084, .38-55 calibre, fancy XXX walnut chequered pistol grip stock with Schuetzen cheekpiece and Helm style buttplate.   £5,151

Winchester model 1885 high wall Schuetzen rifle, serial No. 107041, .22 Short calibre, 28in. #3 octagon barrel fitted with Winchester B-5 telescopic sight, select burl wood with chequered forend fitted with palm rest.
(Butterfield & Butterfield)   £2,759

Rare Winchester 'One of One Hundred' model 1873 rifle, calibre 44–40, 24½in. octagonal barrel, first type with mortised dust cover, engraved and banded on breech and muzzle, top of barrel engraved *One of One Hundred*, deluxe chequered stock and forearm, made in 1876.
(Butterfield & Butterfield)   £34,500

Winchester model 1876 rifle, second model, calibre 50 express (50–95), 26in. round barrel with half magazine, blued finish, case hardened frame, forecap and lever, chequered deluxe stock and forearm, shot gun butt, standard address, serial No. 9901, made in 1880. (Butterfield & Butterfield)   £9,400

Nimschke engraved Winchester model 1866 rifle, serial no. 35866, .44 calibre, Third Model, 24in. octagonal barrel, the frame with fine floral scroll engraving featuring a bold eagle's head on either side by L.D. Nimschke and signed by him behind the trigger. (Butterfield & Butterfield) £6,200

Engraved Winchester model 1866 carbine, serial no. 48763, .44 calibre, Third Model, 20in. round barrel, frame, hammer, lever, buttplate, and barrel bands with floral scroll engraving. (Butterfield & Butterfield) £3,000

Winchester model 1895 rifle, serial no. 4047, .30 calibre, flatside model, 28in. round barrel, frame mounted Lyman peep sight, pistol grip stock with crescent buttplate. (Butterfield & Butterfield) £980

Rare C.F. Ulrich engraved Winchester model 1866 rifle, serial no. 36259, .44 calibre, Third Model, 24in. octagonal barrel, the receiver with floral scroll engraving featuring a panel with an elephant on the left side and two panels on the right side; one with a lioness and one with an elk. (Butterfield & Butterfield) £10,000

Winchester model 1886 line throwing rifle, serial no. 154779A, .45-70 calibre, 14½ octagonal barrel, varnished walnut stock with crescent buttplate. (Butterfield & Butterfield) £800

Winchester High Wall Schuetzen rifle, serial no. 95276, .38-55 calibre, 30in. heavy octagon barrel with matte top flat, standard target sights, double set triggers, elaborate finger lever marked "Jos Singer", Monte Carlo stock with checkered wrist and Schuetzen buttplate. (Butterfield & Butterfield) £2,150

Rare Winchester model 1873 One of One Thousand rifle, serial no. 31270, .44 calibre, early Second Model, 28in. round barrel with scroll engraving at muzzle and at frame with legend in script "One of One Thousand" on top flat. (Butterfield & Butterfield) £50,000

WINCHESTER RIFLES

Winchester model 1892 saddle ring carbine, serial no. 575830, .32 calibre, 20in. round barrel with button magazine, saddle ring in place. (Butterfield & Butterfield) £375

Rare experimental Winchester musket, .30 calibre, 28in. round tapering barrel, musket stock with barrel cover, forward barrel band with integral bayonet lug, stock with carbine style buttplate. (Butterfield & Butterfield) £3,000

Winchester model 1886 short rifle, serial no. 89503, .40-82 calibre, 22in. heavy octagonal barrel with button magazine, varnished walnut stock and forend, crescent buttplate. (Butterfield & Butterfield) £1,700

Rare Winchester model 1876 One of One Hundred rifle serial no. 896, .45 calibre, First Model, 28in. octagonal barrel with scroll engraving at muzzle and at frame with legend in script "One of One Hundred" on top flat. Tang mounted peep sight, select wood with checkered forend and straight checkered wrist stock, crescent buttplate. (Butterfield & Butterfield) £100,000

Winchester trapper's model 1892 carbine, serial no. 895108, .44 calibre, 15in. round barrel, oil finished walnut stock and forend, saddle ring in place. (Butterfield & Butterfield) £925

Winchester trapper's model 1892 carbine, serial no. 290849, .38 calibre, 12in. barrel, oil finished walnut stock and forend, saddle ring in place. (Butterfield & Butterfield) £1,525

Winchester deluxe model 1876 rifle, .50-95 Express, Third Model, 26in. octagonal barrel with full magazine, the dust cover marked "Winchester Express/.50 Cal. 95 Grs", checkered forend and checkered pistol grip stock with shotgun buttplate. (Butterfield & Butterfield) £2,200

WINCHESTER RIFLES

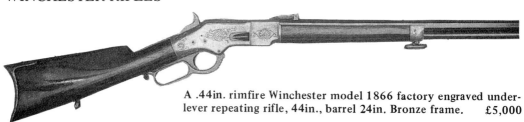

A .44in. rimfire Winchester model 1866 factory engraved underlever repeating rifle, 44in., barrel 24in. Bronze frame.   £5,000

**A good .38in. centre fire Winchester model 1873 full tube
magazine underlever sporting rifle, 41in. overall, round barrel
22in. with London proofs, deluxe walnut stock with finely
chequered fore end and wrist.
(Wallis & Wallis)**   **£950**

A .44in. rimfire Winchester model 1866 underlever repeating rifle,
44in., octagonal barrel 24in., ladder sight to 800 yards. Brass
frame, steel sling swivels, tubular magazine, brass buttcap. £2,750

Winchester first model 1876 rifle, calibre 45-60, 26in. part
round, part octagon with button magazine, blued finish, case
hardened frame, lever, hammer and forecaps, straight uncheck-
ered walnut stock and forearm, shipped in 1880.
(Butterfield & Butterfield)   £3,500

Boxed Winchester model 1892 saddle ring carbine, serial No.
951720, 44 W.C.F. calibre, standard model with 20in. barrel,
blued finish and plain straight stock, in original factory
carton. (Butterfield & Butterfield)   £3,661

Rare Winchester model 1876 short rifle British proofed, third
type, calibre 50-95 express, 22in. round barrel marked 50
calibre, half button magazine, blued finish with case hardened
frame, lever, hammer, trigger and forecap, made in 1883.
(Butterfield & Butterfield)   £5,000

INDEX

INDEX TO ADVERTISERS